The Case Law Compendium

English & European Law

Neil Egan-Ronayne

BLACK LETTER PUBLISHING

18 Bateson Road, Cambridge CB4 3HF
United Kingdom

© Black Letter Publishing 2017

The moral rights of the author have been asserted

ISBN 978-1-5272-1320-3

Printed on acid free paper by
Amazon

This book is entirely dedicated to my wife (and best friend) Natasha and to our two wonderful daughters Cassidy and Neave, without whom I would not have found the courage and conviction to write and publish this first body of work. I can only extend my immense gratitude for their unwavering faith in my writing, and for the incalculable hours that it has taken to write it.

There are I hope, many more titles to follow, and while I can appreciate that such endeavours require time away from those I love most, I always do so in the knowledge that our lives are uniformly enriched, and that my hard work can help others pursue their legal dreams with confidence and inspiration. After all, writing is a universal language that both educates and enlightens.

Preface

The purpose of The Case Law Compendium is quite simply to assist all those studying and researching law. With this edition comes an appreciation of English and European case law as used by most universities at undergraduate level; and while of primary design, the book immediately qualifies as a valuable resource to postgraduate and doctoral researchers needing to 'quick-look' cases they might consider for contextual argument, but without the labour of protracted transcripts.

As a law undergraduate it was all too common to hear complaints about lengthy case judgments that often overwhelmed students assigned the task of writing an essay around a particular field and matter. While I always took enjoyment in reading case material, it was admittedly not without considerable time and concentration; and so it was that after graduating I decided to devote greater time to the cases previously touched upon while attending university. This has allowed me to distill the essence of each matter before clarifying the purpose of the courts, along with the inclusion of key citations; thereby providing students with immediate access to the minds of the judges.

By examining leading cases in their respective fields, I have ultimately compiled an indispensable support for both writing and reference, either as a refresher of what was discussed or when simply examining the courts' summary judgments. In retrospect I can now only imagine the difference such a book would have made not only to myself, but to those struggling with the demands of the degree and who perhaps lacked the courage to ask for help.

I also believe that by allowing students to use this book for their own educational advantage, there is an immediate alleviation of pressure upon tutors compelled to explain at length (i) what these cases illustrate and (ii) how the powers of statute and legal precedent are instrumental in their outcome. I believe this dual appeal organically creates a win-win scenario for students and universities alike, while cumulatively increasing undergraduate confidence, because with The Case Law Compendium in hand, law students can now effectively familiarise themselves with the subject matter in advance, while possessing the tools with which to argue around it both in tutorials, study groups and written assignments.

On a personal note I would like to express my thanks to Dr. Alexander Murray of Anglia Ruskin University Cambridge and Professor John Bell of the University of Cambridge, both of whom were instrumental in my tackling the academic side of law, and whose comments shaped my decision to remain within it. I would also like to extend particular gratitude to Squire Law Library Assistant, Ms Kay Naylor, who always extended her continued encouragement and positive commentary during my time there as an undergraduate.

Neil Egan-Ronayne
August 2017

Contents

5. European Law — 154

Table of Cases

Table of Statutes

Table of Secondary Legislation

European Treaties and Conventions

European Directives and Regulations

1. Constitutional and Administrative Law

1. A v Secretary of State for the Home Department

The unlawful detention of individuals suspected of terrorist activity is central to this collective appeal amidst the unprecedented attacks of September 11 2001 in New York; when in light of this historic event the United Kingdom took swift measures to derogate from their commitment to the Convention on Human Rights (ECHR) and the Human Rights Act 1998.

Following a number of arrests there were nine men of various nationalities detained under s.23 of the Anti-terrorism, Crime and Security Act 2001. In order to facilitate such action the Home Secretary had worked closely with Parliament to both execute and enact Part 4 of the 2001 Act, which provided powers to issue freezing orders upon those suspected of threats to the stability or security of the country. To further support this measure, statutory instrument SI/2001/3644[1] (also known as the 'Derogation Order') was drafted as to allow for specific actions peripheral to the Human Rights Act 1998 where those suspected were subject to the terms of the 2001 Act.

Prior to this amendment it was only possible under para.2(2) of sch.3 of the Immigration Act 1971 for the Secretary of State to detain non-British nationals while awaiting deportation, and such action was only deemed justifiable for a reasonable period of time as this allowed the United Kingdom to remain fully compliant with its obligations to the ECHR, in particular art.5(1) (Right to liberty and security); however in *Chahal v United Kingdom*[2] Parliament attempted to circumvent art.3 of the Convention (No one shall be subjected to torture or to inhuman or degrading treatment or punishment) in order to excessively detain and deport a Sikh separatist on grounds of an affiliation to terrorism, but were overruled by the EU Commission on democratic principles.

In this instance the appellants were challenging the derogation from ECHR principles for the purposes of detainment and deportation of foreign nationals, on grounds that the United Kingdom was not in a state of public emergency as required by art.15(1) of the Convention, and that further clarification of that article had been found in *The Greek Case*, where the Commission explained that:

> "Such a public emergency may then be seen to have, in particular, the following characteristics: (1) It must be actual or imminent. (2) Its effects must involve the whole nation. (3) The continuance of the organised life of the community must be threatened. (4) The crisis or danger must be exceptional, in that the normal measures or restrictions, permitted by the Convention for the maintenance of public safety, health and order, are plainly inadequate."[3]

---

[1] The Human Rights Act 1998 (Designated Derogation) Order 2001, SI 2001/3644

[2] (1996) 23 EHRR 423.

[3] *Greek Case, The* (1969) 12 YB 1 [153] (Commission Decision).

It was thus contended that none of the above elements were visible when derogating from the ECHR and applying the terms of the Anti-terrorism, Crime and Security Act 2001 in order to both arrest and detain the appellants, and further noted that recent ministerial statements indicated that the United Kingdom was under no immediate threat; and so while alert to international attacks, they had no evidence to suggest otherwise.

Having considered the voluminous evidence provided by both sides, and the decision taken by the Court of Appeal, the House of Lords reemphasised the course of action taken by the Secretary of State, who had countered that failure to adopt a pre-emptive state of emergency was tantamount to a breach of national security; and so while no immediate evidence suggested imminent danger to the general public and economic infrastructure, proportionate measures taken, now far outweighed the argument for adherence to Convention policy, despite overwhelming disagreement by the European Commission.

There was also discussion around unlawful use of the Special Immigration Appeals Commission (SIAC) as provided for in s.24 of the 2001 Act, who were granted exclusive jurisdiction over the rights and appeals of detainees, as opposed to referral to the courts; itself another obvious attempt to circumvent due process under principles of national security. With knowledge of deviant use of policy and a flagrant appreciation of the English judicial system, the House unanimously allowed the appeals, while quashing the Derogation Order and declaring s.23 of the Ant-terrorism, Crime and Security Act 2001 incompatible with arts.5 and 14 of the ECHR on grounds of discrimination through the use of immigration status.

Key Citations

"[A] non-national who faces the prospect of torture or inhuman treatment if returned to his own country, and who cannot be deported to any third country and is not charged with any crime, may not under article 5(1)(f) of the Convention and Schedule 3 to the Immigration Act 1971 be detained here even if judged to be a threat to national security."[4]

"Any prediction about the future behaviour of human beings (as opposed to the phases of the moon or high water at London Bridge) is necessarily problematical. Reasonable and informed minds may differ, and a judgment is not shown to be wrong or unreasonable because that which is thought likely to happen does not happen."[5]

"The more purely political (in a broad or narrow sense) a question is, the more appropriate it will be for political resolution and the less likely it is to be an appropriate matter for judicial decision. The smaller, therefore, will be the potential role of the court."[6]

---

[4] *A v Secretary of State for the Home Department* [2004] UKHL 56 [9] (Bingham LJ).

[5] *A v Secretary of State for the Home Department* [2004] UKHL 56 [29] (Bingham LJ).

[6] *A v Secretary of State for the Home Department* [2004] UKHL 56 [29] (Bingham LJ).

"[T]he function of independent judges charged to interpret and apply the law is universally recognised as a cardinal feature of the modern democratic state, a cornerstone of the rule of law itself."[7]

"[S]suspicion of being a supporter is one thing and proof of wrongdoing is another. Someone who has never committed any offence and has no intention of doing anything wrong may be reasonably suspected of being a supporter on the basis of some heated remarks overheard in a pub."[8]

"[T]he Government has a duty to protect the lives and property of its citizens. But that is a duty which it owes all the time and which it must discharge without destroying our constitutional freedoms."[9]

"The real threat to the life of the nation, in the sense of a people living in accordance with its traditional laws and political values, comes not from terrorism but from laws such as these. That is the true measure of what terrorism may achieve."[10]

"Indefinite imprisonment in consequence of a denunciation on grounds that are not disclosed and made by a person whose identity cannot be disclosed is the stuff of nightmares…"[11]

"[I]n the course of argument, a portentous but non-specific appeal to the interests of national security can be used as a cloak for arbitrary and oppressive action on the part of government. Whether or not patriotism is the last refuge of the scoundrel, national security can be the last refuge of the tyrant."[12]

---

[7] *A v Secretary of State for the Home Department* [2004] UKHL 56 [42] (Bingham LJ).

[8] *A v Secretary of State for the Home Department* [2004] UKHL 56 [87] (Nicholls LJ).

[9] *A v Secretary of State for the Home Department* [2004] UKHL 56 [95] (Hoffman LJ).

[10] *A v Secretary of State for the Home Department* [2004] UKHL 56 [97] (Hoffman LJ).

[11] *A v Secretary of State for the Home Department* [2004] UKHL 56 [155] (Scott LJ).

[12] *A v Secretary of State for the Home Department* [2004] UKHL 56 [193] (Walker LJ).

2. Ahmad v United Kingdom

While paving the way for a number of similar 'religious obligations' versus 'Convention rights' cases, this protracted legal discourse reveals a number of indiscretions that in many respects, served to influence legislative and educational policy in the United Kingdom and illustrated how laws evolve through the integration of cultural norms and progressive state cohabitation.

After working as a supply teacher within the mainstream schools arena for a considerable number of years, an Islamic man took issue with the government upon grounds that his need (or at least doctrinal requirement) to attend a mosque on Friday afternoons was being denied by statute, and that subsequent operational policy created the violation of a number of constitutional rights afforded to all citizens of the United Kingdom.

Citing arts.9 (1) of the European Convention on Human Rights (Freedom of thought, conscience and religion) and 14 (Prohibition of discrimination), the applicant protested that s.30 of the Education Act 1994 stood in immediate conflict with the need to manifest his religious beliefs every Friday between the hours of 1.30pm to 2.15pm. After being previously employed by a number of London Borough schools prior to his decision to resign rather than reduce his working hours, the man had been given verbal allowances by one school and shown strict opposition by another, which bore an inconsistent position of unwillingness to accommodate a religious need which until recently, had never been expressed nor discussed at the time of his original appointment.

When it was submitted that the repeated failure of a Muslim man to attend a mosque (subject to relative distances) would likely result in a beheading in a country such as Saudi Arabia, the applicant expected that the same principles would apply under United Kingdom jurisdiction, and that those grounds, along with previous (albeit unofficial) allowances, were sufficient enough to warrant time taken from his contractual duties, despite any inconvenience to teaching staff and pupils.

After failing to find those arguments upheld in the domestic courts, the matter wound up before the European Commission for Human Rights, where it was unanimously decided that the terms of the Convention were constructed in such a fashion as to allow interpretation and consideration of all religions and beliefs, not just those of the applicant. It was further noted that when willingly accepting a position of employment that brings with it a set of express and implied terms, the accepting individual takes ownership of how that agreement might impinge upon their religious requirements or obligations of faith, and so must therefore act accordingly.

Key Citations

"[E]ven a person at liberty may, in the exercise of his freedom to manifest his religion, have to take into account his particular professional or contractual position."[13]

"[T]he applicant, of his own free will, accepted teaching obligations under his contract with the ILEA, and that it was a result of this contract that he found himself unable 'to work with the ILEA and to attend Friday prayers'."[14]

"[T]he freedom of religion, as guaranteed by Article 9, is not absolute, but subject to the limitations set out in Article 9(2). Moreover, it may, as regards the modality of a particular religious manifestation, be influenced by the situation of the person claiming that freedom."[15]

---

[13] *Ahmad v United Kingdom* (1982) 4 EHRR 126 [7] (ECHR).

[14] *Ahmad v United Kingdom* (1982) 4 EHRR 126 [9] (ECHR).

[15] *Ahmad v United Kingdom* (1982) 4 EHRR 126 [11] (ECHR).

3. Associated Provincial Picture Houses Ltd v Wednesbury Corp

Acting ultra vires through the application of executive powers is not something alien to public authority decision-making, but it is equally important that those seeking legal review are clear as to exactly what has constituted a breach of their jurisdiction.

During the period following the World War II there were three Acts that affected the opening times of cinematograph houses across the United Kingdom. The first was the Cinematograph Act 1909, second was the Sunday Entertainments Act 1932 and third was Defence Regulation 42B, which had been introduced during the war, but remained effective until late 1947.

When it was decided by an issuing local authority to grant a trading licence to their local picture house, there came with it, restrictions preventing any attendance by children aged below fifteen years of age, regardless of whether they were accompanied by an adult. While appreciative of the opportunity to open on a day typically reserved for domestic pursuits, the appellants sought judicial review on grounds that such a restriction was self-defeating and thereby 'unreasonable'.

As there were three Acts from which to rely upon, it was agreed that for the purposes of clarity the Sunday Entertainments Act 1932 was the most appropriate, and yet within the terms prescribed, s.1(1) provided that the issue of a licence was "subject to such conditions as the authority think fit to impose."[16] This, it was agreed, allowed the local authority to apply its discretion to the limitations of the permit, and so by extension it had acted accordingly.

When heard in the first instance, the court dismissed the objections brought by the picture house, and after a brief but considered review of that decision, it was reiterated that while the courts are able to question the legal validity of executive decisions, they are not equipped, nor predisposed, to challenge the illegitimacy of those limitations, unless the body in question has applied its powers outside the boundaries of reasonableness and in ignorance of the required objectives.

The Court of Appeal later relied upon the relevant case history behind these matters, and agreed that there was, despite strong opposition by the commercial vendors, no precedent upon which their argument could stand. The Court further held that it was important to hold in mind the scope of discretion afforded local authorities when following statute, before taking up the court's time over a difference of opinion, rather than issues of genuine public interest.

---

[16] Sunday Entertainments Act 1932, s.1(1)

Key Citations

"[T]he court, whenever it is alleged that the local authority have contravened the law, must not substitute itself for that authority."[17]

"If, in the statute conferring the discretion, there is to be found expressly or by implication matters which the authority exercising the discretion ought to have regard to, then in exercising the discretion it must have regard to those matters."[18]

"[A] person entrusted with a discretion must, so to speak, direct himself properly in law. He must call his own attention to the matters which he is bound to consider. He must exclude from his consideration matters which are irrelevant to what he has to consider."[19]

"[T]he task of the court is not to decide what it thinks is reasonable, but to decide whether what is prima facie within the power of the local authority is a condition which no reasonable authority, acting within the four corners of their jurisdiction, could have decided to impose."[20]

"The court is entitled to investigate the action of the local authority with a view to seeing whether they have taken into account matters which they ought not to take into account or, conversely, have refused to take into account or neglected to take into account matters which they ought to take into account."[21]

"The power of the court to interfere in each case is not as an appellate authority to override a decision of the local authority, but as a judicial authority which is concerned, and concerned only, to see whether the local authority have contravened the law by acting in excess of the powers which Parliament has confided in them."[22]

---

[17] *Associated Provincial Picture Houses Ltd v Wednesbury Corp* [1948] 1 KB 223 (CA) 228 (Lord Green MR).

[18] *Associated Provincial Picture Houses Ltd v Wednesbury Corp* [1948] 1 KB 223 (CA) 228 (Lord Green MR).

[19] *Associated Provincial Picture Houses Ltd v Wednesbury Corp* [1948] 1 KB 223 (CA) 229 (Lord Green MR).

[20] *Associated Provincial Picture Houses Ltd v Wednesbury Corp* [1948] 1 KB 223 (CA) 233 (Lord Green MR).

[21] *Associated Provincial Picture Houses Ltd v Wednesbury Corp* [1948] 1 KB 223 (CA) 233 (Lord Green MR).

[22] *Associated Provincial Picture Houses Ltd v Wednesbury Corp* [1948] 1 KB 223 (CA) 234 (Lord Green MR).

4. Attorney-General v Jonathan Cape Ltd

Public interest, national security and the freedom of speech are the ingredients to that which a country and its servants make a United Kingdom. Should one of those elements become endangered, there is an immediate risk that any sense of democracy would be diminished in favour of state control.

When a Cabinet Minister chose to keep an open diary of his time in government, he did so on the acknowledged pretence that it would one day become a published series for public reading. When upon retirement the now deceased author endowed his executors the rights to attain full publication, and with the support of the Treasury solicitors, they did so with the aim of releasing sections of the first volume through a leading national newspaper.

At the outset there was a collaborative effort between the executors and the Secretary of the Cabinet, however after numerous demands to remove what was considered critical text, the partnership dissolved into legal argument and subsequent litigation. In the first instance a writ was issued by the Attorney-General against the executors and publishers, that sought to prevent publication under grounds of a conventional breach of confidence and national safety, while in a second writ, the newspapers were subjected to the same restrictive terms in order to cease printing and publishing the planned articles.

Having previously presented before the courts, it was argued by the claimants that history demonstrated how current and former Ministers served the country in the knowledge that any official discourse was considered secret, and that where permitted for public release, such information was typically held to a thirty-year restraining period. As this was the approach adopted, under any existing law it was honoured through duty rather than enforcement, and thus it was countered that any information contained within the compiled material was now over a decade old, and so posed no real threat to the ongoing operational integrity of the Cabinet, nor compromised national stability to any lasting degree.

Relying upon three primary principles, it was then held that the onus for prohibition fell to the claimants, and that it must be proven beyond doubt that (i) a breach of confidence had occurred (ii) that public interest was that of repression of information and (iii) that any need for public disclosure was insufficient to stand against non-publication. Given time to consider the facts before them, it was agreed that despite strong supposition on the part of the Attorney-General, there had been sufficient examination of the final and edited source material to prevent any interference by the court; and that with appreciation of free speech and the transparency of the author's intentions, the defendants' were free to both publish the first volume and release the preceding articles.

Key Citations

"[T]here may be no objection to a Minister disclosing (or leaking, as it was called) the fact that a Cabinet meeting has taken place, or, indeed, the decision taken, so long as the individual views of Ministers are not identified."[23]

"[I]t must be for the court in every case to be satisfied that the public interest is involved, and that, after balancing all the factors which tell for or against publication, to decide whether suppression is necessary."[24]

"In the present action against the literary executors, the Attorney-General asks for a perpetual injunction to restrain further publication of the diaries in whole or in part. I am far from convinced that he has made out a case that the public interest requires such a draconian remedy when due regard is had to other public interests, such as the freedom of speech…"[25]

"[T]he present defendants are not in breach of the Official Secrets Acts. It seems to me, therefore, that the Attorney-General must first show that whatever obligation of secrecy or discretion attaches to former Cabinet Ministers, that obligation is binding in law and not merely in morals."[26]

"[T]he court must have power to deal with publication which threatens national security, and the difference between such a case and the present case is one of degree rather than kind."[27]

"[W]hen a Cabinet Minister receives information in confidence the improper publication of such information can be restrained by the court, and his obligation is not merely to observe a gentleman's agreement to refrain from publication."[28]

"To leak a Cabinet decision a day or so before it is officially announced is an accepted exercise in public relations, but to identify the Ministers who voted one way or another is objectionable because it undermines the doctrine of joint responsibility."[29]

---

[23] *Attorney-General v Jonathan Cape* [1976] QB 752 (QB) 764 (Lord Widgery CJ).

[24] *Attorney-General v Jonathan Cape* [1976] QB 752 (QB) 765 (Lord Widgery CJ).

[25] *Attorney-General v Jonathan Cape* [1976] QB 752 (QB) 767 (Lord Widgery CJ).

[26] *Attorney-General v Jonathan Cape* [1976] QB 752 (QB) 767 (Lord Widgery CJ).

[27] *Attorney-General v Jonathan Cape* [1976] QB 752 (QB) 769 (Lord Widgery CJ).

[28] *Attorney-General v Jonathan Cape* [1976] QB 752 (QB) 770 (Lord Widgery CJ).

[29] *Attorney-General v Jonathan Cape* [1976] QB 752 (QB) 770 (Lord Widgery CJ).

5. **Council of Civil Service Unions v Minister for the Civil Service**

Executive powers and national security form the footing of this call for judicial review, under the argument that changes to civil servant working conditions were executed without due consideration for those affected.

In a relationship with a chequered history, it was decided by the Minister of the Civil Service (who was also acting Prime Minister Mrs Thatcher) that since the previous strike actions of key staff within the Government Communications Headquarters (GCHQ) had proven destructive beyond purpose, it was necessary to execute instructions to ban any affiliation by government employees with trade unions of any sort. While this unprecedented move to restrict employee rights was carried out under legitimate powers conferred by the sovereign, it stood in direct conflict to the principle that governmental decisions were first offered to consultation with the trade unions as an inherent duty to exercise fairness when carrying out executive function.

These instructions were orally released within the House of Commons, and so naturally reception of this was greeted with anger and confusion as to how it had escaped prior discussions. Carried out under art.4 of the Civil Service Order 1982,[30] the aim of this sudden prohibition was to circumvent discourse in favour of avoiding future disruption through anticipated strike actions that had already been considered a significant threat to national security.

When heard at court level, the presiding judge ruled that the instructions were issued on grounds demonstrating no effort toward consultation and were therefore invalid in their application. With leave to appeal the Court again held that the executive action itself was not exempt from judicial review, because the order came from prerogative powers rather than statute; and that despite the latter source forming the premise for most reviews, the Court saw no distinction between a self-executed order and that of an act of Parliament.

The defence used by the Minister for the Civil Service relied upon operational safety measures, and that under those circumstances it was felt that the same people responsible for the previous compromises were right to be excluded from using consultation as leverage to create further damage; while it was further argued that any discussions between trade unions and The Government would have amounted to the same outcome, regardless of any protestation by those affected. This was also supported by the fact that s.(a) and (a)(ii) of art.4 of the Order in Council 1982 allowed the Minister to create regulations that controlled the conduct of those employed, which translated that denial of trade union membership fell within those remits and was therefore legally sound.

When the actions of the Minister were upheld, the appellants were again granted appeal to the House of Lords, who sought to establish if judicial review was necessary, and whether the respondents had acted in manner that precluded fairness and duty to follow precedent. After careful examination of the facts presented, it was held that while the avoidance of discussion prior to the execution of the order showed a clear breach of that

---

[30] Civil Service Commission, *Civil Service Order in Council* 1982 (Civil Service Commission, 1982)

duty, it was not the responsibility of the courts to determine what constituted a threat to national security; and that the executive itself was empowered to prove, or disprove itself as to its own actions, therefore on this occasion the grounds for immediate execution were tenable.

Key Citations

"In the present case the prerogative power involved is power to regulate the Home Civil Service, and I recognise there is no obvious reason why the mode of exercise of that power should be immune from review by the courts."[31]

"Whatever their source, powers which are defined, either by reference to their object or by reference to procedure for their exercise, or in some other way, and whether the definition is expressed or implied, are in my opinion normally subject to judicial control to ensure that they are not exceeded."[32]

"[T]he evidence shows that, ever since GCHQ began in 1947, prior consultation has been the invariable rule when conditions of service were to be significantly altered."[33]

"[W]here a question as to the interest of national security arises in judicial proceedings the court has to act on evidence."[34]

"I see no reason why simply because a decision-making power is derived from a common law and not a statutory source, it should for that reason only be immune from judicial review."[35]

"I am unable to see, subject to what I shall say later, that there is any logical reason why the fact that the source of the power is the prerogative and not statute should today deprive the citizen of that right of challenge to the manner of its exercise which he would possess were the source of the power statutory."[36]

---

[31] *Council of Civil Service Unions v Minister for the Civil Service* [1985] AC 374 (HL) 398 (Fraser LJ).

[32] *Council of Civil Service Unions v Minister for the Civil Service* [1985] AC 374 (HL) 399 (Fraser LJ).

[33] *Council of Civil Service Unions v Minister for the Civil Service* [1985] AC 374 (HL) 401 (Fraser LJ).

[34] *Council of Civil Service Unions v Minister for the Civil Service* [1985] AC 374 (HL) 406 (Scarman LJ).

[35] *Council of Civil Service Unions v Minister for the Civil Service* [1985] AC 374 (HL) 410 (Diplock LJ).

[36] *Council of Civil Service Unions v Minister for the Civil Service* [1985] AC 374 (HL) 417 (Roskill LJ).

6. Davidson v Scottish Ministers (No.2)

The pollution of judicial impartiality is an issue raised by a prison inmate when campaigning for a transfer on grounds of Convention rights, and when faced with a verdict that ran contrary to his calculated expectations.

While serving sentence in HMP Barlinnie, Scotland, the appellant took issue with the prison when complaining that his living conditions were counter to his rights under art.3 of the European Convention on Human Rights (ECHR) (Prohibition of torture), and that he was justified a transfer to a more suitable prison. Raising both a petition and an order for specific performance along with a claim for damages, the appellant requested that the acting Scottish Ministers arranged for his transfer, and undertook measures of financial compensation for his alleged suffering.

In the first instance the Court of Session refused to issue orders against the Scottish Ministers on grounds that s.21 of the Crown Proceedings Act 1947 prohibited such action in lieu of declaratory rights, which unfortunately on this occasion, were also denied. Having been granted leave to reclaim, the matter was brought before the Extra Division, who again denied his claim for the same reasons.

In accordance with his rights, the appellant then looked to appeal to the House of Lords but this was again dismissed by majority; however it became known to the appellant that one of the presiding judges (Hardie LJ) had, while holding a previous position as a Lord Advocate, been involved in the amendment of the 1947 Act, and that his presence had been contributory to the inclusion of Scottish Ministers when protecting members of the Crown as read in s.38(2):

> ""Civil proceedings" includes proceedings in the High Court or the county court for the recovery of fines or penalties, but does not include proceedings on the Crown side of the King's Bench Division; . . ."Officer", in relation to the Crown, includes any servant of His Majesty, and accordingly (but without prejudice to the generality of the forgoing provision includes a Minister of the Crown *and a member of the Scottish Executive*."[37]

It was for this reason that the appellant cited an 'actual bias' within the reclaim hearing, and that a re-trial was legally binding under the rule of law for the purposes of objectivity and equity. Where judicial bias is suggested, the test established in *Porter v Magill*[38] was relied upon in order to establish clarity and impartiality, and framed the approach through the fair-minded and informed opinion of an observer, as opposed to one of jurisprudence and professional insight.

After careful examination of the actual degree to which Lord Hardie had been involved in the amending of the statute, it was agreed that the origins of that legislative change stemmed directly from the mind of Donald Stewart MP, who was at the time, the Secretary of State for Scotland, and that Lord Hardie had merely been representative of those actions within his professional capacity. This evidence became fatal to the claim of

---

[37] Crown Proceedings Act 1947 s. 38(2) (emphasis added).

[38] [2001] UKHL 67.

bias, and it was on those principles that while the House sympathised to the plight of the now former inmate, there was simply no warrant for quashing the previous decision and thus his appeal was dismissed.

Key Citations

"[P]roblems of apparent bias do not arise where a judge is invited to revisit a question on which he or she has expressed a previous judicial opinion, which must happen in any developed system, but problems are liable to arise where the exercise of judicial functions is preceded by the exercise of legislative functions."[39]

"[A] risk of apparent bias is liable to arise where a judge is called upon to rule judicially on the effect of legislation which he or she has drafted or promoted during the parliamentary process."[40]

"There will be cases where disclosure is called for, but objection will not frequently be taken. Where it is, and the judge thinks it right to stand down, the loss is justified by the need to maintain full confidence in the integrity of the judicial process."[41]

"The quashing of decisions on the ground of apparent bias leads to delay and increased costs and puts at risk the virtue of finality. A balance has to be struck between the demands of the general interest of the community and the requirements of the protection of the individual's fundamental rights between holding and applying the principle and allowing it to run out of control."[42]

"There must be a sufficiently close relationship between the previous words or conduct and the issue which was before the tribunal to justify the conclusion that when it came to decide that issue the tribunal was not impartial or, as the common law puts it, that there was a real possibility that it was biased…"[43]

"[T]he best safeguard against a challenge after the event, when the decision is known to be adverse to the litigant, lies in the opportunity of making a disclosure before the hearing starts. That is the proper time for testing the tribunal's impartiality. Fairness requires that the quality of impartiality is there from the beginning, and a proper disclosure at the beginning is in itself a badge of impartiality."[44]

---

[39] *Davidson v Scottish Ministers (No.2)* [2004] UKHL 34 [10] (Bingham LJ).

[40] *Davidson v Scottish Ministers (No.2)* [2004] UKHL 34 [17] (Bingham LJ).

[41] *Davidson v Scottish Ministers (No.2)* [2004] UKHL 34 [20] (Bingham LJ).

[42] *Davidson v Scottish Ministers (No.2)* [2004] UKHL 34 [49] (Hope LJ).

[43] *Davidson v Scottish Ministers (No.2)* [2004] UKHL 34 [53] (Hope LJ).

[44] *Davidson v Scottish Ministers (No.2)* [2004] UKHL 34 [54] (Hope LJ).

7. Entick v Carrington

In a time following the great revolution it was taken by some occupying ministerial roles that powers typically reserved for the King and courts were equally applicable to his immediate servants. This included the presumed right to issue warrant against those deemed offensive to the Crown, and that might seek to usurp its position through libellous acts.

When a number of gentlemen set about the formation of a newspaper, they were eventually seen to be acting with defamatory intent, and so after the publication of certain articles, a warrant for the seizure of the original works was issued by the Earl of Halifax, who was acting Secretary of State. While the officers despatched were told to include the presence of a police constable, they chose to act alone and used force to enter the claimant's home, before causing significant damage to his property while searching for the relevant documentation. The second part of the warrant required that they brought the claimant and his papers before the Earl himself, so that he could be examined and held to account.

Prior to the revolution, there had been many abuses of power by those so appointed, and so the reemergence of the rule of common law had sought to prevent these flagrant ignorances in favour of equity and the rights of the citizens of the state; yet when the claimant sought relief for the damages caused, it was argued by the defendants that (i) the Secretary of State reserved the right to execute warrants in the interest of the Crown and (ii) that the defendants had subsequently acted under the rights contained within the Constables Protection Act 1750,[45] and were therefore beyond reproach when carrying out the duties contained in the warrant.

When brought before the court, it became clear that despite statute conferring certain protections against those undertaking certain duties under the instruction of the Crown, there was no evidence to support either the Secretary of State or the officers assigned, until it could be proven that the former was legally entitled to issue warrants. It was also evident that no police constable had accompanied the defendants as was requested, and that the evidence gathered was then presented to an employee of the Earl and not the issuer himself, who held no powers of delegation in such circumstances. To further add insult to injury, it was also apparent that the man accused was not even responsible for the libellous comments, and so the whole affair constituted nothing more than trespass and criminal damage.

Having closely evaluated the limitations imposed upon the Secretary of State, it was agreed by the presiding Chief Justice that at no point in time had it been assumed that the post included magisterial or advisory rights, other than to act within matters of high treason, which supported their service as protectors of the public and the state. This translated that the Earl had acted well beyond his remit, and that any such warrant was now void and unenforceable at law. With due consideration for the first point, it then followed that the officers had been acting under illegality, and were therefore guilty of trespass and breaking and entering, and so award was granted in favour of the claimant.

---

[45] Constables Protection Act 1750, 24 Geo. 2c.44.

Key Citations

"[I]f the Secretary of State had claimed any such power then certainly the Petition of Right would have taken notice of it; but from silence on that head we may fairly conclude he neither claimed nor had any such power."[46]

"[T]he whole body of the law seem not to know that Privy Counsellors out of Council had any power to commit, if there had been any such power they could not have been ignorant of it."[47]

"[I]f it appears that he hath power to commit in one case only, how can we then without authority say he has that power in other cases?"[48]

"The Secretary of State is no conservator nor a justice of the peace, quasi secretary, within the words or equity of the Stat. 24 Geo.2 admitting him..."[49]

"[O]ur law holds the property of every man so sacred, that no man can set his foot upon his neighbour's close without his leave; if he does he is a trespasser, though he does no damage at all; if he will tread upon his neighbour's ground he must justify it by law."[50]

"[W]e can safely say there is no law in this country to justify the defendants in what they have done, if there was, it would destroy all the comforts of society; for papers are often the dearest property a man can have."[51]

"[I]f a man is punishable for having libel in his private custody, as many cases say he is, half the kingdom would be guilty in the case of a favourite libel, if libels may be searched for and seized by whomsoever and wheresoever the Secretary of State sees fit."[52]

"[W]e are no advocates for libels, all Governments must set their faces against them, and whenever they come before us and a jury we shall set our faces against them; and if juries do not prevent them they may prove fatal to liberty, destroy governments and introduce anarchy."[53]

---

[46] *Entick v Carrington* (1765) 19 St Tr 1030 (KB) 814 (CJ).

[47] *Entick v Carrington* (1765) 19 St Tr 1030 (KB) 816 (CJ).

[48] *Entick v Carrington* (1765) 19 St Tr 1030 (KB) 817 (CJ).

[49] *Entick v Carrington* (1765) 19 St Tr 1030 (KB) 817 (CJ).

[50] *Entick v Carrington* (1765) 19 St Tr 1030 (KB) 817 (CJ).

[51] *Entick v Carrington* (1765) 19 St Tr 1030 (KB) 817 (CJ).

[52] *Entick v Carrington* (1765) 19 St Tr 1030 (KB) 818 (CJ).

[53] *Entick v Carrington* (1765) 19 St Tr 1030 (KB) 818 (CJ).

8. Ghaidan v Godin-Mendoza

Same-sex relationships and the discrimination of landlords under death of secured tenants, provokes the wisdom of the judiciary when progressive interpretation of existing statute is the only salient answer to a claim for devolved rights by the freeholder.

After living together in a committed homosexual relationship for over thirty years, the respondent had been left facing continued occupancy of the flat under the terms of an assured tenancy, following the death of his partner and secure tenant. By becoming subject to the lesser of the two tenancies, the respondent was now vulnerable to potentially increased rents, with no legal rights to challenge repossession should the freeholder decide to remove him.

Having sought enforcement under sch.2 para.1 of the Rent Act 1977, the appellant landlord argued that same-sex relationships were precluded from the enjoyment of direct succession of statutory tenancy as prescribed in the 1977 Act, but those surviving death could remain in occupation under an assured tenancy, as first held in *Fitzpatrick v Sterling Housing Association Ltd.*[54] As this matter had been raised prior to the Human Rights Act 1998 (HRA), the respondent countered that devolution of rights through the application of the 1977 Act constituted a direct violation of arts.8 (Right to respect for private and family life) and 14 (Prohibition of discrimination) of the European Convention on Human Rights, and that under such conditions, the respondent was free to remain in occupation under the same rights afforded those in sch.1 paras.1, 2 and 3 of the 1977 Act as below:

> "1.Paragraph 2 or, as the case may be, paragraph 3 below shall have effect, subject to section 2(3) of this Act, for the purpose of determining who is the statutory tenant of a dwelling-house by succession after the death of the person (in this Part of this Schedule referred to as "the original tenant") who, immediately before his death, was a protected tenant of the dwelling-house or the statutory tenant of it by virtue of his previous protected tenancy.
>
> 2. If the original tenant was a man who died leaving a widow who was residing with him at his death then, after his death, the widow shall be the statutory tenant if and so long as she occupies the dwelling-house as her residence.
>
> 3. Where paragraph 2 above does not apply, but *a person who was a member of the original tenant's family was residing with him at the time of and for the period of 6 months immediately before his death then, after his death, that person or if there is more than one such person such one of them as may be decided by agreement, or in default of agreement by the county court, shall be the statutory tenant if and so long as he occupies the dwelling-house as his residence.*"[55]

---

[54] [1998] Ch 304.

[55] Rent Act 1977, sch.1 paras 1,2,3 (emphasis added).

For clarification, the Court's view was that para.3 of the Rent Act 1977 was designed to treat women who had been in occupation, yet remained unmarried as family members, so as to allow assured tenancies to permit continuous occupancy when no marriage or family existed. The events in *Fitzpatrick* had allowed the Court to permit unmarried same-sex couples to enjoy the same rights, albeit in diluted form to that of 'traditional' spouses; however social attitudes had continued to evolve, and at the time of this appeal, Parliament was drafting and approving the Civil Partnership Bill, which would later grant same-sex couples the privileges of married heterosexual partners; therefore the inclusion of HRA 1998 principles gave greater weight to the adjustment of the Rent Act 1977, as to allow those freedoms to provide equal rights ahead of the proposed legislation.

In the first hearing, the court made allowances to the interpretation of Convention principles on grounds that overt discrimination was not a virtue welcome in English law, and that rather than declaring incompatibility with the two doctrines, there was sufficient grounds to apply domestic legislation in a manner that provided fairness and equitability. After taking the matter to the Court of Appeal, the appellant was left with the same outcome, before presenting the matter to the House of Lords.

As with all cases of this nature, the facts were given equal attention, and while appreciation of s.3 of the HRA 1998 (Interpretation of legislation) reminded the House that interpretation of domestic statute was subject to 'possible' and not 'reasonable' constraints, the time was considered right to embrace the universal nature of close and loving bonds, and the freedoms of the Convention, without the need for Parliamentary involvement, thus the appeal was allowed by majority.

Key Citations

"[T]he rent payable under an assured tenancy is the contractual or market rent, which may be more than the fair rent payable under a statutory tenancy, and an assured tenant may be evicted for non-payment of rent without the court needing to be satisfied, as is essential in the case of a statutory tenancy, that it is reasonable to make a possession order."[56]

"Discrimination is an insidious practice. Discriminatory law undermines the rule of law because it is the antithesis of fairness. It brings the law into disrepute. It breeds resentment. It fosters an inequality of outlook which is demeaning alike to those unfairly benefited and those unfairly prejudiced."[57]

"Marriage is not now a prerequisite to protection under paragraph 2. The line drawn by Parliament is no longer drawn by reference to the status of marriage. Nor is parenthood, or the presence of children in the home, a precondition of security of tenure for the survivor of the original tenant."[58]

---

[56] *Ghaidan v Godin-Mendoza* [2004] 2 AC 557 [5] (Nicholls LJ).

[57] *Ghaidan v Godin-Mendoza* [2004] 2 AC 557 [9] (Nicholls LJ).

[58] *Ghaidan v Godin-Mendoza* [2004] 2 AC 557 [16] (Nicholls LJ).

"[T]he mere fact the language under consideration is inconsistent with a Convention-compliant meaning does not of itself make a Convention-compliant interpretation under section 3 impossible. Section 3 enables language to be interpreted restrictively or expansively."[59]

"Paragraph 2 of Schedule 1 to the Rent Act 1977 is unambiguous. But the social policy underlying the 1988 extension of security of tenure under paragraph 2 to the survivor of couples living together as husband and wife is equally applicable to the survivor of homosexual couples living together in a close and stable relationship."[60]

"Ordinary principles of statutory construction include a presumption that Parliament does not intend to legislate in a way which would put the United Kingdom in breach of its international obligations."[61]

"In enacting section 3(1), it cannot have been the intention of Parliament to place those asserting their rights at the mercy of the linguistic choices of the individual who happened to draft the provision in question."[62]

"Parliament was not out to devise an entertaining parlour game for lawyers, but, so far as possible, to make legislation operate compatibly with Convention rights. This means concentrating on matters of substance, rather than on matters of mere language."[63]

"[B]ecause section 3(1) is to be operated by many others besides the courts, and because it is concerned with interpreting and not with amending the offending provision, it respectfully seems to me that it would be going too far to insist that those using the section to interpret legislation should match the standards to be expected of a parliamentary draftsman amending the provision…"[64]

"[I]t is a purpose of all human rights instruments to secure the protection of the essential rights of members of minority groups, even when they are unpopular with the majority. Democracy values everyone equally even if the majority does not."[65]

"If it is not legitimate to discourage homosexual relationships, it cannot be legitimate to discourage stable, committed, marriage-like homosexual relationships of the sort which qualify the survivor to succeed to the home."[66]

---

[59] *Ghaidan v Godin-Mendoza* [2004] 2 AC 557 [32] (Nicholls LJ).

[60] *Ghaidan v Godin-Mendoza* [2004] 2 AC 557 [35] (Nicholls LJ).

[61] *Ghaidan v Godin-Mendoza* [2004] 2 AC 557 [60] (Millett LJ).

[62] *Ghaidan v Godin-Mendoza* [2004] 2 AC 557 [123] (Rodger LJ).

[63] *Ghaidan v Godin-Mendoza* [2004] 2 AC 557 [123] (Rodger LJ).

[64] *Ghaidan v Godin-Mendoza* [2004] 2 AC 557 [124] (Rodger LJ).

[65] *Ghaidan v Godin-Mendoza* [2004] 2 AC 557 [132] (Baroness Hale).

[66] *Ghaidan v Godin-Mendoza* [2004] 2 AC 557 [143] (Baroness Hale).

9. Jackson v Attorney General

The implementation of prohibitive statute designed to prevent the hunting of foxes with dogs, was a decision made by the ruling party in a time when the public had seen enough wanton killing to stamp it out for good. Under traditional constitutional processes, the act of passing a bill required full agreement of the House of Commons, the House of Lords and the Monarchy; however on this occasion the Parliament Act 1949 allowed for the creation of the Hunting Act 2004 without the acquiescence of the House of Lords; thus becoming a motion that sparked tremendous outrage from those in favour of the 'sport,' and resulting in this application for judicial review.

In seeking the reversal of this unprecedented ban, the appellants (Chairman of the Countryside Alliance, a professional huntsman and a self-employed farrier) relied upon the mechanism used to establish the 1949 Act in order to undermine its legality, and have the courts permanently remove it; however in order to clarify how the argument gained merit, it is first necessary to understand how the founding Acts came into existence.

The Parliament Act 1911 was first enacted so as to empower the House of Commons to pass certain Bills without the consent of the House of Lords, subject to a predetermined period of time, after which the applicable Act would enter into force with equal effect to that which would have required their consent. This Act was the inevitable product of a previous form of rule so dysfunctional, that without it the country ran risk of complete collapse or civil revolt, therefore it was not designed without a degree of resistance from certain quarters.

Many years passed until the Parliament Act 1949 made some amendments to the 1911 Act, which while considered minor, reduced the period of time in which the House of Commons would need to wait before achieving Royal Assent and subsequent enactment. This itself was brought into effect using the terms of s.2(1) of the 1911 Act, which expressed:

> "*[T]he Bill shall, unless the House of Commons direct to the contrary, be presented to His Majesty and become an Act of Parliament on the Royal Assent being signified,* notwithstanding that the House of Lords have not consented to the Bill."[67]

Therefore despite not following the conventional methods of construction, the 1949 Act was without doubt, primary legislation and beyond reproach of those in opposition; as was the case when the Hunting Act 2004 was passed, as well as the War Crimes Act 1991, the European Parliamentary Elections Act 1999 and the Sexual Offences (Amendment) Act 2000 before it. However, in a bid to dismantle the 2004 Act, the appellants drew attention to the wording, which failed to include obligatory reference to "the Lords Spiritual and Temporal and Commons," but instead used "Queen's most Excellent Majesty by and with the advice and consent of the Commons in accordance with the provisions of the Parliament Acts 1911 and 1949," upon which they claimed the legislation was merely secondary in effect and therefore invalid.

---

[67] Parliament Act 1911 s.1(1) (emphasis added).

Having been dismissed in their first hearing, the appellants continued to the Court of Appeal, which followed suit before allowing leave to the House of Lords. Here the principles of legislative power, along with the chequered history behind the 1911 and 1949 Acts, were clearly defined, along with express clarification of the meaning and purpose of legislation as below:

> "[A] Bill is not there to inform, to explain, to entertain or to perform any of the other usual functions of literature. A Bill's sole reason for existence is to change the law. The resulting Act is the law. A consequence of this unique function is that a Bill cannot set about communicating with the reader in the same way that other forms of writing do. It cannot use the same range of tools. In particular, it cannot repeat important points simply to emphasise their importance or safely explain itself by restating a proposition in different words. To do so would risk creating doubts and ambiguities that would fuel litigation. As a result, legislation speaks in a monotone and its language is compressed."[68]

Reiterating both the origins and validity of the 1911 and 1949 Acts, the House continued to illustrate that regardless of discrepancies of wording, the power and application of the Hunting Act 2004 remained as resolute as the 1911 Act and any before it, and so it was with the greatest of respect, that the appeal was uniformly dismissed.

---

[68] Select Committee, *Explanatory Note from First Parliamentary Counsel to the Select Committee on the Modernisation of the House of Commons* (HC 1997, 389, 2) para 35.

Key Citations

"Legislation under the 1911 Act is not similar to other delegated or subordinate legislation, such as statutory instruments and bylaws made under the authority of statute, but it is delegated or subordinate or derivative in the sense that its validity is open to investigation in the courts, which would not be permissible in the case of primary legislation."[69]

"The 1911 Act did, of course, effect an important constitutional change, but the change lay not in authorising a new form of sub-primary parliamentary legislation but in creating a new way of enacting primary legislation."[70]

"Section I of the 1911 Act involved no delegation of legislative power and authority to the Commons but a statutory recognition of where such power and authority in relation to supply had long been understood to lie."[71]

"The overall object of the 1911 Act was not to delegate power: it was to restrict, subject to compliance with the specified statutory conditions, the power of the Lords to defeat measures supported by a majority of the Commons, and thereby obviate the need for the monarch to create (or for any threat to be made that the monarch would create) peers to carry the Government's programme in the Lords."[72]

"[S]tatutory interpretation is properly cognisable by a court of law even though it relates to the legislative process. Statutes create law. The proper interpretation of a statute is a matter for the courts, not Parliament."[73]

---

[69] *Jackson v Attorney General* [2005] UKHL 56 [22] (Bingham LJ).

[70] *Jackson v Attorney General* [2005] UKHL 56 [24] (Bingham LJ).

[71] *Jackson v Attorney General* [2005] UKHL 56 [25] (Bingham LJ).

[72] *Jackson v Attorney General* [2005] UKHL 56 [25] (Bingham LJ).

[73] *Jackson v Attorney General* [2005] UKHL 56 [51] (Nicholls LJ).

10. Liversidge v Anderson

Reasonableness within the confines of legislation and determination of that principle fall into varying categories. National security under times of war, further compounds the need for subjective action when those bestowed executive powers must act to prevent dissent without fear of reprisal, or leave themselves undermined through abuse of legal recourse.

Acting upon the terms prescribed within the Defence (General) Regulations 1939,[74] it was decided by the Secretary of State, to issue a writ that served to detain a suspected 'threat' while the country was at war with Germany. For reasons undisclosed to the appellant on principle of national safety, the individual was held in indefinite detention in Brixton prison, as an act of subversion against known factions operating to weaken the country's defences.

After almost a year, the appellant sought to challenge the validity of the writ, contesting that his imprisonment was on fraudulent grounds, and that the above legislation conferred limited powers of issue that on this occasion, were in need of evidential support over subjective opinion. In addition to this, he requested that there ought to be proven grounds for his incarceration, and that those reasons needed to determine the eligibility to hold him. In the first hearing, the court dismissed his claim but granted leave to appeal, after which the Court of Appeal also refused to support any action taken against an executive order; however they did allow appeal to the House of Lords for purposes of exploration.

As foundation of the appeal, s.18B of the regulations read that:

> "If the Secretary of State has reasonable cause to believe any person to be of hostile origin or associations or to have been recently concerned in acts prejudicial to the public safety or the defence of the realm or in the preparation or instigation of such acts and that by reason thereof it is necessary to exercise control over him, *he may make an order against that person directing that he be detained.*"[75]

This particular aspect of legislation was now left to the House to examine in detail before establishing if, under circumstances where no written evidence had been submitted to justify the writ, the Secretary of State was liable to produce such material as to satisfy the restricted liberty of an individual innocent of any criminal wrongdoing. While in the immediate sense it ran risk of appearing beyond reproach and without just cause, the judges fully appreciated that in times of conflict it was ultra vires for the courts to expect confidential information to be brought into view in order to resolve what was essentially a claim for damages under the presumption of absolute civil liberty.

---

[74] Parliamentary Counsel to HM Treasury, *The Defence (General) Regulations 1939* (14th edn, HMSO 1943)

[75] Parliamentary Counsel to HM Treasury, *The Defence (General) Regulations 1939* (14th edn, HMSO 1943) (emphasis added)

Despite fully appreciating the need for personal satisfaction and the variances of reasonableness within numerous forms of English law, it was felt that within a position shouldering tremendous responsibility for the safety and welfare of both the state and the public, the phrase "has reasonable cause" was ultimately to be interpreted as subjective to the Secretary of State, and not one for justiciability or those bound to his decision to conclude.

Key Citations

"The argument that when the regulations mean different things they use different language and when they mean the same thing they use the same language breaks down, regrettable as this must be to the drafting purist."[76]

"All the courts today, and not least this House, are as jealous as they have ever been in upholding the liberty of the subject. But that liberty is a liberty confined and controlled by law, whether common law or statute."[77]

"The safeguard of British liberty is in the good sense of the people and in the system of representative and responsible government which has been evolved. If extraordinary powers are here given, they are given because the emergency is extraordinary and are limited to the period of the emergency."[78]

"[I]t was clear from the regulation that the decision on this difficult matter was not to be entrusted to one of His Majesty's judges, or to any ad hoc tribunal, but to the Home Secretary alone."[79]

"In my judgment, a court of law could not have before it the information on which the Secretary acts, still less the background of statecraft and national policy which is what must determine the action which he takes on it."[80]

"[I]f the question whether the Secretary of State had reasonable grounds for the belief on which his order was founded is one for a court of law to determine, it is plain that the court must be placed in full possession of all the relevant facts, and if some of those facts are withheld from it, even though it be by reason of public policy, it will have no option but to say that no reasonable grounds for his belief have been shown to exist."[81]

---

[76] *Liversidge v Anderson* [1942] AC 206 (HL) 256 (Macmillan LJ).

[77] *Liversidge v Anderson* [1942] AC 206 (HL) 260 (Wright LJ).

[78] *Liversidge v Anderson* [1942] AC 206 (HL) 261 (Wright LJ).

[79] *Liversidge v Anderson* [1942] AC 206 (HL) 261 (Wright LJ).

[80] *Liversidge v Anderson* [1942] AC 206 (HL) 267 (Wright LJ).

[81] *Liversidge v Anderson* [1942] AC 206 (HL) 279 (Romer LJ).

11. M v Home Office

Administrative confusion and errors in judgment, were the foundations of a refused application for asylum that at first glance appeared false, until professional evidence revealed otherwise. It was only after a collection of ministerial and administrative mishaps that the refugee brought civil action against the Home Secretary and the Crown.

In autumn of 1990, an African citizen arrived in the United Kingdom, claiming asylum on grounds that he had been a victim of torture while working as a school teacher in Zaire. His story, while sounding hard to imagine, was later corroborated by the attending doctor at the Medical Foundation for the Care of Victims of Torture, whose report stated:

> "I found nothing in his history or its presentation to suggest that it was in any way unreliable. His description of prison conditions has been confirmed innumerable times by other people who have experienced them. The scars he bears are entirely compatible with the causes he ascribes to them. He is suffering a degree of deafness and spinal trouble quite likely to have arisen from his mistreatment. Psychologically he describes symptoms very likely to arise from the experiences he described. He shows some evidence of depression and his continued detention can only aggravate these symptoms and he could easily become a serious suicide risk."

Prior to this disclosure, the Home Office had rejected his previous two submissions and plans were set in motion to return him back to Zaire, whereupon he had applied for judicial review after which time, the deportation arrangements were cancelled in lieu of his appearance before the court. Two months later, the review application was refused, at which point the appellant applied to the Court of Appeal.

Unfortunately his solicitors failed to lodge the application therefore it went unregistered, and while the doctor's report provided sufficient weight to support his claim, it was not received by the Home Office until a day before his planned removal from the country. By luck rather than judgment, the Court of Appeal had already made time to hear the case on the day of deportation, but dismissed the application while unaware of the report, or that the applicant was changing solicitors on grounds that his case had been misrepresented, and that a new application for judicial review was being lodged.

Having been heard before Garland J literally thirty minutes before the assigned plane was due to depart, it was decided that there needed to be further provisions in place to evaluate the matter fairly, so proceedings were adjourned in favour of another session the following day. This led to the cancelling of the flight by the appellant's solicitor who had telephoned the Home Office accordingly. During this period, Garland J interpreted that the Home Office had expressed permission for the appellant to remain in the country and explained:

> "[T]he application for leave to move for judicial review be adjourned on the undertaking by counsel for the Home Office . . . that the applicant would not be removed from the United Kingdom to Zaire."

For one reason or another, the information was never relayed to those accompanying the appellant and he was deported to Paris en route to his home country. Around the time the appellant was leaving there had been a meeting between the Parliamentary Under Secretary of State to the Home Office, Home Office officials and the appellant's representing solicitor, yet no intervening action had been taken with regard to the appellant's departure. This culminated in the appellant's solicitor meeting with Garland J in the midnight hours, whereupon the judge issued a written order requesting the appellant's immediate return and interim protection. Notice of this order then reached numerous state departments and their representatives, including the Home Secretary Kenneth Baker who while acting upon legal advice, declared the order beyond the jurisdiction of the judge (ultra vires), and that an appeal would be lodged against the order on grounds that there was insufficient cause for the appellant to receive asylum and return to the United Kingdom. It was there that the judge held the Home Secretary in contempt of court and declared his actions (or inactions) a breach of statutory duty.

Legal precedence of injunctions or orders served against either the Crown or their representatives dates back to *Feather v The Queen*, where Cockburn CJ remarked:

> "As the Sovereign cannot authorise wrong to be done, the authority of the Crown would afford no defence to an action brought for an illegal act committed by an officer of the Crown."[82]

This continued until the Crown Proceedings Act 1947, whereupon s.1 enabled action against the Crown by petition of right, while s.2 allowed tortious claims upon those identifiable under the Crown's protection. S.17 of Part II of the 1947 Act further provided a list of those Ministers and their departments, to allow civil claims against the department or the position held by those subject to the action. S.21(a) of the 1947 Act also explained that where an injunction or specific performance was sought, the courts would instead allow declaratory rights for those claiming, as to do otherwise would contradict the principle that the Crown can do no wrong.

Under the powers of s.31 of the Supreme Court Act 1981, RSC Ord.53 allowed for judicial review, whereupon s.37(1) of the 1981 Act provided that:

> "The High Court may by order (whether interlocutory or final) grant an injunction ... in all cases in which it appears to the court to be just and convenient to do so."[83]

This translated that irrespective of the violations argued by the Home Secretary, the intentions of Ord.53 were such that allowed the courts to grant interim relief where appropriate, as further expressed in The Supreme Court Practice 1993, which read:

> "Where the case is so urgent as to justify it, [the judge] could grant an interlocutory injunction or other interim relief pending the hearing of the application for leave to move for judicial review. But, if the judge has refused leave to move for judicial review he is functus officio and has no jurisdiction to

---

[82] *Feather v The Queen* (1865) 6 B & S 257 (QB) 296 (Cockburn CJ).

[83] Rules of the Supreme Court (NI)) 1980, SR 1980/346

grant any form of interim relief. The application for an interlocutory injunction or other interim relief could, however, be renewed before the Court of Appeal along with the renewal of the application for leave to move for judicial review."[84]

Having appealed against the charge of contempt, the Court of Appeal held that the Crown, a government department or a Minister were exempt from contempt; whereupon the case was presented to the House of Lords, who declared that Garland J had been acting well within his judicial powers throughout, and that in consideration of the limited knowledge held by the Home Secretary himself, it was only reasonable that the charge of contempt was applicable to the position held, rather than that of his own personal acts, at which point the Home Office appeal was dismissed, subject to amendments.

Key Citations

"[T]he argument that there is no power to enforce the law by injunction or contempt proceedings against a minister in his official capacity would, if upheld, establish the proposition that the executive obey the law as a matter of grace and not as a matter of necessity, a proposition which would reverse the result of the Civil War."[85]

"[C]ircumstances can occur where it is in the interests both of a person who is subject to the powers of government and of the government itself that the courts should be in a position to make an order which clearly sets out either what should or what should not be done by the government."[86]

"If there were no power to make coercive orders, then the need to rely on the law of contempt for the purpose of enforcing the orders would rarely arise."[87]

"[W]hile a citizen is entitled to obtain injunctive relief (including interim relief) against the Crown or an officer of the Crown to protect his interests under Community law he cannot do so in respect of his other interests which may be just as important."[88]

"[A]s long as the plaintiff sued the actual wrongdoer or the person who ordered the wrongdoing he could bring an action against officials personally, in particular as to torts committed by them, and they were not able to hide behind the immunity of the Crown."[89]

---

[84] Sir Jack IH Jacob (ed), *The Supreme Court Practice 1993* (Sweet & Maxwell 1992) 53/1 - 14/24

[85] *M v Home Office* [1994] 1 AC 377 (HL) 395 (Templeman LJ).

[86] *M v Home Office* [1994] 1 AC 377 (HL) 404 (Woolf LJ).

[87] *M v Home Office* [1994] 1 AC 377 (HL) 405 (Woolf LJ).

[88] *M v Home Office* [1994] 1 AC 377 (HL) 407 (Woolf LJ).

[89] *M v Home Office* [1994] 1 AC 377 (HL) 409 (Woolf LJ).

"It has never been suggested that a declaration is not available in proceedings against a minister in his official capacity and if Order 53 and section 31 apply to a minister in the case of declarations then, applying ordinary rules of construction, one would expect the position to be precisely the same in the case of injunctions."[90]

"While it is correct that an application for judicial review cannot be made until leave is granted, this does not mean that section 31(2) restricts the court's jurisdiction to grant interim or final injunctions until after leave has been given and this has been followed by lodging the formal application with the court."[91]

"[T]he language of section 31 being unqualified in its terms, there is no warrant for restricting its application so that in respect of ministers and other officers of the Crown alone the remedy of an injunction, including an interim injunction, is not available."[92]

"A purpose of the courts' powers to make findings of contempt is to ensure that the orders of the court are obeyed. This jurisdiction is required to be coextensive with the courts' jurisdiction to make the orders which need the protection which the jurisdiction to make findings of contempt provides."[93]

"On applications for judicial review orders can be made against ministers. In consequence of the developments identified already such orders must be taken not to offend the theory that the Crown can supposedly do no wrong. Equally, if such orders are made and not obeyed, the body against whom the orders were made can be found guilty of contempt without offending that theory, which would be the only justifiable impediment against making a finding of contempt."[94]

"[T]he Crown's relationship with the courts does not depend on coercion and in the exceptional situation when a government department's conduct justifies this, a finding of contempt should suffice."[95]

---

[90] *M v Home Office* [1994] 1 AC 377 (HL) 418 (Woolf LJ).

[91] *M v Home Office* [1994] 1 AC 377 (HL) 422 (Woolf LJ).

[92] *M v Home Office* [1994] 1 AC 377 (HL) 422 (Woolf LJ).

[93] *M v Home Office* [1994] 1 AC 377 (HL) 425 (Woolf LJ).

[94] *M v Home Office* [1994] 1 AC 377 (HL) 425 (Woolf LJ).

[95] *M v Home Office* [1994] 1 AC 377 (HL) 425 (Woolf LJ).

12. R v Secretary of State for the Home Department *ex p* Brind

Ministerial discretion and the supremacy of European principles, force the judiciary to impose demarcation when the imposition of press regulation extends the powers of the executive beyond what some might consider 'reasonable' bounds.

At a time when the media was becoming central to the lives of the general public, there were numerous attempts by terrorist factions to use television as a means of political propagation. In direct response to this, the Home Secretary of the time issued instructions to both the BBC (British Broadcasting Corporation) and the IBA (Independent Broadcasting Authority) to censor the speech and appearance of those representing such organisations, as to prevent viewers from taking offence and to cripple plans to advocate fear as a means of influence.

These orders fell under the terms of s.29(3) of the Broadcasting Act 1981 and clause 13(4) of the licences agreement between the BBC and IBA respectively, and while stymying the direct effects of terrorist representation, they were flexible enough to allow dubbed voiceovers for the sake of reporting, and also allowed the affected reporters to discuss the comments and associate the parties involved, therefore not entirely curtailing the views and commentary of those included within the Prevention of Terrorism (Temporary Provisions) Act 1984 and the Northern Ireland (Emergency Provisions) Act 1978.

In an abject reaction of professional outrage, a number of prominent and established representatives of the associated media sought a judicial review on grounds that the censorship of those affected, stood in direct violation of art.10 (Freedom of Expression) of the European Convention for the Protection of Human Rights and Fundamental Freedoms 1953, while the use of those powers was disproportionate to their objectives and irrational in design, to the extent that such an abuse of power was in need of legal redress.

Heard first in the Divisional Courts, the application was dismissed on grounds that while the principles of the Convention were recognised, the executive powers granted to those qualified were never given lightly, and that on this occasion there was insufficient evidence to suggest the Home Secretary had acted ultra vires of his position. Taken to the Court of Appeal, the appellants relied upon the principles held in *Associated Provincial Picture Houses Ltd v Wednesbury Corporation* [96] whereby the reasonableness of the decision must reflect the objectives while balancing the needs of public interest; again citing that when allowing the Home Secretary to enforce the orders, the executive must have had the Convention principles in mind, and so therefore had allowed a breach that denied impartiality to those affected.

Having evaluated the arguments presented, the Court dismissed the appeal while allowing leave to the House of Lords, at which point the same contentions were used to urge the judiciary to intervene and quash the restrictions now in place, with particular emphasis on the very principles upon which judicial review was founded. With due consideration of the points raised, the House reminded the appellants that judicial review was a means of management rather than contest for those displeased with case

---

[96] [1948] 1 KB 223.

outcomes, while emphasis was placed upon the almost microscopic levels of disruption the censorship caused the broadcasters when accusations of impartiality, irrationality and unreasonableness were made. When taken collectively, the House dismissed the appeal and ruled unanimously that regardless of what may appear as an abuse of power, was nothing more than a calculated protection of democracy; and that as expressed within art.10(1) of the Convention, those same rights of expression are subject to a degree of restriction where public interest requires it.

Key Citations

"In any civilised and law-abiding society the defeat of the terrorist is a public interest of the first importance."[97]

"In a field which concerns a fundamental human right—namely that of free speech—close scrutiny must be given to the reasons provided as justification for interference with that right."[98]

"Where Parliament has given to a minister or other person or body a discretion, the court's jurisdiction is limited, in the absence of a statutory right of appeal, to the supervision of the exercise of that discretionary power, so as to ensure that it has been exercised lawfully."[99]

---

[97] *R v Secretary of State for the Home Department ex p Brind* [1991] 1 AC 696 (HL) 749 (Bridge LJ).

[98] *R v Secretary of State for the Home Department ex p Brind* [1991] 1 AC 696 (HL) 757 (Ackner LJ).

[99] *R v Secretary of State for the Home Department ex p Brind* [1991] 1 AC 696 (HL) 757 (Ackner LJ).

13. R v Secretary of State for the Home Department *ex p* Fire Brigades Union

In a collective application for judicial review, the actions of the Secretary of State for the Home Department were held to account when a decision was made to override and subsequently remove, existing but as yet unenforced statute, in lieu of a more cost effective solution to criminal offence compensation.

In 1964 the unprecedented Criminal Injuries Compensation Scheme was created under the Crown's prerogative powers, and while described as "one of the most generous state compensation schemes for the victims of crimes of violence anywhere in the world", all payments were made ex gratia through nominated funds reserved by the House of Commons, meaning its operation existed beyond the scope of legislation and remained subject to the discretion of the appointed personal injury assessors.

In 1978 the Pearson Commission on Civil Liability and Compensation for Personal Injury Command Paper[100] proposed that the scheme needed to become statutory and operate upon tortious principles, as had already been applied. In 1986 it was reported that the scheme had now been included within ss.108 - 117 of sch.6 and 7 of the Criminal Justice Act 1988, in which s.171(1) of the Act read:

> "Subject to the following provisions of this section, this Act shall come into force *on such day as the Secretary of State may by order* made by statutory instrument appoint and different days may be appointed in pursuance of this subsection for different provisions or different purposes of the same provision."[101]

This translated that the Secretary of State was afforded a degree of discretion as to exactly when the powers of the scheme were to become fully enforced. In financial terms, the programme had experienced enormous growth, and by 1984 the government was paying out over £35m per year, with a backlog of nearly fifty-thousand claims. Based upon calculated projections, the government concluded that by the year 2000 the annual cost would have risen to around £550m, therefore a proposal was made to replace the existing system with a newly drafted compensation tariff, which was presented through a White Paper titled 'Compensating Victims of Violent Crime: Changes to the Criminal Injuries Compensation Scheme'.[102] In contrast, this system offered claimants a flat-rate compensation tariff that while lower in award levels, expedited the claim process and removed the need for legal advice aside from appeal cases, thus lowering the anticipated costs to an estimated £225m per year. It was also decided that the tariff-based scheme would likewise operate ex gratia, despite calls for statutory implementation of the existing system.

---

[100] Lord Chancellor's Department, *Royal Commission on Civil Liability and Compensation for Personal Injury: Report* (Cmd 7054, 1978)

[101] Criminal Justice Act 1988, s.171(1) (emphasis added).

[102] Home Office, *Compensating Victims of Violent Crime: Changes to the Criminal Injuries Compensation Scheme* (Cmd 2434, 1993)

In light of this unexpected turn, the respondent Fired Brigades Union along with the National Association of Schoolmasters and Union of Women Teachers, UNISON, GMB, the Royal College of Nursing, the Transport and General Workers' Union, the Prison Officers' Association, the Associated Society of Locomotive Engineers and Firemen, the Civil and Public Services Association, the Trades Union Congress and the NatWest Staff Association applied for judicial review on grounds that the decision by the Secretary of State to (i) avoid enforcement of ss.108 - 117 of sch.6 and 7 of the Criminal Justice Act 1988 and (ii) implement the Criminal Injuries Compensation Tariff scheme, constituted a breach of statutory duty and abuse of position, and therefore the courts were required to issue an order of mandamus to enforce the statute, and an interlocutory injunction to prevent the implementation of the tariff.

In the first instance, the respondents were awarded leave for judicial review on the proviso that the tariff scheme remained in stasis until a verdict had been reached, and in lieu of the injunction being dropped; whereupon the court dismissed the application but granted leave to appeal. In the Court of Appeal it was held that the terms of ss.108 - 117 of sch.6 and 7 of the Criminal Justice Act 1988 were in principle effective and so no action was needed, but that the overriding of existing statute in favour of the tariff constituted an abuse of position; at which point the Secretary of State appealed, while the respondents cross-appealed.

Heard before the House of Lords, the facts of the case were given due consideration, however the lines were drawn between political discourse and the powers of the court, in which the suggestion that the House ought to 'enforce' the enactment of a statute already enshrined was held as ultra vires to the judiciary, but that circumvention of the powers of the Criminal Justice Act 1988 amounted to an abuse of prerogative powers, and one representative of a frustration of statute through the actions of those obliged to enforce them with unanimity; whereupon both appeals were dismissed by majority.

Key Citations

"[A]ny decision by the Secretary of State as to whether or not sections 108 to 117 should be brought into effect at any particular time is a decision of a political and administrative character quite unsuitable to be the subject of review by a court of law."[103]

"While no doubt many members of the public may be expected to have hoped that sections 108 to 117 of the Act of 1988 would be brought into force, they had no right to have them brought into force."[104]

---

[103] *R v Secretary of State for the Home Department ex p Fire Brigades Union* [1995] 2 All ER 244 (HL) 544 (Keith LJ).

[104] *R v Secretary of State for the Home Department ex p Fire Brigades Union* [1995] 2 All ER 244 (HL) 545 (Keith LJ).

"[T]he doctrine of legitimate expectation cannot reasonably be extended to the public at large, as opposed to particular individuals or bodies who are directly affected by certain executive action."[105]

"In the absence of express provisions to the contrary in the Act, the plain intention of Parliament in conferring on the Secretary of State the power to bring certain sections into force is that such power is to be exercised so as to bring those sections into force when it is appropriate and unless there is a subsequent change of circumstances which would render it inappropriate to do so."[106]

"[T]he Secretary of State made the attempt to bind himself not to exercise the power conferred by section 171(1) and such attempt was an unlawful act."[107]

"It is for Parliament, not the executive, to repeal legislation. The constitutional history of this country is the history of the prerogative powers of the Crown being made subject to the overriding powers of the democratically elected legislature as the sovereign body."[108]

"[I]f Parliament has conferred on the executive statutory powers to do a particular act, that act can only thereafter be done under the statutory powers so conferred: any pre-existing prerogative power to do the same act is pro tanto excluded."[109]

"[A]lthough during the suspension of the coming into force of the statutory provisions the old prerogative powers continue to exist, the existence of such legislation basically affects the mode in which such prerogative powers can be lawfully exercised."[110]

---

[105] *R v Secretary of State for the Home Department ex p Fire Brigades Union* [1995] 2 All ER 244 (HL) 545 (Keith LJ).

[106] *R v Secretary of State for the Home Department ex p Fire Brigades Union* [1995] 2 All ER 244 (HL) 551 (Browne-Wilkinson LJ).

[107] *R v Secretary of State for the Home Department ex p Fire Brigades Union* [1995] 2 All ER 244 (HL) 551 (Browne-Wilkinson LJ).

[108] *R v Secretary of State for the Home Department ex p Fire Brigades Union* [1995] 2 All ER 244 (HL) 552 (Browne-Wilkinson LJ).

[109] *R v Secretary of State for the Home Department ex p Fire Brigades Union* [1995] 2 All ER 244 (HL) 552 (Browne-Wilkinson LJ).

[110] *R v Secretary of State for the Home Department ex p Fire Brigades Union* [1995] 2 All ER 244 (HL) 554 (Browne-Wilkinson LJ).

14. R v Secretary of State for Transport *ex p* Factortame Ltd (No.2)

Direct effect compatibility and the obligation owed by Member States to transpose Directives and Treaties as binding upon national laws, was a ruling that would soon unearth conflicts of interest. On this occasion, the contention was brought about by aggressive amendment to statute in favour of the fishing industry.

Until 1988, those parties involved in domestic commercial fishing were required to register under the Merchant Shipping Act 1894; an act that allowed overseas companies to operate outside British waters, but still have their fleets registered under United Kingdom incorporation. As a means of preventing 'quota hopping' (over-fishing), it was enacted by Parliament to include Part II of the Merchant Shipping Act 1988 and Merchant Shipping (Registration of Fishing Vessels) Regulations 1988, to the effect that all those trading were to re-register under new conditions.

These terms required that in order to qualify for registration, the company must have a minimum of seventy-five percent British ownership, and where ownership fell outside the United Kingdom, there needed to be a seventy-five percent shareholding by British citizens. This translated that the appellants who had been previously registered for over almost twenty years, were now unable to re-register, as the owners were Spanish and thus exempt from the new legislation.

Having appreciated the United Kingdom's position as a Member State, and subsequent membership to European Community law, the firm sought proceedings under the principle that the choice taken to exclude other EU members from registration had displayed an overt refusal to comply with art.177 of the EEC Treaty. Furthermore, it was claimed that where Community rights were held to have 'direct effect', it was the onus of the national courts to suspend challenged legislation, with the granting of interim relief where proven necessary.

When heard in the Divisional Courts, the claim was supported and provisions made to allow the unfettered trading of the claimants, until such time that clarification was found in the challenge against the amended 1984 Act. However, when appealed by the Secretary of State, the Appeal Court set aside the previous finding, while granting leave of appeal to the House of Lords. In this instance the House agreed that should the claimants fail in their argument, the financial damage would be sufficient enough to cause irretrievable damage to the firm, but that without a preliminary ruling by the European Court of Justice, it was impossible to determine (i) if the courts were empowered to suspend legislative effect and (ii) how best to determine what form the interim relief should take.

Upon deliberate consideration by the Court, it was unanimously agreed that when the objectives of direct effect were designed, they were done so in a way that intended literal application with immediate purpose, and that unless under exceptional circumstances, it was the duty of the national courts to hold the powers of Community law above those of domestic interest; and that when matters required it, they were to construe that any relevance for interim relief would, by extension, be both applied and agreed by the Member States themselves.

Key Citations

"[N]ational courts are required to afford complete and effective judicial protection to individuals on whom enforceable rights are conferred under a directly effective Community provision, on condition that the Community provision governs the matter in question from the moment of its entry into force…"[111]

"Interim protection is intended to prevent so far as possible the damage occasioned by the fact that the establishment and the existence of the right are not fully contemporaneous from prejudicing the effectiveness and the very purpose of establishing the right, which was also specifically affirmed by the Court of Justice when it linked interim protection to a requirement that, when delivered, the judgment will be fully effective…"[112]

"To give priority to the national legislation merely because it has not yet been definitively established as incompatible with Community law (and thus to proceed on the basis merely of a putative compatibility) may amount to depriving the Community rules of the effective judicial protection which is to be afforded to them…"[113]

"[U]nder Community law, the national court must be able to afford interim protection, where the pre-conditions are met, to rights claim by an individual on the basis of provisions of Community law having direct effect, pending the final outcome of the proceedings, including proceedings on a reference to the Court of Justice for a preliminary ruling."[114]

"[T]hat the national court's duty to afford effective judicial protection to rights conferred on the individual by Community law, where the relevant requirements are satisfied, cannot fail to include the provision of interim protection for the rights claimed, pending a final determination."[115]

"[I]t is for the national court, obviously, to determine whether the preconditions for interim protection are met, but also that, in the absence of Community harmonisation, those preconditions must be and must remain those provided for by the individual, national legal systems."[116]

---

[111] *R v Secretary of State for Transport ex p Factortame Ltd (No.2)* [1991] 1 AC 603 (HL) 628 (AG Tesauro).

[112] *R v Secretary of State for Transport ex p Factortame Ltd (No.2)* [1991] 1 AC 603 (HL) 630 (AG Tesauro).

[113] *R v Secretary of State for Transport ex p Factortame Ltd (No.2)* [1991] 1 AC 603 (HL) 636 (AG Tesauro).

[114] *R v Secretary of State for Transport ex p Factortame Ltd (No.2)* [1991] 1 AC 603 (HL) 637 (AG Tesauro).

[115] *R v Secretary of State for Transport ex p Factortame Ltd (No.2)* [1991] 1 AC 603 (HL) 638 (AG Tesauro).

[116] *R v Secretary of State for Transport ex p Factortame Ltd (No.2)* [1991] 1 AC 603 (HL) 638 (AG Tesauro).

15. Regina (SB) v Governors of Denbigh High School

A difference of opinion regarding school uniform found itself thrust into judicial review when a Muslim pupil refused to follow school policy, but insisted freedom to choose under the terms of the Convention. When the claim was counter-challenged, the courts fell into conflict as to procedural requirements, and that of continued mediation between parties.

Seventeen year-old Shabina Begum commenced legal proceedings against Denbigh High School, after the Headmaster refused to let her wear a religious garment known as a 'jilbab' because it was not in accordance with existing school uniform policy; a policy which had been sensitively implemented through consultation with the local Muslim community several years prior to the incident.

The respondent had been aware of this policy for two years, and had worn the approved uniform during school without protest; however, when advised to go home and change or risk staying away from the school, the respondent claimed that such a refusal to let her 'manifest' her religious beliefs and removal from school, directly violated arts.8 (Right to respect for private and family life), 9 (Freedom of thought, conscience and religion) and 14 (Prohibition of discrimination) of the European Convention on Human Rights; and that denying her access to an education was also a breach of art.2 (Right to life) of the Convention.

After numerous solicitors failed to sway the school's decision, and despite every effort being made on the part of the school to help bring the respondent back to her classes, receive home teaching, or move to an alternative school that would allow her to wear her jilbab, the case eventually went to court where the original judgment was found in favour of the appellants.

When subject to the Appeal Court the residing judges reversed the decision back in favour of the respondent, after which the school sought leave to appeal to the House of Lords. Here, after lengthy exploration of the manner in which the Appeal Court approached the case, the House found by majority that while deprivation of the right to observe and manifest art.9 of the Convention prima facie warranted a claim for judicial review, it was equally important to note that art.9(2) gave express terms as to when an institution or local authority policy is deemed to have interfered with that right.

On this occasion, such a claim was simply untenable given the thorough attention to detail shown by the school when designing and approving the uniform worn at the time the respondent sought action; and so for this reason (and many more besides) the appeal was upheld and the original judgment restored, while the House remained mindful of the errors shown by the lower courts throughout the trial.

Key Citations

"The school authorities had statutory authority to lay down rules on uniform, and those rules were very clearly communicated to those affected by them."[117]

"The headscarf was permitted in 1993, following detailed consideration of the uniform policy, in response to requests by several girls. There was no evidence that this was opposed. But there was no pressure at any time, save by the respondent, to wear the jilbab, and that has been opposed."[118]

"It was feared that acceding to the respondent's request would or might have significant adverse repercussions. It would in my opinion be irresponsible of any court, lacking the experience, background and detailed knowledge of the head teacher, staff and governors, to overrule their judgment on a matter as sensitive as this."[119]

"Article 9 does not require that one should be allowed to manifest one's religion at any time and place of one's own choosing."[120]

"[B]y choosing to pursue her higher education in a secular university a student submits to those university rules, which may make the freedom of students to manifest their religion subject to restrictions as to place and manner intended to ensure harmonious coexistence between students of different beliefs."[121]

"[T]he purpose of the Human Rights Act 1998 was not to enlarge the rights or remedies of those in the United Kingdom whose Convention rights have been violated but to enable those rights and remedies to be asserted and enforced by the domestic courts of this country…"[122]

"[A] two-year interruption in the education of any child must always be a subject for profound regret. But it was the result of the respondent's unwillingness to comply with a rule to which, as I have concluded, the school were entitled to adhere, and, since her religious convictions forbade compliance, of her failure to secure prompt admission to another school where her religious convictions could be accommodated."[123]

---

[117] *Regina (SB) v Governors of Denbigh High School* [2007] 1 AC 100 [26] (Bingham LJ).

[118] *Regina (SB) v Governors of Denbigh High School* [2007] 1 AC 100 [33] (Bingham LJ).

[119] *Regina (SB) v Governors of Denbigh High School* [2007] 1 AC 100 [34] (Bingham LJ).

[120] *Regina (SB) v Governors of Denbigh High School* [2007] 1 AC 100 [50] (Hoffman LJ).

[121] *Regina (SB) v Governors of Denbigh High School* [2007] 1 AC 100 [23] (Bingham LJ).

[122] *Regina (SB) v Governors of Denbigh High School* [2007] 1 AC 100 [29] (Bingham LJ).

[123] *Regina (SB) v Governors of Denbigh High School* [2007] 1 AC 100 [36] (Bingham LJ).

16. Ridge v Baldwin (No.1)

'Justice should not only be done, but should manifestly and undoubtedly be seen to be done'[124] is a phrase too often overlooked by those seeking legal remedy, and so when fear and prejudice cloud the flow of proceedings, the outcome is one left wanting. On this occasion, the alleged actions of a police employee provoke a one-sided evaluation of accounts, instead of a balanced discourse between parties.

In 1925, the appellant joined Brighton police force, after which he was regularly promoted until reaching the position of chief constable. At this time, the police were overlooked by the watch committee, who were endowed with powers short of that held by the Secretary of State. In 1957, and at a time close to the point of his retirement, the appellant was embroiled in a conspiracy charge involving himself and four other officers, upon which the the respondent watch committee took steps to suspend him from service under the terms of the Police Discipline (Deputy Chief Constables, Assistant Chief Constables and Chief Constables) Regulations 1952, while allowing him full pay under regulation 15 of the same legal instrument.

Having been tried in the Central Criminal Court, the appellant was acquitted of the charges brought against him, after which his solicitor requested he be reinstated. At the summation of the trial, the presiding judge passed comment as to the qualities shown by the appellant when carrying out his role, by saying to those sentenced:

> "[N]either of you had that professional and moral leadership which both of you should have had and were entitled to expect from the chief constable of Brighton, now acquitted…"

Within a month, the appellant was tried for a second indictment concerning the receipt of £20 from a known criminal, to which he pleaded not guilty, and for which the prosecution offered no evidence with which to convict; whereupon the judge commented again:

> "This prospect and this risk will remain until a leader is given to the force who will be a new influence, and who will set a different example from that which has lately obtained."

The next day the appellant was informed of a watch committee meeting yet was extended no invitation, after which he received a letter informing him of his dismissal. The reasons cited were based upon numerous unfounded statements by members of both the committee and the town clerk, both suggesting his negligence in the discharge of duty, thus being unfit for purpose, and that the decision had been based upon conferred powers of s.191(4) of the Municipal Corporations Act 1882.

That same day, the appellant's solicitor wrote to the Secretary of State contending that the dismissal was unlawful, an affront to the processes of natural justice, and that they were appealing under the Police (Appeals) Act 1927 on grounds that the terms of the dismissal failed to disclose specific details that in turn were subject to his right to

---

[124] *R v Sussex Justices ex p McCarthy* [1924] 1 KB 256 (KB) 259 (Hewart CJ).

provide a statement of defence under regulation 18 of SI 1952 No.1706.[125] In such circumstances, there must also be a tribunal hearing, whereupon submissions by both parties must be evaluated and assessed before the watch committee can, on proof of the evidence, decide the appropriate punishment where justified. By the provisions of the Police Pensions Act 1948, it was then the duty of the Secretary of State to determine if those dismissed were entitled to their pensions where relevant, and on this occasion the appellant was asking for such rights instead of reinstatement.

Having been brought before the courts, the first judge held that that the dismissal was null and void, but subject to the final decision of the Secretary of State, who had at such time, dismissed the appellant's appeal, whereupon a similar fate was found in the Court of Appeal. Presented for a final time to the House of Lords, the facts were explored to a greater extent, at which point it was held by majority that the respondents' were obliged under s.4(1) of the Police Act 1919, to provide the appellant with an opportunity to defend himself against the claims proposed yet unproven, and that to circumvent the legal procedures expected, was tantamount to a violation of natural justice and subsequently void of merit. It was for that reason that the appeal was allowed, and the matter referred back to the courts for revisitation of the facts with note that the appellant sought only his full pension rights and not a return to work.

Key Citations

"In modern times opinions have sometimes been expressed to the effect that natural justice is so vague as to be practically meaningless. But I would regard these as tainted by the perennial fallacy that because something cannot be cut and dried or nicely weighed or measured therefore it does not exist."[126]

"[T]he power of dismissal in the Act of 1882 could not then have been exercised and cannot now be exercised until the watch committee have informed the constable of the grounds on which they propose to proceed and have given him a proper opportunity to present his case in defence."[127]

"The body with the power to decide cannot lawfully proceed to make a decision until it has afforded to the person affected a proper opportunity to state his case."[128]

"There are many cases where two remedies are open to an aggrieved person, but there is no general rule that by going to some other tribunal he puts it out of his power thereafter to assert his rights in court…"[129]

---

[125] Police Discipline (Deputy Chief Constables, Assistant Chief Constables and Chief Constables) Regulations 1952, SI 1952/1706

[126] *Ridge v Baldwin (No.1)* [1964] AC 40 (HL) 64 (Reid LJ).

[127] *Ridge v Baldwin (No.1)* [1964] AC 40 (HL) 79 (Reid LJ).

[128] *Ridge v Baldwin (No.1)* [1964] AC 40 (HL) 80 (Reid LJ).

[129] *Ridge v Baldwin (No.1)* [1964] AC 40 (HL) 81 (Reid LJ).

"[O]nce there was a report or allegation from which it appeared that a chief constable may have committed an offence it was a condition precedent to any dismissal based on a finding of guilt of such offence that the regulations should in essentials have been put into operation."[130]

"It is well established that the essential requirements of natural justice at least include that before someone is condemned he is to have an opportunity of defending himself, and in order that he may do so that he is to be made aware of the charges or allegations or suggestions which he has to meet…"[131]

"[W]here the power to be exercised involves a charge made against the person who is dismissed, by that I mean a charge of misconduct, the principles of natural justice have to be observed before the power is exercised."[132]

"A man may be unfit because he is stupid, vacillating, unable to meet a crisis or generally to command others, but I do not see this as the subject-matter of a charge."[133]

"[E]ach case depends on its own facts, and that here the deprivation of a pension without a hearing is on the face of it a denial of justice which cannot be justified upon the language of the section under consideration."[134]

---

[130] *Ridge v Baldwin (No.1)* [1964] AC 40 (HL) 113 (Morris LJ).

[131] *Ridge v Baldwin (No.1)* [1964] AC 40 (HL) 113 (Morris LJ).

[132] *Ridge v Baldwin (No.1)* [1964] AC 40 (HL) 132 (Hodson LJ).

[133] *Ridge v Baldwin (No.1)* [1964] AC 40 (HL) 132 (Hodson LJ).

[134] *Ridge v Baldwin (No.1)* [1964] AC 40 (HL) 133 (Hodson LJ).

17. Thoburn v Sunderland City Council

In a collective hearing, the facts surrounding national transition between imperial and metric measurements for the purposes of trade, gave rise to claims of unlawful application and subsequent challenge within the High Court as below:

Thoburn v Sunderland City Council

In this matter, a greengrocer was accused of trading without licensed weighing scales as required under s.11(2) of the Weights and Measures Act 1985. It was also alleged that despite a number of warnings to have his scales calibrated in line with the legal requirements, the defendant had continued to operate the machines, until their seizure by the local authority pending litigation. After failing in his defence in the Divisional Court, the defendant applied for referral to the High Court, in order that the legalities of both imperial and metric measurements be further discussed.

Hunt v Hackney London Borough Council

On this occasion, another fruit and vegetable trader was accused of a number of offences under s.4 of the Prices Act 1974 and s.28(1) of the Weights and Measures Act 1985, after commercial standards officers made discreet purchases revealing average product weight losses of twenty percent in favour of the defendant. Having been charged in the first instance, the defendant challenged the validity of the legislation, and sought the opinion of the High Court on grounds that he contended the applicability of the 1974 Act and the unlawfulness of displaying goods under the imperial weights system.

Harman and another v Cornwall County Council

The facts of this matter involved a market trader and a fishmonger who were both accused of selling their produce using imperial units of cost, thus violating art.5 of the Price Marking Order 1999, as found under the Prices Act 1974 and sch.1 of the Weights and Measures Act 1985, as amended by the Weights and Measures (Metrication Amendments) Regulations 1994 (SI 1994/1851). It was also alleged that the two defendants had prevented their attending local authority representative from removing the imperial price stickers when attempting to obtain evidence of their acts. Having both admitted liability, the judge was referred to the outcome of *Thoburn*, and raised the question as to the intention that both imperial and metric systems were to continue to run in parallel to one another, and whether the trading standards officers were acting ultra vires when attempting to obtain pricing stickers from traders, despite no suggestion of dishonesty by those accused.

Collins v Sutton London Borough Council

In a slightly different circumstance, the appellant had argued that the terms of the renewal of his trading licence had been unlawfully amended by the issuing council, and applied for a summons under s.30(1)(a) of the London Local Authorities Act 1990. It was claimed that under the Weights and Measures Act 1985 (Metrication) (Amendment) Order 1994, the Units of Measurement Regulations 1994 and the Weights and Measures (Metrication Amendments) Regulations 2001 (SI 2001/85), the local authority had instructed the appellant that he must display and charge for his produce under the metric weights system, and that such a request constituted a breach of statutory powers and a violation of art.10 of the Human Rights Act 1998 (Freedom of expression). Having again considered the position taken in *Thoburn*, the questions of HRA 1998 breaches and the imposition of metric pricing over imperial, were put before the High Court for evaluation.

S.1(1) of the Weights and Measures Act 1963, provided that both the metric and imperial system of measurements were permitted equal presence within the United Kingdom until the creation of the European Communities Act 1972. With the introduction of Council Directive 80/181/EC in 1989, chapter 1 of the Directive Annex cited that the metre and the kilogram were to become the single legal measurements of both length and mass; however chapter IV provided that certain goods sold loose in bulk were allowed to be measured in pounds and ounces until 31 December 1999.

In the following two years, the Units of Measurement Regulations 2001 (SI 2001/55) provided that imperial measures, while unlawful as primary indicators for sale, were still permitted as secondary indicators until 1 January 2010, while contrastingly, the Price Marking Order 1999 required traders to indicate unit prices in metric measures, and that anything to the contrary was a criminal offence under para.5 of sch.2 of the Prices Act 1974.

When brought before the High Court, the four appellants relied upon the contention that the Weights and Measures Act 1985 (Metrication) (Amendment) Order 1994, Units of Measurement Regulations 1994, Weights and Measures (Metrication Amendments) Regulations 1994 and the Price Marking Order 1999 were all unlawful and thus invalid under the principle of 'implied repeal'. This is applied when Parliament enacts successive statutes containing inconsistent terms, whereupon the former is repealed by the latter in order to avoid future binding and confusion of effect. It was also argued that the 1985 Act had repealed s.2(2) of the European Communities Act 1972, so to prevent future subordinate legislation, as had been used to replace the imperial with the metric measurement system.

Having considered the somewhat unorthodox line of argument taken by the appellants, the Court held that while observation of European Community law remained first and foremost to the function of the sovereign, there was nothing in the European Communities Act 1972 that allowed any outside jurisdiction to compromise the supremacy of Parliament, and that conflicting legislation was exempt from the principle of implied repeal when held to be constitutional in effect; as was the case when both EU and domestic law were at odds. This led to the conclusion that domestic law stipulated how the executive measures of the 1972 Act were only subject to repeal by express and specific decisions and not implication, upon which all four appeals were dismissed.

Key Citations

"Parliament cannot bind its successors, and that is a requirement of legislative sovereignty."[135]

"Parliament cannot bind its successors by stipulating against repeal, wholly or partly, of the 1972 Act. It cannot stipulate as to the manner and form of any subsequent legislation. It cannot stipulate against implied repeal any more than it can stipulate against express repeal."[136]

"[T]here are no circumstances in which the jurisprudence of the Court of Justice can elevate Community law to a status within the corpus of English domestic law to which it could not aspire by any route of English law itself."[137]

"The conditions of Parliament's legislative supremacy in the United Kingdom necessarily remain in the United Kingdom's hands. But the traditional doctrine has in my judgment been modified. It has been done by the common law, wholly consistently with constitutional principle."[138]

"There are now classes or types of legislative provision which cannot be repealed by mere implication. These instances are given, and can only be given, by our own courts, to which the scope and nature of parliamentary sovereignty are ultimately confided."[139]

"[A] constitutional statute is one which (a) conditions the legal relationship between citizen and state in some general, overarching manner, or (b) enlarges or diminishes the scope of what we would now regard as fundamental constitutional rights."[140]

"A constitutional statute can only be repealed, or amended in a way which significantly affects its provisions touching fundamental rights or otherwise the relation between citizen and state, by unambiguous words on the face of the later statute."[141]

"The fundamental legal basis of the United Kingdom's relationship with the EU rests with the domestic, not the European, legal powers."[142]

---

[135] *Thoburn v Sunderland City Council* [2002] EWHC Admin 195 [51] (Laws LJ).

[136] *Thoburn v Sunderland City Council* [2002] EWHC Admin 195 [59] (Laws LJ).

[137] *Thoburn v Sunderland City Council* [2002] EWHC Admin 195 [59] (Laws LJ).

[138] *Thoburn v Sunderland City Council* [2002] EWHC Admin 195 [59] (Laws LJ).

[139] *Thoburn v Sunderland City Council* [2002] EWHC Admin 195 [60] (Laws LJ).

[140] *Thoburn v Sunderland City Council* [2002] EWHC Admin 195 [62] (Laws LJ).

[141] *Thoburn v Sunderland City Council* [2002] EWHC Admin 195 [63] (Laws LJ).

[142] *Thoburn v Sunderland City Council* [2002] EWHC Admin 195 [69] (Laws LJ).

2. Contract Law

1. Bristol and West Building Society v Mothew

During a notable slump in the housing market, breach of contract, negligence and breach of fiduciary duty become central to the misgivings of a solicitor, whose oversight led to financial loss for the lender. For reasons atypical to existing procedures, the lender sought recovery of the loss through equitable principles, where other options failed.

In the late 1980s, a building society entered into a mortgage arrangement with a couple who having realised their previous mortgage, were looking to secure a second property for a sum of £73,000. Conditional to the agreement, the respondent mortgagees stipulated that the £59,000 loaned, was subject to the mortgagors paying the balance of the property from existing capital, as opposed to additional borrowing, so as to reduce any risk of default and retain creditor priority.

This reservation was expressed to the acting appellant solicitor, after which the appellant agreed to undertake the conveyance and provide a full report, as contained in their contract. During the period before completion of the purchase, the mortgagors took out a small charge against their existing property for £3,350 to help raise the funds needed to secure the mortgage, and on principle that the debt would be later secured against the new house. Despite knowledge of this, the appellant failed to report the change in financial circumstances to the respondents, instead continuing to press ahead with the conveyance.

Having completed the purchase, the mortgagors honoured a number of repayments before lapsing into default, whereupon the new house was sold as part of the repossession process. Unfortunately, due to the crash in property values the amount recovered fell short of satisfying the debt by £6,000. This left the respondents with no choice other than to litigate for damages at the expense of the solicitor. When heard in the original trial, the judge considered the novelty of contractual breach, but ruled that such an approach required evidence to show that the respondents would not have loaned the money, had they known the true facts.

This led to a claim under equity, inasmuch as the appellants had acted in breach of their fiduciary duty to the respondents, and that remoteness or proof of causation were irrelevant, as was the requirement for a breach of contract. In conclusion, the judge ruled in favour of the respondents under the principles of equity, and awarded damages to the effect of £59,000, less the funds raised from the sale, while allowing for assessment for damages under breach of contract.

Having been challenged in the Court of Appeal, the appellants contended that the respondents had come to learn about the second small charge prior to the completion of purchase; however it was later established that the report submitted by the appellants had occurred prior to their discovery, and so was after the fact. When discussing damages, it had been agreed in *Banque Bruxelles Lambert SA v Eagle Star Insurance Co Ltd*[143] that failure to take care, give proper advice and provide accurate information

---

[143] [1997] AC 191.

represented scales of award, and that on this occasion the appellants were liable only for the consequences of misinformation and nothing more, while the onus was on the respondents to establish the scope of loss brought about by the appellants error and not the shortfall in sale value when the property was sold, particularly as the two events were unrelated.

Turning to the claim under equity, the court investigated the argument that the appellants had breached their fiduciary duty and therefore held the mortgage funds on constructive trust for the respondents. After careful examination of the principle of fiduciary duties, it was agreed that if construed as a fiduciary relationship, the oversight of the appellant did not constitute a breach of duty to either the mortgagees or the respondents, as the appellants had been consciously acting in good faith throughout the transaction. This translated that any subsequent lapse of skill or application was not deliberate but accidental, which negated the claim of fiduciary breach, and by default, removed any liability for breaching a constructive trust; at which point the appeal was upheld and the previous decision reversed.

Key Citations

"The expression "fiduciary duty" is properly confined to those duties which are peculiar to fiduciaries and the breach of which attracts legal consequences differing from those consequent upon the breach of other duties."[144]

"It is similarly inappropriate to apply the expression to the obligation of a trustee or other fiduciary to use proper skill and care in the discharge of his duties. If it is confined to cases where the fiduciary nature of the duty has special legal consequences, then the fact that the source of the duty is to be found in equity rather than the common law does not make it a fiduciary duty."[145]

"The various obligations of a fiduciary merely reflect different aspects of his core duties of loyalty and fidelity. Breach of fiduciary obligation, therefore, connotes disloyalty or infidelity. Mere incompetence is not enough."[146]

"[I]f a fiduciary is properly acting for two principals with potentially conflicting interests he must act in good faith in the interests of each and must not act with the intention of furthering the interests of one principal to the prejudice of those of the other..."[147]

---

[144] *Bristol and West Building Society v Mothew* [1998] Ch 1 (CA) 16 (Millet LJ).

[145] *Bristol and West Building Society v Mothew* [1998] Ch 1 (CA) 16 (Millet LJ).

[146] *Bristol and West Building Society v Mothew* [1998] Ch 1 (CA) 18 (Millet LJ).

[147] *Bristol and West Building Society v Mothew* [1998] Ch 1 (CA) 19 (Millet LJ).

2. Carlill v Carbolic Smoke Ball Co.

The primary ingredients to a valid and enforceable contract are (i) offer (ii) acceptance (iii) consideration and (iv) performance; and so on this occasion, the sale of medicinal apparatus proved the undoing of what may have at first appeared to be a lucrative use of marketing and false pretence.

In 1891, an advertisement was placed in the Pall Mall Gazette, which boasted the remedial powers of carbolic smoke balls, that when used in accordance with the manufacturers instructions, could prevent users from the effects of influenza. The exact words used were:

> "100*l* reward will be paid by the Carbolic Smoke Ball Company to any person who contracts the increasing epidemic influenza, colds, or any disease caused by taking cold, after having used the ball three times daily for two weeks according to the printed directions supplied with each ball. 1000*l* is deposited with the Alliance Bank, Regent Street shewing our sincerity in the matter."

Having decided to take the challenge, the respondent in this appeal purchased and used the product in full observation of the terms of the advert, yet still caught the virus, whereupon she sued for breach of contract. Having examined the nature of her claim, the court awarded in favour of the respondent before the appellants sought to challenge the existence of a contract.

Arguing against the existence of a breach, the appellants cited that the advert (i) did not constitute a contract (ii) that non-specificity of persons prevented any binding effect on consumers (iii) no acceptance had been notified so as to bind them, and (iv) no consideration had been made by the respondent so as to warrant a claim of right.

After addressing each point sequentially, it was unanimously held that (i) while the advert did not amount to a contract, it did represent an offer to the world entire therefore those who chose to purchase and use the product as prescribed within the published text, were through their participation, demonstrating full and unconditional acceptance of the offer. Similarly, (ii) the money spent and time invested when using the smoke balls (an unpleasant experience in itself), further indicated that consideration had been sufficient enough to allow a claim.

In closing, it was also noted that unlike contracts of an arms-length nature, the all-encompassing design of advertisements were not such that required acceptance for reasons of practicality; and that reasonable application of the promises made prevented revocation by the advertisers on grounds that when drafting the advert, they did so upon the risk that profit may, or may not, have become certain. For those reasons, the arguments against a claim were dismissed and the appeal upheld.

Key Citations

"[T]he true view, in a case of this kind, is that the person who makes the offer shews by his language and from the nature of the transaction that he does not expect and does not require notice of the acceptance apart from notice of the performance."[148]

"[I]f a person chooses to make extravagant promises of this kind he probably does so because it pays him to make them, and, if he has made them, the extravagance of the promises is no reason in law why he should not be bound by them."[149]

"[A]lthough the offer is made to the world, the contract is made with that limited portion of the public who come forward and perform the condition on the faith of the advertisement."[150]

"[I]f the person making the offer, expressly or impliedly intimates in his offer that it will be sufficient to act on the proposal without communicating acceptance of it to himself, performance of the condition is a sufficient acceptance without notification."[151]

"Inconvenience sustained by one party at the request of the other is enough to create a consideration."[152]

"[T]he advertisement was an offer intended to be acted upon, and when accepted and the conditions performed constituted a binding promise on which an action would lie, assuming there was consideration for that promise."[153]

"[A] person becomes a persona designata and able to sue, when he performs the conditions mentioned in the advertisement."[154]

---

[148] *Carlill v Carbolic Smoke Ball Co* (1893) 1 QB 256 (CA) 262 (Lindley LJ).

[149] *Carlill v Carbolic Smoke Ball Co* (1893) 1 QB 256 (CA) 268 (Bowen LJ).

[150] *Carlill v Carbolic Smoke Ball Co* (1893) 1 QB 256 (CA) 268 (Bowen LJ).

[151] *Carlill v Carbolic Smoke Ball Co* (1893) 1 QB 256 (CA) 269 (Bowen LJ).

[152] *Carlill v Carbolic Smoke Ball Co* (1893) 1 QB 256 (CA) 271 (Bowen LJ).

[153] *Carlill v Carbolic Smoke Ball Co* (1893) 1 QB 256 (CA) 273 (Smith LJ).

[154] *Carlill v Carbolic Smoke Ball Co* (1893) 1 QB 256 (CA) 274 (Smith LJ).

3. Central London Properties v High Trees House Ltd

'Equity regards as done that which ought to be done' and in this instance, the maxim is perfectly suited to the exploitative coloration of a business agreement. In September 1937, two firms (the latter of which was a subsidiary of the claimant) entered into a written lease agreement concerning a newly built block of flats.

Shortly after the outbreak of World War II, the buildings became partially occupied due to the obvious risk of bombing; so in order to keep the relationship profitable and fair, the claimants agreed to reduce the rent from 2500*l* per annum to 1250*l* per annum. While the rent reduction was put in writing, it failed to express the end of the revision, yet the original lease agreement was to run for a period of ninety-nine years.

While the defendants had enjoyed the reduced rent for the years up to December 1945, it became clear after the death of the parent company owner, that the rent had not been readjusted to its original rate. In light of the goodwill between the two firms, his business partner sought to claim arrears to the sum of 625*l* for the period between 29 September 1945 and 25 December 1945, whereupon the defendants argued that the letter containing the reduced rent constituted a legally binding contract, and one enforceable for the remainder of the lease.

Under previously existing common law, the terms of the original lease were unalterable when made under seal, and therefore full ground rent was owed without challenge. However, recent advances in the influence of equity had provided that a lease under seal could be amended in writing where evidence was provided and consideration given as determined in *Berry v Berry*,[155] however on this occasion no consideration had been shown by either party.

This left only the option of estoppel, which relied upon representations based on the present, whereas the letter discussed the reduction of rent during a future period, therefore this approach failed on the facts. Referring to the binding effects of a promise, the court balanced the probability of a breach where an agreement to reduce rents was now under challenge, but when embraced within the reasoning of equity there lacked any sense of reasonableness, particularly as the defendants had since profited from rent charges in excess of those originally agreed to the point of claim.

By embracing the virtues of equitable law, the court held that when agreeing to the reduce the rent, it had been constructed with mind to the outset of war, and that no reasonable person would have entered into an arrangement where one party would unlawfully profit at the expense of another for a period far in excess of that originally conceived, and so it was with those concise reasons that the judge upheld the claim and awarded the monies due.

---

[155] [1929] 2 KB 316.

Key Citations

"[A] promise to accept a smaller sum in discharge of a larger sum, if acted upon, is binding notwithstanding the absence of consideration: and if the fusion of law and equity leads to this result, so much the better."[156]

"[S]uch a promise as that to which I have referred, should be enforceable in law even though no consideration for it has been given by the promisee."[157]

"[T]he principle that a promise intended to be binding, intended to be acted on and in fact acted on, is binding so far as its terms properly apply."[158]

---

[156] *Central London Properties v High Trees House Ltd* [1947] KB 130 (KB) 135 (Denning J).

[157] *Central London Properties v High Trees House Ltd* [1947] KB 130 (KB) 135 (Denning J).

[158] *Central London Properties v High Trees House Ltd* [1947] KB 130 (KB) 136 (Denning J).

4. Chartbrook Ltd v Persimmon Homes Ltd

Rectification of contract and the exclusionary rule of pre-contract negotiations when deciphering the intentions of the parties involved, are uneasy bedfellows within English law; yet when the complex and relatively confusing drafting of a multimillion pound construction project amounts to heated litigation, the two legal principles are urgently required.

When an established land dealer and well-known property developer undertake a mixed development scheme, the terms of the arrangement give rise to uncertainty and conflict through opposing interpretations of the contract. By using an overly complicated formulae in sch.6 of the contract, the two firms arrived at differing conclusions that at first glance, stood in favour of the land owners when the calculations produced a profit difference of almost £3.6m. Relying upon the argument of construction to claim their fees, the now respondents took the matter to court, where in the first instance the judge found in favour of the claimants and awarded the amount owed before the defendants appealed, only to find themselves in the same position.

Taking their case to the House of Lords, it was left for the House to decide how best to unravel the tangled mess of text so as to provide clarity of judgment. When discussing the nature of contracts and the intentions of those involved, the courts relied upon *Prenn v Simmonds*,[159] where it was held that submission of pre-contract negotiations offered nothing to the facts at hand and served only to undermine the bargain agreed and signed for when contracting. Unfortunately, due to the numerable errors made when drafting this particular agreement, it ran counter to expediency to ignore the mindsets of the two parties when agreeing to work together, despite tradition suggesting otherwise.

In matters showing a clear disparity between the expectations of those contracting, the common approach is one of rectification of the contract, as defined in *Swainland Builders Ltd v Freehold Properties Ltd*, where Gibson LJ remarked:

> "The party seeking rectification must show that: (1) the parties had a common continuing intention, whether or not amounting to an agreement, in respect of a particular matter in the instrument to be rectified; (2) there was an outward expression of accord; (3) the intention continued at the time of the execution of the instrument sought to be rectified; (4) by mistake, the instrument did not reflect that common intention"[160]

However this principle is based on the presumption that both parties agreed to the terms expressed and that a mistake has since been established; but on this occasion the respondents were adamant that the formulae used was correct despite obvious contention by the appellants, which prevented the application of rectification.

Having closely examined the correspondence prior to contract, and the application of the formulae through the objective expectations of a reasonable man in similar circumstances, the House unanimously agreed that while the respondents were content

---

[159] [1971] 1 WLR 1381.

[160] *Swainland Builders Ltd v Freehold Properties Ltd* [2002] 2 EWCA Civ 560 [71] (Gibson LJ).

to pursue the terms of sch.6 under a misapprehension, there was sufficient reasoning and evidence to support the claim that the appellants' interpretation reflected that of both the House and laymen, thereby allowing the appeal to stand.

Key Citations

"When the language used in an instrument gives rise to difficulties of construction, the process of interpretation does not require one to formulate some alternative form of words which approximates as closely as possible to that of the parties. It is to decide what a reasonable person would have understood the parties to have meant by using a language which they did."[161]

"[I]n deciding whether there is a clear mistake, the court is not confined to reading the document without regard to its background or context."[162]

"[A] rule that prior negotiations are always inadmissible will prevent the court from giving effect to what a reasonable man in the position of the parties would have taken them to have meant."[163]

---

[161] *Chartbrook Ltd v Persimmon Homes Ltd* [2009] UKHL 38 (CA) 1113 (Hoffman LJ).

[162] *Chartbrook Ltd v Persimmon Homes Ltd* [2009] UKHL 38 (CA) 1114 (Hoffman LJ).

[163] *Chartbrook Ltd v Persimmon Homes Ltd* [2009] UKHL 38 (CA) 1117 (Hoffman LJ).

5. Crest Nicholson (Londinium) Ltd v Akaria Investments Ltd

Law of contract operates in a world that extends well beyond the niceties of discourse, and in doing so relies upon certainty of both intention and expression. In this appeal case the confused and often assumptive approach to business between a property owner's asset manager and developer, left the judges with no choice but to reassess the contracting parties interpretations in order to establish a conclusive judgment.

As part of an ongoing development agreement, the two companies had outlined very specific terms to their arrangement, and which due to their complex nature, commanded considerate specificity. While the majority of the schedules to the contract were secure and without contention, the subject of rental values remained less certain due to the poor wording (or at least absent text) within the respondent's letter.

Much like the 'elephant in the room', the discussion around whether unoccupied properties were subject to an expected target rental figure or market-driven rates, was left improperly addressed, while in the letter from the respondents there was also a tone of trying to set the terms of the contract. Clause 18.2.1 of the development agreement required that the developers were bound to seek open market occupation of the properties as soon as possible, and that the target rents (as defined in sch.4 of the agreement) set down by the owners, were to be achieved where reasonable. In addition to this, clause 19.8.1 stated clearly that where no occupation occurred within an agreed period, the appellants would agree to pay a calculable sum, based upon the open market rent value at the time.

Unfortunately, during the exchange of letter and email it was implied by the developer that the sum awarded would be based upon the pre-agreed target rent values, and not (as was expressed within the above clause) the open market value. By the appellant explaining that the proposed terms within the letter were 'acceptable', it was also argued that they had, by virtue of their response, agreed to be bound by the principle that the target rent values were those in effect, and not that of any (as yet undeterminable) open market rent rate.

After consideration of the assumptive wording of the letter, it was concluded within the Supreme Court that no reasonable person, including those with inside knowledge of the working arrangement, would have construed that such a statement was (i) expressed (ii) openly agreed to, and for those two reasons the appeal was upheld.

Key Citations

"A statement to a party to an already existing contract which (incorrectly) purports to set out the legal effect or factual position under that contract is not, without more, to be taken as an offer to be bound by the position as stated."[164]

"An offer is defined as "an expression of willingness to contract on specified terms made with the intention (actual or apparent) that it is to become binding as soon as it is accepted by the person to whom it is addressed.""[165]

"There is nothing in those headings to suggest that any of the four sections is intended to introduce a further purpose in addition to the four which have been identified in the first paragraph."[166]

"[T]here is no sufficient evidential basis for a submission that Ms Smith did, in fact, understand that she was being invited to agree to a proposal that Target Rents should be treated as market rents."[167]

"[I]t would have been impossible for her to reach an understanding that the letter of 21 June 2007 was inviting her to agree to a proposal, advanced for the first time and in the absence of any prior discussion, that the Target Rents shown in the schedule should be taken as the open market rents for the purposes of clause 19.8.1."[168]

---

[164] *Crest Nicholson (Londinium) Ltd v Akaria Investments Ltd* [2010] EWCA Civ 1331 [20] (Sir John Chadwick).

[165] *Crest Nicholson (Londinium) Ltd v Akaria Investments Ltd* [2010] EWCA Civ 1331 [24] (Sir John Chadwick).

[166] *Crest Nicholson (Londinium) Ltd v Akaria Investments Ltd* [2010] EWCA Civ 1331 [32] (Sir John Chadwick).

[167] *Crest Nicholson (Londinium) Ltd v Akaria Investments Ltd* [2010] EWCA Civ 1331 [42] (Sir John Chadwick).

[168] *Crest Nicholson (Londinium) Ltd v Akaria Investments Ltd* [2010] EWCA Civ 1331 [43] (Sir John Chadwick).

6. Davis Contractors Ltd v Fareham UDC

The principle of 'frustration' and the nature of commercial contracts are both given equal consideration when a local authority fails to acknowledge, or pay, costs exceeding the original agreement, despite pleas for reasonability by the claimants.

Shortly after World War II, the appellant building contractors submitted to the respondents, a tender for the construction of a large number of houses over a fixed period. Included was a letter that outlined allowances for rising material costs and labour shortages, which while not atypical to construction projects of the time, remained peripheral to the tender documentation. Having further negotiated before awarding the contract to the respondents, the appellants left them to work the contract until the agreed eight-month period expired, whereupon only a fraction of the total number of houses had been completed.

Citing frustration through inclement weather, delays in materials and shortage of labour, the contractors explained that the project was now going to take much longer than originally anticipated and priced for. The local authority expressed no disagreement with the statement made by the appellants, and the work continued for another fourteen months. Upon completion, the total cost of the work was £115,233 versus the agreed £94,424, therefore the appellants stood to lose around £20,000.

When asked to pay the additional sum on grounds of *quantum meruit* (payment for services rendered and therefore deserved), the respondents refused to pay and offered only the amount contracted for. This led to a claim by the appellants under three grounds: (i) that the letter submitted with the tender was part of the contract, (ii) that the contract was entered into on the proviso that both materials and labour were available, and (iii) that because those key elements were absent, the contract had ceased to exist, and that subsequent work carried out was subject to a *quantum meruit*.

Having been heard before an arbitrator, the doctrine of frustration was given considered significance in favour of the appellants on the strength of the letter, despite no agreement as to exactly when the contract had altered or terminated. When presented to the court, the judge agreed that the letter formed part of the contract and awarded accordingly. Challenged in the Court of Appeal, the Court disagreed, and referred the matter back to the arbitrator for greater clarification of frustration, and in particular, the relevance of this case and that of *Bush v Whitehaven Port and Town Trustees*,[169] which had become the benchmark for 'frustration' cases but was not entirely consistent with the facts of this matter.

With the arbitrator remaining resolute on the *Bush* case and the letter, the Court held that the letter had not formed part of the final contracts, but was merely a facet of negotiations, therefore no frustration had occurred. It was then put before the House of Lords in order that the appellants could advance their contention that where frustration failed, *quantum meruit* ought to succeed.

As was established, the nature of frustration relied more upon unforeseen circumstances that affected both parties to a contract, rather than that where one is at a loss through

---

[169] (1888) 2 Hudson's Building Contracts , 4th ed.,122

unexpected events. As could be seen in this instance, the appellants were aware that labour and material shortages were likely, therefore the onus was on them to navigate that scenario as best as possible. In light of the contract itself, there had, at no point, been any oral, or otherwise, agreement by both parties that the original contract had ceased to exist and that another had begun. This further negated the effect of *quantum meruit*, because unless agreed to, the terms of the original contract had remained unaltered, despite the increased duration of the project and escalating costs incurred by the appellants. Unanimously dismissing the appeal, the House held that this conflict of interests amounted to little more than a seemingly well-drafted plan gone awry, and one that on this occasion, left a financial scar on the contractors.

Key Citations

"[I]t cannot, in the light of later authority, be used to support the proposition that where, without the default of either party, there has been an unexpected turn of events, which renders the contract more onerous than the parties had contemplated, that is by itself a ground for relieving a party of the obligation he has undertaken."[170]

"Construction of a contract and the implication of a term are questions of law, whereas the question whether the basis of a contract is overthrown, if not dependent on the construction of the contract, might seem to be largely a matter for the judgment of a skilled man comparing what was contemplated with what has happened."[171]

"[F]rustration depends, at least in most cases, not on adding any implied term, but on the true construction of the terms which are in the contract read in light of the nature of the contract and of the relevant surrounding circumstances when the contract was made."[172]

"If delays occur through no one's fault that may be in the contemplation of the contract, and there may be provision for extra time being given: to that extent the other party takes the risk of delay. But he does not take the risk of the cost being increased by such delay."[173]

"[F]rustration occurs whenever the law recognizes that without default of either party a contractual obligation has become incapable of being performed because the circumstances in which performance is called for would render it a thing radically different from that which was undertaken by the contract. Non haec in foedera veni. It was not this that I promised to do."[174]

---

[170] *Davis Contractors Ltd v Fareham Urban District Council* [1956] AC 696 (HL) 716 (Simonds VC).

[171] *Davis Contractors Ltd v Fareham Urban District Council* [1956] AC 696 (HL) 719 (Reid LJ).

[172] *Davis Contractors Ltd v Fareham Urban District Council* [1956] AC 696 (HL) 721-722 (Reid LJ).

[173] *Davis Contractors Ltd v Fareham Urban District Council* [1956] AC 696 (HL) 724 (Reid LJ).

[174] *Davis Contractors Ltd v Fareham Urban District Council* [1956] AC 696 (HL) 729 (Radcliffe LJ).

7. Destiny 1 Ltd v Lloyds TSB Bank Plc

As has been previously discussed in *Crest Nicholson*,[175] it is imperative for disputing parties to recognise that the wording of documents and the terms implied behind them, are not to be misconstrued to the detriment of those seeking justice, as is demonstrated in this brief matter.

When a small business owner found himself in a position to expand upon his success as a retail outlet, he began negotiations with a new bank that had shown an interest in helping him secure an additional property with a view to opening a second store. As there were complex requirements within the proposed arrangement, there needed to be a number of component contracts that would collectively form a single binding contract.

These came in a number of different forms, including several small charges against the properties held under title by the applicant, a guarantee of indemnity for a supplier the applicant had chosen for his new store and a re-financing of an existing loan with his current bank, which due to its significant size, formed the footing of the agreement because without it the bank had no means by which to achieve a workable profit.

As part of the pre-contract process, the bank sent a letter that conveyed its agreement to support the package contract on the proviso that the appellant agreed to submit to the terms contained within the letter, and the actions he was required to undertake prior to their commencement. The appellant duly signed and returned the letter to display his compliance with those terms, but unfortunately for reasons not outlined within the appeal hearing, the bank was unable to proceed with the loan refinancing and therefore the proposed arrangement could not be realised.

It was this unexpected withdrawal that promoted the appellant to cite that his business had subsequently suffered pecuniary losses through the inability to expand, and that the banks unwillingness to endorse his guarantee to the potential supplier constituted a clear breach of contract.

When given broad and considered thought in the Court of Appeal, it was again agreed that while the bank and the appellant had drawn up a multi-layered agreement to contract, no such contract could exist without the complete participation of all the arrangements, for without them functioning as a whole, no such contract could be seen to exist. The Court also held that while the bank's letter only outlined that they needed the appellant's agreement to the terms contained within, his acceptance did not by extension, form a binding contract. Furthermore, while the bank's cessation to undertake business with the appellant had left him dissatisfied, there could be no causal link between the failure of the contract to become manifest, and any obstruction of commercial expansion under his own efforts.

---

[175] *Crest Nicholson (Londinium) Ltd v Akaria Investments Ltd* [2010] EWCA Civ 1331.

Key Citations

"[E]ven if the bank was in breach of contract, it had not caused the loss in respect of which Destiny sought to recover."[176]

"[T]he law decides whether a contract has come into existence by looking objectively at what each party said to the other, not at their subjective intentions or understandings."[177]

"There was never any attempt to reach an agreement with Destiny separate from that which was being negotiated with Mr Khalid; the two were inextricably linked."[178]

---

[176] *Destiny 1 Ltd v Lloyds TSB Bank plc* [2011] EWCA Civ 831 [9] (Moore-Bick LJ).

[177] *Destiny 1 Ltd v Lloyds TSB Bank plc* [2011] EWCA Civ 831 [15] (Moore-Bick LJ).

[178] *Destiny 1 Ltd v Lloyds TSB Bank plc* [2011] EWCA Civ 831 [17] (Moore-Bick LJ).

8. Dunlop Pneumatic Tyres Co Ltd v Selfridge & Co Ltd

Enforcement of a contract extending beyond reasonable bounds, proves the undoing of a commercial tyre distributor seeking to retain product values beyond their remit. When action is brought against a third party, the rules of contract move to narrow the scope of claim and protect those party to sub-contracts.

In 1911, the appellant tyre manufacturer set about establishing written agency distributorship agreements with a number of commercial outlets, as to retain control over the sale value of its tyres and accessories. There were a number of stipulations that encompassed the restrictive nature of these contracts, least of all the claimable damages for breach when those agents violated the terms of the agreement. In this matter, the respondents had purchased a Dunlop tyre from an agent who had been privy to an agency agreement providing them with a ten percent discount on Dunlop tyres, subject to a nine percent rebate for purchases exceeding 2000*l* per annum.

In consideration of this, the agency were prevented from selling Dunlop tyres (and accessories) to any other firms, or individuals, for less than the standard list price, with the sole caveat that they could, at their discretion, sell those same products to other trade outlets at a maximum of ten percent discount, provided those outlets entered into and signed, a prohibitive contract similar to the one held by the agency. Schs.2 and 5 of this price maintenance agreement expressly stipulated that:

> "(2) We will not sell or offer any Dunlop motor tyres, covers or tubes to any private customers or to any co-operative society at prices below those mentioned in the said price list…nor give to any such customer or society any… discounts or advantages reducing the same.

> (5) We agree to pay to the Dunlop Pneumatic Tyre Co Ltd, the sum of 5*l* for each and any tyre, cover or tube sold or offered in breach of this agreement, as and by way of liquidated images and not as penalty, but without prejudice to any other rights or remedies you or the Dunlop Pneumatic Tyre Co Ltd may have hereunder."

In December of that year, a known tyre outlet secured an order for a particular Dunlop tyre from a private customer, who naturally asked for the best price possible. For one reason or another, the outlet offered a seven and a half percent discount, at which point the consumer paid in full and took receipt of the tyre. When ordering the tyre from the agency, they were informed that no discount could be offered without the completion of the signed price maintenance agreement, which was later executed by the now respondents. Having learned of this, the appellants sought an injunction and sued the respondents for breach of contract, on grounds that the agency were acting under the principle control of the appellants, and that by selling the tyre to a prohibited party they were liable for damages as contained in the agreement.

When first heard, the judge awarded in favour of the appellants, while granting the injunction as requested. Challenged in the Court of Appeal, the appellants raised the contention that the contract made between the agency and the appellants excluded the right to enforce by a third party, on grounds that no consideration had been given by the respondent tyre manufacturers when the price maintenance agreement had been drafted.

Having lost the appeal, the manufacturers sought to argue the principles relied upon through the same position taken as before, where it was unanimously held that when examined in full, the unwavering fact that the appellants gave no consideration at the point the agreement was made, precluded them from any claim of right under English common law. This was reinforced by the recent outcome of *Humble v Hunter*,[179] and that by virtue of the price maintenance agreement itself, the contract terms were between the agency and the respondent only, and that the appellants relinquished that right when allowing for discretionary discounts on the part of the agency.

Key Citations

"[I]n the law of England certain principles are fundamental. One is that only a person who is a party to a contract can sue on it."[180]

"[I]f a person with whom a contract not under seal has been made is to be able to enforce it consideration must have been given by him to the promisor or to some other person at the promisor's request."[181]

"I do not think that a man can treat one and the same contract as made by him in two capacities. He cannot be regarded as contracting for himself and for another uno flatu."[182]

"But for any contract to the contrary, Messrs. A. J. Dew & Co. were entitled to resell the goods supplied to them by the appellants upon any terms they might think fit, and in reselling as they did there was no breach of any restrictive contract."[183]

"In this transaction nothing moved from the appellants to the respondents. It would have been the same if the other firm had not existed. The appellants have sued on a nudum pactum."[184]

"There is no question that parol evidence is admissible to prove that the plaintiff in an action is the real principal to a contract; but it is also well established law that a person cannot claim to be a principal to a contract, if this would be inconsistent with the terms of the contract itself."[185]

---

[179] (1848) 12 QB 310.

[180] *Dunlop Pneumatic Tyre Co Ltd v Selfridge & Co Ltd* [1915] AC 847 (HL) 853 (Viscount Haldane LC).

[181] *Dunlop Pneumatic Tyre Co Ltd v Selfridge & Co Ltd* [1915] AC 847 (HL) 853 (Viscount Haldane LC).

[182] *Dunlop Pneumatic Tyre Co Ltd v Selfridge & Co Ltd* [1915] AC 847 (HL) 854 (Viscount Haldane LC).

[183] *Dunlop Pneumatic Tyre Co Ltd v Selfridge & Co Ltd* [1915] AC 847 (HL) 860 (Parker LJ).

[184] *Dunlop Pneumatic Tyre Co Ltd v Selfridge & Co Ltd* [1915] AC 847 (HL) 863 (Sumner LJ).

[185] *Dunlop Pneumatic Tyre Co Ltd v Selfridge & Co Ltd* [1915] AC 847 (HL) 864 (Parmoor LJ).

9. Esso Petroleum v Mardon

Prior to the Misrepresentation Act 1967, many cases where mistruths and false inducements occurred, were reliant upon rules of collateral warranty and negligent misrepresentation to establish liability. On this occasion, the expertise of an international oil company fell foul to haste, when embarking upon a project that victimised a willing but inexperienced employee.

In 1961, the respondents were looking to construct a new filling station within the busy streets of Southport. Having considered the location and calculated the potential value of business, it was agreed that once opened, the station could very well expect to turnover around 200,000 gallons of petrol per year within the first three years of business. With such positive numbers influencing their decision, the respondents purchased the site and began work. During the planning permission stage they were delivered an unexpected blow by the the local authority, when it was made expressly clear that the petrol pumps were not permitted to face the road but were instead, to be positioned at the rear of the building.

This change of design was to have a significant impact upon the previous calculations, however, undeterred the respondents sought to recruit a leaseholder for the site. After a successful interview the appellant was offered the post for a determined period, while subject to rents that were based upon the now unrealistic sales volumes. During the interview the appellant queried the figures presented, while admitting his naivety to petroleum industry technicalities, subsequently citing a figure half the size quoted by the respondents. In order to retain his services, the respondents argued that with a collective forty-plus years of experience between the two employers present, there was no cause for concern, and that the original projections remained reliable.

In spite of his concerns, the appellant took the position and continued to work tirelessly for two years, before reaching a point of financial ruin, after not only losing money from the severely reduced sales, but as a result of having invested large sums of money from a business he and his wife owned, along with a sizeable overdraft that could no longer be repaid. Approaching the respondents with every intention to quit, the respondents agreed to reduce the rent and offer bonus payments from the sale of petrol, so as to offset the current losses. As an act of continued faith, the respondent agreed to keep working to a twelve month contract; however nothing changed, and despite offers by the respondents to find him a more profitable station to run, the support dried up and things came to an unfortunate end.

In 1966, the respondents issued a writ for non-payment of petrol supplied during the relationship, at which point the appellant counter-claimed for damages caused through the loss of earnings, damage to his health, lost opportunities through his efforts to make the site a success, breach of warranty through the misleading statements made in relation to sales turnover and negligent misrepresentation and the inducement to take employment where the outcome was never the one presented during the interview.

When first heard, the judge held that the comments from the respondents were tantamount to opinions and not warranties, but that the claim for negligent misrepresentation was enforceable until the date of the revised employment contract in 1964. In the Court of Appeal, the appellant contended that the previous judge had erred in law on a number of counts, and that under the recent ruling in *Hedley Byrne & Co Ltd v Heller & Partners Ltd*,[186] pre-contract negotiations fell under the scope of negligent misrepresentation, and therefore damages foreseeable under that principle extended to those losses claimed by the appellant.

Having examined the finer points of collateral warranty and the limitations of contractual breaches versus tortious remedy, it was unanimously held with absolute certainty that the flow of damages witnessed were unmistakably linked to the claim raised, and that no degree of remoteness could apply when factoring in the sources of revenue used by the appellant as a means to keep the station afloat. This resulted in the negligent misrepresentation of the respondents proving pivotal to an award of damages that far from ending in 1964, continued to the point of litigation, and that such measures remained only to be discussed after the appeal was allowed.

Key Citations

"[I]f such a person makes a forecast, intending that the other should act upon it and he does act upon it, it can well be interpreted as a warranty that the forecast is sound and reliable in the sense that they made it with reasonable care and skill."[187]

"[I]n the case of a professional man, the duty to use reasonable care arises not only in contract, but is also imposed by the law apart from contract, and is therefore actionable in tort."[188]

"[I]f a man, who has or professes to have special knowledge or skill, makes a representation by virtue thereof to another be it advice, information or opinion with the intention of inducing him to enter into a contract with him, he is under a duty to use reasonable care to see that the representation is correct, and that the advice, information or opinion is reliable."[189]

"[T]here is no valid argument, apart from legal technicality, for the proposition that a subsequent contract vitiates a cause of action in negligence which had previously arisen in the course of negotiation."[190]

---

[186] [1964] AC 645.

[187] *Esso Petroleum v Mardon* [1976] QB 801 (CA) 818 (Lord Denning MR).

[188] *Esso Petroleum v Mardon* [1976] QB 801 (CA) 819 (Lord Denning MR).

[189] *Esso Petroleum v Mardon* [1976] QB 801 (CA) 820 (Lord Denning MR).

[190] *Esso Petroleum v Mardon* [1976] QB 801 (CA) 833 (Shaw LJ).

10. Holwell Securities Ltd v Hughes

Conveyance of property and the requisite methods of notice when accepting an offer, are clearly defined under s.196 of the Law of Property Act 1925, so when a buyer elects to take advantage of an option to purchase, they do so in a way that while flirting with the prescribed method, fails to secure the bargain, despite arguments to the contrary.

Having decided to sell his home, the respondent wrote to a prospective buyer, setting out an option to purchase that expired within a six-month period. The specific terms of the offer outlined in clause 2 were as follows:

> "The said option shall be exercisable by notice in writing to the intending vendor at any time within six months from the date hereof..."

Contrastingly, s.196(4) of the Law of Property Act 1925 reads:

> "Any notice required or authorised by this Act to be served shall also be sufficiently served, if it is sent by post in a registered letter addressed to the lessee, lessor, mortgagee, mortgagor, or other person to be served, by name, at the aforesaid place of abode or business, office, or counting-house, and if that letter is not returned through the post-office undelivered; and that service shall be deemed to be made at the time at which the registered letter would in the ordinary course be delivered."[191]

On this occasion the appellant's solicitors drafted a written acceptance of the offer and hand delivered it to the respondent's solicitors, noting within the correspondence that a copy of the written notice of acceptance had been posted to the respondent's home, along with a cheque covering the required deposit. After receiving the letter, the solicitors telephoned the respondent to advise him that they had received the notice, and that a copy of it was on its way to him. The respondent then explained that he had made travel plans, and so having been instructed to leave regardless of the expected letter, he vacated his home for a number of days.

Despite being franked and handed to the post-office, the letter never arrived at the respondent's home, after which the appellant sought legal action to secure the purchase on grounds that a contract for both sale and purchase had been executed, irrespective of whether the posted letter had arrived. It was also argued that the oral communication between the solicitors and the respondent further confirmed acceptance of the offer when factoring in the possession of the letter by the solicitors.

Relying upon the postal rule stated by Herschell LJ in *Henthorn v Fraser*, which expressed:

> "Where the circumstances are such that it must have been within the contemplation of the parties that, according to the ordinary usages of mankind,

---

[191] Law of Property Act 1925, s.196(4).

the post might be used as a means of communicating the acceptance of an offer, the acceptance is complete as soon as it is posted."[192]

The appellant contended that the act of posting was sufficient to effect a contract, however, the court ruled against them before the matter was again discussed in the Court of Appeal. Here the postal rule was acknowledged but overruled, in light of the absence of postal methods expressed within the purchase option provided for by the respondents; while failure of the respondent to physically take receipt and read the notice, became fatal to any claim of right to buy, whereupon for those two reasons the Court held in favour of the respondent and the appeal was dismissed.

Key Citations

"A person does not give notice in writing to another person by sitting down and writing it out and then telephoning to that other saying "listen to what I have just written"."[193]

"If a notice is to be of any value it must be an intimation to someone. A notice which cannot impinge on anyone's mind is not functioning as such."[194]

---

[192] *Henthorn v Fraser* [1892] 2 Ch 27 (CA) 33 (Herschell LJ).

[193] *Holwell Securities Ltd v Hughes* [1974] 1 All ER 161 (CA) 159 (Russell LJ).

[194] *Holwell Securities Ltd v Hughes* [1974] 1 All ER 161 (CA) 160 (Lawton LJ).

11. L'Estrange v Graucob

'Reading the small print' is a phrase familiar to discerning consumers, and in this instance, the value of careful reading serves to remind that contracts of all shapes and sizes require careful attention, especially when the text is not readily visible.

In 1933, two travelling salesmen paid a visit to a small community café in Wales in order to sell them an automatic cigarette vending machine. Having spent a number of hours discussing the user benefits and attached payment terms, the appellant duly agreed to sign the partially completed 'sales agreement', in expectation of a new and fully working product.

Once the deposit had been paid, the respondents returned a signed 'order confirmation' and accompanying eighteen-month guarantee, at which point the contract was well underway and instalments were regularly paid. After a period of less than a few days, the machine began malfunctioning, and several engineer visits followed, while the product intermittently remained operable, before at the point of exhaustion, the appellant requested the item be returned in forfeit of her deposit.

The respondents refused to terminate the transaction, at which point a claim for legal recourse was initiated by the appellant for reclamation of the monies paid to the respondents on grounds that the product had been unfit for purpose and thus contrary to the contract and guarantee.The respondents counter-claimed the remaining costs owed for the purchase of the machine, whereupon the appellant amended her claim to include either (i) repayment for failure to provide full consideration, or (ii) breach of implied condition that the vending machine was functioning at point of sale, and/or (iii) damages for breach of implied warranty that the product was fit for purpose.

The argument cited by the respondents relied upon (i) an absence of failed consideration (ii) non-existence of implied conditions as per the Sale of Goods Act 1893, and (iii) no implied warranty, as the signed sales agreement excluded both condition and warranty within the small print shown at the bottom, which read:

> "…This agreement contains all the terms and conditions under which I agree to purchase the machine specified above, and any express or implied condition, statement, or warranty, statutory or otherwise not stated herein is hereby excluded…"

In reply, the appellant contended that she had been induced through misrepresentation by the respondents to sign the agreement, while never having her attention drawn to the exclusion contained therein; and that on those grounds she was entitled to claim recovery of her payments. When first heard, the judge awarded in favour of the respondents for sum of 70*l* in light of a perceived breach of the warranty, despite her signature and no evidence of misrepresentation, while allowing the appellants the sum of 71*l* for the monies unpaid.

Having appealed, the appellants argued again that no misrepresentation had occurred, and that at any point the respondent was free to note and enquire as to the limitations of the contract, but waived that right when signing to the terms expressed. Relying upon the principles used in *Parker v South Eastern Railway Co*, the Court agreed that:

"In an ordinary case, where an action is brought on a written agreement which is signed by the defendant, the agreement is proved by proving his signature, and, in the absence of fraud, it is wholly immaterial that he has not read the agreement and does not know its contents."[195]

And that despite recognition of the respondent's misfortune, the law could not enforce a claim for misrepresentation based upon the oversight of a willing party to contract. This left the court with no option other than to set aside the respondent's award, and uphold that of the appellants, while further noting that future contracts of a similar nature ought to have larger fonts and include statements of exclusion within the order confirmation forms.

Key Citations

"When a document containing contractual terms is signed, then, in the absence of fraud, or, I will add, misrepresentation, the party signing it is bound, and it is wholly immaterial whether he has read the document or not."[196]

"[T]he plaintiff, having put her signature to the document and not having been induced to do so by any fraud or misrepresentation, cannot be heard to say that she is not bound by the terms of the document because she has not read them."[197]

"[W]hen the order confirmation was signed by the defendants confirming the order form which had been signed by the plaintiff, there was then a signed contract in writing between the parties."[198]

---

[195] *Parker v South Eastern Railway Co* (1877) 2 CPD (CA) 416 (Mellish LJ).

[196] *L'Estrange v Graucob* [1934] 2 KB 394 (KB) 403 (Scrutton LJ).

[197] *L'Estrange v Graucob* [1934] 2 KB 394 (KB) 404 (Scrutton LJ).

[198] *L'Estrange v Graucob* [1934] 2 KB 394 (KB) 406 (Maugham LJ).

12. Maple Leaf Macro Volatility Master Fund v Rouvroy

When consideration is given by at least one party to a contract (whether interlocutory or final), it becomes in principle very hard for the other party to claim no contract existed, irrespective of signatures or third-party withdrawal. In this appeal case, the founder-directors of a beverage firm sought to rescind an agreement between themselves and a hedge fund provider, despite a long-standing commercial history and openly agreed terms of engagement.

After enjoying moderate success as an alcoholic drinks manufacturer, and having recently acquired a smaller company as part of their expansion, it was decided that the time had come to recoup on their investment, and so a controlling share of their business was sold to a large financial holdings company. Within the year, the working relationship between the investors and owners deteriorated to the degree that the appellants moved to buy back their company and regain controlling influence.

As part of this reversion, the terms of the arrangement required them to obtain significant loans in a short period of time, in which the borrowers granted stakeholder rights to the lenders. During the construction of the contract, the defendants took the step of paying the monies borrowed, directly to the controlling firm, as part of their commitment to the loan arrangement and repurchase scheme. When a third party to the draft contract renegotiated a different arrangement with the appellants, they declined to add their signature to the final agreement, leaving only the appellants and defendants ink upon the document.

It was then argued by the appellants, that an absence of a third signature rendered the contract void, and that there now existed no binding obligation on their part, to continue with the loan or invitation to share control. When stripped down and reassembled in its proper context, it was found by the Court of Appeal that due to the consideration given by the defendants, there was sufficient evidence to show that a contract did exist, and which bound both signatories, despite the reluctance of the third party. This was underlined by the words of Steyn J, who explained in *Trentham v Archital Lucifer* that:

> "The fact that the transaction was performed on both sides will often make it unrealistic to argue that there was no intention to enter into legal relations."[199]

---

[199] *Trentham v Archital Lucifer* [1993] 1 Lloyds Rep 25 (CA) 25 (Steyn J).

Key Citations

"In the first place, there was no requirement either within or outside the Funding Agreement that it would only become binding when signed."[200]

"The fact that the agreement envisages a signature and leaves a space for those signatures is not a "prescription" that the agreement can nil become binding on the appending of signatures."[201]

"[A]lthough no contract can be made without an intention to be legally bound, that intention has to be ascertained objectively, not by looking into the parties' minds."[202]

"[T]hat there was objectively an intention to be bound was the fact that the appellants had signed Version 9."[203]

"Maple Leaf were themselves doubtful whether a binding agreement had been made, but nevertheless paid this not inconsiderable sum in the hope that it would in due course be concluded, by a court if necessary, that there was indeed a binding agreement."[204]

---

[200] *Maple Leaf Macro Volatility Master Fund v Rouvroy* [2009] EWCA Civ 1334 [16] (Longmore LJ).

[201] *Maple Leaf Macro Volatility Master Fund v Rouvroy* [2009] EWCA Civ 1334 [16] (Longmore LJ).

[202] *Maple Leaf Macro Volatility Master Fund v Rouvroy* [2009] EWCA Civ 1334 [17] (Longmore LJ).

[203] *Maple Leaf Macro Volatility Master Fund v Rouvroy* [2009] EWCA Civ 1334 [18] (Longmore LJ).

[204] *Maple Leaf Macro Volatility Master Fund v Rouvroy* [2009] EWCA Civ 1334 [20] (Longmore LJ).

13. Moran v University College Salford

Interlocutory discourse between those that apply for, or request, obtainment of services, and the party empowered to grant them, can on the surface, appear to suggest a verbal, or somewhat provisional agreement to contract to one another. Unfortunately, it would seem that under common law, this would be a false assumption, as there is still yet more to require a binding agreement. When the applicant for a university degree course becomes victim to an administrative error, it is left for the courts to clarify the mechanics of these arrangements in a light that might well surprise.

After choosing to study for a recognised qualification in a competitive field, the appellant used a central admissions system to act on his behalf when approaching a number of suitable universities. After facing a volume of rejections, he received an unconditional offer from a provider of notable standing. There were of course, certain conditions attached to the offer, and one of those, was the preclusion from seeking admission through the clearing system, as well as accepting any other offers from universities at a later date. The appellant duly acquiesced to these conditions and returned his acceptance form, both in good time and using the methods prescribed by the university.

During the period between his acceptance and subsequent discovery that his application had been denied due to oversubscription, the appellant had left his position of employment, turned down a second interview for another post, surrendered his tenancy with his landlord and made plans to relocate in order to support his education. In fact, it was due to a phone call to the university that he learned of the error, at which point he was informed that he could try to apply for an alternative course through clearing (which by this time had run its course).

When seeking legal remedy under (i) specific performance (ii) mandatory injunction and (iii) breach of contract, the court found that although the offer had been sent and the acceptance received within the guidelines, there was no guarantee of contract until the enrolment process and payment of fees had occurred. As this fact prevented the existence of a contract, any claim for specific performance was quashed, along with that of a breach or mandatory injunction.

Upon appeal, the details of the arrangement were given a thorough examination and some interesting facts emerged. While it was central admission policy to issue application guidelines to the public, there were similar guidelines issued to the receiving universities that contained within them, important information that upon consideration, warranted inclusion to the former documentation as they outlined the responsibilities of the providers where such errors were found. In addition to this, the failure of the admissions team to properly address the appellants application had denied him any opportunity to enter clearing; an act held by the Court as consideration prior to contract.

Unfortunately, despite the good intention and sufferance of the applicant (under the assumption that a legal contract had been constructed), the court ruled that as with the first judgment, there had been no evidence to suggest a contract existed, because there had been no formal enrolment and agreed payment of fees; a caveat which had been further construed from the terms contained within the central admissions guide.

Key Citations

"[G]iving up the chance of obtaining another place through PCAS clearing in this way was a sufficient detriment to constitute consideration moving from the plaintiff for the purposes of these technical rules of the law of contract."[205]

"[T]he respondents having made their own offer through PCAS, and in accordance with the PCAS scheme, did impliedly request the plaintiff, by inviting his acceptance of their offer, to take a step which to their knowledge necessarily involved his removal from the scheme and with it any opportunity to enter clearing in accordance with its rules."[206]

"[I]t would no doubt come as a surprise to many thousands of applicants who give firm acceptances in response to unconditional offers, were they told that the institution is not bound to provide them with a place, and is free to withdraw the offer at any time before they present themselves for enrolment at the beginning of the academic year."[207]

"Whether or not such an agreement is legally enforceable depends primarily upon the terms of the particular agreement and secondly upon the 'matrix' which is provided by the scheme itself."[208]

---

[205] *Moran v University College Salford* [1994] ELR 187 (CA) 199 (Evans LJ).

[206] *Moran v University College Salford* [1994] ELR 187 (CA) 199 (Evans LJ).

[207] *Moran v University College Salford* [1994] ELR 187 (CA) 203 (Evans LJ).

[208] *Moran v University College Salford* [1994] ELR 187 (CA) 204 (Evans LJ).

14. Royal Bank of Scotland v Etridge (No.2)

Used as an opportunity to tackle the principles surrounding surety for a partners borrowing against a risk of property repossession, this House of Lords appeal took the opportunity to address *Royal Bank of Scotland plc v Etridge (No.2), Barclays Bank plc v Harris, Midland Bank plc v Wallace, National Westminster Bank plc v Gill, UCB Home Loans Corporation Ltd v Moore, Barclays Bank plc v Coleman, Bank of Scotland v Bennett* and *Kenyon-Brown v Desmond Banks & Co*, all of which were at various stages of litigation.

In these instances, the wives of husbands both acting as individuals and owners of their businesses, offered themselves as surety for loans that notwithstanding payment, placed the wives' interest in the matrimonial home in the hands of the lenders upon default. As had become a feature of the courts, it had become common for those co-signatories to deny knowledge of that risk, and claim they were unduly influenced into signing, either through withholding of information, or misrepresentation by the husbands; whereupon recovery of funds through property repossession became almost impossible for the lenders in the absence of overwhelming evidence to the contrary.

Legal precedent for the requisite principles needed to secure repossession, are found in *Barclays Bank plc v O'Brien*,[209] in which it was stated that the bank or lender, is held accountable for disclosure to the co-signing party when (i) the wife is signing despite no financial gain on her part and (ii) the manner in which the husband has induced the wife's assistance represents an inequitably wilful act that enables the wife to withdraw her acquiescence if needed. Having taken this process a stage further, the House of Lords expressed that in such circumstances, the banks or lenders were to insist upon privately held meetings with just the wife; and that a full and comprehensive disclosure of her liabilities were to be explained by a representative of the bank before strongly advising her to seek independent legal advice prior to signing; whereas previous cases (including those below) allowed the lenders to rely upon mere solicitor referral, whose written confirmation of an explanation was sufficient enough to support a possession order.

Royal Bank of Scotland v Etridge (No.2)

Unlike the following cases, the wife's claim of undue influence in similar circumstances fell foul of insubstantial evidence, and was dismissed both in the first hearing and in the Court of Appeal. Having approached the claim under both 'actual' and 'presumed' undue influence, it was ultimately judged in favour of the bank, but not before caution was raised when attempting to exploit legal principles with questionable evidence. Despite this outcome, the matter was presented to the House of Lords in the hope of preventable repossession, whereupon the appeal was unanimously dismissed.

Barclays Bank plc v Harris

In this matter, the wife again stood as surety for her husband's company, however, the solicitor involved was not appointed by her, but did enjoy a close relationship with her husband. Unaware as to the liabilities of her signing, the wife argued that she had been

---

[209] [1994] 1 AC 180.

unduly influenced by her partner to sign the agreement; while the bank itself had never obtained written confirmation from the solicitors that they had fully explained the legal ramifications of her actions, yet were aware that the solicitors felt they had not provided clear enough instruction as to her responsibilities. Having been heard as an interlocutory appeal, the bank had been supported, despite stark evidence to the contrary, and was now before the House of Lords for final judgment, where the appeal was unanimously upheld and the case referred for full trial.

Midland Bank plc v Wallace

In this interlocutory appeal, the lender was put on inquiry after the wife of the borrower stood as surety for her husbands debts, whereupon a solicitor was required to provide independent legal advice as to her liabilities, prior to her signing the document. Under agreed legal principles, a solicitor must be appointed by the wife, or her husband, and act accordingly, so as to remain party to the outcome of the agreement should the need arise. It transpired here that the solicitor had acted alone, therefore the bank had a right to damages for breach of implied warranty of authority against the solicitor, but not the wife. However, the Court of Appeal awarded in favour of the bank, thus being again challenged by the wife on grounds of undue influence, where the House upheld the appeal and referred the case for full trial.

National Westminster Bank plc v Gill

What began as a possible argument for misrepresentation, ended up failing under a claim of 'actual' undue influence, when the wife standing surety to a £36,000 loan was actually party to an advance of around £100,000, but one that demonstrated her approval and acquiescence. This became fatal to her allegation, and thus was brought before the House of Lords, who again unanimously dismissed the appeal.

UCB Home Loans Corporation Ltd v Moore

Varying slightly, this interlocutory matter concerned the actions of both an insurance company and husband, that culminated in the bank agreeing to the loan, despite failing to check and receive confirmation that the signing wife had been made aware of her legal encumbrance. Having induced his wife to sign the agreement through fraudulent means, the husband's acting insurance broker never once communicated with the wife, while the lenders and the solicitors, equally failed to instruct or advise her accordingly. At the point of this appeal, the House ruled that to establish full accountability, the case was required to go to trial.

Barclays Bank plc v Coleman

When a husband and wife who were both members of the Hassidic Jewish community, signed an agreement for monies secured to purchase property, the wife again acted as surety for the loan, despite a lack of knowledge as to the fullness of her legal obligation. When heard at trial, she claimed that an elderly solicitor had been acting for her, but had failed to fully explain her liabilities as legally required. However, when suing for breach of duty, it was established that the gentleman had since died, and so no proceedings on her part could be brought; but other issues remained in contention at the point of this appeal, which despite a degree of reservation, was wholly dismissed.

Bank of Scotland v Bennett

For loans secured against the survival of his company, a husband had again, coerced his wife into signing as surety for a substantial amount before the unavoidable collapse of the firm. Having challenged the validity of the order for repossession, the wife argued that she had been victim to undue influence on the part of her husband, and that the bank had due notice of such impropriety. The trial judge found in her favour before the Court of Appeal again upheld her claim, hence the final appeal by the bank in the House of Lords, who uniformly upheld the argument taken by the bank.

Kenyon-Brown v Desmond Banks & Co

On this occasion, the wife claimed undue influence in that she had reluctantly agreed to sign as surety for her husband's debts at his suggestion, yet unaware that their jointly-owned home was at risk. The wife also argued that she had received no prior legal advice from their acting solicitor, whereupon the solicitor provided legal certification to the bank claiming such advice had been given. Unable to provide sufficient evidence at the Court of Appeal, the solicitor's contention was then presented to the House of Lords, who upheld their appeal in full.

Key Citations

"[W]hatever the legal character of the transaction, it must constitute a disadvantage sufficiently serious to require evidence to rebut the presumption that in the circumstances of the parties' relationship, it was procured by the exercise of undue influence."[210]

"What passes between a husband and wife in this regard in the privacy of their own home is not capable of regulation or investigation as a prelude to the wife entering into a suretyship transaction."[211]

"[I]t is plainly neither desirable nor practicable that banks should be required to attempt to discover for themselves whether a wife's consent is being procured by the exercise of undue influence of her husband."[212]

"If the solicitor considers the transaction is not in the wife's best interests, he will give reasoned advice to the wife to that effect. But at the end of the day the decision on whether to proceed is the decision of the client, not the solicitor."[213]

---

[210] *Royal Bank of Scotland v Etridge (No.2)* [2001] UKHL 44 [25] (Nicholls LJ).

[211] *Royal Bank of Scotland v Etridge (No.2)* [2001] UKHL 44 [37] (Nicholls LJ).

[212] *Royal Bank of Scotland v Etridge (No.2)* [2001] UKHL 44 [53] (Nicholls LJ).

[213] *Royal Bank of Scotland v Etridge (No.2)* [2001] UKHL 44 [61] (Nicholls LJ).

"It goes without saying that the solicitor's explanations should be couched in suitably non-technical language. It also goes without saying that the solicitor's task is an important one. It is not a formality."[214]

"[T]he solicitor must not act for the husband or the bank in the current transaction save in a wholly ministerial capacity, such as carrying out conveyancing formalities or supervising the execution of documents and witnessing signatures."[215]

"As a matter of general understanding, independent advice would suggest that the solicitor should not be acting in the same transaction for the person who, if there is any undue influence, is the source of that influence."[216]

"The bank does not have, and is intended not to have, any knowledge of or control over the advice the solicitor gives the wife. The solicitor is not accountable to the bank for the advice he gives to the wife."[217]

"The creditor must always take reasonable steps to bring home to the individual guarantor the risks he is running by standing as surety."[218]

"Banks and other lenders who take charges from surety wives are certainly purchasers of property rights. But they acquire their rights by grant from the surety wives themselves."[219]

"It is notice of the husband's impropriety that the bank must have, not notice of any prior rights of the wife. It is the notice that the bank has of the impropriety that creates the wife's right to set aside the transaction. The wife does not have any prior right or prior equity."[220]

---

[214] *Royal Bank of Scotland v Etridge (No.2)* [2001] UKHL 44 [66] (Nicholls LJ).

[215] *Royal Bank of Scotland v Etridge (No.2)* [2001] UKHL 44 [69] (Nicholls LJ).

[216] *Royal Bank of Scotland v Etridge (No.2)* [2001] UKHL 44 [72] (Nicholls LJ).

[217] *Royal Bank of Scotland v Etridge (No.2)* [2001] UKHL 44 [77] (Nicholls LJ).

[218] *Royal Bank of Scotland v Etridge (No.2)* [2001] UKHL 44 [87] (Nicholls LJ).

[219] *Royal Bank of Scotland v Etridge (No.2)* [2001] UKHL 44 [144] (Scott LJ).

[220] *Royal Bank of Scotland v Etridge (No.2)* [2001] UKHL 44 [146] (Scott LJ).

15. Scriven Bros & Co v Hindley & Co

Negligence and mistake, are two elements of contract law which conflict as between vendor and purchaser, particularly when the former is unreasonably applied to the buyer. In this very brief but notable case, the issue in hand turns upon the overpayment for a product at auction.

As was typical of the period, many agricultural products were imported for domestic use as the temperate weather of foreign countries provided for larger tonnage and lower prices. On this occasion, the subject matter was Russian industrial grade hemp, which while grown widely across the United Kingdom, remained their largest export at the time, and was a much sought after commodity. Contrastingly, tow is a by-product of hemp, and is thus sold at a much lower price for use as upholstery stuffing and other secondary purposes.

When a dockside auctioneer put out large bales of both hemp and tow, the samples shown to potential bidders were easily confusable. To make matters worse, the two consignments were given similar lot names, therefore for those uninitiated, the possibility of bidding in error was high. On this occasion, the purchaser had recruited a manager to bid on his behalf, at which point he had placed similar bids on both items on the assumption that he was buying hemp. To his further detriment, the auction programmes failed to distinguish the lots, and so only those who had the foresight to inspect them beforehand were spared the embarrassment of overpaying for items of lower market value.

When the purchaser discovered his managers error, he sued the auctioneers for misrepresentation through the principle of 'ad idem' (which is parties not in agreement to the nature of a contract), who themselves counter-sued for negligence on the part of the manager. In the original trial, it was found that there could be no evidence of a contract as per the principle of disagreement, and that no grounds of negligence existed in the absence of any duty of care by the manager to examine the lots prior to bidding.

When brought before a deciding jury it became apparent, despite appreciation of a number of opposing facts, that the auctioneers had been recent victims of fraud, so were simply looking to pass on the loss to another unsuspecting buyer. And so irrespective of any argument that the onus of inspection fell to the buyer's representative, it was held that a contract could not be found to exist where no agreement had been settled between the vendor and the purchaser.

Key Citations

"The second and third findings of the jury shew that the parties were never ad idem as to the subject-matter of the proposed sale; there was therefore in fact no contract of bargain and sale."[221]

"It was natural for the person inspecting the "S.L." goods and being shown hemp to suppose that the "S.L." bales represented the commodity hemp."[222]

"[I]t was peculiarly the duty of the auctioneer to make it clear to the bidder either upon the face of his catalogue, or in some other way which lots were hemp and which lots were tow."[223]

"A buyer when he examines a sample does so for his own benefit and not in the discharge of any duty to the seller."[224]

"Such a contract cannot arise when the person seeking to enforce it has by his own negligence or by that of those for whom he is responsible caused, or contributed to cause, the mistake."[225]

---

[221] *Scriven Bros & Co v Hindley & Co* [1913] 3 KB 564 (KB) 568 (Lawrence J).

[222] *Scriven Bros & Co v Hindley & Co* [1913] 3 KB 564 (KB) 569 (Lawrence J).

[223] *Scriven Bros & Co v Hindley & Co* [1913] 3 KB 564 (KB) 569 (Lawrence J).

[224] *Scriven Bros & Co v Hindley & Co* [1913] 3 KB 564 (KB) 569 (Lawrence J).

[225] *Scriven Bros & Co v Hindley & Co* [1913] 3 KB 564 (KB) 569 (Lawrence J).

16. Williams v Roffey Bros & Nicholls (Contractors) Ltd

Due consideration for the amendment of an existing contract becomes central to the argument between contracting parties, after the lesser of the two stops work and proceeds to litigate. When a main building contractor secures a residential refurbishment project, he accepts the tender of a carpentry subcontractor, despite the low value of his submission.

Having agreed to both first, and second fix, twenty-seven flats within a specified time for the sum of £20,000, the claimant carried out the work on the understanding that payments were made on an arbitrary basis. Within six months, the claimant had first-fixed all twenty-seven flats, but second-fixed only nine, while having been paid £16,200. Aware that his valuation of costs had now become unprofitable, the claimant turned to the defendant in order to renegotiate the contract in order to keep his business afloat, and help avoid the financial penalty clause applied to the main contractor, should the project overrun.

After discussing the needs of both parties, the two agreed to continue working together on the condition that a further £10,300 would be paid in incremental payments of £575 for each flat completed; at which point only an additional £1,500 had been paid at the time the claimant ceased working on the project. This left the defendant no choice but to use alternate subcontractors to finish the flats, after only seventeen of the twenty-seven flats were substantially completed.

Initially seeking around £33,000 in damages, the claimant reduced his claim to around £11,000, citing that the defendant had breached the terms of their oral agreement; whereas the defendants contended that the agreement to pay the additional £10,300, was unenforceable due to their non-completion, and that no consideration had been given by the claimant when the original contract was revised. The judge found that while the flats had not been completed, there had been sufficient consideration as to allow calculable damages of around £11,800, and awarded accordingly.

Presented to the Court of Appeal, the issues around payment for incomplete performance of a contract and the argument for lack of consideration were given closer examination, along with the potential claim for duress on the part of the appellants, which was later dismissed out of hand. Referring to p.126, para.183 of *Chitty on Contracts*, the Court held that:

> "The requirement that consideration must move from the promisee is most generally satisfied where some detriment is suffered by him e.g. where he parts with money or goods, or renders services, in exchange for the promise. But the requirement may equally well be satisfied where the promisee confers a benefit on the promisor without in fact suffering any detriment."[226]

Which translated that the respondent's agreement to continue working toward completion of the flats, provided a degree of benefit to the appellants, as failure to do so rendered them subject to the penalty clause; a principle which more than addressed the question of consideration and became fatal to their appeal. Relying upon the outcome of

---

[226] AG Guest (ed), *Chitty on Contracts* (26th edn, Sweet & Maxwell 1989)

H Dakin & Co Ltd v Lee,[227] the Court again turned to the principle of substantial performance of the contract to justify the payment of costs for work undertaken, as opposed to absolute performance as a qualification for claim. These two approaches left the Court in no doubt as to why the previous judgment must be upheld, and so the appeal was summarily dismissed.

Key Citations

"(i) if A has entered into a contract with B to do work for, or to supply goods or services to, B in return for payment by B; and (ii) at some stage before A has completely performed his obligations under the contract B has reason to doubt whether A will, or will be able to, complete his side of the bargain; and (iii) B thereupon promises A an additional payment in return for A's promise to perform his contractual obligations on time; and (iv) as a result of giving his promise, B obtains in practice a benefit, or obviates a disbenefit; and (v) B's promise is not given as a result of economic duress or fraud on the part of A; then (vi) the benefit to B is capable of being consideration for B's promise, so that the promise will be legally binding."[228]

"[T]he courts nowadays should be more ready to find its existence so as to reflect the intention of the parties to the contract where the bargaining powers are not unequal and where the finding of consideration reflect the true intention of the parties."[229]

"[W]here, as in this case, a party undertakes to make a payment because by so doing it will gain an advantage arising out of the continuing relationship with the promisee the new bargain will not fail for want of consideration."[230]

"[T]he modern approach to the question of consideration would be that where there were benefits derived by each party to a contract of variation even though one party did not suffer a detriment this would not be fatal to the establishing of sufficient consideration to support the agreement. If both parties benefit from an agreement it is not necessary that each also suffers a detriment."[231]

---

[227] [1916] 1 KB 566.

[228] *Williams v Roffey Bros & Nicholls (Contractors) Ltd* [1991] 1 QB 1 (CA) 15 (Glidewell LJ).

[229] *Williams v Roffey Bros & Nicholls (Contractors) Ltd* [1991] 1 QB 1 (CA) 18 (Russell LJ).

[230] *Williams v Roffey Bros & Nicholls (Contractors) Ltd* [1991] 1 QB 1 (CA) 19 (Russell LJ).

[231] *Williams v Roffey Bros & Nicholls (Contractors) Ltd* [1991] 1 QB 1 (CA) 23 (Purchas LJ).

3. Criminal Law

1. Hashman and Harrup v United Kingdom

Does the allegation and summary conviction of a breach of the peace constitute a violation of art.10 of the European Convention on Human Rights (ECHR), and if so must the courts take a more detailed approach to public disorder offences before sweeping aside the individual rights bestowed them? When two hunt saboteurs are impugned under statute dating back centuries, the certainty of this broadly applied restriction was questioned by virtue of it's failing exactness.

While actively demonstrating at a village fox hunt, the methods used by the two appellants included the blowing of horns and hollering around the hunt dogs, so to effect distractive consequences and general confusion to the event. As a consequence of these tactics, a single hound strayed from the pack before winding up killed under the wheels of a passing lorry. Although there were no ensuing fisticuffs or threats of violence, legal action was taken that resulted in a binding over order subject to £100, on grounds of a breach of the peace, while the order was to run for a twelve month period in lieu of a reasonable prison sentence.

Under appeal to the Crown Court, it was agreed that under the terms of the Justices of the Peace Act 1361, there could be no evidence that their conduct qualified a breach of the peace because as previously mentioned, there had been no violence or coercion to violence shown by the protestors. However, it was felt that unless some restrictive measures were in effect, there was a genuine risk of repeat behaviour that could likely end up with criminal sentencing of some measure.

This judgment was then challenged under domestic jurisdiction, but the Crown Court refused leave of appeal to the High Court, which forced proceedings to continue in the European Court of Human Rights. Citing art.10 of the ECHR (Freedom of expression), the appellants refuted the power of the binding over order upon grounds that the nature of the statute was in effect, too vague in construction to provide any genuine clarity as to (i) what the protestors were being asked to refrain from doing and (ii) what behaviour would further constitute a breach of that order.

Despite some compelling dissent, it was found after considered examination of the interfering potential of the order, that while the principle behind the restriction was honourable by design, the prohibitive quality bestowed by the now antiquated and outdated measure of binding over orders, was such that the even the Law Commission had proposed them abolished, and where once public order would be restored without contest, the case had found itself before the European Commission.

Using the powers afforded citizens under the Convention, it was then agreed by majority that when a domestic law fails to provide adequate redress, it does so by effectively interfering with those individual rights, and must therefore fail to find fact. For those reasons, the appeal was upheld and costs awarded against the state.

Key Citations

"The Commission recalls that freedom of expression goes beyond mere speech and considers that the applicants' behaviour was an expression of their disagreement with the hunt, and as such falls within the ambit of Article 10."[232]

"The applicants' behaviour ran counter to neither criminal nor civil law, and it did not have the element of harm or threat of fear of harm which is essential in breach of the peace cases."[233]

"The Commission is struck in the present case by the absence of any judicial or statutory definition of what is "wrong rather than right in the judgment of the vast majority of contemporary fellow citizens"."[234]

"A norm cannot be regarded as a "law" unless it is formulated with sufficient precision to enable the citizen to regulate his conduct."[235]

"[T]he present applicants did not breach of the peace, and given the lack of precision referred to above, it cannot be said that what they were being bound over not to do must have been apparent to them."[236]

---

[232] *Hashman and Harrup v United Kingdom* [2000] 30 EHRR 24 [47] (Commission Decision).

[233] *Hashman and Harrup v United Kingdom* [2000] 30 EHRR 24 [49] (Commission Decision).

[234] *Hashman and Harrup v United Kingdom* [2000] 30 EHRR 24 [55] (Commission Decision).

[235] *Hashman and Harrup v United Kingdom* [2000] 30 EHRR 24 [31] (Commission Decision).

[236] *Hashman and Harrup v United Kingdom* [2000] 30 EHRR 24 [40] (Commission Decision).

2. R v Ahluwalia

Victim to an arranged marriage, and having endured years of systematic and debilitating abuse at the hands of her husband, the defendant in this appeal case found herself subjected to yet further suffering through the absence of vital medical evidence when her case was presented at trial.

Having been introduced by her brother and sister-in-law while abroad, the defendant, who had been previously studying towards a degree in law, was by cultural obligation and the wishes of her family, forced into marrying the man who later became the subject of her actions. Prior to their starting a family, the husband began a campaign of mental and physical abuse spanning a decade, until such time as her spirit was broken and death seemed the only solution.

After two failed suicide attempts, the defendant, who herself had been subjected to continuous death threats and physical battery, discovered that her husband was now having an affair with another woman, while uncompromisingly flaunting it with little thought to how degrading and shameful such deceit was to both them and their children.

It was after pleading for him to remain in the marriage, that the defendant set aside a bucket of petrol and a bottle of caustic soda until the time came for her to retaliate. Unable to sleep one evening, the defendant entered the marital bedroom and proceeded to throw the contents of the bucket over the husband, before lighting a stick and igniting the petrol, whereupon the husband ran screaming from the house before being taken to hospital suffering major burns and dying days afterwards.

At trial, the court found itself with no evidence to support her actions, and after examining both defences offered, the judge explored the argument that her actions represented the cumulative effect of years of provocation by the husband, and that the jury should interpret her actions as that of manslaughter and not murder.

Relying on the changes made to the Homicide Act 1957, there was greater emphasis on the expanse of time between causative actions and those of the defendant, rather than instantaneous responses to attacks. However, insufficient emphasis was placed upon the mental state of the defendant at the time the act took place, which subsequently resulted in a murder charge, despite the background to the matter.

When taken to the Appeal Court, the judges held that arguments of misdirection were insubstantial to the effect that the jury might have mitigated the verdict. However, there was the discovery of medically professional evidence that relied upon the Mental Health Act 1983 when describing the defendant as suffering from 'a major depressive disorder', thus allowing for diminished responsibility as an alternate defence. Although the Court typically frowned upon the late presentation of key evidence, it made allowances on this occasion under the powers of s.23(1) of the Criminal Appeal Act 1968, before moving to request a new trial on grounds that fair and balanced representation was critical to the maxim that 'Justice should not only be done, but should manifestly and undoubtedly be seen to be done'.[237]

---

[237] *R v Sussex Justices ex p McCarthy* [1924] 1 KB 256 (KB) 259 (Hewart CJ).

Key Citations

"The phrase "sudden and temporary loss of self-control" encapsulates an essential ingredient of the defence of provocation in a clear and readily understandable phrase."[238]

"Where a particular principle of law has been re-affirmed so many times and applied so generally over such a long period, it must be a matter for Parliament to consider any change."[239]

"[T]he existence of a mandatory life sentence for all murders is a matter for Parliament, not for this court and we cannot bend the law in an individual case or class of cases where it may be thought the mandatory life sentence operates harshly."[240]

---

[238] *R v Ahluwalia* [1992] 4 All ER 889 (CA) 138 (Lord Taylor CJ).

[239] *R v Ahluwalia* [1992] 4 All ER 889 (CA) 139 (Lord Taylor CJ).

[240] *R v Ahluwalia* [1992] 4 All ER 889 (CA) 142 (Lord Taylor CJ).

3. R v Bree

The premise of statutory rape relies upon the principles of informed consent, and such legalities further rely upon the effects of the Sexual Offences Act 2003 when establishing guilt. On this occasion, the defendant contended that the act of sex between himself and the complainant began and ended with reasoned determination, and not forcible violation.

When a group of university undergraduates chose to have a night out, they did so in the knowledge that drinking to excess brings consequences that while not unexpected, can lead to actions which in the aftermath of intoxication, can give rise to shame and regret.

After drinking a voluminous amount of alcohol and liquid stimulant, the complainant paired off with the defendant before both of them returned to her lodgings, whereupon the complainant began vomiting. Having cleaned her up and placed her in her bed, the defendant sat with her before the two began physically enjoying each other (albeit through physical cues and minimal dialogue). Having discussed the availability of contraception, they proceeded to engage in intercourse, again with the defendant relying upon visual and audible cues as to the complainant's consent.

For preventative reasons, the act of intercourse ceased before the defendant left the property after having asked if the complainant wished him to stay the night. It was shortly afterwards that the complainant contacted friends and family whilst intoxicated, to explain her distress at what had occurred. Citing statutory rape, the case was brought before the Crown Court, where the jury were asked to consider the ramifications of s.74 of the Sexual Offences Act 2003, which outlined in instances where rape under s.1 of the Act has been claimed:

> "[A] person consents if he agrees by choice, and has the freedom and capacity to make that choice."[241]

It was this distinction, that when held against the facts of the case, that was of primary importance to the minds of the jury when determining guilt; and so as the finer points of the complainant's statement were examined, it became apparent that despite being heavily intoxicated prior to her vomiting, her state was such that she was aware enough to know that she, and the defendant, were engaging in sex, and that at no point did she express her unwillingness to have unprotected sex, further to the defendant withdrawing from the act while absent of ejaculation.

In the first hearing, the jury found the defendant guilty of statutory rape, yet upon appeal the Court examined the subtleties of the judges direction, and noted that inadequate emphasis had been placed upon the complaint's conscious acquiescence in lieu of the defendant's persistence; differences that persuaded the verdict rather than apportioning responsibility on both parties as consenting adults. In light of these oversights, and in addition to a number of secondary mitigating factors, it was then agreed that for those reasons the conviction was to be quashed.

---

[241] Sexual Offences Act 2003, s.74.

Key Citations

"[F]or the purposes of the 2003 Act "capacity" is integral to the concept of "choice", and therefore to "consent".[242]

"There is nothing abnormal, surprising, or even unusual about men and women having consensual intercourse when one, or other, or both have voluntarily consumed a great deal of alcohol. Provided intercourse is indeed consensual, it is not rape."[243]

"[W]hen someone who has had a lot to drink is in fact consenting to intercourse, then that is what she is doing, consenting: equally, if after taking drink, she is not consenting, then by definition intercourse is taking place without her consent. This is unexceptionable."[244]

"If, through drink (or for any other reason) the complainant has temporarily lost her capacity to choose whether to have intercourse on the relevant occasion, she is not consenting, and subject to questions about the defendant's state of mind, if intercourse takes place, this would be rape."[245]

---

[242] *R v Bree* [2007] EWCA Crim 804 (CA) 137 (Sir Igor Judge P).

[243] *R v Bree* [2007] EWCA Crim 804 (CA) 138 (Sir Igor Judge P).

[244] *R v Bree* [2007] EWCA Crim 804 (CA) 140 (Sir Igor Judge P).

[245] *R v Bree* [2007] EWCA Crim 804 (CA) 140 (Sir Igor Judge P).

4. R v Collins

A conviction of burglary with intent to rape becomes convoluted when under appeal, the defendant places the burden of proof upon a building fixture.

In an unprecedented case, the defendant was a teenager who for one reason or another, took it upon himself to enter a teenage girl's bedroom before engaging in sexual intercourse. What distinguishes this impulsive act from one that many might expect at that age, is the fact that the complainant allowed his entry on the mistake that she believed him to be her boyfriend, and not a complete stranger.

Having first consumed a large amount of alcohol, the defendant decided that one way or another, he was going to have his way with a willing girl, somewhere. On this occasion, he selected the home of a girl who, while not directly known to him, he had seen when working on her parents house sometime before. Having climbed a ladder to her bedroom window, the defendant saw her lying naked in her bed and removed his clothes, while fully aroused.

The complainant was also inebriated to some degree, and therefore beckoned him into her bed, while physically pulling him in before they began to have sex. After a period of time, the complainant realised that the person she was having sex with was not her boyfriend, upon which she slapped him and ran to her bathroom. Following his arrest the following morning, the defendant confessed to his actions but denied that he intended to rape her; instead noting that she had willingly invited him into her bedroom (much to his surprise) on the pretence that they were to have sex.

When heard before a jury the charge brought before them relied upon s.9(1)(a) of the Theft Act 1968, which explained that burglary was an act requiring trespass with intent to commit an offence, which in this instance fell under s.9(2) as rape. Having explained the nature of his entry and the preceding acts, the judge left the jury to consider whether his trespass was intentional or reckless, upon which it was agreed that the former applied.

Having appealed, the defendant challenged the conviction on grounds that it had been unproven as to whether the entry was undertaken based upon the complainant's words and actions, and thus remained unproven as to whether the defendant was (i) outside the window frame or (ii) inside the bedroom when she invited him in. In light of the fact that insufficient evidence existed when establishing that fact, it was decided by the Court that a degree of misdirection had occurred in the original hearing, and so without the full disposal of the truth the conviction for burglary could not stand.

Key Citations

"[F]or the purposes of section 9 of the Theft Act, a person entering a building is not guilty of trespass if he enters without knowledge that he is trespassing or at least without acting recklessly as to whether or not he is unlawfully entering."[246]

"[T]here cannot be a conviction for entering premises "as a trespasser" within the meaning of section 9 of the Theft Act unless the person entering does so knowing that he is a trespasser and nevertheless deliberately enters, or, at the very least, is reckless as to whether or not he is entering the premises of another without the other party's consent."[247]

"Unless the jury were entirely satisfied that the defendant made an effective and substantial entry into the bedroom without the complainant doing or saying anything to cause him to believe that she was consenting to his entering it, he ought not to be convicted of the offence charged."[248]

---

[246] *R v Collins* [1973] QB 100 (CA) 104 (Davies LJ).

[247] *R v Collins* [1973] QB 100 (CA) 105 (Davies LJ).

[248] *R v Collins* [1973] QB 100 (CA) 106 (Davies LJ).

5. R v G and R

Reckless culpability and the innocence of youth cross swords in a case that both rewrote the powers of legislation and allowed subjective reasoning to prevail. When two young boys aged eleven and twelve spent the night camping, they wound up playing in the rear storage yard of a Co-operative store. What began as tomfoolery with matches and newspaper, wound up as criminal damage and arson, totalling over £1m in damages. However, with equal consideration of English criminal law and precedent relating to the facts, it also became a matter destined to reach the House of Lords.

Having decided to spend the night camping outside, the two appellants trespassed into the refuse area of the store, and began reading discarded newspapers. For reasons best known to themselves, the boys then set alight to a bundle of newspapers before placing them underneath a large plastic dustbin. Without staying to watch the flames extinguish, the defendants left the yard and presumably returned home.

Unfortunately, as is the nature of fire, the flames ignited the bin, which subsequently ignited the adjacent bin, before the fire spread to the roof and beyond. When first heard at trial, the judge rightly relied upon the exacting terms of s.1(1) of the Criminal Damage Act 1971, which reads:

> "A person who without lawful excuse destroys or damages any property belonging to another intending to destroy or damage any such property or being reckless as to whether any such property would be destroyed or damaged shall be guilty of an offence."[249]

While the term 'reckless' remains subjectively difficult to ascertain, the application of this measure failed to discriminate between the range of comprehension created through age, disability, or intelligence. This absence of evaluation forced the jury to determine the boys' guilt on the objective reasoning of an adult, as established in *R v Caldwell*[250] and earlier in *R v Cunningham*[251] (albeit a case more reliant upon maliciousness than ignorance). In *Caldwell*, the defendant had been intoxicated prior to choosing to set fire to his employer's hotel, thereby putting the guests and staff in great danger while noting that he had paid little mind to the consequences when starting the fire.

It was this case that led to an objective reasoning test, that while applicable to most mature adults, offered little consideration for children or vulnerable adults in similar circumstances. Having deliberated on the certainty of a fair conviction, the judge and jury were left finding guilt, although not without concern for the limitations of the 1971 Act.

Having been dismissed by the Court of Appeal, the appellants were granted leave to present to the House of Lords, where greater attention was placed upon the disparity of

---

[249] Criminal Damage Act 1971, s.1(1)

[250] [1982] AC 341.

[251] [1957] 2 QB 396.

the Criminal Law Act 2003 and art.40(1) of the European Convention on Human Rights (Public hearings and access to documents), which expressed:

> "States parties recognise the right of every child alleged as, accused of, or recognised as having infringed the penal law to be treated in a manner consistent with the promotion of the child's sense of dignity and worth, which reinforces the child's respect for the human rights and fundamental freedoms of others and which takes into account the child's age and the desirability of promoting the child's reintegration and the child's assuming a constructive role in society."[252]

It was then with appreciation of the narrowness that recklessness previously enjoyed, that the House examined the relevance of continuing to broaden the scope of reckless behaviour, so as to avoid the need for deliberate and considered forethought to the mindset of those accused. Having revisited the case history preceding the Criminal Damage Act 1971, it became clear that overlooking the objective test, as subjectively interpreted by the courts, had prevented fair and reasoned judgment, and that this particular case was the vehicle upon which to amend that error. It was with that collective ethos that the House (by majority) declared the boys' innocence and upheld the appeal.

---

[252] European Convention for the Protection of Human Rights and Fundamental Freedoms (1953)

Key Citations

"[I]t is a salutary principle that conviction of serious crime should depend on proof not simply that the defendant caused (by act or omission) an injurious result to another but that his state of mind when so acting was culpable."[253]

"It is neither moral nor just to convict a defendant (least of all a child) on the strength of what someone else would have apprehended if the defendant himself had no such apprehension."[254]

"It is one thing to decide whether a defendant can be believed when he says that the thought of a given risk never crossed his mind. It is another, and much more speculative, task to decide whether the risk would have been obvious to him if the thought had crossed his mind."[255]

"*R v Caldwell* adopted an interpretation of section 1 of the 1971 Act which was beyond the range of feasible meanings."[256]

"[I]f the law is to operate with the concept of recklessness, then it may properly treat as reckless the man who acts without even troubling to give his mind to a risk that would have been obvious to him if he had thought about it."[257]

---

[253] *R V G and R* [2002] EWCA Crim 1992 [32] (Bingham LJ).

[254] *R V G and R* [2002] EWCA Crim 1992 [33] (Bingham LJ).

[255] *R V G and R* [2002] EWCA Crim 1992 [38] (Bingham LJ).

[256] *R V G and R* [2002] EWCA Crim 1992 [51] (Steyn LJ).

[257] *R V G and R* [2002] EWCA Crim 1992 [69] (Rodger LJ).

6. R v Ghosh

Subjective dishonesty (or honesty) is both a key ingredient to conviction of a criminal act and a frustration for the jury when reaching fair and reasoned judgment. When the deceitful acts of a professional lead him to court, it is not without a degree of debate that the verdict is clear.

Having worked as a locum tenens (substitute doctor), the appellant used his position to charge and receive payments for services carried out under public health principles, or on occasion, not at all. When taken to court, the appellant claimed that he had performed a pregnancy termination, and subsequently charged the hospital consultancy fees; a service that while claimed as honest, had in fact been freely available and performed under the National Health Service (NHS).

Under ss.15(1) and 20(2) of the Theft Act 1968 the court ruled (i) that the appellant had acted fraudulently through his dishonest appropriation of monies under false pretences, and (ii) that such deception rendered him liable for theft. In his defence, it was argued that the meaning of dishonesty as per s.1 of the Theft Act 1968, was one of subjective reasoning and so not subject to the objective test applied by the jury.

In response, the Court of Appeal examined the meanings and applications for both fraud and theft in their respective terms. While fraud (or conspiracy to commit fraud) followed a subjective test, there had been concerns as to why an objective test was applied for theft. These two principles were first established in *R v Landy*,[258] where those preparing or conspiring to defraud were judged not on their actions, but on their mens rea (mindset preceding the crime); whereas in theft cases as laid down in *R v Greenstein*,[259] the jury were asked instead to view the motives of the defendant from that of a reasonable person; the reason for this being that the theft had been established, therefore guilt was apparent unless the action was deemed innocent by the jury.

The position adopted by the appellant was that rather than allowing a jury to determine guilt using their own perspective, it ought to be viewed instead from the mind of the appellant himself, who on this occasion claimed to have been acting honestly, despite stark evidence to the contrary. This play on words gave no rise to review the current position on dishonesty for a number of reasons, one of which being that subjective determination by a defendant provides nothing more than the ability to act as judge, jury and executioner (so to speak), thus manipulating the rule of law for criminal gain. It was for this reason alone that the Court dismissed the appeal and upheld the conviction for theft, before noting that regardless of which test had been applied, the outcome would have remained the same.

---

[258] [1981] 1 WLR 355.

[259] [1975] 1 WLR 1353.

Key Citations

"[T]he subjective test is appropriate where the charge is conspiracy to defraud, but in the case of theft the test should be objective."[260]

"It is no defence for a man to say "I knew that what I was doing is generally regarded as dishonest; but I do not regard it as dishonest myself. Therefore I am not guilty." What he is however entitled to say is "I did not know that anybody would regard what I was doing as dishonest.""[261]

"It is dishonest for a defendant to act in a way which he knows ordinary people consider to be dishonest, even if he asserts or genuinely believes that he is morally justified in acting as he did."[262]

"If the judge had asked the jury to determine whether the defendant might have believed that what he did was in accordance with the ordinary man's idea of honesty, there could have only been one answer - and that is no…"[263]

---

[260] *R v Ghosh* [1982] QB 1053 (CA) 1058 (Lane CJ).

[261] *R v Ghosh* [1982] QB 1053 (CA) 1064 (Lane CJ).

[262] *R v Ghosh* [1982] QB 1053 (CA) 1064 (Lane CJ).

[263] *R v Ghosh* [1982] QB 1053 (CA) 1065 (Lane CJ).

7. R v Hinks

An amendment to the Theft Act 1968 in relation to appropriation, becomes central to the discussion when a single mother takes advantage of a vulnerable adult. As a single parent, the appellant befriended an older man who while living alone, was of low intelligence and in need of daily care. Through the course of their relationship, the appellant manipulated the man into withdrawing small sums of money from his £60,000 inheritance, almost to the point of exhausting his funds, before walking away with his television set.

Having been caught and convicted of theft under s.1 of the 1968 Act, the appellant continued to claim that her actions were honest, inasmuch as he had agreed to give her the money, and had accompanied her to the building society in order to facilitate the withdrawals. In addition to this, she claimed that those gifts were for the betterment of herself and her young son, and that the television set was simply another act of charity on his part.

With her contention dismissed by the Court of Appeal, it was left to the House of Lords to examine the precision of the Theft Act 1968, and those terms applicable to appropriation. Prior to the drafting of the 1968 Act, it was expressed in s.1(1) of the Larceny Act 1916, that:

> "A person steals who, *without the consent of the owner*, fraudulently and without a claim of right made in good faith, takes away and carries away anything capable of being stolen with intent, at the time of such taking, permanently to deprive the owner thereof."[264]

However, when examining the terms of the Theft Act 1968, s.1(1) instead reads:

> "A person is guilty of theft if he *dishonestly appropriates property belonging to another wth the intention of permanently depriving the other of it*; and 'thief' and 'steal' shall be construed accordingly."[265]

This variance (or absence) of words was what the appellant relied upon when claiming that the monies given were gifts, and that despite any subjective opinion that her receipt of them constituted a criminal act, she was in fact innocent and therefore wrongly convicted.

When considering the finer points of theft and the decision by Parliament to broaden the effect of theft under the 1968 Act, it had already been agreed that in both *R v Lawrence*[266] and *R v Gomez*,[267] appropriation of property belonging to another under dishonest circumstances was still tantamount to theft, even where knowing consent had been provided. In *Lawrence*, a taxi driver had overcharged a foreign student in the

---

[264] Larceny Act 1916, s.1(1) (emphasis added).

[265] Theft Act 1968, s.1(1) (emphasis added).

[266] *R v Lawrence* [1972] AC 626 (HL).

[267] *DPP v Gomez* [1993] AC 442.

knowledge that the fare ought to have been less, at which point the student duly paid. In *Gomez*, a shop owner allowed payment for goods by cheque on the pretence that the cheques were valid, particularly after his conspiring employee confirmed their authenticity.

Those two cases were identical in context inasmuch as the victims were misled into parting with property on the assumption that the transactions were honest. In this case however, the appellant had induced her victim into believing that (i) he had the funds to give away and (ii) that the cause of his donations was genuine as opposed to one of her simple greed. This raised further questions around his ability to understand his decision making, and whether her appropriation under false pretences allowed her to circumnavigate the law and avoid penalty.

With a degree of division within the House, it was finally decided that despite any argument that relinquishing property under conscious knowledge could not amount to theft, the dishonest intentions of the recipient were encompassed by s.1 of the Theft Act 1968, regardless of whether the donors believed the act to be lawful.

Key Citations

"If the law is restated by adopting a narrower definition of appropriation, the outcome is likely to place beyond the reach of the criminal law dishonest persons who should be found guilty of theft."[268]

"In practice the mental requirements of theft are an adequate protection against injustice."[269]

---

[268] *R v Hinks* [2000] 4 All ER 833 (HL) 252 (Steyn LJ).

[269] *R v Hinks* [2000] 4 All ER 833 (HL) 253 (Steyn LJ).

8. R v Howe

In a conjoined appeal, the murder of two men in separate circumstances led to enquiry as to the extent of duress in criminal acts; and where used as a defence to murder, whether it was capable of effecting sentencing reduction or even acquittal where two parties were liable for the act.

Howe and Bannister

In the first matter, it was argued by two of four defendants, that their participation in a number of killings and acts of abhorrent violence, was based upon a fear of retribution by the older of the men (M). There were two counts of murder and one of conspiracy to murder, as the third man narrowly escaped death; and on both occasions the two named appellants were present, albeit jointly culpable only for the killing of the second victim. After the third defendant and M pleaded guilty to murder under s.1 of the Criminal Law Act 1977, it was then left to the appellants to submit pleadings that they had acted under duress while subject to the instructions of M; and that subsequently, their conviction for murder should be one reduced to manslaughter.

Burke and Clarkson

In this instance, the premeditated killing of a man was brought about through fear of his providing evidence against the second appellant in court. It was argued by the first appellant, that his willingness to shoot the man was tempered by his fear of what might happen to him if he didn't act on the second appellant's instructions. Further to this was the contention that when confronted on his doorstep, the victim was killed through accidental firing of the gun, and not by a deliberate act. For this reason, the first appellant pleaded manslaughter through accidental death, while the second appellant claimed to have had nothing to do with the shooting whatsoever.

When first argued, the jury were directed as to the merits of manslaughter under duress, and on both occasions found the appellants equally liable for murder. When taken to the Court of Appeal, the jury were again asked to take an objective view when considering the influence of those providing instructions and those that committed the criminal acts; where again, the appeals were dismissed and the convictions upheld.

When presented to the House of Lords, it was argued that where objective reasoning for the crime of murder could not allow for a reduction through duress, it was only fair that the appellants were afforded the right to subjectively defend their actions in the face of perceived threats. This approach ran contrary to English criminal law and was subject to previous instances where similar claims had been presented and denied (*R v Kray*[270] and *R v Lynch*[271] as two such examples). In *Lynch* however, the Court of Appeal had been willing to allow a defence of duress, when the appellant had merely driven the killer(s) to their destination.

---

[270] *R v Kray* (1969) 53 Cr App R 569.

[271] *Lynch v DPP* [1975] AC 653 (HL).

Through careful examination of the facts behind *Lynch*, the House found that while duress was acknowledged in matters of serious wounding, it would constitute an affront to the principles of law if those accused of murder, or even as accomplices to murder, were entitled to reason away their actions on grounds of weakness or fear. For that reason the appeals were dismissed, whilst a deeper conviction of the all-encompassing weight of murder remained firm.

Key Citations

"[D]uress is only that species of the genus of necessity which is caused by wrongful threats. I cannot see that there is any way in which a person of ordinary fortitude can be excused from the one type of pressure on his will than the other."[272]

"[T]here is a valid distinction to be drawn in ordinary language between a man who actually participates in the irrevocable act of murder to save his own skin or that of his nearest and dearest and a man who simply participates before or after the event in the necessary preparation for it or the escape of the actual offender."[273]

"[W]hile there can never be a direct correspondence between law and morality, an attempt to divorce the two entirely is and has always proved to be, doomed to failure, and, in the present case, the overriding objects of the criminal law must be to protect innocent lives and to set a standard of conduct which ordinary men and women are expected to observe if they are to avoid criminal responsibility."[274]

"The justification for allowing a defence of duress to a charge of murder is that a defendant should be excused who killed as the only way of avoiding death himself or preventing the death of some close relation such as his own well-loved child."[275]

"To say that a defence in respect of which so many questions remain unsettled should be introduced in respect of the whole field of murder is not to promote certainty in the law."[276]

"While I appreciate fully the gradual development that has taken place in the law relating to the defence of duress I question whether the law has reached a sufficiently precise definition of that defence to make it right for us sitting in our judicial capacity to introduce it as a defence for an actual killer for the first time in the law of England."[277]

---

[272] *R v Howe* [1987] Crim LR 480 (HL) 429 (Lord Hailsham LC).

[273] *R v Howe* [1987] Crim LR 480 (HL) 429 (Lord Hailsham LC).

[274] *R v Howe* [1987] Crim LR 480 (HL) 430 (Lord Hailsham LC).

[275] *R v Howe* [1987] Crim LR 480 (HL) 453 (Mackay LJ).

[276] *R v Howe* [1987] Crim LR 480 (HL) 454 (Mackay LJ).

[277] *R v Howe* [1987] Crim LR 480 (HL) 455 (Mackay LJ).

9. R v Ireland

While s.20 of the Offences Against the Person Act 1861 provides that certain physical acts of violence are grounds for a conviction of grievous bodily harm, the psychological fear of impending violence through the use of words or silence, can prove difficult to sustain as a claim for assault occasioning actual bodily harm. In this conjoined appeal, the House of Lords was required to assess exactly where the terms of the 1861 Act ended, particularly when the use of modern technology produced fears capable of physical manifestation.

R v Ireland

In this matter, the appellant had been tried and convicted of assault occasioning actual bodily harm under s.47 of the Offences Against the Person Act 1861. Having repeatedly called three women during the night on a number of occasions, and each time remaining silent or breathing heavily so as to induce fear and anxiety, his actions had the effect of causing prolonged psychiatric distress. In a previous case (*R v Chan-Fook*),[278] the court had agreed that non-physical acts are capable of amounting to actual bodily harm where the victim had been mentally affected (albeit the conviction was quashed upon appeal), however in this instance, the question was whether such a charge could extend so as to qualify for assault.

R v Burstow

On this occasion, the appellant had been in a relationship with a woman, which for a number of reasons, came to an end. In the months following their separation, the appellant went to great lengths in order to frighten her and give cause for her personal safety after making abusive (and silent) phone calls, distributing libellous pamphlets around the community, taking unsolicited photographs of the appellant and her family and making unannounced visits to her workplace and home. As appreciated, the net result of his threatening behaviour left the woman in a depressive state and in constant fear of a violent attack. When tried in court the judge agreed that while no physical contact had been made, the collective damage of his actions was sufficient to uphold a charge of maliciously inflicting grievous body harm under s.20 of the Offences Against the Person Act 1861.

With both appellants seeking to overturn the charges, they took their cases to the Court of Appeal, who while dismissing their claims, allowed leave to appeal to the House of Lords. In *Burstow*, it was argued that causing and inflicting harm are distinguishable, and that as no physical contact was made the charges were unsustainable. However, the House examined the differences and held that infliction was, by connotation, a word suggesting suffering of the recipient, and so his appeal was dismissed. In *Ireland*, the meaning of assault was explored inasmuch as the second element of assault was one where anticipation of violence is sufficient enough to warrant a charge, and that the appellant had simply used a combination of telecommunications and silence with which to install immediate dread and uncertainty as to what he would do next.

---

[278] [1994] 1 WLR 689.

Key Citations

"[I]t is essential to bear in mind that neurotic illnesses affect the central nervous system of the body, because emotions such as fear and anxiety are brain functions."[279]

"[A]lthough out of considerations of piety we frequently refer to the actual intention of the draftsman, the correct approach is simply to consider whether the words of the Act of 1861 considered in the light of contemporary knowledge cover a recognisable psychiatric injury."[280]

"The proposition that a gesture may amount to an assault, but that words can never suffice, is unrealistic and indefensible. A thing said is also a thing done."[281]

"[T]here is no reason why a telephone caller who says to a woman in a menacing way 'I will be at your door in a minute or two' may not be guilty of an assault if he causes his victim to apprehend immediate personal violence."[282]

"[I]t is not a necessary ingredient of the word 'inflict' that whatever causes the harm must be applied directly to the victim. It may be applied indirectly, so long as the result is that the harm is caused by what has been done."[283]

"If the words or gestures are accompanied in their turn by gestures or by words which threaten immediate and unlawful violence, that will be sufficient for an assault. The words or gestures must be seen in their whole context."[284]

---

[279] *R v Ireland* [1998] Crim LR 810 (HL) 156 (Steyn LJ).

[280] *R v Ireland* [1998] Crim LR 810 (HL) 158 (Steyn LJ).

[281] *R v Ireland* [1998] Crim LR 810 (HL) 161 (Steyn LJ).

[282] *R v Ireland* [1998] Crim LR 810 (HL) 161 (Steyn LJ).

[283] *R v Ireland* [1998] Crim LR 810 (HL) 164 (Hope LJ).

[284] *R v Ireland* [1998] Crim LR 810 (HL) 166 (Hope LJ).

10. R v Kennedy

The domestic criminal law principle of 'free will' within the confines of substance abuse, is a question that by extension remains fraught with uncertainty (with particular regard to Class A substances). In this drug-related death case, the issue before the court was fundamentally one of autonomy versus conjoined culpability.

When two drug users were engaging in social discourse, the now deceased party asked the appellant to prepare a syringe of heroin so that he might be able to sleep that evening. After preparing the drug in the manner requested, the appellant left the room before the deceased self-injected the measured dose. Minutes afterwards, the user was found breathless and pronounced dead upon arrival at the nearest hospital.

When heard during the original trial, the appellant was convicted of supplying a class A drug under s.4(1) of the Misuse of Drugs Act 1971, and administering the drug under s. 23 of the Offences Against The Person Act 1861. These two offences were then tantamount to a charge of manslaughter and sentence was set at eight years, with five of those under imprisonment. When the defendant appealed, the judges unflinchingly upheld the conviction, and it so was that when the Criminal Cases Review Commission studied the finer details of the case, it was bought again before the Court of Appeal, where despite strongly presented contentions, it was summarily dismissed and left to the defendant to seek final appeal in the House of Lords.

With a need for investigation surrounding the notion that administration of drugs implied contributory action on the part of the supplier, it was eventually made clear that the previous judges had become victim to self-misdirection, despite distinguishing case citations presented throughout the appeals. Ultimately the doctrine of '*novus actus interveniens*' was sufficiently present enough for the injecting party to have acted under free will with appreciation of the inherent risks associated with heroin abuse; and that while the first offence, which itself carried a prison sentence remained intact, the charge of manslaughter could not stand when held against the perhaps better appreciated evidence now on display.

Key Citations

"The criminal generally assumes the existence of free will."[285]

"[G]enerally speaking, informed adults of sound mind are treated as autonomous beings able to make their own decisions how they will act…"[286]

"Questions of causation frequently arise in many areas of the law, but causation is not a single, unvarying concept to be mechanically applied without regard to the context in which the question arises."[287]

"[T]hat the deceased freely and voluntarily administered the injection to himself, knowing what it was, is fatal to any contention that the appellant caused the heroin to be administered to the deceased out taken by him."[288]

"At the trial of the present appellant there was no consideration of section 23 and the trial judge effectively stopped defence counsel submitting to the jury that the appellant had not caused the death of the deceased."[289]

"[T]he court gave no detailed consideration to the terms of section 23, and it is now, accepted that the deceased's injection of himself was not an unlawful act."[290]

---

[285] *R v Kennedy* [2007] UKHL 38 [14] (Bingham LJ).

[286] *R v Kennedy* [2007] UKHL 38 [14] (Bingham LJ).

[287] *R v Kennedy* [2007] UKHL 38 [15] (Bingham LJ).

[288] *R v Kennedy* [2007] UKHL 38 [18] (Bingham LJ).

[289] *R v Kennedy* [2007] UKHL 38 [21] (Bingham LJ).

[290] *R v Kennedy* [2007] UKHL 38 [21] (Bingham LJ).

11. R v Kingston

Sexual assault and involuntary intoxication of the accused become central to the question of defence when the mens rea remains equally present despite the influences of a third party. In this House of Lords appeal, the idea that perhaps existing criminal law has overlooked the subjective effects of those liable for acts against the person, is explored before deciding how best to answer it.

In this case, the actions of two men were complicit to the sexual assault and degradation of a fifteen year-old boy, while under the influence of a powerful sedative. The background to the matter stemmed from a business arrangement gone sour, and that left the respondent victim to the subterfuge of his colleague, who unknown to him, was acting on behalf of the slighted party. Having been paid to place the respondent in a compromising position, the man had arranged for them to invite the teenager to a room, before using a number of drugs to induce the victim into a state of unconsciousness, whereupon the respondent engaged in a variety of lewd and sexually abusive acts as his colleague secretly filmed and took pictures of his assault upon the boy.

When the images and recorded film were obtained by the police, the two men were taken to court and charged with indecent assault. Upon conviction, the the respondent pleaded a defence of involuntary intoxication, on grounds that the co-defendant had also plied him with a similar drug, and that by extension, his actions upon the victim were as a result of diminished responsibility. It was on this premise that the respondent pleaded his innocence and sought acquittal on the fact that as previous case law provided, involuntary intoxication was sufficient enough to remove the contributory effect of mens rea; and so while the intention to carry out an indecent sexual act was latent within the respondent, it was only manifested through the actions of another, and not by conscious choice.

Precedent for a defence under voluntary intoxication rested upon the outcome of *R v Majewski*,[291] where the court found that the informed decision to drink excessive amounts of alcohol was not suffice to exemption from the consequences of damage caused afterwards. However, where a defendant has lost conscious reasoning through the act of another, it was held that mens rea could not logically exist as the decision to act unlawfully was not one of full cognisance but diminished thinking.

In this instance, the capability to sexually abuse minors was knowingly present within the respondent, and so reliance upon an unwittingly ingested drug prior to the act, reduced the foundation of that defence when used as a means of acquittal. Having subsequently been challenged in the Court Appeal, the conviction was quashed, after which the Crown appealed to the House for reasons of public interest.

The question raised was whether a predilection for young boys negated the defence of involuntary intoxication, and if so, whether it was for the prosecution to establish, or that of the defendant. Having traced the legal position from as far back as 1830, the idea that temporary insanity or 'lunacy' could provide sufficient defence to a criminal act was rebuked when it appeared that certain generosities were afforded those accused, albeit in

---

[291] [1977] AC 443.

circumstances contrary to their normal course of behaviour. In this instance there was clear evidence that the respondent was predisposed to engaging in deviant sexual acts, and so regardless of what volume or form of intoxication preceded the acts, it was not such that became the source of that unlawfulness, but rather the mindset and neurology of the accused at the point of origin when establishing mens rea. For that reason, the House denied that the current boundaries of involuntary intoxication defence were to extend further than as before, and that in light of that fact the Crown's appeal was to be upheld.

Key Citations

"[I]t is no answer for the defendant to say that he would not have done what he did had he been sober, provided always that whatever element of intent is required by the offence is proved to have been present."[292]

"[I]rresistible impulse of a solely internal origin (not necessarily any more the fault of the offender) does not in itself excuse although it may be a symptom of a disease of the mind…"[293]

"[I]n the field of road traffic the "spiked" drink as a special reason for not disqualifying from driving is a regular feature. Transferring this to the entire range of criminal offences is a disturbing prospect."[294]

"[T]he interplay between the wrong done to the victim, the individual characteristics and frailties of the defendant, and the pharmacological effects of whatever drug may be potentially involved can be far better recognised by a tailored choice from the continuum of sentences available to the judge than by the application of a single yea-or-nay jury decision."[295]

---

[292] *R v Kingston* [1994] Crim LR 846 (HL) 369 (Mustill LJ).

[293] *R v Kingston* [1994] Crim LR 846 (HL) 376 (Mustill LJ).

[294] *R v Kingston* [1994] Crim LR 846 (HL) 377 (Mustill LJ).

[295] *R v Kingston* [1994] Crim LR 846 (HL) 377 (Mustill LJ).

12. R v Lambert

'Innocent until proven guilty' is a phrase common to both English and European law, however when the conviction of possession of controlled drugs required a reverse burden of proof upon the the defendant, it ran risk of violating the rights afforded citizens under the Convention.

Having been arrested and convicted of possession of £140,000 worth of class A drugs under s.5(3) of the Misuse of Drugs Act 1971, the appellant challenged the trial judges direction and that of the jury under art.6(2) of the European Convention for the Protection of Human Rights (ECHR) (Right to a fair trial), while further citing that s.28 of the 1971 Act placed an unfair burden of proof, that when taken in context with s.6 of the newly introduced Human Rights Act 1998 (HRA) (Right to a fair trial), rendered the actions of the court void and thereby unlawful.

As point of fact, the HRA 1998 had been drafted and given royal assent in November 1998, but had not taken legal affect until 2 October 2000. Contrastingly, the appellant had been convicted on 9 April 1999 and so relied upon the effects of the Convention and the HRA 1998 in order to undermine the courts decision to pass sentence. Domestic legal position at the time prior to the 1998 Act, was that when accused of possession of controlled drugs, the defendant was afforded reasonable protection through s.28(2) of the Misuse of Drugs Act 1971, which read:

> "[I]n any proceedings for an offence to which this section applies it shall be a defence for the accused to prove that he neither knew of nor suspected nor had reason to suspect the existence of some fact alleged by the prosecution which it is necessary for the prosecution to prove that he is to be convicted of the offence charged."[296]

This allowed the defendant to prove by balance of probability, that possession of such substances arose from ignorance of it's existence rather than conscious choice. S.28(3)(b)(i) further allowed the defendant to seek acquittal by proving that he had no reason to suspect that whatever substance he possessed was a controlled drug.

When heard before the first court, the judge applied existing criminal procedure by directing the jury to assume that the defendant knew he had possession of the drugs, and that by reverse burden of proof it was for the defendant to demonstrate otherwise. It was this approach that the appellant relied upon when citing the Convention rights and HRA 1998 principles, inasmuch as art.6(2) of the Convention stated that "everyone charged with a criminal offence shall be presumed innocent until proven guilty according to law." Despite his protestations, the court reached summary conviction and he was sentenced to seven years in prison.

Having brought his case before the Court of Appeal, his appeal was dismissed, while a number of questions were raised concerning both the presumption of innocence and the retroactive nature of the HRA 1998. This allowed his case to be heard again in the House of Lords, where consideration of the hearing date (April 2001) enabled the House to examine the validity of his claim, after the effects of the HRA 1998 had begun.

---

[296] Misuse of Drugs Act 1971, s.28(2)

Through the powers of s.6(1) of the HRA 1998, it was possible for individuals to hold a local authority liable for violations of the Convention, and that under English law, the House of Lords was exactly that. However, the caveat to this argument was that the initial conviction was in fact prior to the 1998 Act, and that for perhaps obvious reasons, no express provision had been made to allow retroactive effect upon previously decided cases. It was for that primary reason that the appeal, while occurring inside the watershed of human rights protection, was considered by extension, as nothing more than a decisive aspect to the whole case; while s.7(6) of the HRA 1998 alone denoted that appeals against the decisions of a court applied only to those matters brought by public bodies and not convicted criminals. This translated that regardless of hypothetical arguments, the outcome would have remained the same, and so the appeal was again dismissed.

On an additional note, the imposition of legal burden upon defendants under s.28 of the Misuse of Drugs Act 1971, was compared to the empowering effects of the Convention, and the House agreed that while the duty of the prosecution was an establishment of guilt, failure to convince a jury that the accused was ignorant as to the existence of an illegal substance should not determine the verdict, and ran counter to the principles of the 1998 Act.

Key Citations

"[S]ection 7(6) distinguishes between proceedings brought by a public authority and "an appeal against the decision of a court" whereas section 22(4) extends the application of section 7(1)(b) only where proceedings are brought by a public authority. This appears to indicate that an appeal by an unsuccessful defendant is not to be treated as a proceeding brought by or at the instigation of a public authority…"[297]

"[W]here there is a specific time-extension of the applicability of a Convention right, which is limited in content and which does not apply to an appeal like the present, it would be surprising if section 6, which has no express provision extending its effect, produced a contrary result so as to be applicable to acts which took place before the Convention rights became part of domestic law."[298]

"[B]y the 1998 Act Parliament has provided that, subject to the ultimate constitutional principle of the sovereignty of Parliament, inroads on the presumption of innocence must be compatible with article 6(2) as properly construed. If incompatibility arises, the subtle mechanisms of the 1998 Act come into play."[299]

"[A] true constituent element can be removed from the definition of the crime and cast as a defensive issue whereas any definition of an offence can be reformulated so as to include all possible defences within it. It is necessary to concentrate not on technicalities and niceties of language but rather on matters of substance."[300]

---

[297] *R v Lambert* [2001] 3 WLR 206 (HL) 561 (Slynn LJ).

[298] *R v Lambert* [2001] 3 WLR 206 (HL) 562 (Slynn LJ).

[299] *R v Lambert* [2001] 3 WLR 206 (HL) 569 (Steyn LJ).

[300] *R v Lambert* [2001] 3 WLR 206 (HL) 571 (Steyn LJ).

13. R v Miller

'Actus reus' and 'mens rea' are two very widely used criminal law maxims that once were essential for the clarification of intention, but sadly over the passage of time, the former has become victim to legal abuses by lawyers seeking to bend a virtue that perhaps warrants review after hundreds of years of application.

In this matter, the accused was a homeless man who after drinking a reasonable amount of alcohol, entered an empty home before taking up occupancy in an upstairs room. After lighting a cigarette, he fell asleep on a mattress, at which point the cigarette began to ignite the mattress fibres, thereby causing it to slowly smoulder.

Upon waking, the appellant saw what was happening, but chose to simply get up from the mattress and walk into an adjacent room before returning to sleep. It was not until the arrival of the local fire brigade that he awoke again to discover that the room he had since left was now ablaze, and that significant fire damage had resulted from his failure to extinguish the burning mattress.

Upon summary, the appellant stood accused of recklessness causing criminal damage to another's property, that in turn led to a conviction of arson under s.1(1)(3) of the Criminal Damage Act 1971. While under appeal, it was argued that both mens rea and actus reus are key elements to a criminal conviction, and that because the appellant had left the room, he could not be found liable through inaction as opposed to action (actus reus); while further arguing that he was under no obligation to extinguish the burning mattress, and that his mens rea was ultimately irrelevant to the proceeding fire.

The crux of this defence misdirection was that while actus reus explores the actions of a defendant, the reality of life is that inaction by its own virtue is an equally destructive process when the party in question can see very clearly that it was his previous actions that started the cause of the offence; and that here there were sufficient steps available to the defendant to prevent the damage from spreading (including seeking the assistance of third parties to that effect). Therefore a defence based upon the interpretation of a word, does nothing to circumvent the social responsibility of those faced with potentially (yet avoidable) damaging situations.

While the appeal was dismissed, it was again put before the House of Lords, who listened intently to a bargaining application for the quashing of an arson charge, before succinctly explaining that with no quarter for doubt, it was evident that the appellant had elected to recklessly avoid his personal obligation to prevent the fire from growing, in favour of distancing himself from his original action, regardless of the foreseeable consequences that followed.

Key Citations

"[I]t is the use of the expression "actus reus" that is liable to mislead, since it suggests that some positive act on the part of the accused is needed to make him guilty of a crime and that a failure or omission to act is insufficient to give rise to a criminal liability unless some express provision in the stature that creates the offence so provides."[301]

"I see no rational ground for excluding from conduct capable of giving rise to a criminal liability, conduct which consists of failing to take measure that lie within one's power to counteract a danger that one has oneself created."[302]

"[I]n a case where the relevant state of mind is not intent but recklessness I see no reason in common sense and justice why mutatis mutandis a similar principle should not apply to impose criminal liability upon him."[303]

"I cannot see any good reason why, so far as liability under criminal law is concerned, it should matter at what point of time before the resultant damage is complete a person becomes aware that he has done a physical act which, whether or not he appreciated that it would be at the time when he did it, does in fact create a risk that property of another will be damaged..."[304]

"I would commend the use of the word "responsibility" rather than "duty" which is more appropriate to civil than to criminal law, since it suggest an obligation owed to another person, i.e. the person to whom the endangered property belongs, whereas a criminal statute defines combinations of conduct and state of mind which render a person liable to punishment by the state."[305]

---

[301] *R v Miller* (1983) 77 Cr App R 17 (HL) 174 (Diplock LJ).

[302] *R v Miller* (1983) 77 Cr App R 17 (HL) 176 (Diplock LJ).

[303] *R v Miller* (1983) 77 Cr App R 17 (HL) 177 (Diplock LJ).

[304] *R v Miller* (1983) 77 Cr App R 17 (HL) 176 (Diplock LJ).

[305] *R v Miller* (1983) 77 Cr App R 17 (HL) 179 (Diplock LJ).

14. R v Steer

Criminal damage to another's property when endangering the lives of those in possession, are simultaneous acts that while seemingly joined, are determinable only by the mens rea attached. In this matter, the defendant appealed against such a conviction on grounds that while capable of the crime itself, he could not be charged for an offence based on subjective opinion, as opposed to lawfully submitted evidence.

After falling out with his business partner, the appellant arrived at his colleague's home brandishing a rifle. Having rung the doorbell, he then proceeded to aim and fire the gun at the bedroom window, living room window and front door. No harm was caused to the occupiers, however, once arrested and indicted, he was charged with three offences: (i) possession of a firearm with intent to endanger life under s.16 of the Firearms Act 1968 (ii) criminal damage to property with intent under s.1(1) of the Criminal Damage Act 1971 and (iii) criminal damage to property while endangering the lives of others, whether through recklessness or intent under s.1(2) of the 1971 Act.

Having pleaded guilty to charges (i) and (ii), the appellant argued that (iii) was superfluous to the crime, as the damage caused to the property was not such as to endanger lives, whereas the firing of the gun was evidently sufficient. Basing his decision on the interpretation of s.1(2) as including not just the physical damage, but the mental intention (mens rea) to endanger lives, the judge dismissed the claim and directed the jury accordingly. This prompted the appellant to plead guilty, before seeking redress in the Court of Appeal, who allowed the appeal, before the Crown moved to seek the wisdom of the House of Lords.

While asking the House to determine if, under s.1(2)(b) of the 1971 Act, the prosecution were obliged to establish guilt of endangering life by either the property damage, or the actions of the accused, the House held that the respondent had accepted the recklessness of his actions and so despite the contention of the Crown, it was implausible to suggest that the draftsmen of the 1971 Act had imagined that s.1(2)(b) was to be construed so as to consider the actus reus of the defendant when carrying out the crime, as being sufficient to establish endangerment of life, as opposed to endangerment arising from the physical damage caused. In the alternative, it was further suggested by the House that the respondent had become culpable for an additional charge under s.17(2) of the Firearms Act 1968, and so the application of s.1(2) of the 1971 Act was both irrelevant and by construction void of effect, while concluding that:

> "Upon the true construction of section 1(2)(6) of the Criminal Damage Act 1971 the prosecution are required to prove that the danger to life resulted from the destruction of or damage to property, it is not sufficient for the prosecution to prove that it resulted from the act of the defendant which caused the destruction or damage."[306]

It was thus upon those grounds that the House dismissed the appeal by a majority.

---

[306] *R v Steer* (1987) 85 Cr App R 352 (HL) 119 (Bridge LJ).

Key Citations

"[I]t seems to me impossible to read the words "by the damage" as meaning "by the damage or by the act which caused the damage." Moreover, if the language of the statute has the meaning for which the Crown contends, the words "by the destruction or damage" and "thereby" in subsection (2)(b) are mere surplusage."[307]

"If A and B both discharge firearms in a public place, being reckless as to whether life would be endangered, it would be absurd that A, who incidentally causes some trifling damage to property, should be guilty of an offence punishable with life imprisonment, but that B, who causes no damage, should be guilty of no offence."[308]

"A person who, at the time of committing an offence under section 1 of the Act of 1971, has in his possession a firearm commits a distinct offence under section 17(2) of the Act of 1968..."[309]

---

[307] *R v Steer* (1987) 85 Cr App R 352 (HL) 117 (Bridge LJ).

[308] *R v Steer* (1987) 85 Cr App R 352 (HL) 117 (Bridge LJ).

[309] *R v Steer* (1987) 85 Cr App R 352 (HL) 118 (Bridge LJ).

15. R v Stone; R v Dobinson

In this landmark criminal law case, the distinction between indifference to, and perception of risk, are carefully weighed in order to appreciate that when compared for their relevance to recklessness, the outcome remains the same, despite differing routes to dire consequences.

In 1972, an eccentric sibling moved into the home of her older disabled brother after a falling out with her sister. The terms of the living arrangement were that of a landlord and tenant, inasmuch as rent was paid, and each were free to live their lives independently of one another. While the brother lived with his mistress and housekeeper along with his mentally challenged son, the sister occupied the front room of the home and maintained a high degree of privacy, despite openly suffering from undiagnosed *anorexia nervosa*; a condition that precluded regular meals in favour of a low bodyweight, and that in many instances, was known to result in premature death or at best, extreme immobility.

After a period of almost nearly three years, the sister's health deteriorated to a point that she became permanently bedridden and unable to clean or feed herself. Despite repeated express concerns from the mistress to the brother regards his sister's condition, there were no attempts made by either party to extend their efforts in seeking medical help beyond that of unsuccessfully trying to locate her doctor. When matters continued with no real intervention, the now seriously ill woman was eventually found dead in her bed, amidst evidence that no care had been taken to tend to her toiletry needs or physical health requirements prior to her death.

When reported to the police, the two defendants were summoned and convicted of manslaughter upon grounds of a breach of duty of care through recklessness; whereupon the two parties appealed under the presumption of diminished responsibility. When considered under appeal, the judges found that irrespective of whether the couple claimed to have taken limited steps to get the deceased help, there was insufficient evidence to avoid the conviction of recklessness as (i) there was adequate foresight of the risk posed to the dying woman while under the assumed care of her brother and mistress, and (ii) that the conduct taken to redress such a risk was made with little regard to the seriousness of her condition.

Ultimately, and when taken in context, the Court felt that it mattered not which route had been taken, only that the destination resulted in her death; and that both parties had been made aware of possible options, yet continued to ignore the duty bestowed upon those assigned the care of a vulnerable person; particularly a close relative with a history of self-neglect and malnutrition.

Key Citations

"Whether Fanny was a lodger or not she was a blood relation of the appellant Stone; she was occupying a room in his house; the appellant Dobson had undertaken the duty of trying to wash her, of taking such food to her as she required."[310]

"The defendant must be proved to have been indifferent to an obvious risk of injury to health, or actually to have foreseen the risk but to have determined nevertheless to run it."[311]

"It is clear that a sentence of immediate imprisonment was unavoidable, if of nothing else at least to mark the public disapproval of such behaviour."[312]

---

[310] *R v Stone; R v Dobinson* (1977) 64 Cr App R 186 (CA) 361 (Lane LJ).

[311] *R v Stone; R v Dobinson* (1977) 64 Cr App R 186 (CA) 363 (Lane LJ).

[312] *R v Stone; R v Dobinson* (1977) 64 Cr App R 186 (CA) 364 (Lane LJ).

16. R v Woollin

Loss of life arising from recklessness or deliberate action, is one decided by a jury. However, when the scope of murder is extended beyond reasonable bounds, the verdict does not always reflect the evidence.

When a father became enraged to the point of throwing his three-month old son onto a hard surface, his actions resulted in a fractured skull and death. When indicted, the evidence presented to the jury left questions as to the mens rea of the defendant, and so it was then left to the presiding judge to direct them accordingly.

In previously similar cases, the test for murder relied upon guidance constructed in *R v Nedrick*,[313] and one which asked that any jury must avoid the implication of intent, unless they could believe that death or serious bodily harm was 'virtually certain' as a result of the defendant's actions. This approach narrowed the charge of murder, while allowing for anomalies (such as those presented in the evidence) to contribute towards an alternate conviction for manslaughter.

On this occasion however, the judge derogated from the explicitness of the *Nedrick* test, using instead, guidance that the appellant:

> "[M]ust have realised and appreciated when he threw that child that there was a *substantial risk* that he would cause serious injury to it…"[314]

The jury found the appellant guilty of murder and dismissed the defence of provocation, and so when taken to the Court of Appeal, the appellant argued that the widening of the mens rea of murder by the judge, amounted to a gross misdirection and error in law. The Court dismissed the appeal, while holding that the virtual certainty of death or serious bodily harm was one reserved for cases with limited evidence relating to the actus reus of the accused, and that on this occasion, there was sufficient grounds for a widening of the meaning of murderous intent. However, questions were raised around the need for jury direction in the absence of compelling evidence; in particular (i) whether the defendant intended to kill or cause serious bodily harm, and (ii) whether it was virtually certain that in such events, death or serious bodily harm would occur, and that it had been appreciated by the defendant at the time of the act.

Having been brought before the House of Lords, the integrity of the *Nedrick* test was scrutinised, along with the relevance of judicial direction in matters where the balancing of evidence, and the mens rea of the defendant, were pivotal to a fair conviction, as outlined in s.8 of the Criminal Justice Act 1967. Here it was found that during the twelve years that the courts had relied upon the *Nedrick* test, there had been no difficulties in it's application due to it's simplicity; and despite some shortcomings in terrorism cases, the test itself was adaptable enough to withstand changes in circumstance. It was also agreed that by widening the scope of the test through the misuse of words, the trial judge had himself been reckless in his misdirection, and that the conviction was to be quashed in lieu of a manslaughter charge.

---

[313] *R v Nedrick* [1986] 1 WLR 1025 (CA).

[314] *R v Woollin* [1998] Crim LR 890 (HL) 88 (Steyn LJ) (emphasis added).

Key Citations

"*Nedrick* does not prevent a jury from considering all the evidence: it merely stated what state of mind (in the absence of a purpose to kill or to cause serious harm) is sufficient for murder."[315]

"It may be appropriate to give a direction in accordance with *Nedrick* in any case in which the defendant may not have desired the result of his act."[316]

"A jury cannot be expected to absorb and apply a direction which attempts to deal with every situation which might conceivably arise."[317]

---

[315] *R v Woollin* [1998] Crim LR 890 (HL) 94 (Steyn LJ).

[316] *R v Woollin* [1998] Crim LR 890 (HL) 95 (Steyn LJ).

[317] *R v Woollin* [1998] Crim LR 890 (HL) 97 (Hope LJ).

17. Sheldrake v DPP

By revisiting two criminal appeal cases, the principle of burden of proof reversal is investigated using drink-driving and terrorism, in order to establish justification of such approaches within domestic law.

Director of Public Prosecutions v Sheldrake

In this matter, the defendant stood accused of being intoxicated while in charge of a parked motor vehicle, and yet despite having no evidence to suggest he intended to drive the car, he was convicted under s.5(1) of the Road Traffic Act 1988, at which point the case was appealed.

Attorney General's Reference No 4 of 2002

In the second case, the defendant was accused under s.11(1) of the Terrorism Act 2000 of holding membership to a proscribed terrorist organisation, and publicly expressing his affiliation in such a way that could incite tensions between the public and the state, although subjective opinion cast doubts as to the credibility of the claims.

Art.6(2) of the Human Rights Act 1998 (HRA) (Right to a fair trial) provides that under criminal law, any person accused of a criminal act will be entitled to a fair trial. This rests upon the principle that all those accused are considered innocent until proven guilty. However, in the majority of criminal cases, the burden of proof rests with the prosecution, who must prove beyond any reasonable doubt, that the conviction stands.

In the former case, s.5(2) of the Road Traffic Act 1988 requires that in order to serve as a defence, the accused must be able to show that there was never any intention drive the vehicle, and that under the majority of circumstances, such proof would be evidential or persuasive enough to grant exoneration.

In the latter case, s.11(2) of the Terrorism Act 2000 allows a defendant to show that while a member of a prohibited organisation, their affiliation began prior to the faction's illegality, and that at no point did the defendant take part in any activities that supported their cause.

Given that on both occasions the burden of proof was contested on grounds of conflict with the HRA 1998, it was down to the House of Lords to take a thorough view of reversed burden, before deciding if those matters that demonstrate an incompatibility of legislation with Convention rights can continue to exist for the greater good and welfare of public safety and interest.

Following a meticulous speech by Bingham LJ, it was agreed by a majority that despite the challenges brought before the House, there was already sufficient grounds under ss. (1) of both Acts to secure a judgment, and that any burden of proof presented by the defendants was required to be legal if it were to withstand conviction.

Key Citations

"The defendant can exonerate himself if he can show that the risk which led to the creation of the offence did not in his case exist. If he fails to establish this grounds of exoneration, a possibility (but not a probability) would remain that he would not have been likely to drive."[318]

"I do not regard the burden placed upon the defendant as beyond reasonable limits or in any way arbitrary. It is not objectionable to criminalise a defendant's conduct in these circumstances without requiring a prosecutor to prove criminal intent."[319]

"[T]he defence in section 11(2) imposed a legal rather than evidential burden and was compatible with article 6(2) of the Convention and would not, save perhaps in circumstances difficult to envisage in the abstract, infringe upon a person's rights under Article 10."[320]

"There can be no doubt that Parliament intended section 11(2) to impose a legal burden on the defendant, since section 118 of the Act lists a number of sections which are to be understood as imposing an evidential burden only…"[321]

"Criminalising membership serves a legitimate purpose by making it difficult for members of the organisation to demonstrate publicly in a manner that affronts law-abiding members of the public."[322]

"[G]iven the murderous aims of the proscribed organisations, it is open to the legislature, without in any way infringing a defendant's rights under the Convention, to make it a punishable offence for someone simply to be a member of, or to profess to belong to, such an organisation in the United Kingdom."[323]

"The reversal of the ordinary burden of proof resting upon the prosecution may accordingly be justified in some cases and will not offend against the principle requiring a fair trial."[324]

---

[318] *Sheldrake v DPP* [2005] 1 AC 264 [40] (Bingham LJ).

[319] *Sheldrake v DPP* [2005] 1 AC 264 [41] (Bingham LJ).

[320] *Sheldrake v DPP* [2005] 1 AC 264 [45] (Bingham LJ).

[321] *Sheldrake v DPP* [2005] 1 AC 264 [50] (Bingham LJ).

[322] *Sheldrake v DPP* [2005] [62] (Rodger LJ).

[323] *Sheldrake v DPP* [2005] [66] (Rodger LJ).

[324] *Sheldrake v DPP* [2005] [80] (Carswell LJ).

4. Equity and Trust Law

1. Agip (Africa) Ltd v Jackson

Constructive trustees, and the effectiveness of traceability through multiple recipients under the pretence and knowledge of fraud, form the basis of this Appeal Court hearing. Through the formation of seven companies that undertook no business other than to allow payments into their nominated bank accounts, the chief accountant of an oil drilling company systematically defrauded his employer of over $10m during a period of just two years.

This was carried out through a network of directors and business partners, who acted as authorised signatories for the sham companies, and who once a small number of deposits were made, closed the accounts, before opening new accounts that would then transfer the funds to a central account held in France. This account belonged to a company that presented itself as a jewellery supplier, and which was owned by a French lawyer, who was the head of the fraudulent operation.

Party to this, was the manager of Lloyd's Bank Holborn Street, whose role it was to receive funds from the chief accountant through his employer's bank on a regular basis, before awaiting instructions as to which of the seven accounts the funds were to be transferred. It was only after a money order destined for a shipping container firm was fraudulently altered, that the scheme became apparent and proceedings commenced.

In the first hearing, the respondent firm sued for payment under mistake of fact, and claimed that recovery was due either by the bank, or the account holders, who themselves took receipt of the funds under knowing deceit. While relying upon the traceability of the monies paid out, it was held by the court that there had been too many displacements in both time and transactions to establish a clear path, therefore recovery under common law was too remote. However, when turning to equity the issue took an another form altogether.

While tracing through equity requires evidence of a fiduciary relationship, the chief accountant had by extension, held a fiduciary role, and so it fell to the Court of Appeal to first explore knowing receipt and knowing assistance; after which it was held that while the appellants received the funds on behalf of their clients, they did so in the knowledge that the money had been obtained through fraud, and so for that reason were liable as constructive trustees for the respondent; particularly as no real effort was made to return the money once notification had been made by the issuing bank.

Key Citations

"I do not think that persons who need to demonstrate that they have acted honestly can shelter behind transactions or objects which were themselves disreputable."[325]

"If the known facts indicate a lack of frankness, the person assisting in effecting the transaction in question must take the risk in the absence of further explanation that it is fraudulent."[326]

"A person may be liable, even though he does not himself receive trust property, if he knowingly assists in fraudulent design on the part of a trustee (including a constructive trustee). Liability under this head is not related to the receipt of trust property by the person sought to be liable."[327]

"Both common law and equity accepted the right of the true owner to trace his property into the hands of others while it was in identifiable form...equity on the other hand will follow money into a mixed fund and charge the fund."[328]

---

[325] *Agip (Africa) Ltd v Jackson* [1992] 4 All ER 385 (CA) 14 (Fox LJ).

[326] *Agip (Africa) Ltd v Jackson* [1992] 4 All ER 385 (CA) 14 (Fox LJ).

[327] *Agip (Africa) Ltd v Jackson* [1992] 4 All ER 385 (CA) 12 (Fox LJ).

[328] *Agip (Africa) Ltd v Jackson* [1992] 4 All ER 385 (CA) 11 (Fox LJ).

2. Armitage v Nurse

Breach of duty and accusations of fraud may appear to seem related, yet the truth is that when put before a court, the facts are both distinct and separate. In this instance, the younger of three beneficiaries took issue with the conduct of her appointed trustees and sued for damages, despite no evidence of foul play.

Upon the death of her grandfather, the appellant was granted a trust of both land and capital, subject to her coming of age at twenty-five, after which a number of trustees were to provide interim payments so as to increase the life of the trust. The trust itself was the product of a successful farming business, now run by the appellant's mother and grandmother, while assisted by the nominated trustees of their marriage settlement under the Variation of Trusts Act 1958. Clauses 9 and 15 contained within the original marriage settlement, provided that:

> "(9) [T]he trustees ... shall have power to carry on or join or assist in carrying on or directing any business of farming ... with power for that purpose ... to employ or engage ... any managers or agents ... and to delegate all or any of the powers vested in them in relation to the business ... [A]nd the trustees shall be free from all responsibility and be fully indemnified out of Paula's fund in respect of any loss arising in relation to the business.

> (15) No trustee shall be liable for any loss or damage which may happen to Paula's fund or any part thereof or the income thereof at any time or from any cause whatsoever *unless such loss or damage shall be caused by his own actual fraud...*"[329]

In the course of litigation, the appellant claimed (i) that the trustees had wrongfully farmed her portion of land at a cost to her trust funds, but to the benefit of her mother and grandmother, (ii) that the trustees had thus failed to manage her trust in accordance with their obligations, (iii) the trustees failed to establish why her portion of land was sold for less than that of her mother's and (iv) that the trustees failed to set a suitable interest rate when loaning trust funds to her mother. These four incidents were then collectively presented under a claim of fraudulent breach of duty at the expense of the appellant's interests, and that clause 15 failed to protect them from such liability.

The respondents counter-claimed that clause 15 did provide exemption from liability, and that clause 9 provided similar protections when examining the variation in land valuations and loan interests granted in the course of their duties. The respondents also contended that the appellant's allegations were statute barred under s.21 of the Limitation Act 1980, and thus unlawful. In the first instance, the judge held that clause 15 was correctly applied, but that clause 9 did not allow for such indiscretions, and that the appellant's claims were not subject to the statute of limitations. After which the judge awarded the respondents eighty percent of the costs, but held that the remaining twenty percent was to be paid directly from them, as a number of points raised and lost fell outside the scope of the trust and were therefore exempt from recovery from the trust funds.

---

[329] (emphasis added).

When the matter was presented to the Court of Appeal, the Court went to considerable lengths to clarify the definition of fraud and its relationship to breach of duty, and it became evident that while allegations of gross and general negligence, honest incompetence, indolence and misapplication of funds were feasible, there was simply no tenable reason to suggest that the respondents had acted with anything less than honest intent.

With regard to the barring under statute, it was explained how s.21(1)(a) of the Limitation Act 1980 clearly stipulated that:

> "No period of limitation prescribed by this Act shall apply to an action by a beneficiary under a trust, being an action (a) in respect of any fraud or fraudulent breach of trust to which the trustee was a party or privy; ..."[330]

Therefore, the appellant was well within her rights to bring a claim of fraud, despite the findings of the court. Having reconsidered the position taken by the trial judge for cost apportionment, it was also held that while relying upon RSC Ord.62 r.6(2)[331] to deny recovery on grounds that the trustee acted for reasons of self-interest over that of the trust fund, the judge had overlooked the principle that trustees are entitled to claim from trust funds when successfully defending themselves against a claim of breach; and so to discriminate upon issues proved unsuccessful, ran counter to natural justice and therefore funds were set aside for full payment. In closing, the Court granted the appellant a right to amend her claims, however the House of Lords later dismissed her right to appeal.

Key Citations

"Breaches of trust are of many different kinds. A breach of trust may be deliberate or inadvertent; it may consist of an actual misappropriation or misapplication of the trust property or merely of an investment or other dealing which is outside the trustees' powers; it may consist of a failure to carry out a positive obligation of the trustees or merely of a want of skill and care on their part in the management of the trust property; it may be injurious to the interests of the beneficiaries or be actually to their benefit."[332]

"It is the duty of a trustee to manage the trust property and deal with it in the interests of the beneficiaries. If he acts in a way which he does not honestly believe is in their interests then he is acting dishonestly."[333]

"A trustee who acts with the intention of benefiting persons who are not the objects of the trust is not the less dishonest because he does not intend to benefit himself."[334]

---

[330] Limitation Act 1980, s.21(1)(a)

[331] Supreme Court of Judicature, *The Rules of the Supreme Court 1965* (HMSO 1966)

[332] *Armitage v Nurse* (1995) The Independent, 3 July; [1997] 2 All ER 705 (CA) 251 (Millett LJ).

[333] *Armitage v Nurse* (1995) The Independent, 3 July; [1997] 2 All ER 705 (CA) 251 (Millett LJ).

[334] *Armitage v Nurse* (1995) The Independent, 3 July; [1997] 2 All ER 705 (CA) 251 (Millett LJ).

3. Attorney-General for Hong Kong v Reid

The phrase 'two wrongs do not make a right' is virtuous to the truth that misdeeds can never amount to anything more than loss, yet when adopted for equitable purposes, the exact opposite can be found.

After rising through the ranks of Hong Kong administration, a solicitor turned Director of Public Prosecutions, positioned himself whereby he was able to accept sporadic bribes in exchange for his obstruction of justice through the failed convictions of known criminals. Having taken over HK $12m in payments, the respondent in this matter invested the funds into three properties, two of which were in title to himself and his wife, and a third to his solicitor.

The discovery of his fraudulent behaviour and subsequent criminal prosecution, raised the question of whether by his breach of fiduciary duty as a servant of the Crown, the sums paid were now held upon trust for his former employers, and that any monetary gain following the purchase of the homes, was composite to that trust.

Common law principles surrounding fiduciary breach and profit from such breaches, have been long held to apply in favour of the trust beneficiary, despite the illegality on the part of the fiduciary when in receipt of bribes from third parties. This is because when acting beyond the remit of the trustee, and in a manner that is dishonest, the action itself becomes legitimate, if only for the benefit of those the fiduciary or trustee was appointed to serve.

This translates that although the respondent allowed himself to selfishly receive bribes in exchange for personal profit, equity would ascribe that his deceit was immediately converted into a positive gesture conferring direct gain to his employers, as no fiduciary can be seen to profit from his breach, as previously mentioned. This, by virtue of the fact of those principles, altered the manner in which the respondent not only executed his plans, but provided the Crown with privilege to acquire beneficial interest in the properties purchased, along with any increase in their value since initial conveyance.

When considered by the Privy Council, it was quickly agreed that any conditions imputed by the respondents, upon the entitlement of his employers to seek recovery of the debts through the homes, failed to override the fundamental obligations owed to him while serving and acting under fiduciary capacity, despite any notion of separateness or mixed investment on his part, therefore his appeal was dismissed.

Key Citations

"A fiduciary is not always accountable for a secret benefit but he is undoubtedly accountable for a secret benefit which consists of a bribe. In addition a person who provides the bribe and the fiduciary who accepts the bribe may each be guilty of a criminal offence. In the present case the first respondent was clearly guilty of a criminal offence."[335]

"Equity considers as done that which ought to have been done. As soon as the bribe was received, whether in cash or in kind, the false fiduciary held the bribe on a constructive trust for the person injured."[336]

"[T]here is no reason why equity should not provide two remedies, so long as they do not result in double recovery. If the property representing the bribe exceeds the original bribe in value, the fiduciary cannot retain the benefit of the increase in value which he obtained solely as a result of his breach of duty."[337]

"Property acquired by a trustee as a result of a criminal breach of trust and the property from time to time representing the same must also belong in equity to his *cestui que trust* and not to the trustee whether he is solvent or insolvent."[338]

"[P]roperty which a trustee obtains by use of knowledge acquired as trustee becomes trust property. The rule must, a fortiori, apply to a bribe accepted by a trustee for a guilty criminal purpose which injures the *cestui que trust*."[339]

"If in law a trustee, who in breach of trust invests trust moneys in his own name, holds the investment as trust property, it is difficult to see why a trustee who in breach of trust receives and invests a bribe in his own name does not hold those investments also as trust property."[340]

"[A] fiduciary acting dishonestly and criminally who accepts a bribe and thereby causes loss and damage to his principal must also be a constructive trustee and must not be allowed by any means to make any profit from his wrongdoing."[341]

---

[335] *Attorney-General for Hong Kong v Reid* [1994] 1 All ER 1 (CA) 330 (Templeman LJ).

[336] *Attorney-General for Hong Kong v Reid* [1994] 1 All ER 1 (CA) 331 (Templeman LJ).

[337] *Attorney-General for Hong Kong v Reid* [1994] 1 All ER 1 (CA) 331 (Templeman LJ).

[338] *Attorney-General for Hong Kong v Reid* [1994] 1 All ER 1 (CA) 331 (Templeman LJ).

[339] *Attorney-General for Hong Kong v Reid* [1994] 1 All ER 1 (CA) 332 (Templeman LJ).

[340] *Attorney-General for Hong Kong v Reid* [1994] 1 All ER 1 (CA) 333 (Templeman LJ).

[341] *Attorney-General for Hong Kong v Reid* [1994] 1 All ER 1 (CA) 338 (Templeman LJ).

4. Blackwell v Blackwell

Verbal instructions that are then attested and complied with by the named trustees before the death of a testator, fall neatly between the rules of wills and probate, and the equitable field of trust. On this occasion, the wish of a dying man was such that a large sum of money was to be held upon trust for a party outside of his marriage while unknown to his widow.

Having long agonised over his duty to make provisions for a mother and child borne out of wedlock, it was decided by the testator to set aside several thousand pounds, in the wish that five of his closest friends would act as trustees with the express purpose of investing the funds for profit. Those profits would then be passed to the two named individuals, until such time that the trustees chose to pay two thirds of the initial sum to them, before placing the remaining third back into the residuary estate of his final will.

Upon the testator's death, his widow discovered the bequest, and looked to dismiss it's validity upon grounds of fraud and contradiction to the terms of the will where his widow and their son were to benefit from his complete estate. As was common to domestic legislation, s.9 of the Wills Act 1837 read that no will (or codicil) shall be valid unless set in writing and signed by the testator in accordance with statute. On this occasion, the instructions given by the deceased were initially verbal, and only put to writing by means of a memorandum drafted by his solicitor, who himself signed as a trustee and submitted it in support of the codicil.

Using the terms contained within the 1837 Act, it was argued that while the trust memorandum was indeed written, the execution of the codicil was oral, and therefore fell outside the powers granted beneficiaries, unless it was in effect designed to stand for the sole benefit of the widow through the residual estate; in which case, the trustees would be acting in fraud should they look to enforce the terms of the codicil.

While decided twice in favour of the trustees, it was put before the House of Lords, where the rules of equity were scrutinised in conjunction with proven case law. Having examined the principle that 'equity will not permit statute to be used as a cloak for fraud' it was found that where a testator propounds a desire to execute a trust, and then proceeds to provide explicit instruction as to its use, any argument that seeks to undermine the intentions of that person through the use of legislation, must then find themselves party to fraud, if they would instead stand to benefit from the funds expressly requested for the enjoyment of another.

In circumstances such as this, it was historically preferred that equity imputes the same responsibility as that agreed to by the original trustee, so that they would then act under the same instructions as to permit the objective of the deceased to be realised. This transference circumvents the fraud and makes right that, which is prima facie, claimed wrong.

Resting upon this proven application of jurisprudence, the presiding Lords established that far from looking to dissect the flaws proposed by the appellants, it was clear that any conflict arising from a lack of signatory validation, was insufficient when looking to overrule the will of the testator against a trust, that by all accounts, left no illusions as to its purpose and means of delivery.

Key Citations

"The necessary elements, on which the question turns, are intention, communication, and acquiescence. The testator intends his absolute gift to be employed as he and not as the donee desires…"[342]

"For the prevention of fraud equity fastens on the conscience of the legatee a trust, a trust, that is, which otherwise would be inoperative; in other words it makes him do what the will in itself has nothing to do with…"[343]

"Why should equity forbid an honest trustee to give effect to his promise, made to a deceased testator, and compel him to pay another legatee, about whom it is quite certain that the testator did not mean to make him the object of this bounty?"[344]

"[E]quity would not set up the statute for itself to prevent the devisee from doing what it would have itself compelled him to do…"[345]

"The frame of s.9 of the Wills Act seems to me to carry on its face, that the legislation did not purport to interfere with the exercise of a general equitable jurisdiction, even in connection with secret dispositions of a testator, except in so far as reinforcement of the formalities required for a valid will might indirectly limit it."[346]

"It is communication of the purpose to the legatee, coupled with acquiescence or promise on his part, that removes the matter from the provision of the Wills Act and brings it within the law of trusts…"[347]

"[W]hat is enforced is not a trust imposed by the will, but one arising from the acceptance by the legatee of a trust, communicated to him by the testator, on the faith of which acceptance the will was made or left unrevoked, as the case might be."[348]

"It is the fact of the acceptance of the personal obligation which is the essential feature, and the rest of the evidence is merely for the purpose of ascertaining the nature of that obligation."[349]

---

[342] *Blackwell v Blackwell* [1929] AC 318 (HL) 334 (Sumner VC).

[343] *Blackwell v Blackwell* [1929] AC 318 (HL) 335 (Sumner VC).

[344] *Blackwell v Blackwell* [1929] AC 318 (HL) 335 (Sumner VC).

[345] *Blackwell v Blackwell* [1929] AC 318 (HL) 337 (Sumner VC).

[346] *Blackwell v Blackwell* [1929] AC 318 (HL) 339 (Sumner VC).

[347] *Blackwell v Blackwell* [1929] AC 318 (HL) 339 (Sumner VC).

[348] *Blackwell v Blackwell* [1929] AC 318 (HL) 342 (Warrington LJ).

[349] *Blackwell v Blackwell* [1929] AC 318 (HL) 342 (Warrington LJ).

5. Boardman v Phipps

Fiduciary duty and the exploits of commercial enterprise often run counter to each other, and in this instance the opportunistic actions of a solicitor produces a profitable outcome for all involved, but not without a cost to the integrity of their working relationships.

Upon the death of a successful business owner, the second appellant and respondent's father, the widow and surviving children were bestowed relatively equal portions of a company shareholding totalling 8,000 shares of a possible 30,000 held. This particular firm operated in two countries, and control was divisible between two families, namely that of the deceased (Phipps) and another named Harris, who were the majority shareholders.

Having read their latest financial returns, the trustee accountant Mr. Fox suggested that the company was in poor financial health, and that if one of the beneficiaries, Tom Phipps (the second appellant), were to the be appointed as director, they could look to improving the status of the firm, thereby increasing the annuity drawn by the children from the existing 8,000 shares. Following a meeting with the family solicitor Thomas Boardman (the first appellant), it was agreed that the two men would attend the forthcoming annual meeting in order to secure Tom's appointment, however their bid was unsuccessful due to board hostilities.

In the face of defeat, it was then suggested that the two appellants' could offer to buy the remaining 30,000 shares in order to gain sufficient control and to improve the company's financial standing. This idea was rejected by the accountant trustee on grounds that such a move would require an application to the court, which on the face of the matter, would be dismissed as throwing good trust money after bad. Left with no other options, the appellants arranged to self-finance the initiative, and set about writing to the shareholders, offering above-market purchase rates.

After first securing 2,925 shares, the appellants went on to successfully buy all 21,986 shares at prices that proved to be significantly profitable to the beneficiaries, while explaining to the children that they were doing so not as representatives of the trust, but as private buyers acting in the best interests of the trust and those standing to profit from it. Upon successful redistribution of the shares to the beneficiaries, the older son issued a writ, claiming that the appellants had simply been acting as constructive trustees, and therefore any profits made on the 21,986 shares were proportionately owed to the beneficiaries on grounds that the solicitor had been acting within a fiduciary capacity when making representations to the shareholders, and while accessing company information that would have otherwise been denied him when making his enquiries.

In the first hearing, the appellants argued that they had made it clear on a number of occasions that their commercial strategies and undertakings were beyond that of the trust, and that support and acknowledgement of this had been given by the majority of the trustees and the respondent. Relying upon the principles held in *Aas v Benham*, it was contended that:

"To hold that a partner "(or trustee)" can never derive any personal benefit from information which he obtains as a partner would be manifestly absurd."[350]

And, that the source of such information was secondary as to how it was applied; whereupon the respondent used the opinion of Russell LJ in *Regal (Hastings) Ltd v Gulliver* to explain that:

"I have no hesitation in coming to the conclusion, upon the facts of this case, that these shares, when acquired by the directors, were acquired by reason, and only by reason of the fact that they were directors of Regal, and in the course of their execution of that office."[351]

Which underlined the argument that by abuse of their positions, the appellants worked together to extract information privy only to the trustees and beneficiaries, in order to secure financial gain, while partially disclosing their intentions to a percentage of the trustees, as opposed to the whole. The first court found in favour of the respondents and the same outcome was found in the Court of Appeal, before arriving at the House of Lords.

By a close margin, the House held that while the appellants conducted themselves with reasonable transparency, there had been oversights as to who was informed and how much they knew, and that despite professing that they had acted outside the scope of the trust, there had also been a number of instances where veiled threats and coercive statements were used under the pretence of the trustees, in order to gain important (and private) information, prior to the negotiations and successful procurement of the outstanding shares. It was for those reasons that the appeal was dismissed, before noting that the appellants were afforded measurable profits based upon the care and skill applied to increase the wealth of the trust.

---

[350] *Aas v Benham* [1891] 2 Ch 244 CA 256 (Lindley LJ).

[351] *Regal (Hastings) Ltd v Gulliver* [1942] 2 All ER 378 (HL) 134 (Russell LJ).

Key Citations

"[I]t does not necessarily follow that because an agent acquired information and opportunity while acting in a fiduciary capacity he is accountable to his principals for any profit that comes his way as the result of the use he makes of that information and opportunity."[352]

"[A]n agent is, in my opinion, liable to account for profits he makes out of trust property if there is a possibility of conflict between his interest and his duty to his principal."[353]

"[N]o person standing in a fiduciary position, when a demand is made upon him by the person to whom he stands in the fiduciary relationship to account for profits acquired by him by reason of his fiduciary position and by reason of the opportunity and the knowledge, or either, resulting from it, is entitled to defeat the claim upon any ground save that he made profits with the knowledge and assent of the other person."[354]

"[A] person in a fiduciary capacity must not make a profit out of his trust which is part of the wider rule that a trustee must not place himself in a position where his duty and his interest may conflict."[355]

"[A] solicitor can deal in shares in a company in which the client is a shareholder, subject always to the general rule that the solicitor must never place himself in a position where his interest and his duty conflict…"[356]

"In general, information is not property at all. It is normally open to all who have eyes to read and ears to hear. The true test is to determine in what circumstances the information has been acquired."[357]

---

[352] *Boardman v Phipps* [1966] 3 All ER 721 (HL) 102 (Viscount Dilhorne).

[353] *Boardman v Phipps* [1966] 3 All ER 721 (HL) 103 (Viscount Dilhorne).

[354] *Boardman v Phipps* [1966] 3 All ER 721 (HL) 105 (Hodson LJ).

[355] *Boardman v Phipps* [1966] 3 All ER 721 (HL) 123 (Upjohn LJ).

[356] *Boardman v Phipps* [1966] 3 All ER 721 (HL) 126 (Upjohn LJ).

[357] *Boardman v Phipps* [1966] 3 All ER 721 (HL) 127 (Upjohn LJ).

6. *Re* Denley

Purpose trusts, and those with intended beneficiaries, are, and can be, hard to distinguish. And so it can often fall to the courts to reexamine the intention of the settlor, so as to avoid failure where none need exist. In a case involving a company trust deed, appointed trustees, valued employees and a forfeiture clause, the contained terms were challenged when the company itself, looked to sell the granted land for profit, as was prescribed in the deed.

In 1917, aircraft manufacturing companies Airco (A) and H.H Martyn (H) merged to become Gloster Aircraft Co Ltd; and in 1936 a trust deed was constructed between H and a number of trustees, which provided that some land and a right of way had been conveyed to the trustees to be held on trust for H, and that the trustees were to allow H to take out a mortgage on the land in order to pay A.

In another part of the deed, it was agreed that the trustees were empowered to manage the land, and grant use of it to the employees (and others by agreement) for sports and recreational purposes by way of weekly subscriptions. The caveat to this arrangement was that when the subscription percentage dropped below seventy-five percent of the male workforce, or the company fell into insolvency, the land reserved was to be sold to Cheltenham General Hospital, and the proceeds used to settle the mortgage owed to A.

Around thirty years later, H decided to sell a portion of the land to pay for maintenance work, and at this point the question arose as to (i) any liability to pay any excess funds to the Hospital, (ii) whether the trust allowed the trustees to sell any part of the land and (iii) the integrity of the trust, as the exactness of the beneficiaries was held to be undeterminable and therefore void.

When the details of the trust were examined, it was argued that as the nature of the trust was one of purpose and not benefit, it could not be enforced, as the purpose was not one of charity but general enjoyment. For this reason, it was contended that the trust must fail, and that H was now free to use the land as it wished. However, the court took a different view and explained that while governance of the trust did include the use of the land by parties beyond the employees, it was at the discretion of the trustees, and was therefore a power, rather than a specific point of benefit.

This interpretation changed the nature of the trust from one of purpose, into one of direct benefit, as the names and identities of the employees (including those unsubscribed) were readily ascertainable. This translated that the trust was in every sense valid, and that to the knowledge of the court, the subscription levels had remained above that of the percentage set, while s.61(d) of the Law of Property Act 1925 also outlined how "the masculine included the feminine and vice versa".

Key Citations

"[C]lause 2(d) of the trust deed expressly states that, subject to any rules and regulations made by the trustees, the employees of the company shall be entitled to the use and enjoyment of the land."[358]

"Where, then, the trust, though expressed as a purpose, is directly or indirectly for the benefit of an individual or individuals, it seems to me that it is in general outside the mischief of the beneficiary principle."[359]

"[T]he provision as to "other persons" is not a trust but a power operating in partial defeasance of the trust in favour of the employees which it does not therefore make uncertain."[360]

"The court can, as it seems to me, execute the trust both negatively by restraining any improper disposition or use of the land, and positively by ordering the trustees to allow the employees and such other persons (if any) as they may admit to use the land for the purpose of a recreation or sports ground."[361]

---

[358] *Denley, re* [1969] 1 Ch 373 (Ch) 383 (Goff J).

[359] *Denley, re* [1969] 1 Ch 373 (Ch) 383 (Goff J).

[360] *Denley, re* [1969] 1 Ch 373 (Ch) 387 (Goff J).

[361] *Denley, re* [1969] 1 Ch 373 (Ch) 388 (Goff J).

7. Gissing v Gissing

The imputation of beneficial rights to property based upon the conduct of the contending parties, has been a delicate issue for the courts for many years. On this occasion, the lines of demarcation were drawn by the House of Lords, in order to prevent further abuses of equity and its associated maxims.

After marrying at a young age in 1935, the respondent in this appeal joined her husband in the purchase of their first home in 1951 for a sum of £2,695. The mortgage was held in sole title by her appellant husband, who contributed £500 by way of a loan, and £45 from his own savings; while the respondent paid £220 for a new lawn, household appliances and furniture. During the time of their marriage, the mortgage was paid by the appellant, who also provided the respondent with regular weekly payments for housekeeping costs, while repaying the loan furnished him by his employer.

Prior to the purchase, the appellant had served time in the military, and after finding himself discharged following the war, the respondent secured him a position with a printing firm that she herself worked at. While the respondent's earnings remained at a stable £500 p.a, the appellant was successful in his endeavours, and soon established himself as director of the firm, with earnings of around £3,000 p.a.

After twenty-five years of marriage and the raising of their son, the appellant committed adultery with a younger woman, before leaving the home and beginning a life with her. This led to their divorce, during which the appellant continued to pay the mortgage, loan and outgoings on their marital home, until the loss of his job and subsequent financial troubles. Around this time, the respondent issued a summons declaring absolute ownership of the home, based upon the oral promise by the appellant that she could keep the house.

Under s.53(1) of the Law of Property Act 1925, any declaration of trust wth regard to beneficial interest in property must be written, however the courts can find the existence of such an agreement by equitable principles of resulting, implied and constructive trusts where sufficient evidence allows. In order to establish this, the court would seek to infer through the conduct of the parties, reasonable proof that when engaging in the purchase of the home there had either been (i) agreement as to how to apportionment of interest was to be divided or (ii) the financial contributions made by each party for the duration of the marriage or occupancy.

In the first hearing, the court awarded that the appellant was, by extension of his financial payments and obvious legal title, the sole owner of the property, and allowed for repossession under law. In the Court of Appeal, the decision was reversed by a majority, who held that the respondent was entitled to a fifty percent share of the home. Presented to the House of Lords, the recent outcome of *Pettitt v Pettitt*[362] was taken under consideration, along with the principles of *cestuis que trusts*.

In *Pettitt*, the former wife pursued proprietary interest of the sole legal title held by her ex-husband under s.17 of the Married Woman's Property Act 1882, on a home still subject to an outstanding mortgage. Her contention was that having occupied the home

---

[362] [1970] AC 777.

for ten years, she was entitled to a beneficial interest due to her substantial contributions to both the deposit and subsequent repayments during the time of their marriage; whereupon the husband countered that his individual improvements to the house afforded him an equal share of the property.

While on that occasion the judgment fell in favour of the wife, there was little with which to compare it to this case, and so the equitable nature of trusts were explored through the conduct of the respondent. Here it was held by majority, that while an oral declaration by the appellant suggested otherwise, there was absolutely no evidence that the respondent did, at any time, intend to contribute to the purchase of the home, or the upkeep of mortgage repayments, even when the appellant had suffered financial setbacks. And so it was for those reasons, that suggestions of trusts of any kind were simply obiter dictum, and that for the purposes of natural justice, the appeal was upheld with costs.

Key Citations

"One cannot counteract the absence of any common intention at the time of acquisition by conclusions as to what the parties would have done if they had thought about the matter. If such a common intention is absent, in my opinion the law does not permit the courts to ascribe to the parties an intention they never had and to hold that property is subject to a trust on the ground that that would be fair in all the circumstances."[363]

"Any claim to a beneficial interest in land by a person, whether spouse or stranger, in whom the legal estate in the land is not vested must be based upon the proposition that the person in whom the legal estate is vested holds it as trustee upon trust to give effect to the beneficial interest of the claimant as *cestui que trust*."[364]

"An express agreement between spouses as to their respective beneficial interests in land conveyed into the name of one of them obviates the need for showing that the conduct of the spouse into whose name the land was conveyed was intended to induce the other spouse to act to his or her detriment upon the faith of the promise of a specified beneficial interest in the land and that the other spouse so acted with the intention of acquiring that beneficial interest."[365]

"[I]n the branch of English law relating to constructive, implied or resulting trusts effect is given to the inferences as to the intentions of parties to a transaction which a reasonable man would draw from their words or conduct and not to any subjective intention or absence of intention which was not made manifest at the time of the transaction itself."[366]

---

[363] *Gissing v Gissing* [1970] 2 All ER 780 (HL) 900 (Viscount Dilhorne).

[364] *Gissing v Gissing* [1970] 2 All ER 780 (HL) 904 (Diplock LJ).

[365] *Gissing v Gissing* [1970] 2 All ER 780 (HL) 905 (Diplock LJ).

[366] *Gissing v Gissing* [1970] 2 All ER 780 (HL) 906 (Diplock LJ).

8. Grey v IRC

The creation of trusts run closely to dispositions of interest unless properly worded and executed in accordance with English law. In this matter, the settlor elected to draft and duly sign a declaration of trust, while orally providing the exact nature of the trusts to his trustees. It was this indiscretion that caused the Inland Revenue to seek proportionate stamp duty, on grounds that the gesture amounted to a disposition of property and nothing less.

Having chosen to leave consideration for his grandchildren, the settlor created six trusts on two separate occasions, each leaving 3,000 company shares per beneficiary, along with particular instructions as to their use. When looking to officialise his request, he brought together his trustees, before instructing them as how best to manage the trusts. Having then finalised six declarations of trust, he signed and sealed them in witness of his solicitor. A key part of his participation was that as of the date the deeds were completed, the settlor had agreed to renounce his continued beneficial, equitable (and therefore legal) interest in the trust property, and that the trustees were now holding them on trust for the benefit of his grandchildren.

Unfortunately, s.53 (1) of the Law of Property Act 1925 reads that:

> "Subject to the provisions hereinafter contained with respect to the creation of interest in land by parol, . . . (c) a disposition of an equitable interest or trust subsisting at the time of the disposition, must be in writing signed by the person disposing of the same, or by his agent thereunto lawfully authorised in writing or by will."[367]

The question then raised, was whether by virtue of their release, the actions of the settlor and the construction of the declarations of trust, were tantamount to voluntary dispositions, that under the terms of statute, attracted stamp duty (or *ad valorem* duty as referred to at the time), or that by lack of written instructions as to their use, the trusts were ineffective and thus exempt from taxation?

When first heard, the judge awarded in favour of the trustees, and cited that no duty was applicable because no 'disposition' had been intended nor indicated, except for the choice of words used by the settlor. Upon appeal, the Court reversed the decision and took the opposing view that despite the intentions of the settlor, the manner in which the trusts were created altered the nature of the relationship between executor and trustee, in so much that the settlor had granted beneficial and equitable ownership to the trustees, and could no longer see himself as a trustee of the property, until such time as the grandchildren took title upon his death.

Presented again before the House of Lords, much greater focus was placed upon the consolidation of the Law of Property Act 1924 and The Statute of Frauds, which under s. 9 explained:

---

[367] Law of Property Act 1925, s.53(1)

"[A]ll grants and assignments of any trust or confidence shall likewise be in writing, signed by the party granting or assigning the same, or by such last will or devise, or else shall likewise be utterly void and of none effect..."[368]

The appellants relied this time upon the terms 'grants and assignments' to circumvent the requirements of the Law of Property Act 1925, in that because the terms of the trust had failed to take written form, the trusts were both invalid and therefore exempt from duty, and that reliance upon the term 'disposition' was an overextension of the facts and a misdirection of law.

Upon generous consideration, it was unanimously agreed that despite the intimation that the actions of the settlor were misconstrued, it was relatively easy to interpret that the renunciation of interest was equatable to a disposition, and that under those circumstances the relevant statutory duty was owed.

Key Citations

"...If the word "disposition" is given its natural meaning, it cannot, I think, be denied that a direction given by Mr. Hunter, whereby the beneficial interest in the shares theretofore vested in him became vested in another or others, is a disposition."[369]

"[I]t is incredible that the legislature intended in the Act of 1925 to make further and radical changes in the law as enacted in preceding Acts, the question is what changes had been effected in those Acts."[370]

"Something had to happen to that equitable interest in order to displace it in favour of the new interests created by the direction: and it would be at any rate logical to treat the direction as being an assignment of the subsisting interest to the new beneficiary or beneficiaries or, in other cases, a release or surrender of it to the trustee."[371]

---

[368] Statute of Frauds, s.9

[369] *Grey v IRC* [1959] 3 All ER 603 (HL) 12 (Viscount Simonds).

[370] *Grey v IRC* [1959] 3 All ER 603 (HL) 14 (Viscount Simonds).

[371] *Grey v IRC* [1959] 3 All ER 603 (HL) 16 (Radcliffe LJ).

9. McPhail v Doulton

Specificity within discretionary trusts is a virtual prerequisite should the settlor wish to enjoy its success; as while the courts are empowered to dispense as the creator intended, they are still subject to restrictive criteria that can often render them ineffective.

When a company owner took the liberty of constructing a trust deed for the benefit of past and present employees and their relatives and children, the duties assigned to the trustees were flexible enough to allow for common sense and equity to steer their decisions. This was because the funds within the trust were limited, and therefore issue to selected employees was restricted on a yearly basis, with further provision for continuous investment in order to extend the lifetime of the trust.

Over twenty years after execution of the deed, and following the death of the owner, the validity of the trust was brought into question by his widow and certain family members, who having found themselves exempt from the pleasures of regular payments from the trustees, sought to challenge the terms of the instrument contained within clause 9, which read that:

> "(a) The trustees shall apply the net income of the fund in making at their absolute discretion grants . . . in such amounts at such times and on such conditions (if any) as they think fit . . . (b) The trustees shall not be bound to exhaust the income of any year or other period in making such grants . . . and any income not so applied shall be . . . [placed in a bank or invested], (c) The trustees may realise any investments representing accumulations of income and apply the proceeds as though the same were income of the fund and may also . . . at any time prior to the liquidation of the fund realise any other part of the capital of the fund . . . in order to provide benefits for which the current income of the fund is insufficient."

Here it was argued that while the trust designated that a class of people were intended as beneficiaries, the list was wide enough to introduce uncertainty at to whether the discretion offered the trustees was construed as a power, rather than trust instructions. And so under those circumstances, the trust had prima facie failed, and that whatever funds existed fell within the deceased's estate.

When heard in the Court of Chancery, the judge upheld the idea that such a power exceeded the delicate framework of a trust, and that clause 10 of the same deed indicated that the interest in the trust lay solely in the hands of the trustees; therefore any disposition of funds were in accordance with their discretion, which resulted in uncertainty as to exactly whom the beneficiaries were. Heard again at the Court of Appeal, the original judgment was upheld, while granting leave to appeal to the House of Lords.

Here, the issues surrounding the true intention of the settlor were given greater consideration, with particular regard to the limitations of the trust fund use, and the relatively ascertainable identity of the employees and their family members. When looked at again in context, it was apparent that the aim of the trust was one that afforded creativity of the funds after the needs of the beneficiaries were met; therefore it could not be construed as self-serving and objective to the intended purpose. Rather it boiled down to poor drafting, that while in the immediate sense lent to initial confusion of those unfamiliar with trusts and fiduciary duties, did not prevent the House from clarifying that the same degree of uncertainty could be removed in lieu of a perfectly functional instrument of generosity.

Key Citations

"I cannot for myself resist the conclusion reached by Russell L.J. that clause 9 is a provision for the distribution of the whole with power to accumulate. There is a complete disposition with a primary duty to distribute, a trust for the whole period of its existence with a power to carry forward from year to year."[372]

"[W]here there is a trust there is a duty imposed upon the trustees who can be controlled if necessary in the exercise of their duty. Whether the trust is discretionary or not the court must be in a position to control its execution in the interests of the objects of the trust. Where there is a mere power entirely different considerations arise. The objects have no right to complain."[373]

"[I]t is in the public interest that trusts of the nature of the present should be saved, if possible, because of the great benefit conferred on the beneficiaries."[374]

"It is striking how narrow and in a sense artificial is the distinction, in cases such as the present, between trusts or as the particular type of trust is called, trust powers, and powers."[375]

"A trustee of an employees' benefit fund, whether given a power or a trust power, is still a trustee and he would surely consider in either case that he has a fiduciary duty…"[376]

"Any trustee would surely make it his duty to know what is the permissible area of selection and then consider responsibly, in individual cases, whether a contemplated beneficiary was within the power and whether, in relation to other possible claimants, a particular grant was appropriate."[377]

---

[372] *McPhail v Doulton* [1970] 2 All ER 228 (HL) 438 (Hodson LJ).

[373] *McPhail v Doulton* [1970] 2 All ER 228 (HL) 441 (Hodson LJ).

[374] *McPhail v Doulton* [1970] 2 All ER 228 (HL) 446 (Guest LJ).

[375] *McPhail v Doulton* [1970] 2 All ER 228 (HL) 448 (Wilberforce LJ).

[376] *McPhail v Doulton* [1970] 2 All ER 228 (HL) 449 (Wilberforce LJ).

[377] *McPhail v Doulton* [1970] 2 All ER 228 (HL) 449 (Wilberforce LJ).

10. Milroy v Lord

When a man of standing sought to create a trust for the purposes of a relative's benefit, he was careful enough to provide specific instructions to his trustee, but unfortunately erred in putting them into action. A number of years after his death, the beneficiary challenged the assigned executor, on grounds that his written desire for her to gain lawful receipt was sufficient enough to constitute an enforceable covenant, and that the courts were inter alia wrong to deny it.

In 1852, the settlor drafted a deed-poll that enabled fifty shares of his stock held in the Louisiana Bank to be transferred to his associate, who had become his appointed trustee, on the proviso that under a number of specific conditions, he was to hold the shares upon trust for the benefit of his beloved niece. During the time between his grant and the date of her marriage or his death, the trustee was to manage the trust and pay any profits arising from the dividend interest to the beneficiary.

During this period, the settlor also granted the trustee power of attorney over all of his financial matters, and so while it was possible for the trustee to complete the request, he never managed to fully execute transferral under the banking practice policy, which required the participation of either the settlor himself, or a qualified solicitor. Where neither was found, the power of attorney rested not with the trustee, but with the bank instead.

When her contest was heard in the first trial, the presiding judge awarded that by virtue of the deed construction, a valid trust had existed, and that the fifty shares were to be reissued by the executor to the existing trustee, whereupon they would be again held upon trust for the niece, as had been the case before the settlor's death.

Upon appeal, the Court took the equitable view that a legally incomplete gesture cannot be enforced (equity will not perfect an imperfect gift), and that it was impossible for the settlor to become a self-appointed trustee for the shares discussed. Rather, it was declared that the funds were to be held upon trust by the executor, until amendments could be made to the deed that provided for redistribution in the manner first intended, or until the trustee and beneficiary chose to take individual action against him.

Key Citations

"I am of the opinion that according to our law the instrument of the 2d April 1852 was not sufficient to constitute and did not constitute Mr. Medley a trustee of the bank shares."[378]

"[I]n order to render a voluntary settlement valid and effectual, the settlor must have done everything which, according to the nature of the property comprised in the settlement, was necessary to be done in order to transfer the property and render the settlement binding upon him."[379]

"[I]n order to render the settlement binding, one or other of these modes must, as I understand the law of this Court, be resorted to, for there is no equity in this Court to perfect an imperfect gift."[380]

"If it is intended to take effect by transfer, the Court will not hold the intended transfer to operate as a declaration of trust, for then every imperfect instrument would be made effectual by being converted into a perfect trust."[381]

"[T]here does not appear to me to be any sufficient ground to warrant us in holding that the settlor himself became a trustee of these bank shares for the purposes of this settlement."[382]

"A Court of Equity could not, I think, decree the agent of the settlor to make the transfer, unless it could decree the settlor himself to do so, and it is plain that no such decree could have been made against the settlor."[383]

"The certificates for the shares would follow the legal title, and as to the fifty bank shares would therefore belong to the Defendant…"[384]

"There is no express covenant in the settlement, and whatever might be done as to implying a covenant to do no act in derogation of the settlement, it would, I think, be going too far to imply a covenant to perfect it."[385]

---

[378] *Milroy v Lord* (1862) 4 De GF & J 264 (CA) 272 (Knight-Bruce LJ).

[379] *Milroy v Lord* (1862) 4 De GF & J 264 (CA) 274 (Knight-Bruce LJ).

[380] *Milroy v Lord* (1862) 4 De GF & J 264 (CA) 274 (Knight-Bruce LJ).

[381] *Milroy v Lord* (1862) 4 De GF & J 264 (CA) 274 (Knight-Bruce LJ).

[382] *Milroy v Lord* (1862) 4 De GF & J 264 (CA) 276 (Knight-Bruce LJ).

[383] *Milroy v Lord* (1862) 4 De GF & J 264 (CA) 277 (Knight-Bruce LJ).

[384] *Milroy v Lord* (1862) 4 De GF & J 264 (CA) 277 (Knight-Bruce LJ).

[385] *Milroy v Lord* (1862) 4 De GF & J 264 (CA) 278 (Knight-Bruce LJ).

11. *Re* Bucks Constabulary Widow's and Orphans Fund Friendly Society

Variances in the formation of societal funds are capable of determining the receipt of unaccounted monies, when those organisations are dissolved through death of its members, or as part of a change in structure and administration. In such instances, the Crown treasury will be quick to adopt the residual capital under the principle of *bona vacantia*, therefore the courts are required to discriminate between the powers of legislation and those of the surviving trustees/members when deciding the destination of such sums.

On this occasion, a widows and orphans trust fund had been formed for the benefit of serving county police officers, which operated under the terms of the Friendly Societies Act 1896 and was used both for loss of life and sickness of those subscribed. In 1968, the society members agreed to wind up the fund as part of an amalgamation with a larger benevolent fund, whereupon it was decided that the £87,000 held would be used to (i) fund ongoing annuities for those claiming under right for the sum of £35,000, and (ii) provide £40,000 so as to gain entry into the new fund, whereupon the remaining £12,000 would be distributed between the surviving members, as provided for by s. 49(1) of the 1896 Act, which reads:

> "All property belonging to a registered society, whether acquired before or after the society is registered, *shall vest in the trustees for the time being of the society, for the use and benefit of the society and the members thereof*, and of all persons claiming through the members according to the rules of the society."[386]

While in the event that no such preparation has been made, there was also adequate authority to suggest that:

> "[I]f on the termination of a society no provision has been made by the rules for the distribution of its funds, such funds are divisible among the existing members at the time of the termination or dissolution in proportion to the amount contributed by each member for entrance fees and subscriptions, but irrespective of fines or payments made to members in accordance with the rules."[387]

Which prima facie, prevented the recovery of money by the Treasury, as might be expected in such instances. In an originating summons submitted by the sole trustee to the fund, the court was asked to determine whether the £40,000 planned for payment should instead be held upon trust for the widows and orphans fund, before being equally distributed amongst the surviving members, or if as was suggested, the monies were due to the Crown under a loss of ownership through the dissolution of the fund.

---

[386] Friendly Societies Act 1896, s.49(1) (emphasis added).

[387] Frank Baden Fuller, *The Law Relating To Friendly Societies* (William Clowes and Sons 1896) 186

Having considered the weight behind such prominent cases as *re Recher's Will Trusts*[388] and *Cunnack v Edwards*,[389] Walton J concluded that unless the society had been reduced to just a single remaining member, there was little to indicate that anything less than an equal distribution between both the existing members and those surviving members that had previously died, would be a suitable application of law, and awarded judgment accordingly.

Key Citations

"[I]t appears to me quite clear that, unless under the rules governing the association the property thereof has been wholly devoted to charity, or unless and to the extent to which the other trusts have validly been declared of such property, the persons, and the only persons, interested therein are the members."[390]

"The assets must continue to be held, the society having been dissolved and the widows and orphans being out of the way, simply for the use and benefit of the members of the society, albeit they will all now be former members."[391]

"The friendly societies legislation does not incorporate the friendly society in any way and the only effect that it has is, as I pointed out in my previous judgment in this case, that there is a section which makes it crystal clear in the Friendly Societies Act 1896 that the assets are held upon trust for the members."[392]

---

[388] [1972] Ch 526.

[389] [1895] 2 Ch 679 CA.

[390] *Bucks Constabulary Widows' and Orphans' Fund Friendly Society (No.2), re* [1979] 1 All ER 623 (Ch) 940 (Walton J).

[391] *Bucks Constabulary Widows' and Orphans' Fund Friendly Society (No.2), re* [1979] 1 All ER 623 (Ch) 942 (Walton J).

[392] *Bucks Constabulary Widows' and Orphans' Fund Friendly Society (No.2), re* [1979] 1 All ER 623 (Ch) 952 (Walton J).

12. *Re* Hallett's Estate

The tracing of funds through the principles of equity are now integral to the protection of trusts and beneficiaries, however in the late nineteenth century things were not as clear cut. In this matter, the discrepancies of a solicitor left both his family and a third party investor out of pocket, and forced to argue over the remaining bank balance upon his death.

Prior to his passing in 1878, Mr Henry Hughes Hallett was in the habit of investing money on behalf of private clients, whereupon he would take a commission as payment for services rendered. In addition to this, he had an existing marriage settlement for the benefit of his wife and children to the sum of £2,300, which had been placed into his personal bank account before being used for a number of other small investments. A Mrs Cotterill employed the deceased for general legal duties, but also to receive and invest sums of money for her eventual profit. On this occasion, she had allowed Mr. Hallett to invest £2,692 for Russian bonds, while he himself used £2,590 of the marriage settlement trust funds to do the same.

Having taken £1,554 worth of the trust bonds for himself before depositing the remaining £1,036 worth of bonds into his bank account, Mr.Hallett proceeded to sell £450 and £2,442 of Mrs Cotterill's bonds, and £1,036 of the trust funds, subject to his taking a commission on all three. Following a number of other transactions, the bank balance on the date of his demise was £3,029, of which £2,600 had been paid into a court relating to the administration of his estate. At the point of litigation, there were claims by both the trustees for his marriage settlement for £770 and £1,554, as used for the purchase of bonds, along with that of Mrs.Cotterill for £1,708.

Previous to this case, the law surrounding recovery of funds once mixed, was not one that favoured the claimant, and in many instances the court awarded against recovery on grounds that unless the money was ear-marked, it was simply indistinguishable from that which it had joined, thus to reach into the account and take it arbitrarily was simply untenable. This changed in the case of *Pennell v Deffell*,[393] in which the Court of Appeal held that the claim of the trustees or *cestui que trusts*, were of greater weight than that of a creditor. However, in the later *Clayton's Case*,[394] the Court of Appeal then held that in such instances the court would determine the first sum of money drawn out from a bank account as that belonging to the first sum paid in, therefore unless there were grounds to suspect fraud on the part of Mr. Hallett, £2,324 of the money left in the account was that of the marriage settlement, while the remaining £705 was that of Mrs. Cotterill.

In the first instance, the Judge awarded priority of claim in favour of Mrs. Cotterill, on grounds that a fiduciary relationship existed between her and the deceased; whereupon the trustees for Mr.Hallett's estate appealed, while Mrs. Cotterill also appealed. On this occasion, the Court of Appeal reversed the decision, awarding priority to the trustees for Mr. Hallett's estate on the equitable grounds that when a trustee mingles assets with that of his own, he is held to withdraw that which is his property when leaving a balance behind. This translated that whatever money Mr. Hallett had taken out prior to his death

---

[393] 4 DM & G 372.

[394] 1 Mer 572.

was that to which he was entitled, therefore the residual balance was that of the trustees and not one of a mere creditor.

Key Citations

"[W]here a trustee has mixed the money with his own, there is this distinction, that the *cestui que trust*, or beneficial owner, can no longer elect to take the property, because it is no longer bought with the trust-money simply and purely, but with a mixed fund. He is, however, still entitled to a charge on the property purchased, for the amount of the trust-money laid out in the purchase; and that charge is quite independent of the fact of the amount laid out by the trustee."[395]

"[I]f the debt were of such a nature as that, between the creditor and the debtor, you could not sever the debt into two, so as to shew what part was trust money, then the *cestui que trust* would have a right to a charge upon the whole."[396]

"[W]herever a specific chattel is intrusted by one man to another, either for the purposes of safe custody or for the purpose of being disposed of for the benefit of the person intrusting the chattel; then, either the chattel itself, or the proceeds of the chattel, whether the chattel has been rightfully or wrongfully disposed of, may be followed at any time, although neither the chattel itself, or the money constituting the proceeds of that chattel, may have been mixed and confounded in a mass of the like material."[397]

"[W]here a man does an act which may be rightfully performed, he cannot say that that act was intentionally and in fact done wrongly. A man who has a right of entry cannot say he committed a trespass in entering. A man who sells the goods of another as agent for the owner cannot prevent the owner adopting the sale, and deny that he acted as agent for the owner."[398]

"If specific coins, the proceeds of trust property, are deposited by a trustee in a box, either in his own custody or in that of another person, and in that box are mixed confusedly with coins, in every sense the property of the trustee, and being so mixed are subjected to dealings analogous to the drawings out and payings in of moneys standing in a banker's account, the trust is impressed upon the coins remaining in the box to the full amount of the proceeds of the trust property, if it be that at no time the mixed fund has been reduced below that amount, or if the mixed fund has at any time been reduced below that amount, then to any lesser amount below which it can be shewn that the mixed fund has never been reduced."[399]

---

[395] *Hallett's Estate, re* (1880) 13 Ch D 696 (Ch) 709 (Lord Jessel MR).

[396] *Hallett's Estate, re* (1880) 13 Ch D 696 (Ch) 711 (Lord Jessel MR).

[397] *Hallett's Estate, re* (1880) 13 Ch D 696 (Ch) 723 (Thesiger LR).

[398] *Hallett's Estate, re* (1880) 13 Ch D 696 (Ch) 727 (Lord Jessel MR).

[399] *Hallett's Estate, re* (1880) 13 Ch D 696 (Ch) 745 (Thesiger LR).

13. *Re* Montagu

Aristocracy and the burden of constructive trusteeship, are brought to bear when the misinterpretation of an appointed solicitor allows for the sale of valuables designated a place within the family trust.

By the actions of a family re-settlement drafted in 1923 by Viscount Mandeville (the future tenth Duke of Manchester), for the purposes of himself and each successive Duke, it was stated under clause 14 that the existing trustees to the estate were required, upon death of the ninth Duke of Manchester, to compile an inventory of goods deemed inheritable by the Viscount, prior to including them into the settlement, while para.B further expressed they should be held:

> "Upon trust after the death of the present Duke or (if and so far as may be found practicable and convenient) during his lifetime to select and make an inventory or inventories of such of the chattels hereby assigned as the trustees in their absolute discretion may consider suitable for inclusion in the settlement hereby made (which selected chattels are hereinafter called 'the selected chattels') and to hold the residue (if any) of the said assigned chattels in trust for Viscount Mandeville absolutely."

After the ninth Duke's passing, the trustees handed the Viscount a number of items with the intention that he would look to sell them, yet he failed to compile a list of valuables for retention into the settlement for future Dukes. When the tenth Duke died in 1977, those items remaining came into possession by his widow, the Dowager Duchess of Manchester, whereupon in 1979, the eleventh Duke of Manchester issued a writ for breach of trust by the surviving trustees of the 1923 settlement, on grounds of having delivered the property to the deceased in the knowledge of their duties under clause 14 of the 1923 settlement, and so by virtue of his having sold them, the tenth Duke was also held accountable as a constructive trustee, and liable for payment of the proceeds to the value of those items sold, as was his widow. It was also argued that failure to compile the list resulted in all items of value falling within the scope of the settlement, and that both repossession of those items and recompense for any property sold was due.

Heard over a lengthy ten-day hearing, judge Megarry V-C took pains to explore the definition of constructive trustees, along with the term 'notice', as had been claimed by the eleventh Duke. When the chain of communication was examined, it became apparent that during the lifetime of the tenth Duke, his solicitor had written to him to explain his obligations, but in way that failed to fully embrace the limitations of the settlement, as illustrated below:

> "I had a long conversation with Nicholl on Thursday last, and the trustees have agreed that the heirlooms should be released, except the pictures. Under the resettlement executed by you on 20 December 1923 there is a clause by which *the trustees can in their discretion release a large quantity of heirlooms and make a new list of such articles as are to remain as heirlooms. The amount obtained for the sale of any articles will be your personal property and the proceeds of sale will not have to be considered as capital trust money.*"[400]

---

[400] (emphasis added).

From this it was easily construed that the lack of legal knowledge on the part of the tenth Duke would have left him reliant upon the professional expertise of his solicitor, who on this occasion had neglected to mention that the trustees were under a lawful obligation to draft a comprehensive list prior to any passing of estate property. This meant that prima facie, the deceased was by extension, a constructive trustee by imputation. However, his ignorance of the facts raised strong argument for his exemption, with particular regard to the five principles of 'knowing' as set down by Gibson J in *Baden, Delvaux and Lecuit v Société General pour Favoriser le Développement du Commerce et de l'Industrie en France SA*,[401] which included (i) actual knowledge (ii) wilfully shutting one's eyes to the obvious (iii) wilfully and recklessly failing to make honest and reasonable enquiries as to the facts (iv) reasonable and honest knowledge of circumstances indicative of the facts and (v) honest and reasonable knowledge of circumstances as to cause inquiry.

While the claimants preferred to impute the knowledge of clause 14 upon the Duke, it was clear by the evidence presented, that the deceased was largely ignorant to his legal requirements, and instead wholly dependent on the instructions of his acting solicitor. It was also noted that ss.199 and 205 (1)(xxi) of the Law of Property Act 1925 specifically exempts beneficiaries under trust from the powers of constructive notice; which left the court little recourse other than to hold that in this instance, the tenth Duke of Manchester was not liable as a constructive trustee, and therefore no action against him could be sustained.

Key Citations

"In determining whether a constructive trust has been created, the fundamental question is whether the conscience of the recipient is bound in such a way as to justify equity in imposing a trust on him."[402]

"Even under the ordinary doctrine of purchaser without notice, a purchaser does not have imputed to him notice of everything of which his solicitor has notice, but only the notice that the solicitor has acquired in the particular transaction: see section 199(l)(ii) (6) of the Law of Property Act 1925."[403]

---

[401] [1923] BCLC 325.

[402] *Montagu's Settlement Trusts, re* [1987] Ch 264 (Ch) 277 (Megarry V-C).

[403] *Montagu's Settlement Trusts, re* [1987] Ch 264 (Ch) 283 (Megarry V-C).

14. *Re* Pryce

When a number of parties choose to create multiple contracts across two generations, there will always be problems trying to control the flow of assets when the moment requires it. In this matter, the sheer volume of trusts, contracts, covenants, wills and gifts left the trustees to one marriage agreement, confused as to exactly what they were under duty to do, and to whom any decided benefit belonged.

In 1887, a married couple entered into an agreement requiring that any property left by the husband upon death, was to be held in trust for their children, and would be thus managed by two appointed trustees. The husband also contracted with his wife that any funds left for him in his father's will, would then be held in the same trust and managed by the trustees.

In the terms of his father's will, the husband was legally entitled to a one-third share of two large sums of money, which had been expressed by action of a family deed in 1849; while in a deed of gift in 1904, the husband then conferred that certain other properties would now be held upon trust for his wife's enjoyment in a separate trust. When his father died in 1891, the husband was duly paid his one-third share of the first of the two sums, although his wife and the trustees of the 1887 marriage contract had no knowledge of this, despite his prior acquiescence to the terms of his gift.

The husband later died in 1907, leaving them no children to benefit from the 1887 marriage trust, after which the specific properties and his other one-third share of money came into his possession through the death of his mother in 1913. These assets were subsequently held by the appointed trustees of his parents own 1889 agreement and the family deed created in 1849. By this time, the residue of the 1887 marriage trust was now held in trust by the trustees, while the property and monies from his parents wills and 1849 deed, were now held on absolute trust, despite his passing.

At this point, the 1887 marriage agreement trustees sought to claim the property and monies held in absolute trust, in order that they now became part of the 1887 trust, while asking whether by virtue of the fact that no children were created during the lifetime of their marriage, the 1849 deed funds were now held upon trust for the benefit of the widow's next of kin upon her death.

When considered by the court, the equitable maxim 'equity will not assist a volunteer' was put to good effect when explaining that despite any suggestion of default to the widow's relatives, it did not fall to the judges, or the appointed trustees, to attempt enforcement of the 1887 agreement, when the widow was legally entitled to benefit from the funds and property now held upon trust by the parent's trustees. It was also noted that despite not having children of their own, no evidence of a declaration of trust could be manufactured between the respondent and her next of kin, so there could be no argument of a breach to the contrary.

Key Citations

"[V]olunteers have no right whatever to obtain specific performance of a mere covenant which has remained as a covenant and has never been performed."[404]

"[T]he next of kin could neither maintain an action to enforce the covenant nor for damages for breach of it, and that the settlement is not a declaration of trust constituting the relationship of trustee and *cestui que trust* between the defendant and the next of kin."[405]

---

[404] *Pryce, re* [1917] 1 Ch 234 (Ch) 241 (Eve J).

[405] *Pryce, re* [1917] 1 Ch 234 (Ch) 241 (Eve J).

15. *Re* **Recher's Will Trusts**

As is not uncommon to the bequests of those organised enough to prepare a will, there are times when beneficiaries such as charitable organisations, evolve into larger bodies with differing names at the point of death, and so on this occasion, the court was required to determine if the nature of the gift was such as to allow application, despite a change of identity on the part of the legatees.

By her will of May 23 1957, the deceased Mrs. Recher had expressed in clause 7 that upon the death of her husband, any residual funds were to be placed upon trust for a number of charities including The London and Provincial Anti-Vivisection Society, 76 Victoria Street, London SW1, and distributed in equal shares to those stated. Upon the death of her husband in 1968, it was discovered that as of January 1 1956, the London and Provincial Anti-Vivisection Society had become absorbed by The National Anti-Vivisection Society, who operated from 27 Palace Street, London SW1, and that amongst the terms provisional to the amalgamation it read:

> "3. (i) *On the appointed day every life member of L. & P. shall become an annual member of N.A.V.S. F.* . . (v) Subject as aforesaid, every person becoming a member of N.A.V.S. under this provision shall be entitled to all the rights and subject to all the liabilities of the other members of the class to which he belongs."[406]

Which translated that at the point of Mrs. Recher's death, all members of the London and Provincial Anti-Vivisection Society were in fact members of The National Anti-Vivisection Society, which itself was no longer a charitable institution but a limited company.

Having been presented to the court under a summons by the acting executor to Mrs. Recher, the point was raised as to whether the apportioned monies were payable to the London and Provisional Anti-Vivisection Society, or if by virtue of the fact that the recipients had been incorporated into a larger organisation, the gift was now left to fail under common law.

Despite existing arguments to the former, it was explained in *Leahy v Attorney-General for New South Wales* that:

> "A gift can be made to persons (including a corporation) but it cannot be made to a purpose or to an object: so also, a trust may be created for the benefit of persons as *cestuis que trust* but not for a purpose or object unless the purpose or object be charitable. For a purpose or object cannot sue, but, if it be charitable, the Attorney-General can sue to enforce it."[407]

Through the terms of the will it was construed by the court that the gift was one for the purposes of the London and Provincial Anti-Vivisection Society and not a limited company, and while there were a number of caveats in favour of passing the gift to the

---

[406] (emphasis added).

[407] *Leahy v Attorney-General for New South Wales* [1959] AC 457 (PC) 478 (Viscount Simonds).

original charity, it was impossible to hold that the testatrix Mrs.Recher, had ever intended to benefit anybody else other than the charity expressed, therefore the gift was to fail.

Key Citations

"[W]here you have a gift to an unidentified institution bearing a name suggesting charitable purposes, particularly if found in the company of a number of gifts to identified charitable institutions, the court may save the unidentified gift by assuming that the testator's bounty is not directed towards the particular institutions named by him but is directed towards a purpose."[408]

"[I]n the absence of words which purport to impose a trust, the legacy is a gift to the members beneficially, not as joint tenants or as tenants in common so as to entitle each member to an immediate distributive share, but as an accretion to the funds which are the subject-matter of the contract which the members have made inter se."[409]

---

[408] *Recher's Will Trusts, re* [1971] 3 All ER 401 (Ch) 537 (Brightman J).

[409] *Recher's Will Trusts, re* [1971] 3 All ER 401 (Ch) 539 (Brightman J).

16. *Re* Rose

Voluntary corporate dispositions, and the prerequisite of company procedures are inextricably linked, yet where discrepancies arise, it falls to equity to resolve the inadequacies argued, before choosing to act. In this instance, the two gestures of a settlor were challenged by the Crown in the hope of securing estate duties post-mortem.

In 1943, an unlimited company owner took the practical steps of transferring two amounts of 10,000 shares to both his wife on the first count, and his wife and secretary on the second. Acting under strict observation of the associated articles of memorandum, namely art.9 which read:

> "[T]he company shall be entitled to treat the person "whose name appears upon the register in respect of any share" as the absolute owner thereof, and shall not be under any "obligation to recognize any trust or equity or equitable claim" to or interest in such share, whether or not it shall have "express or other notice thereof.""

And art.28 which also read:

> "[T]he transferor shall be "deemed to remain the holder of such share until the name of" the transferee is entered in the register in respect thereof."

It was further indicated by art.29 that:

> "Shares in the company shall be transferred in "the following form, or as near thereto as circumstances will "permit.""

On this occasion, the documentation used was fully compliant with the terms prescribed by the company articles, and such that by sealed written instruction the husband had willingly relinquished himself of any proprietary and beneficial ownership, so that in order for legal title to succeed, along with liability for estate duty fees, the company would only need to register the transfer before a specified date.

For one reason or another, the registration was incomplete until two days after the exemption period, and so a number of years after the settlor's death, the Inland Revenue sought to recover the duties on both transfers, under the combined effects of the Customs and Inland Revenue Act 1881, the Customs and Inland Revenue Act 1889 and the Finance Act 1894.

When first heard, the judge awarded in favour of the transferees, whereupon it was appealed by the Inland Revenue Commissioners, who primarily relied upon *Milroy v Lord*[410] to argue against the previous decision. Having considered the facts of both matters, the Court refused to support the far-reaching contradiction of the appellants, who contested (i) that as the transfer had not been successfully completed by registration within the determined period it was non-effectual, and so represented nothing more than a promissory gesture, and yet (ii) once completed, the settlor was unable to reverse the transfer and so held the shares in death as he did in life.

---

[410] (1862) 4 De GF & J 264.

While in *Milroy* the deed-poll constituted little more than a written instruction, the explicit nature of the instrument of transfer in this instance had made it quite clear that at the date of execution (roughly ten days before the exemption threshold lapsed), the husband had expressly ceased to hold any beneficial or proprietary interest in the shares, and that by virtue of the gift, all beneficial ownership rights were now conferred to the wife and secretary, despite the absence of legal title. It was this minor, yet crucial technicality that distinguished itself from *Milroy*, and thus negated the position taken by the appellants when seeking payment.

Deciding in unison, the previous judgment was vehemently upheld, while the point made clear that when a settlor acts within his duties, and in as exhaustible a manner as possible, any uncertainty of legal title does not preclude the completion of a gift; and that where duty commands it, beneficial ownership is sufficient answer when legal title is peripheral to judicial determination.

Key Citations

"[A]ny transaction of gift imports a donor and a donee, a disposition by the donor and receipt of the subject-matter of the disposition by the donee."[411]

"[T]he directors of the company, when they registered the transfers, registered them, because, by virtue of the transfers, the transferees had become owners of the shares, and as such had become entitled to get in the legal estate by being put on the register in respect of the shares."[412]

"[T]hese transfers were nothing more nor less than transfers of the whole of the deceased's title, both legal and equitable, in the shares, and all the advantages attached to the shares, as from the date on which he executed and delivered the transfers…"[413]

"[T]he effect of these transactions, having regard to the form and the operation of the transfers, the nature of the property transferred, and the necessity for registration in order to perfect the legal title, coupled with the discretionary power on the part of the directors to withhold registration, must be that, pending registration, the deceased was in the position of a trustee of the legal title in the shares for the transferees."[414]

"[I]t is a fallacy to adduce from that the conclusion that there can be no complete gift of shares as between transferor and transferee unless and until the transferee is placed on the register."[415]

---

[411] *Rose, re* [1952] 1 All ER 1217 (Ch) 515 (Jenkins LJ).

[412] *Rose, re* [1952] 1 All ER 1217 (Ch) 516 (Jenkins LJ).

[413] *Rose, re* [1952] 1 All ER 1217 (Ch) 517 (Jenkins LJ).

[414] *Rose, re* [1952] 1 All ER 1217 (Ch) 518 (Jenkins LJ).

[415] *Rose, re* [1952] 1 All ER 1217 (Ch) 518 (Jenkins LJ).

17. Rochefoucauld v Boustead

Does the creation of a trust rely upon written acknowledgement, or can the verbal promises of another to act in many respects as a fiduciary, provide evidence enough of an intention to serve as a trustee? In an unusual arrangement between a lady of nobility and her business associate, the latter was asked to purchase an estate that she might otherwise lose through the rigours of her recent divorce.

While once a thriving coffee plantation, the land in question was by all accounts operational but subject to increased crop damage, yet without the revenue historically provided, there was little chance that the appellant could continue to live within means accustomed to. This led to her asking her colleague to secure a conveyance of the property from the mortgagees, on the proviso that she would over time, reimburse him for (i) the cost of the purchase and (ii) any additional costs incurred during the management and administration of the business.

Although not expressly stated in any official correspondence at the time, this verbal arrangement served to create a settlor and trustee relationship that benefitted both parties, albeit with overall beneficial interest remaining in the hands of the appellant.

After a number of years, the company deteriorated into insolvency, whereupon the appellant made claim for her beneficial title so as to avoid any loss to creditors. It was then argued that the mortgage had enabled the respondent full title to the land (upon which he had previously mortgaged out portions for personal profit), and that this deed protected any claim to the contrary. The right was claimed in addition to the twelve years during which no legal proceedings were instigated by the appellant; a delay which was ultimately denied through the statute of limitations and the estoppel of laches.

When first heard, the judge awarded in favour of the defendant with little investigation of the collected evidence, and so when taken to appeal, the Court was more diligent when reaching a verdict. Having looked closely at the correspondence both before and after the initial conveyance, it became clear that while nothing had been set to paper, there was never any indication that anything less than a trust/trustee arrangement had been effected, and that the appellant's beneficial interest was never held in question. Adding to the fact that the respondent had acted in a clandestine manner when selling land for gain before destroying the business accounts, there was little upon which he could rely when claiming 'reasonable' behaviour.

With collective agreement that the appellant did have a right to claim title upon grounds of an express trust, the only stumbling block was the length of time in which it took her to seek remedy. Having then explained that financial difficulties, faith in the defendant's honesty and conflicting legal advice had dissuaded her from pursuing it in the courts; the judges concluded that there was nothing justiciable to prevent her from recovery of the estate, and so reversed the previous judgment and awarded in her favour.

Key Citations

"[I]t is a fraud on the part of a person to whom land is conveyed as a trustee, and who knows it was so conveyed, to deny the trust and claim the land himself."[416]

"[I]t is competent for a person claiming land conveyed to another to prove by parol evidence that it was so conveyed upon trust for the claimant, and that the grantee, knowing the facts, is denying the trust and relying upon the form of conveyance and the statute, in order to keep the land himself."[417]

"The Bankruptcy Act then in force the Act of 1869, and by s.49 of that Act bankrupt trustees were not discharged from the claims of their *cestuis que trust*."[418]

"[T]he plaintiff has done nothing actively to lead the defendant to suppose that she abandoned any claim she might have against him as her trustee."[419]

"It must be declared that the defendant purchased the Delmar estates as a trustee for the plaintiff, but subject to a charge for the amount paid to the Dutch company."[420]

---

[416] *Rochefoucauld v Boustead* [1897] 1 Ch 196 (Ch) 206 (Lindley LJ).

[417] *Rochefoucauld v Boustead* [1897] 1 Ch 196 (Ch) 206 (Lindley LJ).

[418] *Rochefoucauld v Boustead* [1897] 1 Ch 196 (Ch) 208 (Lindley LJ).

[419] *Rochefoucauld v Boustead* [1897] 1 Ch 196 (Ch) 211 (Lindley LJ).

[420] *Rochefoucauld v Boustead* [1897] 1 Ch 196 (Ch) 212 (Lindley LJ).

18. Royal Brunei Airlines v Tan

Breach of trust by a third party to a trustee, is something that while frustrating at common law, becomes punishable under equity where sufficient evidence is presented. On this occasion, the director of a travel agent privy to a fiduciary relationship with a leading airline, took it upon himself to mingle trust assets with those of his company, in order to balance the books and keep his own affairs in order.

Royal Brunei Airlines entered into an agreement with Borneo Leisure Travel on the proviso that the agent would secure bookings for both passenger and cargo flights in exchange for a commission. In addition to this, it was decided that the now respondents were to hold the booking payments in a standalone bank account, before paying the funds to the appellants every thirty days.

Having agreed to operate under those terms, the respondent chose instead to keep the money either in his sole deposit account, or his company account, while using the capital for disbursements that profited his firm. After six years, the appellants terminated their agreement with the respondent, and began litigation on grounds that the director himself had acted in breach of trust as a third party, and that the travel agents had also acted in breach of their duties as trustees to the airline.

The footing of the claim rested upon the long-standing statement by Lord Selbourne LC in *Barnes v Addy*, who stipulated that:

> "[The responsibility of a trustee] may no doubt be extended in equity to others who are not properly trustees, if they are found . . . actually participating in any fraudulent conduct of the trustee to the injury of the *cestui que trust*. But. . . strangers are not to be made constructive trustees merely because they act as the agents of trustees in transactions within their legal powers, transactions, perhaps of which a court of equity may disapprove, unless those agents receive and become chargeable with some part of the trust property, *or unless they assist with knowledge in a dishonest and fraudulent design on the part of the trustees.*"[421]

This translated that even though the respondent was acting outside the duties of the trustee company, he was equally liable under law for the process which the agent had dishonestly employed when using trust funds for unintended purposes. Such a position was further strengthened by the words of Thomas J in *Powell v Thompson*, who stressed:

> "Once a breach of trust has been committed, the commission of which has involved a third party, the question which arises is one as between the beneficiary and that third party. If the third party's conduct has been unconscionable, then *irrespective of the degree of impropriety in the trustee's conduct, the third party is liable to be held accountable to the beneficiary as if he or she were a trustee.*"[422]

In the first instance, the court awarded in favour of the airline, yet in the Court of Appeal the judgment was reversed on grounds that a mere breach of trust was no indication of

---

[421] *Barnes v Addy* (1874) LR 9 Ch App 244 (Ch) 251-252 (Selbourne LC) (emphasis added).

[422] *Powell v Thompson* [1991] 1 NZLR 597 (HC) 613 (Thomas J) (emphasis added).

dishonesty, and unless such conduct was proven, there could be no justifiable reasons for imputing dishonesty for the sake of remedy. Having then appealed before the Privy Council, the facts were reconsidered along with the objective standards of honesty. Here it was once again found that despite protestations of accidental misplacement of trust funds, the respondent had admitted to a breach of trust, and although he intended to repay the appellants the princely sum of $335,000, there had been sufficient knowledge shown by the respondent that his improper use of trust property was wrong, and that his actions had been critical to the travel agent's breach of trust, therefore the original judgment was restored with costs.

Key Citations

"Liability as an accessory is not dependent upon receipt of trust property. It arises even though no trust property has reached the hands of the accessory. It is a form of secondary liability in the sense that it only arises where there has been a breach of trust."[423]

"[A] trust is a relationship which exists when one person holds property on behalf of another. If, for his own purposes, a third party deliberately interferes in that relationship by assisting the trustee in depriving the beneficiary of the property held for him by the trustee, the beneficiary should be able to look for recompense to the third party as well as the trustee."[424]

"The standard of what constitutes honest conduct is not subjective. Honesty is not an optional scale, with higher or lower values according to the moral standards of each individual. If a person knowingly appropriates another's property, he will not escape a finding of dishonesty simply because he sees nothing wrong in such behaviour."[425]

"[D]ishonesty is a necessary ingredient of accessory liability. It is also a sufficient ingredient. A liability in equity to make good resulting loss attaches to a person who dishonestly procures or assists in a breach of trust or fiduciary obligation."[426]

---

[423] *Royal Brunei Airlines v Tan* [1995] 3 All ER 97 (PC) 382 (Nicholls LJ).

[424] *Royal Brunei Airlines v Tan* [1995] 3 All ER 97 (PC) 386 (Nicholls LJ).

[425] *Royal Brunei Airlines v Tan* [1995] 3 All ER 97 (PC) 389 (Nicholls LJ).

[426] *Royal Brunei Airlines v Tan* [1995] 3 All ER 97 (PC) 392 (Nicholls LJ).

19. Twinsectra Ltd v Yardley

Dishonesty, or knowing assistance, are two distinguishable phrases, yet seem to have become tarred with the same brush within civil and equitable matters. In this instance, the defendant solicitor was accused of enabling a breach of duty by subjectively distancing themselves from their actions; while the question remained as to whether this had been through deviance, or self-appointed exclusion.

When a property developer expressed an interest in the considerable purchase of a selection of properties, he approached his bank for a loan of £1m. When the bank failed to respond as anticipated, he looked further afield in order to secure the homes with haste. Having consulted an alternative lender, a loan was agreed on the condition that a solicitor underwrote the arrangement, in order to provide the required level of security. When the developer's solicitor (solicitor A) refused to support the loan, he turned instead to another local practice (solicitor B), with whom he had a trading history, and one that had resulted in solicitor B owing a debt to the developer of £1.5m.

In order to circumvent the complexities of the planned loan, solicitor B took it upon themselves to borrow the money directly, on the pretence that they were acting on behalf of the developer, but in truth it was to help clear the substantial debt owed to the developer. The terms of the loan were such that the developer was eligible for the sum determined on the proviso that the loan was to be used for property acquisition, and that B was under a duty to ensure that those terms were adhered to.

Under acceptance of the contracted agreement, solicitor B entered into to dealings wth the lenders, after which solicitor B informed solicitor A that it would be sending the money to them to hold on trust for the developer until required. Solicitor A was also aware of the express terms of the loan after receiving a draft copy of the agreement letter from solicitor B, and so agreed to receive the funds on behalf of the developer until such time as they were needed, despite solicitor B contracting to hold the funds themselves when taking out the loan.

What transpired was that the developer then obtained release of the funds from solicitor A, in the knowledge that only part of those funds were to be used for property purchases, and without solicitor A making enquiries to ascertain their use, as per the terms of the loan. When the loan failed to be repaid through the insolvency of solicitor B, the lenders sought damages against solicitor A, for having dishonestly assisted in a breach of contract, that left them liable for almost £360,000 in unrecovered debt.

When heard in the original trial, it was found by the judge that under the unusual terms of the arrangement, and through uncertainty as to the beneficiaries, (i) no trust could be held to exist and (ii) solicitor A's ignorance of his obligations was insufficient enough to warrant dishonesty when releasing the funds to the developer. When challenged, the Court of Appeal reversed the decision in favour of the lender, and held that solicitor A had been fully converse to the terms of the loan when forgoing them in subjective dissonance to his own responsibility, and therefore knowingly enabled a breach of trust arising by virtue of the loan's construction.

Finally brought before the House of Lords, the notion of 'dishonesty' as a subjective trait was given weighted evaluation, while the exact nature of beneficial interest was equally debated. Having considered the exhaustive previous cross-examination of solicitor A, along with the conflict of criminal and civil law interpretations of dishonesty, it was felt that despite lingering uncertainty as to his self-determined innocence, it would be remiss of the House to undermine the mens rea of the first judge on both counts, therefore the appeal was upheld with only one (albeit compelling) dissension.

Key Citations

"[D]ishonesty requires knowledge by the defendant that what he was doing would be regarded as dishonest by honest people, although he should not escape a finding of dishonesty because he sets his own standards of honesty and does not regard as dishonest what he knows would offend the normally accepted standards of honest conduct."[427]

"[A] loan to a borrower for a specific purpose where the borrower is not free to apply the money for any other purpose gives rise to fiduciary obligations on the part of the borrower which a court of equity will enforce. It is unconscionable for a man to obtain money on terms as to its application and then disregard the terms on which he received it. Such conduct goes beyond a mere breach of contract."[428]

"[A] person who makes money available on terms that it is to be used for a particular purpose only and not for any other purpose thereby places his trust and confidence in the recipient to ensure that it is properly applied. This is a classic situation in which a fiduciary relationship arises, and since it arises in respect of a specific fund it gives rise to a trust."[429]

"[I]f the borrower is treated as holding the money on a resulting trust for the lender but with power (or in some cases a duty) to carry out the lender's revocable mandate, and the lender's object in giving the mandate is frustrated, he is entitled to revoke the mandate and demand the return of money which never ceased to be his beneficially."[430]

"[E]quity looks to a man's conduct, not to his state of mind."[431]

"Where a third party with knowledge of a contract has dealings with the contract breaker which the third party knows will amount to a breach of contract and damage results, he commits an actionable interference with the contract."[432]

---

[427] *Twinsectra Ltd v Francis John Yardley* [2002] 2 All ER 377 [36] (Hutton LJ).

[428] *Twinsectra Ltd v Francis John Yardley* [2002] 2 All ER 377 [68] (Millett LJ).

[429] *Twinsectra Ltd v Francis John Yardley* [2002] 2 All ER 377 [76] (Millett LJ).

[430] *Twinsectra Ltd v Francis John Yardley* [2002] 2 All ER 377 [98] (Millett LJ).

[431] *Twinsectra Ltd v Francis John Yardley* [2002] 2 All ER 377 [123] (Millett LJ).

[432] *Twinsectra Ltd v Francis John Yardley* [2002] 2 All ER 377 [128] (Millett LJ).

20. Vandervell v IRC

Avoidance of duty through the floatation of a private business, was the driving force behind what some might describe as a text book error in accounting procedure, and one that on this occasion, left the owner (and his trusted colleagues) feeling less than savvy.

Having already positioned himself as a controlling shareholder, the director of a vibrant engineering company took steps to create a trust company, before appointing his three friends as trustees for the purpose of two previously created trusts. When explained that making the firm open to public investment would attract increased wealth, the appellant expressed that he was now looking to set up another trust using 100,000 shares, in order to circumvent excess taxation through estate duty after his passing.

The initial plan was that an employee trust could serve to not only benefit his workers, but help avoid the inevitable revenue claims, however nothing went beyond the drafting stage. After looking further afield, the appellant then chose to secure a pharmacology chair at a nearby surgical college, and set out to establish this at a cost of £150,000, as per the terms set by the institution. When in many instances a simple cash payment would suffice, the appellant (under advisement by one of his accountant trustees), elected to have his bank transfer the shares to the college, whereupon dividends to the amount of £150,000 would be paid over a specific period.

With consideration of the plan to go public, the trustee then advised that the best course of action would be to request that the college allow for an option to repurchase the shares for a small sum, in order to prevent any concerns by potential stock market investors when assessing the pattern of ownership. In light of this, the college were asked for their compliance, at which point they duly acquiesced, as their interests were purely fiscal. This led to a deed of variation comprising payment of £145,000, followed by the immediate repurchase of the 100,000 shares for a sum of £5,000; after which the property would be held upon trust by the trust company, until such time as it would be decided by the trustees to place them in a suitable trust of their choice.

When carrying out the transfer, the bank were asked to leave the transferee name space blank, while following all other legal requirements for a successful gift. It was made expressly clear by his letter, that the appellant had relinquished any interest whatsoever in the shares, and that the trustees were to act as they saw fit. Upon receipt of the share certificates, the college signed themselves as shareholders, and were duly added to the company register, in accordance with company laws.

When the Inland Revenue learned of this transaction, it was claimed that the appellant had failed to act outside of his settlor obligations, and that under s.415 of the Income Tax Act 1952, it was declared that any income generated under a settlement paid to another person other than the settlor, and where the settlor has not released himself of his legal and equitable interest, the money will be construed as that of the settlor and taxed accordingly.

When brought before the courts, it was first found that the appellant had acted in error, and that liability to taxation was due. When appealed, the outcome was much the same, and so granted leave to present before the House of Lords, the judges took steps to examine the finer points of the transaction.

While arguments as to s.53 of the Law of Property Act 1925 rested upon written dispositions (or a lack of it in this case), the root of the matter was more about the assignation of the shares, with the intention to recoup equitable and legal title upon the final dividend sum. This was where the appellant contested that there had been no retention of interest, but rather an alternate means of investment and transferral to his trustees.

With a fiercely divided judgment, it was found on the facts, rather than any principle of law, that while the construction of a repurchase option was not entirely fatal to the existence of a disposition, the absence of a named transferee meant that until such time as one appeared, the shares and any revenue attached to them, remained the property of the appellant settlor, therefore the implications of s.415 of the Income Tax Act 1952 remained in effect, and any undeclared revenue was now taxable.

Key Citations

"The directors were not lawyers and clearly knew nothing about the legal position. But in any event it is the intention of the donor and not the belief of the donee that matters."[433]

"The grant of an option to purchase is very different from a grant of a legal estate in some real or personal property without consideration to a person nominated by the beneficial owner."[434]

"If, owning the entire estate, legal and beneficial, in a piece of property, and desiring to transfer that entire estate to another, I do so by means of a disposition which ex facie deals only with the legal estate, it would be ridiculous to argue that section 53(1)(c) has not been complied with, and that therefore the legal estate alone has passed."[435]

"To extract from the findings a conclusion that the trustee company was to hold free from any trust but possibly subject to some understanding or gentleman's agreement seems to me, rather than even a benevolent interpretation of the evidence, a reconstruction of it."[436]

"[H]e had, as the direct result of the option and of the failure to place the beneficial interest in it securely away from him, not divested himself absolutely of the shares which it controlled."[437]

---

[433] *Vandervell v IRC* [1966] Ch 261 (HL) 309 (Reid LJ).

[434] *Vandervell v IRC* [1966] Ch 261 (HL) 314 (Upjohn LJ).

[435] *Vandervell v IRC* [1966] Ch 261 (HL) 317 (Donovan LJ).

[436] *Vandervell v IRC* [1966] Ch 261 (HL) 328 (Wilberforce LJ).

[437] *Vandervell v IRC* [1966] Ch 261 (HL) 329 (Wilberforce LJ).

5. European Law

1. Adeneler and others v Ellinikos Organismos Galaklos (ELOG)

Workers rights directly related to the powers conferred under a Framework Agreement annexed to Council Directive 1999/70/EC, were given new protections in instances where fixed-term employment contracts were no longer seen as helpful, but in fact deemed contrary to the security of European citizens.

In this matter, a collective claim was put before the Greek Monomeles Protodikio Thessalonikis (Court of the First Instance) by eighteen publicly employed staff of the Greek Milk Organisation (ELOG), after the firm failed to renew their fixed-term contracts.

The aim of the Framework Agreement was to reduce inherent abuses found in all forms of employment, and so by reducing the duration of recurring fixed-term contracts, it was intended that unless an employer could demonstrate that repeated fix-term employment contracts served both the employer and employee, it was required by the terms of the agreement that they were to become contracts of 'indefinite duration'.

While it is agreed under Community law principles that Member States are expected to transpose Directives within a predetermined period, the Greek government applied under para.2 of Directive 1999/70 for an extension of two years, in which to adopt the terms prescribed. It was however, not fully transposed until April 2003, under the Presidential Decree No.81/2003, which was later superseded by Presidential Decree 164/2004.

Protections for public employees found in the Framework Agreement were then presented in such a way as their employers could continue using fixed-term employment contracts for 'seasonal purposes', or in times requiring periodic or temporary needs, as explained in art.21 of Law No.2190/1994. This was further supported by art.5 of Presidential Decree 164/2004, which provided that successive contracts of employment enjoyed by the same worker were prohibited if contract renewal periods were greater than three months.

On this occasion, the claimants had worked under contracts lasting no more than eight months, and whose renewals ranged between twenty-two days and eleven months; therefore they argued that cessation of their employment constituted a breach under the terms of the Framework Agreement and Directive 1999/70, as they had all been employed for fixed and permanent needs, as opposed to those described in art.21 of Law No.2190/1994.

When referred to the European Court of Justice under art.234 EC, the court sought preliminary ruling as to four questions, namely (i) the exact date of effect of Directive 1999/70, (ii) the definition of 'objective reasons' as per clause 5(1)(a) of the Framework Agreement when determining the renewal of fixed-term contracts, (iii) the practicality of Presidential Decree 81/2003 when interposed with the terms of the Directive, and (iv) whether the limitations of art.21 of Law No.2190/1994 allowed for abuses in contrast to the reductive effects of the Framework Agreement.

Having appreciated the somewhat unnecessary aims of the questions, it was agreed by the Court of Justice that (i) the date of effect was that of the publication of the Directive, which was July 1999 and not April 2003, (ii) that national legislation cannot overrule the aims of objective reasoning, as prescribed within the framework agreement, (iii) that clause 5(1)(a) to (c) offered a number of available measures to the Member States in order to reduce contractual abuses, and (iv) that the same clause again offered sufficient remedies in order to fully support the effects of Directive 1999/70 and the Framework Agreement.

Key Citations

"[T]he definition of 'fixed-term workers' for the purposes of the Framework Agreement, set out in clause 3(1), encompasses all workers without drawing a distinction according to whether their employer is in the public, or private, sector."[438]

"[T]o admit that a national provision may, automatically and without further precision, justify successive fixed-term employment contracts would effectively have no regard to the aim of the Framework Agreement, which is to protect workers against instability of employment, and render meaningless the principle that contracts of indefinite duration are the general form of employment relationship."[439]

"[D]irectives are either (i) published in the Official Journal of the European Communities in accordance with Article 254(1) EC and, in that case, enter into force on the date specified in them or, in the absence thereof, on the 20th day following that of their publication, or (ii) notified to those to whom they are addressed, in which case they take effect upon such notification, in accordance with Article 254(3) EC."[440]

"[F]rom the date upon which a Directive has entered into force, the courts of the Member States must refrain as far as possible from interpreting domestic law in a manner which might seriously compromise, after the period for transposition has expired, attainment of the objective pursued by that Directive."[441]

---

[438] *Adeneler and others v Ellinikos Organismos Galaklos (ELOG)* [Case C-212/04] [2006] ECR I-6057, para 56 (ECJ).

[439] *Adeneler and others v Ellinikos Organismos Galaklos (ELOG)* [Case C-212/04] [2006] ECR I-6057, para 73 (ECJ).

[440] *Adeneler and others v Ellinikos Organismos Galaklos (ELOG)* [Case C-212/04] [2006] ECR I-6057, para 118 (ECJ).

[441] *Adeneler and others v Ellinikos Organismos Galaklos (ELOG)* [Case C-212/04] [2006] ECR I-6057, para 123 (ECJ).

2. CILFIT and Lanificio di Gavardo SpA v Ministry of Health

Member State compliance with Community law is brought into question, when an Italian national court seeks to address the contention of their Ministry for Health that domestic laws preclude a right to claim, and that no Regulatory terms could provide a different outcome.

When a claim was made by a number of textile firms against the excessive taxation of imported wool, it relied upon the powers conferred by Regulation 827/68/EEC, and not the discriminatory rules set down by national statute. Under the powers of Law No.30, the companies had been forced to pay levies ten times the amount intended, until the amendment under Law No.1239, after which the action began.

Having been dismissed of a right to recover in the Tribunal di Roma (District Court), the claimants were also told that the adoption of Regulation 827/68 had, by extension of the products listed, excluded wool from the scope of that Community law, and that no such claim could stand. When pursued in the Corte d'Appello (Court of Appeal), the entire claim was rejected in conjunction with the argument presented by the Ministry of Health, that the terms of the Regulation did not encompass wool, therefore no compensation was owed.

When further appealed to the Court of Cassation, the Ministry of Health cross-appealed, while attempting to persuade the Court to decide the outcome without referring to the European Court of Justice for a preliminary ruling under art.177 EC.

This was construed by the Court that by virtue of the fact that the Ministry of Health had claimed there was no need to consult the Court of Justice, there must be a degree of uncertainty as to the effect of Regulation 827/68, and that while no national legislation provided a remedy, such a duty existed. In accordance with its perceived obligations, the Court of Cassation asked whether para.3 of art.177 EC required, under circumstances such as the one presented, the national courts (or courts of first instance) to seek a preliminary ruling, where uncertainty or doubt as to the interpretation of a Regulation existed.

Having evaluated the intentions and possible variances of art.177 EC, it was agreed by the European Court of Justice, that while certain discretions were provided for when adopting and applying the terms of Community law, the obligation to seek a preliminary ruling was one designed to establish clarity; and so even if the questions arose from claimants, government or the courts themselves, it was important that the courts looked at the complexity of the doubt, and sought where relevant, the assistance of the Court of Justice, so that (i) the effect of the Regulation or Directive was established and (ii) the aims of Community law remained superior to those of national significance.

Key Citations

"[T]here is no reason why the court's power to submit a question for a preliminary ruling of its own motion should be confused with its discretion to determine whether it is appropriate to submit such a question."[442]

"[T]he oft-repeated latin maxim *"in claris not fit interpretatio"* should be abandoned, since it is through the interpretation of a provision that it is possible to ascertain whether its meaning is clear or obscure."[443]

"[T]he claim for wider powers for the judiciary in relation to certain prerogatives of the executive is quite distinct from the division between the tasks of interpretation entrusted to the national courts of last instance, on the one hand, and those entrusted to the Court of Justice of the European Communities, on the other."[444]

"The requirement that courts or tribunals of last instance must always refer questions to the Court of Justice for a preliminary ruling is supported by the specific technical and formal characteristics of Community law…"[445]

"[T]he obligation to refer a matter to the Court for a preliminary ruling comes into existence, in the case of courts of last instance, only where there is an interpretative doubt…"[446]

"A uniform interpretation of Community law by the Court is objectively in the public interest, which may not be subordinated to the existence or otherwise of agreement between the national courts in the previous stages of an action or to the assent or dissent of the parties."[447]

"[T]he course of a specific action before a national court cannot affect the scope of the obligation laid down by the third paragraph of Article 177."[448]

---

[442] *CILFIT and Lanificio di Gavardo SpA v Ministry of Health* [Case 283/81] [1982] ECR 3415, Opinion of AG Capotorti, para 3.

[443] *CILFIT and Lanificio di Gavardo SpA v Ministry of Health* [Case 283/81] [1982] ECR 3415, Opinion of AG Capotorti, para 4.

[444] *CILFIT and Lanificio di Gavardo SpA v Ministry of Health* [Case 283/81] [1982] ECR 3415, Opinion of AG Capotorti, para 4.

[445] *CILFIT and Lanificio di Gavardo SpA v Ministry of Health* [Case 283/81] [1982] ECR 3415, Opinion of AG Capotorti, para 6.

[446] *CILFIT and Lanificio di Gavardo SpA v Ministry of Health* [Case 283/81] [1982] ECR 3415, Opinion of AG Capotorti, para 9.

[447] *CILFIT and Lanificio di Gavardo SpA v Ministry of Health* [Case 283/81] [1982] ECR 3415, Opinion of AG Capotorti, para 9.

[448] *CILFIT and Lanificio di Gavardo SpA v Ministry of Health* [Case 283/81] [1982] ECR 3415, Opinion of AG Capotorti, para 9.

3. Commission v United Kingdom [Excise Duties on Wine]

Member State obligations to observe the fairness of the European market when allowing for competition, were crystallised in this taxation matter surrounding the importation and domestic production of alcoholic drinks.

The terms of art.95 EC (in particular para.1) were constructed so as to allow, and support, the freedom of competition between Member States when selling comparable products, including alcoholic beverages in their various forms. During a period between 1973 and 1981, the United Kingdom had deliberately increased the taxation rates for bottled wines over that of bottled beers, and the margin between the two had remained disproportionate for a considerable period, thus hampering the sale of affordable imported wines, versus the proliferation of domestic low-volume beers.

When addressed by the European Commission, and under the inference that such disparity amounted to a breach of para.2 of art.95 EC, it was suggested that while running contrary to the harmonisation of Community law, the Member State was, under art.169 EC, now required to submit its own observations in defence of its failure to follow the terms prescribed.

In response, the United Kingdom contested the findings, but with little supporting evidence, prompting the Commission to apply to the European Court of Justice on the strength of the breach, and that by way of reparation, the United Kingdom was to pay the costs of the action. It was shortly afterwards, that the Court allowed Italy to intervene in support of the Commission under art.37 of the Protocol on the Statute of the Court of Justice, and to which the Court then instructed the three parties to reexamine their arguments, and submit relevant chronological sales data before reconvening for judgment.

Having established that the manufacturing processes for beer and wine were comparable, it was then revealed that due to the complex structure of the British market, it was only possible to compare prices through the taxation rates applicable to the volume (strength) of the alcohol in hand. It was this contradistinction that showed clear support for the suggestion that protective measures had been implemented so as to deprive the import of affordable wines from other Member Sates, despite the measures laid down under art.95 and the obligation to follow them.

Citing numerous and unsustainable arguments for the heavy taxation of wines (including manufacturing costs as previously ruled out, and 'social' reasons), the Court held that a serious breach of art.95 EC had been in existence not only for a considerable period, but that recent attempts to narrow the margin were indicative of reasons beyond that expected from a Member State when observing their duty to encourage, and support, free movement of goods and the equality of competition between states.

Key Citations

"[A] Member State may lay down differing tax arrangements even for identical products on the basis of objective criteria provided that such arrangements pursue objectives of economic policy which are themselves compatible with Community law and that they are not discriminatory or protective in nature."[449]

"[W]ine production is not in my opinion afforded indirect protection by higher taxation on beer provided that the price of beer including tax is no higher than the price of the competing wines."[450]

"[I]t seems to me in principle that the symmetrical application of the second paragraph of Article 95 with regard to countries producing mainly beer and those producing mainly wine does not, on the grounds given, lead to consequences which are unacceptable for the Community."[451]

"[T]he tax burden on imported products is so much higher than the tax burden on domestic substitute products that it must be assumed that domestic production of the substitute products is indirectly protected by the taxation on the imported products."[452]

"[D]ifferences in production costs will, as stated above, be expressed in differences in price, so that in the use of the criterion of price they are automatically taken into account in the comparison of the tax burden."[453]

"From the objective of the second paragraph of Article 95 together with the general scheme of the Treaty it in fact follows that proof of a clear restriction of competition with regard to imported products which separately or collectively have an appreciable share of the market in those products is of itself sufficient to establish an infringement of that provision."[454]

---

[449] *Commission v United Kingdom [Excise Duties on Wine]* [Case 170/78] [1980] ECR 417, Opinion of AG Verloren van Themaat, para 1.5.

[450] *Commission v United Kingdom [Excise Duties on Wine]* [Case 170/78] [1980] ECR 417, Opinion of AG Verloren van Themaat, para 2.5.

[451] *Commission v United Kingdom [Excise Duties on Wine]* [Case 170/78] [1980] ECR 417, Opinion of AG Verloren van Themaat, para 2.5.

[452] *Commission v United Kingdom [Excise Duties on Wine]* [Case 170/78] [1980] ECR 417, Opinion of AG Verloren van Themaat, para 2.6.

[453] *Commission v United Kingdom [Excise Duties on Wine]* [Case 170/78] [1980] ECR 417, Opinion of AG Verloren van Themaat, para 3.1.

[454] *Commission v United Kingdom [Excise Duties on Wine]* [Case 170/78] [1980] ECR 417, Opinion of AG Verloren van Themaat, para 3.1.

4. Courage Ltd v Crehan

Under English law, the courts refuse to endorse a claim for damages when the claimant was a party to a contract borne from illegal principles. This is echoed in equity under the maxim 'he who comes to equity must come with clean hands', and reminds those considering such arrangements that they do so without the aid of the judiciary.

In this matter the claimant was a party to a publican agreement drawn up through the merger of a large brewery and owners of a number of public houses across the United Kingdom. As part of this agreement, the claimant brewery supplied beer to existing tenants (publicans) under a non-negotiable tariff, purportedly designed to protect the interests and profits of those purchasing.

After the tenant amassed a debt of around £15,000, the brewery sought recovery through the courts. Having previously discovered that the brewery was supplying the same beers for lower prices to non-contracted third parties, it was counter-claimed that the agreement demonstrated a breach of art.85 EC, and that damages were owed, while no payment for beers previously provided was due.

Having reached the Court of Appeal, it was decided that due to the conflict between national and Community law, a preliminary ruling to the European Court of Justice under art.234 EC was necessary in order to reach summary judgment. With this came four questions asking (i) whether art.85 EC allowed a party to a prohibited agreement to claim damages, (ii) whether a party can claim when relying upon their own adherence to the agreement, (iii) whether a national law preventing recovery under prohibited agreements remained consistent with Community law, and (iv) where deemed incompatible, which situations allowed national law to apply.

Having evaluated the aims of national law, and determining the validity of claim under such circumstances, it was noted that while those contracting in the distortion of fair competition are themselves contributors to their own demise, there are scenarios that demonstrate an inequality of bargaining power and therefore grounds for reconsideration. In this instance, the tenant was subjected to the terms of the agreement with little no room for bargain, and so while it was agreed that the terms of art.85 EC precluded claims of that nature, it did so on the proviso that the claimant was proportionately liable for the market distortion.

On this occasion, it was clear that where no such arrangement existed, the effects of art. 85 EC, which provided for direct effect and application between individuals, were sufficient enough to allow for a claim, despite the objections raised under English law.

Key Citations

"[P]ursuant to the principle of cooperation laid down in Article 10 EC, it is the national courts which are entrusted with ensuring the legal protection which citizens derive from the direct effect of the provisions of Community law."[455]

"[W]here a party is too small to resist the economic pressure imposed on it by the more powerful undertaking - there is no reason to deny that party the protection of Article 81 EC."[456]

"[A]rticle 81 EC protects not only third parties from the effects of an agreement but also, in exceptional circumstances, a party to the agreement where that party bears no significant responsibility for the distortion of competition."[457]

"[C]ommunity law precludes a rule of national law which prevents a party subject to a clause in a contract which infringes Article 81 EC from recovering damages for the loss suffered by it on the sole ground that it is a party to that contract."[458]

"[T]he circumstances in which a person's own illegal actions can be invoked to bar his right to seek damages should be limited to cases where the party seeking relief is indeed *in pari delicto* in having at least equal responsibility for the restriction of competition from which it seeks relief."[459]

---

[455] *Courage Ltd v Crehan* [Case C-453/99] [2001] ECR I-6297, Opinion of AG Mischo, para 46.

[456] *Courage Ltd v Crehan* [Case C-453/99] [2001] ECR I-6297, Opinion of AG Mischo, para 43.

[457] *Courage Ltd v Crehan* [Case C-453/99] [2001] ECR I-6297, Opinion of AG Mischo, para 44.

[458] *Courage Ltd v Crehan* [Case C-453/99] [2001] ECR I-6297, Opinion of AG Mischo, para 60.

[459] *Courage Ltd v Crehan* [Case C-453/99] [2001] ECR I-6297, Opinion of AG Mischo, para 65.

5. Defrenne v SABENA

The effects of art.119 EC, and the stark inequality between men and women in the workplace, were brought together in a case that demonstrated the power of law, and showcased the equitability of the European Community.

When employed as an air hostess in 1963 by Belgian Société Anonyme Belge de Navigation Aérienne (SABENA), the appellant to the Court of Justice was re-contracted as a Cabin Steward and Air Hostess that translated as a Principal Cabin Attendant. The caveat to this contract was that unlike her male counterparts, she was expected to return from her duties at the age of forty. Upon termination of her employment, she also received twelve months severance pay, but was denied any pension rights, as per the contract.

Shortly afterwards, the appellant initiated proceedings against her former employers, claiming discrimination for a number of matters, including the assertion of her rights to equal pay under the terms of art.119 EC. Despite her ardent contentions, the Tribunal du Travail of Brussels dismissed her claims outright, which resulted in her appeal to the Cour du Travail of Brussels, where the majority of her claims were denied, with the exception of inequality of salary. While the court was in a position to overrule its own legislation in favour of the Treaty article, it chose instead to seek a preliminary ruling by the Court of Justice.

First introduced in 1957, the Treaty of Rome included within art.119 EC, the express requirement that every Member State would ensure, and maintain, the application of the principle that men and women should receive equal pay for equal work. The initial adoption period was set at two years, and yet Belgium never amended its own legislation to reflect the values of the Treaty Article until 1967, in which s.14 of Royal Decree 40 enabled women in such situations, the rights to seek remedy within the national courts.

The defence put forward by the Belgian government was that while art.119 conferred powers to those women paid less than men in similar roles, the effect of that principle was construed as narrow to the limitations of public office, and thus private contractual negotiations were beyond that remit. This argument was founded upon the implied financial costs of regulating matters that might be placed before the courts, and the time spent correcting those deficiencies within the judicial system.

The claimant countered that by all accounts the direct effect of art.119 EC had existed since 1957, and as such provided her with retrospective rights of recovery, where previously challenged. While the direct effect of that power was held in question, it was clarified by the Advocate General, that direct effect relied upon the clarity of the regulation, and that when addressing matters of inequality between men and women it was clear that the purpose of such a principle rested upon the individual differences cited, therefore no obstacle to its effectiveness could stand.

In closing, the Court ruled that as of the date of the hearing, the national courts were to refrain from reference to art.177 EC in order to seek preliminary rulings, when there was sufficient cause within art.119 EC to overrule (where needed), domestic legislation in full accordance with the rule of Community law. Despite wishing to allow backdated claims for pay-related matters, the Commission was the first to admit that a lack of enforcement of art.119 EC, had denied them the right to extend recovery for predated instances, separate from those that had been previously raised.

Key Citations

"[T]he fact that the concepts relied upon in a provision require interpretation by the national court, which may, inter alia, avail itself of the procedure in Article 177 of the Treaty, constitutes no obstacle to recognition of its direct effect."[460]

"From the precedents established by this Court it is clear that an Article of the Treaty does not cease to have direct effect merely because it imposes on the States an obligation to act, provided that the obligation is expressed clearly and unconditionally, its tenor is precise and no real discretion is left to the Member States with respect to the application of the provision."[461]

"Article 119, despite the fact that it is restricted to imposing an obligation on the States, is primarily concerned with the relationship between individuals. The discrimination which the provision sets out to prohibit will, in the majority of cases, consist of discriminatory action by a private undertaking against women workers."[462]

"The decisive factor in determining what the effects of a Community provision are in national law is not the identity of those to whom it is addressed but its nature, which the Court defines on the basis of 'the spirit, the general scheme and the wording' of the provision itself."[463]

"It is no more difficult for the national court to disallow a discriminatory contractual agreement than to disallow a national law which is incompatible with the Treaty or to award compensation to an individual who has suffered damage as the result of such a law."[464]

"[T]he fact that certain provisions of the Treaty are formally addressed to the Member States does not prevent rights from being conferred at the same time on any individual who has an interest in the performance of the duties thus laid down."[465]

---

[460] *Defrenne v SABENA* [Case 43/75] [1976] ECR 455, Opinion of AG Trabucchi, para 4.

[461] *Defrenne v SABENA* [Case 43/75] [1976] ECR 455, Opinion of AG Trabucchi, para 5.

[462] *Defrenne v SABENA* [Case 43/75] [1976] ECR 455, Opinion of AG Trabucchi, para 6.

[463] *Defrenne v SABENA* [Case 43/75] [1976] ECR 455, Opinion of AG Trabucchi, para 6.

[464] *Defrenne v SABENA* [Case 43/75] [1976] ECR 455, Opinion of AG Trabucchi, para 7.

[465] *Defrenne v SABENA* [Case C 43/75] [1976] ECR 455, para 31 (ECJ).

6. Faccini Dori v Recreb Srl

Private contracts between individuals are often overlooked in terms of actual rights, so when an Italian consumer entered into an agreement to purchase an English language course while visiting a railway terminal, the vendor looked to enforce the contract when notified that her order was to be cancelled.

Relying upon Doorstep Selling Directive 85/577/EEC, the applicant issued proceedings against the vendor, and contended to the Giudice Concilliatore (Judge-Concillaitor) that arts.1(1), 2 and 5 conferred protective measures that allowed for rescindable notice within a period of seven days between consumers and private companies; which on this occasion was undertaken through written instruction to the contracting parties.

While the Directive had been in force for a number of years, the Italian government had failed to transpose it within the time allowed, therefore no domestic legislation existed concerning the facts of the case. As was common knowledge to Member States, a failure to adopt Directives in the prescribed period results in a loss of profit to the Member State, when defending against direct effect claims by their citizens. In this instance however, the terms of the Directive, while both clear and precise, were related to dealings between individuals, and therefore not subject to the benefit of protection, unless transposed under the guidance of Community law, and within the adoption window.

This presented the national court with a dilemma, inasmuch as they were unable to determine exactly what rights the claimant had when seeking cancellation of the contract, and if consideration was ultimately due to the vendor, as per the terms of their agreement. For this reason, the court sought a preliminary ruling under art.177 EC, and requested that the European Court of Justice clarify (i) if the terms of the Directive were clear and precise enough to provide direct effect, and (ii) whether despite a failure to adopt the measures in accordance with the Treaty, the claimant could rely upon them to enforce her individual right to cancel.

Having examined the arguments around horizontal effect between parties, and the power of Directives, it was agreed that for reasons of legal certainty, future consideration must be given to broaden the scope of those entitlements when applying them to private and not public matters. That aside, it was still held that although the terms of the Directive were relative to horizontal dealings, it was not possible for the claimant to rely upon them when seeking to terminate her agreement with the vendor. However, because the Italian government had failed to adopt the Directive, and in light of the fact that there existed no domestic legislation to settle the matter, it was now possible for the national courts to transpose the effects of the Doorstep Selling Directive, in order that a remedy could be provided in favour of the consumer.

Key Citations

"The obligation to ensure the effectiveness of Community law by way of interpretation does not relate only to the legislation adopted in order to implement a Directive, but to the national legal system as a whole."[466]

"In the case of Directives whose content is intended to have effects in relations between private persons and which embody provisions designed to protect the weaker party, it is obvious that the failure to transpose a Directive deprives it of effet utile."[467]

"Member States are not entitled to invoke, after the expiry of the period for transposition, freedoms which were conferred on them only for the purposes of the due implementation of the Directive within the time limit laid down."[468]

"Directives are not measures of lesser quality but are addressed, with a view to their implementation, to the Member States, which are under an obligation under the Treaty to transpose them into national law in full and in good time."[469]

"For reasons of *legal certainty*, which is a fundamental right of the citizen on whom a burden is imposed, the public must be prepared as of now for the fact that Directives will in future have to be recognised as having horizontal direct effect…"[470]

"[H]orizontal effect seems to me to be necessary, subject to the limits mentioned, in the interests of the uniform, effective application of Community law. In my view the resulting burdens on private individuals are reasonable, since they do not exceed the constraints which would have been applied to them if the Member State concerned had acted in conformity with Community law."[471]

"[I]n the absence of measures transposing the Directive within the prescribed time limit, consumers cannot derive from the Directive itself a right of cancellation as against traders with whom they have concluded a contract or enforce such a right in a national court."[472]

"Where damage has been suffered and that damage is due to a breach by the State of its obligation, it is for the national court to uphold the right of aggrieved consumers to obtain reparation in accordance with national law on liability."[473]

---

[466] *Faccini Dori v Recreb Srl* [Case C-91/92] [1994] ECR 1-3325, Opinion of AG Lenz, para 36.

[467] *Faccini Dori v Recreb Srl* [Case C-91/92] [1994] ECR 1-3325, Opinion of AG Lenz, para 54.

[468] *Faccini Dori v Recreb Srl* [Case C-91/92] [1994] ECR 1-3325, Opinion of AG Lenz, para 59.

[469] *Faccini Dori v Recreb Srl* [Case C-91/92] [1994] ECR 1-3325, Opinion of AG Lenz, para 60.

[470] *Faccini Dori v Recreb Srl* [Case C-91/92] [1994] ECR 1-3325, Opinion of AG Lenz, para 66.

[471] *Faccini Dori v Recreb Srl* [Case C-91/92] [1994] ECR 1-3325, Opinion of AG Lenz, para 73.

[472] *Faccini Dori v Recreb Srl* [Case C-91/92] [1994] ECR 1-3325, para 25 (ECJ).

[473] *Faccini Dori v Recreb Srl* [Case C-91/92] [1994] ECR 1-3325, para 29 (ECJ).

7. Foster v British Gas

In the same vein as *Marshall*[474] determined the rights of female employees under the protections of Directive 76/207/EEC, this class action matter extended the scope of the principles, so as to allow those claiming the right to recover damages for untimely dismissal through the purposes of retirement.

When six former workers were forced to retire at the age of sixty, they took the collective steps of seeking remedy through the industrial tribunals, on grounds that their employer British Gas Plc, had violated its obligation to observe the principles of equality contained under the Directive, and that as such, they were entitled to compensatory payment for significant financial loss.

When first heard, their claims were dismissed on the strength that British Gas Corporation had since 1986, become a private entity, and therefore fell outside the scope of the Directive, while operating under the validity of s.6(4) of the Sex Discrimination Act 1975. A subsequent appeal to the Employment Appeal Tribunal met with the same fate, before pursuance in the Court of Appeal was again fatal.

In 1989, the applicants appealed to the House of Lords, whereupon it was decided that before any judgment could pass, a referral to the European Court of Justice under art. 177 EC was required. There were again, two questions raised, in which the House asked (i) whether the manifestation of British Gas at the time of the claim, was within the terms of the meaning "state", and if so, (ii) what form the award might take. The position of the respondents was that unlike the period where it was state controlled, it had been released of executive powers, and was to all intents and purposes, a privately owned organisation acting within its policy rights.

Having listened to both sides of the argument, the House held that when Directive 76/207 first came into force, it was ignored by the United Kingdom, and subsequently failed to become part of domestic legislation within the timeframe provided. This translated that the respondents were state owned, and subject to the terms of the Gas Act 1972 when the Directive first applied. Therefore, when the state failed to transpose the terms of the Directive, it left itself open to the Community law doctrine that no state can profit from its own failure.

This resulted in an outcome favourable to the appellants, in that the terms of the Directive were fully applicable to the now privately owned corporation, as they qualified as an emanation of the state, and were thus subject to the effects provided under it. When addressing the issue of financial remedy, the House once again reiterated that any decision to measure damages must come from the national court, and when reaching such a figure, it must hold in mind that the payment must run parallel to the injuries suffered, and not remain subject to nominal tariffs.

---

[474] *Marshall v Southampton and South West Area Health Authority [No1]* [Case 152/84] [1986] ECR 723.

Key Citations

"The point is not who is the state or an individual in the abstract, but against whom the failure of a Member State to implement a Directive correctly and in good time in its own legal system can be pleaded, having regard to the underlying reasons."[475]

"[W]henever, in the light of the underlying purpose of the measure, the concept of "the State" is given a broad interpretation, reference is made to the criterion of actual control, dominating influence and the possibility on the part of the authorities to give binding directions, regardless of the manner in which such control is exercised..."[476]

"[T]he assumption is thus that there is a "core" of authority (broadly defined to include all central, regional and local authorities) which, for the purpose of the measure concerned, imparts a public character by its control and influence to other bodies or transactions, even where these are governed by private law."[477]

"[B]oth the criterion "exercise of a public function" and that of "real control" can bring a person, in this case an employer, within the concept of "the State...""[478]

"[T]he concept of a public body must be understood very broadly and that all bodies which pursuant to the constitutional structure of a Member State can exercise any authority over individuals fall within the concept of "the State."[479]

"Once the State (in the broad sense) has retained such a power to exercise influence over a person (in this case the B.G.C.) with regard, inter alia, to the subject matter of the relevant provision of a Directive, from the point of view of individuals it has brought that person within its sphere of authority."[480]

"[T]he State may not benefit from its default in respect of anything that lies within the sphere of responsibility which by its own free choice it has taken upon itself, irrespective of the person through whom that responsibility is exercised."[481]

"[C]ompliance with the law, including Community law binding on the Member State, is an objective of national interest, so that binding instructions could have been given to the B.G.C. to comply with the provisions of Directive (76/207/E.E.C), which at the material time had not been formally implemented in national law."[482]

---

[475] *Foster v British Gas* [Case C-188/89] [1990] ECR 1-3313, Opinion of AG Gerven, para 10.

[476] *Foster v British Gas* [Case C-188/89] [1990] ECR 1-3313, Opinion of AG Gerven, para 16.

[477] *Foster v British Gas* [Case C-188/89] [1990] ECR 1-3313, Opinion of AG Gerven, para 16.

[478] *Foster v British Gas* [Case C-188/89] [1990] ECR 1-3313, Opinion of AG Gerven, para 20.

[479] *Foster v British Gas* [Case C-188/89] [1990] ECR 1-3313, Opinion of AG Gerven, para 21.

[480] *Foster v British Gas* [Case C-188/89] [1990] ECR 1-3313, Opinion of AG Gerven, para 21.

[481] *Foster v British Gas* [Case C-188/89] [1990] ECR 1-3313, Opinion of AG Gerven, para 21.

[482] *Foster v British Gas* [Case C-188/89] [1990] ECR 1-3313, Opinion of AG Gerven, para 22.

8. Francovich and others v Italy

The adoption of EU Directives, is a prerequisite for all Member States, and so when ignorance of the duty to transpose those obligations into the fabric of national and Community law remains unaddressed, there comes along the perfect vehicle with which to underline it.

The importance of employee rights is one frequently contested in all forms of commerce so when Italy failed to adopt Directive 80/97/EEC (which contained inherent direct effects), it was the joint action of a group of factory workers, that drew the attention of the European Community towards the heart of industry, and the anger of those being abused within the market system.

After serving as a loyal employee for an electronics firm, the claimant found himself redundant through the process of liquidation, and yet left (i) unpaid in full for the work he had undertaken and (ii) uncompensated for loss of earnings, that had the Directive been in effect within the national legislature, would have arisen by default. In a conjoined hearing, Danila Bonifaci and thirty-three other employees (case C-9/90) had fallen victim to a similar fate, and were thus embraced within the same matter.

Following the request for a preliminary hearing, the first approach taken by the Court of Justice was to determine if, by failing to recognise it's obligations to adjust domestic laws in line with Community Directives, the Italian government had rendered itself liable to individual enforcement of accountability for payment of lost earnings (within a discretionary period). Or failing that approach, whether the pecuniary losses sustained by the employees as a result of State avoidance, provided grounds enough to claim damages-based sums instead.

Through observance of the qualifying criteria for direct effect claims, the Court established that the identity of the individual suffering detriment of unadopted rights, the details of those rights lost, and the party liable for grant of those rights, was conclusive; with the exception that through non-adoption, the Member State had not fulfilled a key term of the Directive requiring proper identification of the companies subscribed to those duties. This left the Commission unable to determine who the two employers were, and how they would be obliged to provide payment, or legally defer the onus to the Italian government for issue, which subsequently impacted the claim for damages.

Under well-established case law including *Simmenthal*,[483] precedent showed quite clearly, that the inability to reflect EU laws will not be overlooked, but again used as an example when serving the interests of the Community. This is a principle that not only bears the inherent purpose of collective agreement, but permits restorative justice to those otherwise abused by legislative apathy. When concluding, the Court unanimously agreed that the national courts were held to a duty to redress the inequity of failed transposition, and so full state funded compensation was awarded to the claiming parties.

---

[483] *Simmenthal SpA v Italian Minister of Finance* [Case 35/76] [1976] ECR 1871.

Key Citations

"[I]t seems incompatible with the concept of the direct effect of Directives that where a Directive precisely defines the rights of individuals a Member State should be able to rely on its own failure to comply by asserting that if it had implemented the directive it could properly have set the individual's rights to a lower level."[484]

"[W]herever the provisions of directive appear, as far as their subject matter is concerned, to be unconditional and sufficiently precise, those provisions may, in the absence of implementing measures adopted within the prescribed period, be relied upon as against any national provision which is incompatible with the directive or in so far as the provisions define rights which individuals are able to assert against the State."[485]

"It must be held that the full effectiveness of Community rules would be impaired and the protection of the rights which they grant would be weakened if individuals were unable to obtain compensation when their rights are infringed by a breach of Community law for which a Member State can be held responsible."[486]

"It follows from the foregoing that it is a principle of Community law that the Member States are obliged to pay compensation for harm caused to individuals by breaches of Community law for which they can be held responsible."[487]

---

[484] *Francovich and others v Italy* [Cases C-6 & 9/90] [1991] ECR 1-5357, Opinion of AG Mischo, para 19.

[485] *Francovich and others v Italy* [Cases C-6 & 9/90] [1991] ECR 1-5357, para 11 (ECJ).

[486] *Francovich and others v Italy* [Cases C-6 & 9/90] [1991] ECR 1-5357, para 33 (ECJ).

[487] *Francovich and others v Italy* [Cases C-6 & 9/90] [1991] ECR 1-5357, para 37 (ECJ).

9. Internationale Handelsgesellschaft mbH v Einfuhr-und Vorratsstelle für Getreide und Futtermittel

The implementation of regulatory measures is questioned by the German courts, when an import/export firm is subjected to forfeiture of a deposit, as required by Community law. Under art.12(1) of Regulation 120/67/EEC, the equilibrium of the European market is protected through the issuing of export and import licences. In order to allow for the stability of the grains, cereals and rice values, it was established by the European Council that those traders wishing to operate in this field, must obtain a licence that would clarify the amounts and costs of those products, whilst subject to a predetermined duration.

The reason for this window, was to enable the Commission to anticipate and adjust, market prices, so as to protect the Member States from over saturation of non-community products, and to allow for the effects of arts.40(3) and 43 EC to be applied. These were principles that followed the aims of art.39 EC, inasmuch as it provided that Member States were to work to maintain, and help stabilise, agricultural markets, in order to ensure fair living standards through reasonable pricing. Art.40(3) EC further focussed on the need to apply certain measures where necessary, which on this occasion included the forfeiture of licence deposits, where no planned exportation or importation had occurred during the licence period.

When the claimant in this case had continued exporting maize beyond their licence expiration date, a percentage of their deposit was forfeited by the Einfuhr-und Vorratsstelle für Getreide und Futtermittel, under the terms of art.12(1) of Regulation 120/67. When challenged in the national courts, there was uncertainty as to how best to reconcile German law with the Treaty Regulations, and so a preliminary ruling was sought under art.177 of the Treaty. The two questions raised enquired as to (i) whether the requirement to forfeit licence deposits subject to the terms of art.12(1) was legal, and (ii) whether art.9 of Regulation 473/67/EEC (which had been adopted in conjunction with Regulation 120/67/) was legal, in that it included the exclusion of forfeiture in matters subject to *force majeure*.

It was also argued, that while the terms of Community law were inherent to the existence of a Member State, it was felt that the superiority of German constitutional law contradicted the presence of deposit forfeitures, on the pretence that such measures were considered penal, as opposed to valuable to the aims of German freedom laws.

When evaluating the views of the court, and the questions set down for clarification, it was first held by the Court of Justice (after providing lengthy and very exhaustive reasoning), that under no circumstances did the forfeiture of deposits serve any other purpose than that of market stability, as outlined in art.40(3) EC, despite claims to the contrary. This translated that Regulation 120/67 was legal and thus did not interfere with the aims and objectives of arts.40 and 43 EC.

With regard to the exemption of forfeiture under the presence of *force majeure* (frustrations beyond control of the licence holder), it was again held that while the context of the exemption was subject to wider meaning, it was deliberate, in that it allowed for a number of prevailing circumstances to determine whether in each instance, the claimant had taken sufficient steps to apply for the licence, before citing any inability to use it. This by extension, allowed for full support of the aims prescribed in art.39 EC, therefore no breach, or conflict of interests, could be found.

Key Citations

"The legality of a Community measure can be judged only in the light of the ordinary law, whether written or unwritten, but never in the light of the national law, even if that is a constitutional law."[488]

"[T]he fundamental principles of the national legal systems contribute to enabling Community law to find in itself the resources necessary for ensuring, where needed, respect for the fundamental rights which form the common heritage of the Member States."[489]

"[I]t is not only necessary but indispensable, if it is desired to maintain the economic freedom of the importers and exporters, both to subject their transactions to the issue of an import or export licence and to lay down that that document is not just a vague declaration of intent and that the condition for its issue is an undertaking to carry out the transaction decided upon, an undertaking which is guaranteed by a deposit."[490]

"[T]o allow certain licences to be requested without a real intention to carry out the transaction would be to distort the whole forecasting system which, as I have tried to show, is indispensable to the regularization of the market as it has been, very liberally, organized."[491]

"It is because the forfeiture of the deposit is seen as a sanction that the Court is asked to lay down that it can only be imposed after taking into account all the mental factors, subjective or circumstantial, which explain the non-completion of the transaction for which the licence was issued."[492]

---

[488] *Internationale Handelsgesellschaft mbH v Einfuhr-und Vorratsstelle für Getreide und Futtermittel* [Case 11/70][1970] ECR 1125 [1146], Opinion of AG Dutheillet de Lammte, para II.

[489] *Internationale Handelsgesellschaft mbH v Einfuhr-und Vorratsstelle für Getreide und Futtermittel* [Case 11/70][1970] ECR 1125 [1146], Opinion of AG Dutheillet de Lammte, para II.

[490] *Internationale Handelsgesellschaft mbH v Einfuhr-und Vorratsstelle für Getreide und Futtermittel* [Case 11/70][1970] ECR 1125 [1146], Opinion of AG Dutheillet de Lammte, para II.

[491] *Internationale Handelsgesellschaft mbH v Einfuhr-und Vorratsstelle für Getreide und Futtermittel* [Case 11/70][1970] ECR 1125 [1146], Opinion of AG Dutheillet de Lammte, para II.

[492] *Internationale Handelsgesellschaft mbH v Einfuhr-und Vorratsstelle für Getreide und Futtermittel* [Case 11/70][1970] ECR 1125 [1146], Opinion of AG Dutheillet de Lammte, para II.

10. Köbler v Austria

Art.48 EC and liability for breach of Community law by a Supreme Court, form the basis of a claim for indirect dissemination by an academic employee. An act which further provokes a preliminary ruling by the regional courts, in order to clarify the exacting powers of the Treaty.

Having worked as an Austrian university professor for over a decade, the claimant sought an application for a conditional length-of-service salary increment, as entitled to those serving for a period of fifteen years or more. The terms of this benefit expressly required that any qualifying employment must occur within Austria, whereas the claimant applied on grounds that his employment had been within the European Community, and so refusal for inclusion constituted indirect discrimination under art.48 EC (freedom of movement for workers) (now art.39 EC), and Regulation 1612/68 (freedom of workers within the Community).

Having been rejected by the deciding authorities under para.50(a) of the 1956 Salary Law, his claim was brought before the Verwaltungsgerictschof (Supreme Administrative Court), where despite his citing discrimination under the rights afforded him through Community law, there was insufficient clarity to reach judgment; therefore a preliminary ruling was sought under art.234 EC, with the aim of determining if employment within other Member States was qualification for a payment scheme designed and operated under Austrian jurisdiction.

During the period between the claimant's rejection and subsequent appeal, the Court of Justice notified the Supreme Court that a similar case had been recently decided in support of the claimant's position, and after reviewing the details of the matter, the application for preliminary ruling was withdrawn, and judgment made against the claimant on grounds that the salary increments were tantamount to bonuses, and were therefore exempt from the protection of art.48 EC.

In light of the court's dismissal, the claimant then took action for compensatory payment for the loss of earnings arising from a national judgment that stood contrary to the effects of art.48 EC, whereupon the Austrian government opposed the claim, on grounds that the decision of a Supreme Court does not provide for State liability where proven unlawful.

Having considered the facts represented, the Landesgericht für Zivilrechtssachen Wien (State Court) submitted five questions under art.234 EC, for the Court of Justice to establish (i) whether a breach of Community law by a national court applied to all courts, (ii) if such a breach was applicable to a Supreme Court, (iii) if the classification of a special length-of-service benefit as an employee bonus constituted a breach of art. 48 EC, (iv) if the effects of art.48 EC enabled individual claim before a national, court, and (v) if the Supreme Court had jurisdiction enough to answer the questions raised, or whether the State Court needed to pass judgment.

Distilled down to four main points, the European Court of Justice held that:

I. Irrespective of arguments for the narrowness of Community law upon Member State judiciaries, the findings in *Francovich and others v Italy*[493] and *R v Secretary of State for Transport ex p Factortame*,[494] clearly established the liability for reparation by Member States to individual claims, and that such scope included the courts when categorising public authorities.

II. The nature of the breach was vital to the right to individual remedy and while excusable (or inexcusable) errors weigh heavily on the the burden of liability, the circumstances of this claim required little adjudication, other than recognition of a clear violation of art.48 EC through the withdrawal of a reference to the Court.

III. With regard to the damage caused by the breach, it was held that evidence of the breach constituted sufficient grounds for damages payable by the State under individual claim, and such reparation must come from domestic legislation, provided it offered equal rights, as those prescribed under the Treaty.

IV. As with any preliminary ruling, it was not for the Court to determine the method of legal summation, but to advise how best to serve the principles of Community law. And so on this occasion, it was the duty of the courts to review and establish, the appropriate measure for compensation through the existing case law provided.

Key Citations

"[S]tate liability for any type of public authority stems from both the Treaty (Article 10 EC and the second and third paragraphs of Article 249 EC) and the Court's settled case-law according to which it is for each Member State to ensure that individuals obtain redress for loss and damage caused to them by non-compliance with Community law, whichever public authority is responsible for the breach."[495]

"That indissoluble and irreducible link between the principle of State liability and the system of the Treaty results from the specific nature of the Community legal order."[496]

"Just as it imposes burdens on individuals, Community law is also intended to give rise to rights which become part of their legal patrimony. Those rights arise not only where they are expressly granted by the Treaty but also by virtue of obligations which the Treaty imposes in a clearly defined manner both on individuals and on the Member States and the Community institutions."[497]

---

[493] [Cases C-6 & 9/90] [1991] ECR I-5357.

[494] [1991] 1 AC 603.

[495] *Köbler v Austria* [Case C-224/01] [2003] ECR I-10239, Opinion of AG Léger, para 23.

[496] *Köbler v Austria* [Case C-224/01] [2003] ECR I-10239, Opinion of AG Léger, para 28.

[497] *Köbler v Austria* [Case C-224/01] [2003] ECR I-10239, Opinion of AG Léger, para 29.

"[U]nder Article 5 of the EC Treaty (now Article 10 EC), the Member States are required to nullify the unlawful consequences of a breach of Community law."[498]

"[I]t is not sufficient for individuals to be entitled to invoke Community law before a supreme court or for that court to be required to apply Community law correctly. It is also necessary, if a Supreme Court renders a decision contrary to Community law, for individuals to be in a position to obtain redress, at least where certain conditions are fulfilled."[499]

"[R]equirement in respect of state liability for the acts or omissions of the legislature or the administrative authorities is transposable to liability for the acts or omissions of Supreme Courts."[500]

"[S]tate liability cannot be prima facie precluded in the case of a supreme court's manifest disregard for its obligation to make a reference for a preliminary ruling where, for example, there is no case law of the Court on the point of law at issue at the time when the national court gives its decision."[501]

"[M]anifest breach by a Supreme Court of an obligation to make a reference for a preliminary ruling is, in itself, capable of giving rise to State liability."[502]

"[I]t would be excessive to require a national court, which was seised of an action for reparation of alleged material damage, to refer a question to the Court for a preliminary ruling in order to know the response which it might have given if it had in fact been seised of such a question."[503]

"[P]rinciple of institutional autonomy, subject to the reservation that effective judicial protection be ensured, is also applicable to any actions for damages brought by individuals against the Member States on the basis of their liability for the acts or omissions of a Supreme Court."[504]

---

[498] *Köbler v Austria* [Case C-224/01] [2003] ECR I-10239, Opinion of AG Léger, para 32.

[499] *Köbler v Austria* [Case C-224/01] [2003] ECR I-10239, Opinion of AG Léger, para 37.

[500] *Köbler v Austria* [Case C-224/01] [2003] ECR I-10239, Opinion of AG Léger, para 124.

[501] *Köbler v Austria* [Case C-224/01] [2003] ECR I-10239, Opinion of AG Léger, para 144.

[502] *Köbler v Austria* [Case C-224/01] [2003] ECR I-10239, Opinion of AG Léger, para 148.

[503] *Köbler v Austria* [Case C-224/01] [2003] ECR I-10239, Opinion of AG Léger, para 152.

[504] *Köbler v Austria* [Case C-224/01] [2003] ECR I-10239, Opinion of AG Léger, para 162.

11. Marleasing SA v La Comercial Internacional de Alimentación SA

The composition and function of incorporated companies, coupled with the fraudulent and deceptive manner in which the assets are contained, becomes central to the contention between founders and creditors, when nullity is sought before the national court.

When creditor and claimant (Marleasing SA) discovers that one of the three founders of La Comercial Internacional de Alimentación SA had used the company in such a way as to avoid third party recovery of assets, it took action against the firm, in order to expose the company as an illegally created organisation, as defined under arts.1261 and 1275 of the Spanish Civil Code.

In response, the defendant founder sought the protection of art.11 of Directive 68/151/EEC (also known as the 'First Directive'), in which was an exhaustive list of qualifying conditions for company nullity, none of which included the grounds relied upon by the claimant. When debated by the Juzgado de Primera Instancia e Instrucción, it was agreed that as transposition of the Directive had not been undertaken, the issue presented remained unsolved without reference to the European Court of Justice under art.177 of the Treaty.

The question asked, was whether the relevant terms contained in art.11(2) of Directive 68/151 were enforceable between individuals, despite a failure to adopt them into national Spanish law. In response to this, and after observing the disparities between existing domestic statute and the meaning of the Directive, the European Court of Justice explained that under Community law principles, it was agreed that no terms of a Directive can be used between individuals, with the exception that a failure to transpose a Directive can result in individual action against the Member State, where clarity and specificity of the Directive is clear. However, it was the obligation of the Member State to align the principles of the Directive against existing statute, in order that the Directive's effect superceded domestic laws.

In relation to the protection of nullity under art.11(2)(b) of Directive 68/151, it was further held that nullity may be provided for where the objects of the company are unlawful or contrary to public policy, or where the number of founding members is less than two. It was also outlined in art.12 that nullity entailed dissolution, and thereby did not affect the validity of the company or its dealings, despite the presence of unlawful operation or intent. This translated that it was down to the discretion of the national courts to determine how best to meet the needs of both the claimant and the defendant, while observing the meaning and effect of Directive 68/151.

Key Citations

"[O]bligation on the part of the national courts to interpret their national law in conformity with a Directive, which has been reaffirmed on several occasions, does not mean that a provision in a Directive has direct effect in any way as between individuals."[505]

"[M]ember States, are required, in the light of Article 5 of the EEC Treaty, to seek to achieve the result pursued by the Directive by all appropriate measures within their power."[506]

"[T]he requirement that an interpretation must be consistent with a Directive precludes the application to public limited companies of the provisions on nullity under ordinary law in such a way as to permit a declaration of nullity of such a company on grounds other than those exhaustively listed in Article 11 of the First Directive."[507]

"[A] declaration of nullity as a result of infringements arising from the contractual relationship between the members of the company or between the members and the company is a penalty which must be avoided as far as possible."[508]

"[I]f the company's real activity, as carried on from the outset, is unlawful or contrary to public policy, the ground of nullity provided for in Article 11(2)(b) can be relied upon, even though that activity is not in accordance with the company's presumably lawful objects as described in the instrument of incorporation or the statutes."[509]

"[T]he national court can easily, when applying national law, apply the exhaustive list of grounds in Article 11 and possibly should a declaration of nullity of the company nevertheless be made the restriction on the retroactive effect of nullity pursuant to Article 12 of the First Directive."[510]

---

[505] *Marleasing SA v La Comercial Internacional de Alimentación SA* [Case C-106/89] [1990] ECR I-4135, Opinion of AG Van Gerven, para 7.

[506] *Marleasing SA v La Comercial Internacional de Alimentación SA* [Case C-106/89] [1990] ECR I-4135, Opinion of AG Van Gerven, para 9.

[507] *Marleasing SA v La Comercial Internacional de Alimentación SA* [Case C-106/89] [1990] ECR I-4135, Opinion of AG Van Gerven, para 10.

[508] *Marleasing SA v La Comercial Internacional de Alimentación SA* [Case C-106/89] [1990] ECR I-4135, Opinion of AG Van Gerven, para 16.

[509] *Marleasing SA v La Comercial Internacional de Alimentación SA* [Case C-106/89] [1990] ECR I-4135, Opinion of AG Van Gerven, para 17.

[510] *Marleasing SA v La Comercial Internacional de Alimentación SA* [Case C-106/89] [1990] ECR I-4135, Opinion of AG Van Gerven, para 20.

12. Marshall v Southampton and South West Area Health Authority (No.1)

Dismissal upon grounds of sexual discrimination, and the direct effect of Community law Directives in issues of state employment, are the key ingredients to this matter, when a former employee of the South-West Hampshire Area Health Authority is subjected to unexpected termination of her employment, despite intimations that her post was secure beyond policy requirements.

Having joined the department in 1974, the applicant had enjoyed working as a Senior Dietician until she reached the contracted retirement age, which was five years earlier than her male colleagues. At this point, it was agreed that she could continue working, although there was no specific end date discussed. With no prior notice, the applicant was dismissed two years later, upon grounds that she was a woman, and that she was now considered beyond retirement age, and therefore surplus to requirements.

Immediately after her departure, the applicant sought to challenge the decision through the enforcement of Council Directive 76/207/EEC, which supports the 'principle of equal treatment' inasmuch as art.1(1), (2), 2(1) and 5, collectively confer Member State obligations to apply and maintain, the equal treatment of men and women with regard to employment, promotion, training, working conditions, social security and dismissal. This also included the prohibition of any discrimination, whether directly or indirectly, and that the above applied to all manner of employment arrangements.

When heard in the lower courts, her claim was denied under the s.6(4) of the Sex Discrimination Act 1975, which provided that discrimination by an employer was exempt under retirement conditions, and that the pensionable age of women under s. 27(1) of the Social Security Act 1975 supported the age of retirement through the availability of state pensions as of sixty years of age. While her claim under EEC law was upheld, it was subsequently dismissed under appeal, on grounds that such a claim could not be heard in English courts.

Taken to the Court of Appeal, the court was forced to raise two questions with a view to a preliminary ruling under art.177 EC, namely (i) whether the appellant's dismissal after reaching retirement age on the basis that she was a woman, constituted sexual discrimination under Directive 76/207, and (ii) if agreed, whether the terms of the Directive allowed for direct effect, given the conflict between domestic legislation and Community law.

Having examined the facts of the case, it was held by the Court of Justice, that while the Health Authority relied upon the narrowness of meaning when determining the powers of legislation, they failed to appreciate that all Member States are obliged to adopt the principles of a Directive within a designated period (which on this occasion had long since elapsed); and that when doing so, must adjust or if necessary, remove the applicable statute, so as to give full effect to the meaning of the Directive. On this occasion, the Health Authority also sought to avoid the duties called for under Community law, while expanding the terms of the Social Security Act 1975 beyond their meaning when deciding that pensionable age was a prerequisite to retirement, which was unsustainable as a legal argument. This amounted to nothing more than overt sexual discrimination, and to which the appellant had a right of claim.

Looking next to the effect of Directive 76/207, it was argued by the Health Authority and the United Kingdom, that the terms within were prescribed for the benefit, or use of the Member State, and not the individual; and that the terms of an non-implemented Directive excluded contracts between private parties. While it was further argued, that the State was entitled to be seen as a private employer for the purposes of the case. It was thus contended that the appellant was denied the right to bring action against the State, and that what was required was a review of the Sex Discrimination Act 1975 before the continuation of proceedings.

In stark contrast, the Court held that a failure to adopt the Directive had rendered the Health Authority liable for penalty, and therefore accountable at law as an emanation of the state, whereupon a citizen can claim such rights within the domestic court in lieu of their non-implementation.

Key Citations

"[D]irectives are capable of conferring rights on individuals which may be relied upon directly before the courts of the Member States; national courts are obliged by virtue of the binding nature of a Directive, in conjunction with article 5 of the E.E.C. Treaty, to give effect to the provisions of Directives where possible…"[511]

"[W]herever the provisions of a Directive appear, as far as their subject matter is concerned, to be unconditional and sufficiently precise, those provisions may be relied upon by an individual against the State where that State fails to implement the Directive in national law by the end of the period prescribed or where it fails to implement the Directive correctly."[512]

"[A] Member State which has not adopted the implementing measures required by the Directive within the prescribed period may not plead, as against individuals, its own failure to perform the obligations which the Directive entails."[513]

"[W]here a person involved in legal proceedings is able to rely on a Directive as against the state he may do so regardless of the capacity in which the latter is acting, whether employer or public authority. In either case it is necessary to prevent the State from taking advantage of its own failure to comply with Community law."[514]

---

[511] *Marshall v Southampton and South West Area Health Authority [No1]* [Case 152/84] [1986] ECR 723, para 41 (ECJ).

[512] *Marshall v Southampton and South West Area Health Authority [No1]* [Case 152/84] [1986] ECR 723, para 46 (ECJ).

[513] *Marshall v Southampton and South West Area Health Authority [No1]* [Case 152/84] [1986] ECR 723, para 47 (ECJ).

[514] *Marshall v Southampton and South West Area Health Authority [No1]* [Case 152/84] [1986] ECR 723, para 49 (ECJ).

13. R v HM Treasury *ex p* British Telecommunications Plc

The successful transposition of EU Directives requires delicate application when ensuring that the overriding objective of the Directive remains intact. On this occasion, the rules of Directive 90/531/EEC while specific in their construction, caused immediate conflict between the domestic government and a dominant telecommunications provider.

Basing their argument on the principles examined in *Francovich and others v Italy*,[515] British Telecom (or BT as they were commonly known) took issue with Parliament's decision to edit the transposed Directive in a way that precluded them from perceived equal rights in a highly competitive industry. In fact, by all accounts the telecommunications giant was already bound to cap its tariff rates, provide connection services irrespective of national geography, and publish its commercial intentions for all to see. However, when put in its proper context, the domestic market was disparagingly divided in such a way that afforded BT a ninety-percent share, while those new to the field were limited to only a collective three-percent stake hold.

This extended enormous advantage to the applicants, and yet they still felt that under the prescribed terms of the Directive, the Commission had intended that any exclusions to the benefit of Community law were decidable between those contracting, and not at the discretion of the Member State. It was understood that in circumstances providing a balanced economic market, the Directive required no degree of intervention, as the playing field would, in many events, present itself fairly, yet the United Kingdom government, having enjoyed the monopoly of BT as a state funded enterprise, were only too aware that without marshalling of the transposition, the essence of equality would be lost in translation, and the integrity of domestic contract law held to account.

By the British government exercising its discretion, the applicants were (rightly or wrongly) denied access to the terms of the Directive, and therefore unable to determine for themselves, which services they felt were excludable and why; a process that would have inevitably relied upon the wisdom of the EU Commission to decide, and so was not in any way affected by those preventative measures.

When transposing Directives, it is the duty of Member States to incorporate the relevant terms 'as far as possible', which on this occasion, it was deemed that the steps taken reflected that ethos. This resulted in the Court of Justice reserving the rights of the legislature to act where appropriate, and that despite any sufferance on the part of the applicants, there were no grounds for either 'direct effect' damages, nor compensatory award for economic loss, as the ends ultimately justified the means.

---

[515] *Francovich and others v Italy* [Cases C-6 & 9/90] [1991] ECR I-5357.

Key Citations

"[T]he operation of the system envisaged by the Directive, as interpreted herein, is sufficiently guaranteed by the supervisory role which the Directive itself entrusts to the Commission, also and above all as regards the possible abuses to which the United Kingdom refers."[516]

"[M]ember States are in a much better position than the Commission to assess whether competition exists in the telecommunications market as regards a specific service and, consequently, that the determination by those States of the matters covered by Article 8(1) will permit the exercise of more effective control than that exercised by the Commission..."[517]

"[A] breach is sufficiently serious where, in the exercise of its legislative powers, an institution or a Member State has manifestly and gravely disregarded the limits on the exercise of its powers."[518]

"[C]ommunity law does not require a Member State which, in transposing the Directive into national law, has itself determined which services of a contracting entity are to be excluded from its scope in implementation of Article 8, to compensate that entity for any loss suffered by it as a result of the error committed by the State."[519]

---

[516] *R v HM Treasury ex p British Telecommunications plc* [Case C-392/93] [1996] ECR 1-1631 [639], Opinion of AG Tesauro, para 16.

[517] *R v HM Treasury ex p British Telecommunications plc* [Case C-392/93] [1996] ECR 1-1631, para 21 (ECJ).

[518] *R v HM Treasury ex p British Telecommunications plc* [Case C-392/93] [1996] ECR 1-1631, para 42 (ECJ).

[519] *R v HM Treasury ex p British Telecommunications plc* [Case C-392/93] [1996] ECR 1-1631, para 46 (ECJ).

14. R v Ministry of Agriculture, Fisheries and Food *ex p* Hedley Lomas

The application of a Treaty article while a harmonising Directive precludes the right to endorse sanctions for Member State non-compliance, results in a loss of licence for Ireland, when exporting sheep for slaughter. This led to a preliminary ruling to ascertain if such a Directive could reasonably deny, or even restrict, exportation to Member States failing to uphold the aims of the assigned article.

Arts.43 and 100 EC, were designed to reduce the suffering of animals sent for slaughter, and prescribed the timely use of stunning and killing within specific guidelines, as enacted by Directive 74/577/EEC. In contrast, art.36 EC explains that restrictive measures surrounding the importation and exportation of products (including livestock), can be applied when acting in the interests of public safety, security and protection of human, animal and plant life.

When Spain transposed Directive 74/577, it did so by Royal Decree while mirroring the terms of art.1 of the Directive, with the exception of sanctions for non-compliance. As a result, the United Kingdom Ministry of Agriculture, Fisheries and Food, whose view was that Spanish law allowed for the suffering of animals, took steps to prohibit exportation through the denial of export licences for livestock. This reaction resulted in an Irish sheep farmer being refused a licence to export to a compliant Spanish slaughterhouse.

When taken to the High Court under appeal for judicial review, and in pursuit of damages, it was agreed by the court that in order to achieve summary judgment in light of the Ministry's reliance upon art.36 EC, there needed to be a preliminary ruling under art.177 EC to the European Court of Justice. There were three questions raised that sought to address (i) whether the terms of Directive 74/577 prevented restrictive measures under art.36 EC, (ii) whether the effects of art.36 EC had universal effect, or were subject to specific criteria, and (iii) where ineffective, whether the Member State applying the article, was liable for compensation where an export licence was denied.

In answer to the questions raised, the Court held that:

I.   The terms of Directive 74/577 were such that did not expressly outline the penalties for non-compliance, but instead conferred such measures to the Member States, in order for legislative powers to ensure the observation of those terms. Unfortunately, the actions taken by the United Kingdom were based upon subjective conviction, as opposed to evidence that demonstrated a breach by the Spanish government, therefore to rely upon the effects of art.36 EC was to act ultra vires, and against the spirit and purpose of Community law when denying the free movement of goods by another Member State.

II. The terms of art.36 EC were not designed to allow one Member State to exercise restrictive powers over another, particularly with no evidence to support a claim of breach, and no investigative powers with which to rely upon. Instead, the route taken must be one of either action, or complaint to the Commission under arts.170 or 186 EC, while allowing for the movement of goods until proven otherwise.

III. When acting in breach of art.43 EC, it is the obligation of the acting Member State to provide reparation for damage caused by the breach, as established in *Francovich*[520] and *Van Gend en Loos*,[521] and when deciding the measure of compensation, it must rely upon its own domestic legislation, while observing the principles of non-discrimination and effective remedy when discussing the matter in the courts, and when calculating the amount payable.

Key Citations

"[I]n so far as there has not been full harmonization in the area of protection of animals regarding their export to other Member States, it is for Member States to adopt the necessary measures of control within the context of Article 36 of the Treaty."[522]

"A Member State cannot take unilateral action against defaults by other Member States. The Treaty of Rome created an original legal order in which the procedures necessary for establishing and penalizing a breach of its provisions are strictly regulated."[523]

"[N]ational measures adopted on the basis of Article 36 of the Treaty are justified only if they take into account the requirements of the free movement of goods as laid down by the Treaty and, in particular, by the last sentence of Article 36."[524]

"[N]ational courts must have the power to ensure the necessary interim protection for rights which an individual derives from Community law, even if those courts do not have that power under their domestic law."[525]

"An individual who brings an action for damages against a State on the ground that there has been a breach of a directly effective provision of Community law can, by definition, show that rights were granted for his benefit and that their content is identifiable."[526]

---

[520] *Francovich and others v Italy* [Cases C-6 & 9/90] [1991] ECR 1-5357.

[521] *Van Gend en Loos v Nederlandse Administratie de Belastingen* [Case 26/62] [1963] ECR 1.

[522] *R v Ministry of Agriculture, Fisheries and Food ex p Hedley Lomas* [Case C-5/94] [1996] ECR I-2553, Opinion of AG Léger, para 17.

[523] *R v Ministry of Agriculture, Fisheries and Food ex p Hedley Lomas* [Case C-5/94] [1996] ECR I-2553, Opinion of AG Léger, para 24.

[524] *R v Ministry of Agriculture, Fisheries and Food ex p Hedley Lomas* [Case C-5/94] [1996] ECR I-2553, Opinion of AG Léger, para 42.

[525] *R v Ministry of Agriculture, Fisheries and Food ex p Hedley Lomas* [Case C-5/94] [1996] ECR I-2553, Opinion of AG Léger, para 61.

[526] *R v Ministry of Agriculture, Fisheries and Food ex p Hedley Lomas* [Case C-5/94] [1996] ECR I-2553, Opinion of AG Léger, para 88.

15. Simmenthal SpA v Italian Minister of Finance

This 1978 case involved the unfair application of import fees upon a business owner, regardless of existing Community law enabling the free movement of goods between Member States. After the matter was bought before the national courts, the fees were requested to be paid back to the claimant, but the Italian finance administration disagreed on constitutional grounds.

Under guidance of art.32 of the Italian consolidated health laws, a Monza-based meat supplier was subjected to inspection fees for a beef consignment purchased in France, despite operating within the framework of Community law. Three years after the charge, the supplier sought action against the Italian government, upon grounds that it had acted ultra vires to its Member State obligations, and now rightfully owed the fees taken, to the claimant.

When first heard, the local court (Pretura di Susa) referred the matter to the Court of Justice by means of a preliminary ruling under art.177 EC, where it was held by the Court that importation charges levied against its citizens, amounted to little more than quantitive restrictions within the scope of art.30 EC, and were therefore illegal and repayable with interest.

The Amministrazione Delle Finanze Dello Stato (Finance Administration) subsequently appealed, citing incompatibility with Italian national law (no.1239/70), which then resulted in the issue of direct effect and the reluctance of Member States, and their Constitutional courts, to enforce Community laws when national laws obstruct the blanket protections afforded individual citizens. At the time of discussion, the only options available to the judiciary were the immediate repeal of the relevant legislation, or declaration of incompatibility by the Constitutional Court.

This approach had been favoured by the Italian government, but having considered the ramifications of waiting for national laws to 'catch up' with Community law, it was held by the Court of Justice that the 'principle of the precedence of Community law' must be held in highest regard, and that in order for this to continue, it was paramount that the lower courts were given the power to enforce Community law, irrespective of any jurisdictional contradictions that might surface.

Key Citations

"[D]irectly applicable Community provisions must, notwithstanding any internal rule or practice whatsoever of the Member States, have full, complete and uniform effect in their legal systems in order to protect subjective legal rights created in favour of individuals…"[527]

"These provisions are therefore a direct source of rights and duties for all those affected thereby, whether Member States or individuals, who are parties to legal relationships under Community law."[528]

"[A]ny recognition that national legislative measures which encroach upon the field within which the Community exercises its legislative power or which are otherwise incompatible with the provisions of Community law had any legal effect would amount to a corresponding denial of the effectiveness of obligations undertaken unconditionally and irrevocably by Member States pursuant to the Treaty…"[529]

---

[527] *Simmenthal SpA v Italian Minister of Finance* [Case 35/76] [1976] ECR 1871, para 7 (ECJ).

[528] *Simmenthal SpA v Italian Minister of Finance* [Case 35/76] [1976] ECR 1871, para 15 (ECJ).

[529] *Simmenthal SpA v Italian Minister of Finance* [Case 35/76] [1976] ECR 1871, para 18 (ECJ).

16. Van Duyn v Home Office

Literally months after joining the European Union, a Dutch citizen attempted to enter the United Kingdom with the aim of working for the Church of Scientology. At the time it was commonly agreed under legislation, that no foreign nationals were permitted to enter the country where government policy dictated, and that the immigration department were conferred powers to refuse entry where applicable.

Achieved through two arms, the first applied where the institution was deemed harmful to public policy, and the second was based upon an individual's character, conduct or association with such undesirables. In this instance, the Scientology movement were deemed by the Home Office to be harmful, and were subsequently struck off as a recognised educational body. This was the primary reason behind the claimant being refused entry when arriving to start her new job, after which she returned home, before taking legal action against their decision.

Membership of the European Union meant that under art.48 EC, European citizens were granted freedom of movement between Member States, and thus entitled to seek and secure employment without challenge, as expressed in Regulation 1612/68. Contrastingly, Directive 64/221/EEC determined that policy decisions made by Member States were based upon the personal conduct of individuals alone, and not any associations or attachments to institutions considered bothersome.

The claimant subsequently enforced her rights under the Treaty, and it was this contention which gave rise to the question of compatibility, and the possible need for a preliminary ruling under art.177 EC. Meanwhile. the United Kingdom defended its decision to deny entry on grounds that while the Scientology movement itself was not subject to the terms of art.48 EC, the claimant's previous history of studying, practicing and seeking employment with the Church, demonstrated an unsavoury character that qualified her inclusion under art.3 of the Directive.

When faced with the obvious conflict, the judge found himself unable to reach summary judgment when there appeared to be uncertainty as to the direct effect of Directive 64/221; and thus determined that in order for a fair hearing to be realised, there needed to be questions addressed to the European Court, so that clarity of interpretation could be found. It would after appraisal, then be possible for the evidence presented to be both properly examined, before the rights bestowed both the Member State and the individual were fairly applied.

Key Citations

"It is well established that the function of the European Court is confined to the interpretation of the Treaty of Rome, and no doubt secondary legislation, and that once the relevant provisions have been interpreted it is for the national court to apply that interpretation to the particular case in point."[530]

---

[530] *Van Duyn v Home Office* [Case 41/74] [1974] ECR 1337, [1974] 1 WLR 1107 (Ch) 1118 (Pennycuick V-C).

17. Van Gend en Loos v Nederlandse Administratie de Belastingen

When a Dutch importer of ureaformaldehyde fell victim to domestically manipulated customs tariffs, the question of both 'direct effect' and the individual right to challenge an abuse of EU Treaties (in particular those laid down in the Treaty of Rome), became subject to a preliminary ruling under art.177 EC.

Because of the supranational nature of the case, it was first believed inapplicable when challenges to increased (or recategorised) tax rates were put into effect by national statutes. However, the argument made by the claimant was that at the time of the original Treaty, taxation of the affected product was set at three percent.

After domestic reclassification set to increase the rate to eight percent, the claimant challenge the adjustment by citing art.12 EC, which explained that:

> "Member States shall refrain from introducing between themselves any new customs duties or imports or exports or any charges having equivalent effect and from increasing those which they already apply in their trade with each other."[531]

In addition to the terms of art.12 EC, it was equally held in art.95 EC that:

> "A Member State shall not impose, directly or indirectly, on the products of other Member States any internal charges of any kind in excess of those applied directly or indirectly to like domestic products."[532]

During the hearing at the European Court of Justice, there was mixed opinion as to the direct effect of art.12 EC. However, the Court held that were the protective principles of Community law to remain excluded from violations of Member States, it would defeat their very purpose. It was thus held that the inherent meaning and purpose of art.12 EC, was one designed to afford unequivocal rights to individuals, who, when taking issue with matters such as this, would do so in the knowledge that their rights were protected by the national courts.

In closing, it was expressed by the Court that all Member States would from thereon, refrain from increasing levies and customs duties that conflicted with those put forward in the original Treaty of Rome. And while the reclassification of that specific tariff was held to be illegal, the the matter was referred back to the national courts, so as to establish how best to reclassify the products involved, while mindful of the rates set at the time when the EEC Treaty first came into effect.

---

[531] TEEC 1957, The elimination of customs duties as between Member States, art.12

[532] TEEC 1957, Fiscal Provisions, art.12

Key Citations

"[T]he Community constitutes a new legal order of international law for the benefit of which the States have limited their sovereign rights, albeit within limited fields, and the subjects of which comprise not only Member States but also their nationals."[533]

"Independently of the legislation of Member States, Community law therefore not only imposes obligations on individuals but is also intended to confer upon them rights which become part of their legal heritage. These rights arise not only where they are expressly granted by the Treaty, but also by reason of obligations which the Treaty imposes in a clearly defined way upon individuals as well as upon the Member States and upon the institutions of the Community."[534]

"[A]ccording to the spirit, the general scheme and wording of the Treaty, Article 12 must be interpreted as providing direct effects and creating individual rights which national courts must protect."[535]

"A restriction of the guarantees against an infringement of Article 12 by Member States to the procedures under Article 169 and 170 would remove all direct legal protection of the individual rights of their nationals."[536]

"It is of little importance how the increase in customs duties occurred when, after the Treaty entered into force, the same product in the same Member State was subjected to a higher rate of duty."[537]

---

[533] *Van Gend en Loos v Nederlandse Administratie de Belastingen* [Case 26/62] [1963] ECR 1, para II (ECJ).

[534] *Van Gend en Loos v Nederlandse Administratie de Belastingen* [Case 26/62] [1963] ECR 1, para II (ECJ).

[535] *Van Gend en Loos v Nederlandse Administratie de Belastingen* [Case 26/62] [1963] ECR 1, para II (ECJ).

[536] *Van Gend en Loos v Nederlandse Administratie de Belastingen* [Case 26/62] [1963] ECR 1, para II (ECJ).

[537] *Van Gend en Loos v Nederlandse Administratie de Belastingen* [Case 26/62] [1963] ECR 1, para III (ECJ).

18. Viamex Agrar Handels GmbH v Hauptzollamt Hamburg-Jonas

Principles of proportionality and the transport of live animals for the purpose of sale beyond the borders of the European Community, lie at the heart of this joint request for a preliminary ruling under art.234 EC. On this occasion, there were two claims brought before the Finanzgericht (Fiscal Court) by livestock exporters, who had been refused export refunds, on grounds that the manner in which they were transported was in breach of Community law.

With regard to the first claimant, it was found that while art.1 of Regulation 615/98 determines the criteria in which a business can claim export cost refunds, it was applied in conjunction with art.3(1) of Directive 91/268/EC, which outlined animal travel-time limitations and further governance of their physical wellbeing through nutrition and hydration. Having submitted their paperwork, it was discovered by the Hauptzollamt Kiel (Customs Office) that contrary to the prescribed rest periods set out under art.48(5) of Chapter VII of the Annexe to Directive 91/628, the animals had been given insufficient treatment as to meet the terms laid down. In argument, the claimants contested that they had been acting under instruction of the official veterinarian at the outset of the journey.

In the second claim, it was found that while advanced reimbursement of export costs had been granted prior to the animals exportation, the subsequent paperwork revealed that the second leg of the drive had exceeded the fourteen-hour threshold contained in the same Annexe of Directive 91/628, and thereby rendered them void of any refund, thus resulting in the Customs Office seeking recovery of payment with interest.

When presented with the material facts, the court raised two questions for the European Court of Justice, namely (i) whether the power of Regulation 615/98 enabled jurisdiction over the terms of Directive 91/268 and (ii) if so, whether it was tantamount to a violation of the principle of proportionality, inasmuch as the terms of a Directive must override any subsidiary limitations, which in this case was the refusal of export costs in light of a regulatory breach.

Having examined the case history behind both concerns, it was agreed by the Court that while Regulation 615/98 ran parallel to the Directive, it did so for the specific purpose of animal protection and the enforcement of Member State conformity, but nothing more. It was also found that this caveat served itself well with regard to legal certainty, and was therefore not in contradiction of the Directive objectives.

In relation to the matter of Community law proportionality, it was agreed that while the terms of Regulation 615/98 conferred a right to deny export cost refunds, it was executed with the express intention that national courts and legislature, applied discretion when determining if a claimant had a right to recover costs where no animal had been harmed.

Key Citations

"[I]mplementing Directive 91/628 had shown that the welfare of live animals was not always respected in animal exports and that it was necessary, for practical reasons, to entrust the Commission with the task of laying down detailed implementing rules for the application of the rules on this matter."[538]

"[E]fforts to achieve objectives of the common agricultural policy cannot disregard requirements relating to the public interest such as the protection of the health and life of animals, requirements which the Community institutions must take into account in exercising their powers, in particular in relation to common organisations of the markets."[539]

"[I]t cannot be precluded, in principle, that the provisions of a Directive may be applicable by means of an express reference in a regulation to its provisions, provided that general principles of law and, in particular, the principle of legal certainty, are observed."[540]

"[W]hen there is a choice between several appropriate measures, recourse must be had to the least onerous, and the disadvantages caused must not be disproportionate to the aims pursued."[541]

"[B]earing in mind the wide discretionary power enjoyed by the Community legislature in matters concerning the common agricultural policy, the legality of a measure adopted in that sphere can be affected only if the measure is manifestly inappropriate in terms of the objective which the competent institution is seeking to pursue."[542]

"[E]xamination of the conditions for granting export refunds has disclosed nothing which would make it possible for Article 5(3) of Regulation No 615/98 to be regarded as manifestly inappropriate in terms of the objective pursued, namely that of ensuring the protection of live animals during transport under the rules on export refunds."[543]

---

[538] *Viamex Agrar Handels GmbH and another v Hauptzollamt Hamburg-Jones* [Cases-C37 & 58/06] [2008] ECR 1-69, para 20 (ECJ).

[539] *Viamex Agrar Handels GmbH and another v Hauptzollamt Hamburg-Jones* [Cases-C37 & 58/06] [2008] ECR 1-69, para 23 (ECJ).

[540] *Viamex Agrar Handels GmbH and another v Hauptzollamt Hamburg-Jones* [Cases-C37 & 58/06] [2008] ECR 1-69, para 28 (ECJ).

[541] *Viamex Agrar Handels GmbH and another v Hauptzollamt Hamburg-Jones* [Cases-C37 & 58/06] [2008] ECR 1-69, para 35 (ECJ).

[542] *Viamex Agrar Handels GmbH and another v Hauptzollamt Hamburg-Jones* [Cases-C37 & 58/06] [2008] ECR 1-69, para 36 (ECJ).

[543] *Viamex Agrar Handels GmbH and another v Hauptzollamt Hamburg-Jones* [Cases-C37 & 58/06] [2008] ECR 1-69, para 45 (ECJ).

19. Von Colson and Kamann v Land Nordrhein-Westfalen

Sexual discrimination, and the right to enforce Directive 76/207/EEC when applying for a position, was an approach not previously taken within the European Community, and so when reaching a reasoned interpretation of the Directive, it was required that the Arbeitsgericht Hamm (German Labour Court) referred a number of questions to the European Court of Justice under art.177 EC.

When two well-qualified female social workers applied for similar posts at the Land Nordrhein-Westfalen (a male populated prison), they were refused employment on grounds of their gender. Having referred to the principles of Directive 76/207/EEC, governing equal access to employment, training, promotion and working conditions, the claimants contended that denial of this particular post was tantamount to a breach of Member State obligations, and that legal remedy should constitute either six months full pay, or the creation of another position with the offer of employment. In addition to this, it was claimed that travel costs were also owed under the terms of para.611a of the Bürgerliches Gesetzbuch (Civil Code), as drafted to support the Directive.

While German law had been amended to incorporate the Directive measures, it was executed with a degree of discretion, inasmuch as evidence of sexual discrimination within the recruitment process, provided only that any resulting sanction was one of travel costs, and not those allowing compensatory damages, or the employment provision sought. This led to the formulation of interrelated questions, that relied upon clarification for conclusive judgment within the national judiciary.

The court asked (i) whether under breach of the anti-discrimination Directive, the employer was liable to provide for, and offer, employment to those parties affected, and if so, (ii) whether it was on grounds that the claimant could provide evidence of greater qualification than those offered employment, and (iii) whether equal competence was acceptable as grounds for the provision of additional employment, or whether the claimant was entitled to employment, irrespective of qualifying ability. Question (v) sought clarification as to whether Directive 76/207/EEC provided clear instruction as to the form of remedy awarded where discrimination occurred, but no employment was required; while question (vi) asked whether the terms of the Directive could be relied upon by an individual when the discrimination was between private individuals.

When examining the facts and the exactness of the Directive, it was held by the Court that while the effects of Community law must be observed by Member States, and that transposition of those Directives follows the principles contained, it was not the intention of the Commission that where discriminatory acts are proven, that an employer is imposed with any obligation to create positions outside of those advertised. In terms of clarity of legal remedy, it was put back to the German court that while para.611a (2) of the Bürgerliches Gesetzbuch allows for remedial costs recovery, it was insufficient to the requirements of the Directive, therefore further national debate was needed in order to amend the legislation in line with a fair and balanced level of compensation. It was also held that the terms of the Directive were too ambiguous as to offer individual powers to enforce against another party, where such provisions were not already in place.

Key Citations

"The principle of the effective transposition of the Directive requires that the sanctions must be of such a nature as to constitute appropriate compensation for the candidate discriminated against and for the employer a means of pressure which it would be unwise to disregard and which would prompt him to respect the principle of equal treatment."[544]

"[D]irective No.76/207 does not require discrimination on grounds of sex regarding access to employment to be made the subject of a sanction by way of an obligation imposed upon the employer who is the author of the discrimination to conclude a contract of employment with the candidate discriminated against."[545]

"[F]ull implementation of the Directive does not require any specific form of sanction for unlawful discrimination, it does entail that that sanction be such as to guarantee real and effective judicial protection."[546]

"[N]ational provisions limiting the right to compensation of persons who have been discriminated against as regards access to employment to a purely nominal amount, such as, for example, the reimbursement of expenses incurred by them in submitting their application, would not satisfy the requirements of an effective transposition of the Directive."[547]

"[I]n applying the national law and in particular the provisions of a national law specifically introduced in order to implement Directive No.76/207, national courts are required to interpret their national law in the light of the wording and the purpose of the Directive in order to achieve the result referred to in the third paragraph of Article 189."[548]

"[I]f a Member State chooses to penalize breaches of that prohibition by the award of compensation, then in order to ensure that it is effective and that it has a deterrent effect, that compensation must in any event be adequate in relation to the damage sustained and must therefore amount to more than purely nominal compensation such as, for example, the reimbursement only of the expenses incurred in connection with the application."[549]

---

[544] *Von Colson and Kamann v Land Nordrhein-Westfalen* [Case14/83] [1984] ECR 1891, para 14 (ECJ).

[545] *Von Colson and Kamann v Land Nordrhein-Westfalen* [Case14/83] [1984] ECR 1891, para 19 (ECJ).

[546] *Von Colson and Kamann v Land Nordrhein-Westfalen* [Case14/83] [1984] ECR 1891, para 23 (ECJ).

[547] *Von Colson and Kamann v Land Nordrhein-Westfalen* [Case14/83] [1984] ECR 1891, para 24 (ECJ).

[548] *Von Colson and Kamann v Land Nordrhein-Westfalen* [Case14/83] [1984] ECR 1891, para 26 (ECJ).

[549] *Von Colson and Kamann v Land Nordrhein-Westfalen* [Case14/83] [1984] ECR 1891, para 28 (ECJ).

20. Wagner Miret v Fondo de Garantía Salarial

Directive 80/987/EEC was drafted to protect the lost earnings of employees subject to the liquidation of their employers. The scope of the Directive was designed to embrace all forms of employment as considered so under national law, and required Member States to designate specific bodies for the payments due to claimants under the protection of Community law, while art.1 of the Directive enabled a degree of discretion when adopting the measures contained therein.

When a higher management employee was later made redundant through company dissolution, he was subsequently denied lost earnings under Spanish law, because when adopting the effects of Directive 80/987, it had been decided by the government to exclude domestic servants from the guarantees afforded them under the Directive. While this exclusion did not apply to the claimant, it had been applied when deciding his case in the Juzgado de lo Social (Social Courts), upon which his recovery of over £2,000 was refused.

Taken to the Tribunal Superior de Justice (Superior Court of Justice), it was argued that when applying the terms of Directive 80/987 the legislature had, under Royal Decree No.1382/85, deliberately avoided the inclusion of higher management to the rights afforded other employees through the pay guarantee fund established under art.33 of Law No 8/80 ('The Employees' Statute'), by allowing employment contract caveats to circumvent the essence of the Directive.

This left the Court unable to fully address the claim, without reference to the European Court of Justice for a preliminary ruling under art.177 EC. In this, were three questions relating to the claim, namely (i) whether the terms of Directive 80/987 included all employees of the Member States, (ii) whether the failure of the Spanish government to encompass higher management staff within the annexe excluding domestic servants, provided for prevention of a claim, and (iii) if the answer to the first question was yes, whether the payment should come from the guarantee fund or State compensation.

Having considered the historic debate surrounding this contentious matter, it was held by the Court that when transposing the terms of the Directive, the Member States should determine what constitutes employment under the meaning of national law, and where agreed, those employees are to be protected under the effects of art.1(2) of the Directive.

In relation to the exclusion of higher management, it was agreed that unless expressly contained in the annexe to Directive 87/987 (later amended to Directive 87/164), those occupying such roles were entitled to received compensatory payment; while with regard to the source of payment, it was clarified by the Court that in instances similar to this, it was the role of the Member State to devolve payment to the fund created, or if such a fund had not been established, the compensation was due from the Member State itself.

Key Citations

"[I]n so far as national law classifies members of the higher management staff as employees, a Member State cannot exclude that category of employee from the scope of application of Directive 80/987/EEC, as amended by Directive 87/164/EEC, if it is not included in the Annex to that directive."[550]

"[T]he application of the guarantees provided for by Directive 80/987/EEC to the higher management staff of undertakings who are wrongly excluded from the payment of such guarantees by national law devolves in principle upon the body normally prescribed for other employees."[551]

"The principle of interpretation in conformity with Directives must be followed in particular where a national court considers, as in the present case, that the pre-existing provisions of its national law satisfy the requirements of the Directive concerned."[552]

---

[550] *Wagner Miret v Fondo de Garantía Salarial* [Case C-334/92] [1993] ECR I-6911, para III (Joliet J).

[551] *Wagner Miret v Fondo de Garantía Salarial* [Case C-334/92] [1993] ECR I-6911, para IV (Joliet J).

[552] *Wagner Miret v Fondo de Garantía Salarial* [Case C-334/92] [1993] ECR I-6911, para 21 (ECJ).

6. Family Law

1. AI v MT (Alternative Dispute Resolution)

With the introduction of Alternative Dispute Resolution (ADR) in 2010, the essence of divorce and family proceedings became less governed by the rigours of litigation, and more attuned to continuous and considered discourse between parties, while on provisional terms that embraced the welfare of children and respect for individual rights.

After marrying relatively young, and moving quickly into starting a family, two devout members of the Jewish faith found themselves in stark opposition as to how best they could live their lives, and in turn, end the marriage before occupying different countries.

When the matter of how contact could be set between the father and the two small children arose, it quickly became a matter of contention, and one that ultimately drew guidance from the Jewish community (Beth Din), with overall authority from from the English courts. When adopting ADR strategies, the emphasis is typically placed upon expedience and reduced costs, however, due to such vast geographical differences and intrinsic religious constraints, the process of divorce ran over a period of years versus months, and was certainly not without its frustrations.

What eventually emerged however, was that through a combination of delicate communication, respect for doctrinal traditions, cohesive written agreements and the balancing of the needs of the children, it was possible to overcome the potential pitfalls of cross-jurisdictional conflict and move matters to a much more mature and objective conclusion. This became an outcome that had at times, seemed unlikely, given the inclination by the parties involved to build walls between them, which served only to harm the children, and drain financial resources more than was necessary.

When summarising the importance of mediation, the court referred to the words of Thorpe LJ, who explained in *Al Khatib v Masry*:

> "[T]here is no case, however conflicted, which is not potentially open to successful mediation, even if mediation has not been attempted or has failed during the trial process"[553]

Ultimately it all came down to a successful collaboration of the Jewish authorities, domestic courts and continued willingness of the parents to collectively work toward a resolution, that the case now stands as testament to the transcendence of ideology in favour of a united family, even after the dissolution of marriage.

---

[553] *Al Khatib v Masry* [2004] EWCA Civ 1353 (CA) [17] (Thorpe LJ).

Key Citations

"[S]ave where statute provides otherwise, when considering issues concerning the upbringing of children, it is the child's welfare that is the paramount consideration."[554]

"[T]he parties are able to select the arbitrator as opposed to litigation where the parties are obliged to accept the judge allocated to hear the case."[555]

"[P]rimary responsibility for children rests with their parents who should be entitled to raise their children without the intrusion of the State save where the children are suffering, or likely to suffer significant harm."[556]

"[A]t a time where there is much comment about the antagonism between the religious and secular elements of society, it was notable that the court was able not only to accommodate the parties' wish to resolves their dispute by reference to their religious authorities, but also buttress that process at critical stages…"[557]

"So far as the financial settlement was concerned, the terms of the agreement were unobjectionable. The parties' devout beliefs had been respected. The outcome was in keeping with English law whilst achieved by a process rooted in the Jewish culture to which the families belong."[558]

---

[554] *AI v MT (Alternative Dispute Resolution)* [2013] EWHC 100 (Fam) [28] (Baker J).

[555] *AI v MT (Alternative Dispute Resolution)* [2013] EWHC 100 (Fam) [32] (Baker J).

[556] *AI v MT (Alternative Dispute Resolution)* [2013] EWHC 100 (Fam) [32] (Baker J).

[557] *AI v MT (Alternative Dispute Resolution)* [2013] EWHC 100 (Fam) [35] (Baker J).

[558] *AI v MT (Alternative Dispute Resolution)* [2013] EWHC 100 (Fam) [37] (Baker J).

2. Evans v Amicus Healthcare Ltd and Others

In vitro fertilisation (IVF), and the unilateral consent of the potential mother, is a circumstance that invokes both legislative and Convention rights for both parties, prior to the actual process of childbirth. On this occasion, the needs of a single woman are driven to exhaustion, despite knowledge that her former partner has made his position clear.

Having both met in their twenties, the parties to this case were engaged to be married, while at the time, equally excited about the possibility of raising children. Before conception could begin, the appellant was diagnosed with cancerous tumours to both her ovaries, at which point her world quite literally turned upside down. Following a medical consultation, the appellant learned that due to slow tumour growth, there was hope that IVF treatment might permit her the chance to carry a child to birth, and thus have the life she had hoped for.

As part of the process, the two parties were asked to complete consent forms for the use and storage of sperm and embryos, as prescribed by the Human Fertilisation and Embryology Act 1990 (HFEA). Upon completion of the harvesting and fertilisation process, six embryos were cryogenically frozen for use by the donors, at a time two years from the treatment, and as advised by the clinic. Roughly six months after their participation, the couple separated, and the man wrote to the clinic, expressly notifying them of his wish to withdraw from the arrangement, and to request that the embryos be destroyed.

Upon learning of this, the appellant issued proceedings against him by injunction, on the stipulation that (i) he could not withdraw from the agreement, (ii) that the embryos were to be kept frozen for ten years as per the terms of the agreement, and (iii) that the appellant was lawfully entitled to receive the embryos, despite his obvious disagreement. By declaration of incompatibility with sch.3 of the 1990 Act, it was further claimed that anything to the contrary was a violation of arts.2 (Right to life), 8 (Right to respect for private and family life) and 14 (Prohibition of discrimination) of the European Convention on Human Rights (ECHR), and that the embryos were afforded equal rights under arts.2 and 8 accordingly.

Sch.3 of the HFEA 1990 Act was drafted to address all matters relating to consent and use of gametes or embryos, and while it was contended that para.2(1)(a) provided that consent allowed for the treatment of two people acting 'together', it is also clearly provided for in s.4(1)(b) that no person shall:

> "[I]n the course of providing treatment services for any woman, *use the sperm of any man unless the services are being provided for the woman and the man together* or use the eggs of any other woman, except in pursuance of a licence."[559]

This translated that the written withdrawal by the appellant's former partner had vetoed the use of the embryos in the absence of his consent, and the family court adopted the same line of argument, before dismissing her claim. Having been appealed before the

---

[559] Human Fertilisation and Embryology Act 1990, s.4(1)(b) (emphasis added).

Supreme Court, the implications of Convention rights and incompatibility were given greater consideration, along with commentary by the Secretary of State, as required under s.5(2) of the Human Rights Act 1998.

Adopting the position that the case revolved around the right to bring life into being as opposed to a right to life, the Court held that the appellant needed to recognise the complexities of the IVF process, and that careful scrutiny of the *Warnock Report*[560] demonstrated that the rights of fathers had been exercised with due caution to the rights of potential mothers. It was also held that while denial of the treatment to the appellant was a violation of art.8 of ECHR, the same principles equally applied were the Court to allow the appellant to proceed without the consent of her former partner. Therefore in circumstances of public policy, it was deemed justifiable to encroach upon certain Convention rights where the best interests of the people applied. While accusations of discrimination levelled under art.14 ECHR were also valid, there were unavoidably distinct differences between natural conception and the rigours of IVF, therefore a right to withdraw from consent was fundamental to the mechanics of such treatment, and thus did not prejudice the appellant on grounds of gender.

With regard to the rights of the embryos, it was determined under art.2 of ECHR (Everyone's right to life shall be protected by law), that in accordance with s.37(1)(a) of the HFEA Act 1990, a twenty-four week old foetus was eligible to legal rights, but not before, and so any declaration that non-enforcement of rights was incompatible with the Convention could not be sustained. It was on these numerous grounds that the appeal was dismissed, with note to the need for greater clarification of individual rights during the IVF registration process, so as to avoid further painful outcomes for those involved.

Key Citations

"If the Human Rights Act is concerned with the protection of individuals from particular incursions by the state into fundamental rights now accorded to them by law, it must be open to a single individual to challenge as disproportionate the effect of legislation on her alone."[561]

"[W]hile legislation modifying individuals' private law liabilities can be expected not to infringe their Convention rights without clear justification, legislation directed to the implementation and management of social policy may well have to infringe some individuals' Convention rights in the interests of consistency."[562]

---

[560] Mary Warnock, *Report of the Committee of Enquiry into Human Fertilisation and Embryology* (White Paper, Cm 9314, 1984)

[561] *Evans v Amicus Healthcare Ltd and Others* [2004] 3 All ER 1025 [54] (Thorpe and Sedley LJJ).

[562] *Evans v Amicus Healthcare Ltd and Others* [2004] 3 All ER 1025 [65] (Thorpe and Sedley LJJ).

3. Fitzpatrick v Sterling Housing Association Ltd

The phrase 'family' has seen a number of changes over the last century, and so it is that the common law of the United Kingdom is expected to accommodate cultural shifts and the cosmopolitain nature of intimate relationships, when reaching a fair and balanced decision.

In this House of Lords appeal case the relationship between a private tenant and potential successor was that of two men, and upon the death of the elder partner, it was found that despite their twenty-year history, and the deeply caring bonds shared between them, the wording of the Rent Act 1977 (as amended into the Housing Act 1988) prevented the surviving party from inheriting the assured tenancy, and thereby remaining in occupation of the home they had shared together.

Because of the widening of interpretation concerning the proximity required to uphold succession, it became possible to appeal to the original judgment; and so the appellant relied upon two sections of sch.1 of the 1977 Act, namely para.2(1) which reads:

> "The surviving spouse (if any) of the original tenant, if residing in the dwelling-house immediately before the death of the original tenant, shall after the death be the statutory tenant if and so long as he or she occupies the dwelling-house as his or her residence."[563]

And para.3(1) which reads:

> "Where paragraph 2 above does not apply, but a person who was a member of the original tenant's family was residing with him in the dwelling-house at the time of and for the period of two years immediately before his death then, after his death, that person or if there is more than one such person such one of them as may be decided by agreement, or in default of agreement by the county court, shall be entitled to an assured tenancy of the dwelling-house by succession."[564]

The issue then presented to the House was not one of spousal qualification, but rather agreement that despite the homosexual relationship between the two men, there did exist an intimacy that by all accounts, could be construed as familial.

In *Ross v Collins*, it was stated by Russell LJ that:

> "[T]wo strangers cannot, it seems to me, ever establish artificially for the purposes of this section a familial nexus by acting as brothers or as sisters, even if they call each other such and consider their relationship to be tantamount to that. Nor, in my view, can an adult man and woman who establish a platonic relationship establish a familial nexus by acting as a devoted brother and sister or father and daughter would act, even if they address each other as such and

---

[563] Rent Act 1977, sch.1 para.2(1)

[564] Rent Act 1977, sch.1 para.3(1)

even if they refer to each other as such and regard their association as tantamount to such."[565]

Yet in *Watson v Lucas*,[566] the Court of Appeal held by a majority that a woman that had cohabited with a man, despite his remaining married to his wife, was considered a family member under sch.1 of the Rent Act 1977; while in *Chios Property Investment Co Ltd v Lopez*,[567] the Court stressed that a sufficient state of permanence and stability would suffice to claim for succession of tenancy under the pretence of family.

Similarly, in *Dyson Holdings Ltd v Fox*[568] the defendant had resided with the tenant for over twenty years, despite never marrying or having children, and yet the Court of Appeal reversed the original judgment, and ruled in favour of the defendant existing as family for the purposes of the 1977 Act.

Later in *Barclays Bank Plc v O'Brien*, the need for appreciation of same-sex relationships was expressed by Browne-Wilkinson LJ, who espoused that:

> "The 'tenderness' shown by the law to married women is not based on the marriage ceremony but reflects the underlying risk of one cohabitee exploiting the emotional involvement and trust of the other. Now that unmarried cohabitation, whether heterosexual or homosexual, is widespread in our society, the law should recognise this."[569]

While in the American case *Braschi v Stahl Associates Co*, the majority of the New York Court of Appeals held that:

> "The intended protection against sudden eviction should not rest on fictitious legal distinctions or genetic history, but instead should find its foundation in the reality of family life. In the context of eviction, *a more realistic, and certainly equally valid, view of a family includes two adult lifetime partners whose relationship is long term and characterised by an emotional and financial commitment and interdependence.*"[570]

With these progressive judgments, and the knowledge that extension of the meaning of family by the court was not an affront to Parliament, but instead a call to arms in the need for legislative review, the House ruled by a majority that while the appellant could not qualify as successor of a statutory tenancy under para.2 of sch.1 of the Rent Act 1977, he did now succeed as a family member under para.3 of the Housing Act 1988, and so allowed the appeal accordingly.

---

[565] *Ross v Collins* [1964] 1 WLR 425 (CA) 432 (Russell LJ).

[566] [1980] 1 WLR 1493.

[567] (1987) 20 HLR 120.

[568] [1976] QB 503.

[569] *Barclays Bank Plc v O'Brien* [1994] 1 AC 180 (CA) 198 (Browne-Wilkinson LJ).

[570] *Braschi v Stahl Associates Co* (1989) 544 NYS2d 784, 788-789 (emphasis added).

Key Citations

"The onus on one person claiming that he or she was a member of the same-sex original tenant's family will involve that person establishing rather than merely asserting the necessary indicia of the relationship. A transient superficial relationship will not do even if it is intimate. Mere cohabitation by friends as a matter of convenience will not do."[571]

"[T]wo people of the same sex can be regarded as having established membership of a family, one of the most significant of human relationships which both gives benefits and imposes obligations."[572]

"[I]t cannot make sense to say that, although a heterosexual partnership can give rise to membership of a family for Rent Act purposes, a homosexual partnership cannot. Where sexual partners are involved, whether heterosexual or homosexual, there is scope for the intimate mutual love and affection and long-term commitment that typically characterise the relationship of husband and wife."[573]

"[T]he morality of a lawful relationship is not now regarded as relevant when the court is deciding whether an individual qualifies for protection under the Rent Acts."[574]

"The element of a free mutual choice of a close intimate relationship and the voluntary determination to spend one's life with another is one form of a family bond."[575]

"It would be wrong to regard the present case as one about the rights of homosexuals. It is simply a matter of the application of ordinary language to this particular statutory provision in the light of current social conditions."[576]

[571] *Fitzpatrick v Sterling Housing Association Ltd* [2000] 1 FCR 21 (HL) 40 (Slynn LJ).

[572] *Fitzpatrick v Sterling Housing Association Ltd* [2000] 1 FCR 21 (HL) 40 (Slynn LJ).

[573] *Fitzpatrick v Sterling Housing Association Ltd* [2000] 1 FCR 21 (HL) 44 (Nicholls LJ).

[574] *Fitzpatrick v Sterling Housing Association Ltd* [2000] 1 FCR 21 (HL) 46 (Nicholls LJ).

[575] *Fitzpatrick v Sterling Housing Association Ltd* [2000] 1 FCR 21 (HL) 49 (Clyde LJ).

[576] *Fitzpatrick v Sterling Housing Association Ltd* [2000] 1 FCR 21 (HL) 53 (Clyde LJ).

4. Jones v Kernott

The inference or imputation of equitable and proprietary rights, are two very distinct approaches within the remit of court discretion, and so it is that this family law appeal case serves the merits of such distinctions well.

When an unmarried couple chose to purchase their first family home, it was done so under joint legal title. While this itself is not an uncommon approach to home-buying, the eventual separation that followed, fractured the robustness of their intentions, and raised questions around the true feelings of the parties at the time the mortgage began.

During their time together, and the period in which they started to raise children, the couple remained unmarried for reasons best known to themselves. After nearly nine years of shared occupancy (albeit with disproportionate financial contributions), the decision was made by the father to separate and leave the family. When a failure to sell the property after the split led him to purchase a property of his own, his previously meagre financial contributions to the home and family, were now redirected toward his new purchase, while the mother and children remained in occupation, while she upheld the mortgage repayments without interruption.

Thirteen years after his departure, the respondent took steps to claim his share of the equitable interest held within the home previously shared, whereupon his former partner initiated proceedings to prevent it. Counter claiming under s.14 of the Trusts of Land and Appointment of Trustees Act 1996, it was her opinion that she was now the sole beneficiary of their family home, and that should the respondent feel he held any beneficial interest in that property, she was subsequently entitled to an equal share percentage of his.

The issues faced by the courts, ultimately stemmed from a fundamental lack of communicated intention (written or otherwise) by either party when purchasing the family home, and a traditional reliance upon the precedence of *Stack v Dowden*[577] when deciding the true intentions of cohabiting couples that have decided to terminate their relationship before dividing the assets of the property enjoyed. In cases that meet the requirements of such an approach, the outcome is fairly predictable, but on this occasion the home discussed did not fall under sole legal title, and so the inclination to apply it was reserved.

In the first hearing, the judge concluded that the shares held were ninety percent for the mother and ten percent for the father, based upon his agreement to sell, and the numerous events that followed (including his leaving and full investment into a solely occupied property of his own). When challenged, the Court of Appeal found in favour of the *Stack* assumption that regardless of financial difference, the intention to purchase under joint title provides that equal shares are afforded the signing parties.

Now in further contention within the Supreme Court, the question was whether automatic imputation of equitable rights could reasonably stand, when the actions shown by the father were indicative of a cessation of interest in a home that he no longer shared and had ceased contributing towards when he left. After a close examination of the

---

[577] [2007] UKHL 17.

validity of inference, it was agreed that there were indeed sufficient grounds to approximate beneficial interest, despite appreciation of the history behind unmarried couples, and the nature of intention by virtue of individual action.

Key Citations

"Financial contributions are relevant but there are many other factors which may enable the court to decide what shares were either intended…or fair…"[578]

"It would be difficult (and, perhaps, absurd) to imagine a scenario involving the circumstances from which, in the absence of express agreement, the court will infer a shared or common intention which is unfair."[579]

"As soon as it is clear that inferring an intention is not possible, the focus of the court's attention should be squarely on what is fair."[580]

"[I]t is impossible to infer that the parties intended that their shares in the property be apportioned as the judge considered they should be but that such an intention should be imputed to them."[581]

---

[578] *Jones v Kernott* [2011] UKSC 53 [51] (Walker & Hale JJSC).

[579] *Jones v Kernott* [2011] UKSC 53 [66] (Collins LJ).

[580] *Jones v Kernott* [2011] UKSC 53 [75] (Kerr LJ).

[581] *Jones v Kernott* [2011] UKSC 53 [77] (Kerr LJ).

5. Mabon v Mabon

The right for a minor to enjoy autonomous representation within family law proceedings, is enshrined under both the Care of Children Act 2004 and the Family Proceedings Rules 1991. While English common law functions within a patriarchal system, it is sometimes counter-productive to fetter the needs of the child, when a recognition of aptitude and resilience to parental influence, permits those involved to speak for themselves.

In this matter, a couple had enjoyed a marriage bearing six children, until such time as they parted company. This produced an almost equal split between the children, with the father remaining with the three eldest boys aged thirteen, fifteen and seventeen. It was after her departure, that the mother applied for residence orders, so as to enjoy spending time with her sons, whereupon the CAFCASS officer became the legal guardian of all six children, prior to proceedings.

Following a lengthy and somewhat protracted hearing, the three boys approached their acting solicitor, so as to remove the presence of the CAFCASS officer in lieu of direct representation. This was requested under Rule 9.2A(4) of the Family Proceedings Rules 1991, which reads:

> "Where a minor has a next friend or guardian ad litem in proceedings and the minor wishes to prosecute or defend the remaining stages of the proceedings without a next friend or guardian ad litem, *the minor may apply to the court for leave for that purpose and for the removal of the next friend or guardian* ad litem ..."[582]

At which point the court must evaluate the merits of such a request under Rule 9.2A(6), which reads:

> "Where the court is considering whether to
>
> (a) ...
>
> (b) grant leave under paragraph (4) and remove a next friend or guardian ad litem, it shall grant the leave sought and as the case may be remove the next friend or guardian ad litem *if it considers that the minor concerned has sufficient understanding to participate as a party in the proceedings concerned or proposed without a next friend or guardian* ad litem."[583]

On this occasion, the trial judge found himself unable to reconcile the boys' request with his own consideration of both time constraints and the value of their own personal insight to the matter (a decision compounded by subjective concerns for their safety and wellbeing in such emotional litigation), and subsequently dismissed their application, before passing judgment.

---

[582] Family Proceedings Rules 1991, rule 9.2A(4) (emphasis added).

[583] Family Proceedings Rules 1991, rule 9.2A(6) (emphasis added).

In response, the boys' countered by appeal to the Supreme Court that failure to allow for the removal of the appointed guardian, stood in direct conflict with art.12 of the United Nations Convention on the Rights of the Child 1989, and art.8 of the European Convention on Human Rights (ECHR) (Right to privacy and family life), with particular focus on autonomy. Having also received a doctors report, the Court were reassured to learn that:

> "What is clear is that all three boys are very able. They are quick in terms of being articulate and perceptive. Andrew is perhaps the more articulate of the three boys; being the middle of the three he tends to be the spokesman, whilst Craig is the more quiet and thoughtful of the three."

Which on the facts, allowed for greater appreciation of Rule 9.2A(6) and confirmation that to prevent the independent and separate representation of the three boys, was counter to the purposes of the Family Proceedings Act 1991 and both Conventions. This was a view supported by s.6(2)(a)(b) of the Care of Children Act 2004, which reads:

> "6 Child's views
>
> (2) In proceedings to which subsection (1) applies,
>
> (a) A child must be given reasonable opportunities to express views on matters affecting the child; and
>
> (b) Any views the child expresses (either directly or through a representative) must be taken into account."[584]

It was with full consideration of not only the statutory powers afforded children, but the advances in family law since 1991, that the Court recognised the need to embrace the advocacy of children's views within family cases, and that while s.42. of the Children Act 1989 affords guardians powers to investigate the views of minors within trial environments, it was unnatural to override the tenacity and endurability of children for the sake of adult overprotection; whereupon the appeal was upheld, and the order of Rule 9.2A(4) of the Family Proceedings Act 1991 allowed.

Key Citations

"Unless we in this jurisdiction are to fall out of step with similar societies as they safeguard Article 12 rights, we must, in the case of articulate teenagers, accept that the right to freedom of expression and participation outweighs the paternalistic judgment of welfare."[585]

---

[584] Care of Children Act 2004, s.6(2)(a)(b)

[585] *Mabon v Mabon and others* [2005] 2 FCR 354 [28] (Thorpe LJ).

6. Miller v Miller

While the principle of fairness is central to the conjoined appeals determined (see here also *McFarlane v McFarlane*),[586] the two cases required differing approaches, due to the duration of each marriage and the financial circumstances surrounding them.

Miller v Miller

In the first appeal, the arrangement of the marriage and financial footing of the two parties were unequal from the outset, and with consideration of the reasons cited for divorce, the presented facts displayed evidence of a self-entitlement that undoubtedly polluted the relationship and led to a generous settlement in favour of the weaker party.

When entering the relationship, the wife occupied a highly paid position that while enviable to most, paled in comparison to the recently acquired wealth of her new husband, who himself was now a multi-millionaire, and on his way to significantly increasing that sum through strategic investment in hedge funds management and a new business partnership. After less than three years, the couple separated and divorce proceedings began on the part of the husband. While he filed under accusations of her unreasonable behaviour, the wife cross-petitioned on grounds of adultery, given his disclosure of intent to re-marry, while noting that she never sought to end the marriage, nor conducted herself in any way to suggest otherwise.

When bought before the judge, it was found that with consideration given for both his estimated current wealth of around £17.5m, and the potential resale value of his company shares which rested around £16m, his wife's position was that of having debts above £200,000, should she be liable for her costs. Through a division of matrimonial assets of both a property and lump sum award, the wife was legally entitled to a £5m settlement that (i) enabled her to remain living in the home shared by both parties during their brief marriage, and (ii) provided enough capital to sustain the standard of living afforded her throughout the course of their relationship. This decision was felt to represent the fairest terms on which to end their marriage, and one that was uniformly upheld under appeal to the House of Lords.

McFarlane v McFarlane

While bearing some similarities to *Miller v Miller*,[587] the couple enjoyed over fifteen years of marriage, and the joy of having three children of their own. Of particular note is that at the outset of their time together, the wife and mother of the children had a successful law career, and at that time earned more than her husband, who was himself about to become partner of a well established accountancy firm.

It was later decided by them both, that in order for the children to benefit from a grounded upbringing, the wife would surrender her position as a solicitor, and become a full-time mother until they had grown into secondary school age; after which she would return to paid work, or retrain for a new career. At the point of their separation, the

---

[586] [2005] Fam 171.

[587] [2006] 2 AC 618.

annual household income was over £1m, but this was made up from the husband's income, with average family living costs of around £150,000 p.a.

When deciding how best to end matters, the court felt that in addition to the equal division of join assets worth £3m (made up of three properties), a joint lives order would best suffice as the estimated annual living costs of the wife (and children) fell around £215,000 p.a. The husband countered that £160-180,000 p.a would sustain a comfortable life for the family, at which point the wife then claimed for £345,000 p.a, whereupon the judge settled upon £310,000 p.a, which was a figure he deemed fair and reasonable.

The husband duly appealed, whereupon the Court of Appeal held that the amount determined was far in excess of the wife's actual living expenses, and was such that would allow her to invest, and thereby accumulate, increased capital from his payments. In light of this perceived inequality, the figure was readjusted down to £240,000 p.a, whereupon the wife cross-appealed, and the Court again upheld on grounds that in specific instances, periodic payment orders can be used as a means to enable recipient accumulation of monies, albeit with a determined liability period of only five years.

When submitted by the wife for final consideration at the House of Lords, it was wholly agreed that the original judgment must remain. And so while the essence of a 'clean break' was observed through the ability of each party to secure a tenable degree of financial freedom, it was done so under the assumption that at some point in the future, the joint lives arrangement would be mutually terminated through the reasoning of fairness.

Key Citations

"A rigid application of the clean break principle, as enacted in section 9(1)(d), has the advantage of certainty. But it runs the risk of becoming outdated as social conditions change and the reasoning behind it no longer fits in with modern concepts of fairness."[588]

"Achieving a clean break in the event of divorce remains as desirable now as it was then. But if this means one party must adjust to a lower standard of living, the result is that a clean break is being achieved at the expense of fairness."[589]

"The courts should have the discretion to provide for a longer period where, in exceptional circumstances and applying the overriding criterion of fairness, the judge finds that one party to the marriage whose contribution to the marriage has resulted in a reduction of his or her earning capacity ought to be compensated out of the other party's future income because the capital needed to provide this is not available."[590]

---

[588] *Miller v Miller* [2006] UKHL 24 [115] (Hope LJ).

[589] *Miller v Miller* [2006] UKHL 24 [120] (Hope LJ).

[590] *Miller v Miller* [2006] UKHL 24 [121] (Hope LJ).

7. Prest v Petrodel Resources Ltd

'Piercing the corporate veil' and the lawful applicability of s.24(1)(a) of Part II of the Matrimonial Causes Act 1973, are uneasily paired to establish liability in this post-matrimonial conflict of property transition, while the extensive evaluation of this mis-applied doctrine in cases of reminiscent yet distinguishable natures, gives rise to ponder its continued relevance.

Following the lengthy divorce of a shrewd businessman and his estranged wife, the order of the court to transfer title of a number of properties to the appellant, was met with continued evasion and somewhat aggressive objection, when the ex-husband consistently went to great lengths in order to frustrate proceedings, and by his refusal to permit the submission of evidence in order to expedite the legal obligation put before him.

First developed in *Re Barcelona Traction Light and Power Co Ltd*,[591] the intended effect of 'piercing the corporate veil' was to stymie the deliberate and fraudulent actions of those parties holding controlling shares of limited companies for the sole purpose of self-interest and avoidance of legal duties. In contrast, the powers conferred under s.24 of the 1973 Act provide if not imply, that the defending party is to transfer the specified property to the claimant, to whom title is now owed under the terms of the marriage and through the act of divorce.

On this occasion, there were a number of properties acquired by the respondent through his established companies, yet with the majority of those funds sourced individually (albeit alleged more than proven given the chaotic administration executed throughout their years of existence). While it was accepted that the matrimonial home would be handed over, the time wasted by the respondent in clarifying his legal and beneficial entitlement to the remaining seven properties, led the original judge to use the principle discussed to establish precise liability, and enforce the transfer in absence of conveyance documentation.

When discussed at appeal, the issue raised was (by virtue of the fact that the respondent showed evidence of beneficial ownership on the assumption that the properties were held on trust by the company used to secure their purchase) whether it was necessary to invoke the piercing of the corporate veil, and whether such application was wholly relevant, given the nature of the case and the narrowness of the principle's design.

After discussing previous judicial exercise of this rigid and yet shoe-horned legal moral, it was decided that the appeal could be readily upheld on grounds of beneficial interest alone; and that transfer of title could take effect through statute, rather than a principle requiring more considered use in the future.

---

[591] [1970] ICJ 3.

Key Citations

"[P]rovided the limits are recognised and respected, it is consistent with the general approach of English law to the problems raised by the use of legal concepts to defeat mandatory rules of law."[592]

"[W]here say, the terms of acquisition and occupation of the matrimonial home are arranged between the husband in his personal capacity and the husband in his capacity as the sole effective agent of the company (or someone else acting at his direction), judges exercising family jurisdiction are entitled to be sceptical about whether the terms of the occupation are really what they are said to be, or are simply a sham to conceal the reality of the husband's beneficial ownership."[593]

"The question nevertheless arises as to whether in a case such as this, the courts have power to prevent the statutes under which limited liability companies may be established as separate legal persons, whether in this or some other jurisdiction, being used as an engine for fraud."[594]

"[T]he court only has power to pierce the corporate veil when all other more conventional remedies have proven to be of no assistance."[595]

"[T]he situations in which piercing the corporate veil may be available as a fall-back are likely to be very rare and that no-one should be encouraged to think that any further exception, in addition to the evasion principle, will be easy to establish."[596]

---

[592] *Prest v Petrodel Resources Ltd and Others* [2013] UKSC 34 [27] (Sumpton LJ).

[593] *Prest v Petrodel Resources Ltd and Others* [2013] UKSC 34 [52] (Sumpton LJ).

[594] *Prest v Petrodel Resources Ltd and Others* [2013] UKSC 34 [89] (Hale LJ).

[595] *Prest v Petrodel Resources Ltd and Others* [2013] UKSC 34 [103] (Clarke LJ).

[596] *Prest v Petrodel Resources Ltd and Others* [2013] UKSC 34 [103] (Clarke LJ).

8. *Re* A (A Child)

Parental contact is key to the successful and balanced growth of every child, regardless of whether the family unit is compromised through divorce or separation, and so when the Family Justice System is left wanting, important questions must be addressed as to how and why the very institution appointed to preserve the sanctity of familial cohesion, failed to provide fair and reasoned justice to a man whose accountability was an example to estranged fathers everywhere.

Having been in a relationship for over a decade prior to the birth of their daughter, the appellant and respondent had never committed to marriage, only cohabiting for a brief period, both before and after becoming parents. Less than two years later, they separated, after which the father applied for a contact order. In a matter spanning twelve years, the two parties fought for their individual rights, as their daughter became a teenager. At the age of fourteen, matters had reached a point where the daughter expressly refused any further contact with her father, and so the court was willing to concur through the issue of a disposal order under s.91(14) of the Children Act 1989, which would render the litigants unable to request further orders of any kind in regard to the needs and interests of the child.

Basing his appeal on the systemic failure of the family courts to preserve his rights under arts.6 (Right to a fair trial) and 8 (Right to respect for private and family life) of the European Convention on Human Rights (ECHR), and that his daughters views were polluted through the calculated manipulation of her mother, the father requested that the Family Law Division make a full and proper reevaluation of the facts as to his claim for contact/residence, and restore the outcome so as to allow his rightful enjoyment of a natural and healthy relationship with his daughter, despite her protestations to the contrary.

To summarise, the matter had been heard by numerous divisional judges, while two CAFCASS (Children and Family Court Advisory and Support Service) guardians retired through ill-health, an appointed child, adolescent and family psychiatrist retired, the local authority withdrew from the case, the mother ceased to attend court and the replacement NYAS (National Youth Advocacy Service) worker had never met the mother, nor provided any evidence in court. In addition to this, the mother herself was alcohol and drug dependant, while suffering from a paranoia and depression-inducing personality disorder coupled with Crohn's disease, and who on one occasion, had been charged with possession of a knife and subjected to a community order, prompting an investigative report under s.37 of the Children Act 1989.

Contrastingly, throughout proceedings, the father had shown impeccable conduct, while being repeatedly subjected to unfounded accusations of abuse, irresponsibility, deviance and selfishness, despite making several allowances in favour of the mother and their child, when others might easily have done otherwise.

Presented to the Supreme Court, it was with great sympathy that the facts of the appeal were given yet another examination, along with the willingness of the previous trial judge to waive enforcement of a large number of orders issued to the mother, and her continued breach of them. Under r52(11)(3) of the Civil Procedure Rules (CPR) it is stated that the Appeal Court will allow an appeal where the decision of the lower court was either wrong, or unjust because of a serious procedural or other irregularity. It was clear that on this occasion, denial of the appellant's rights to spend time with his daughter, and the omission of the judge to enforce the court orders, were both violations of the natural course of justice and therefore subject to investigation.

With regard to the actions of the judge, it was held that the principles outlined by Munby J in *Re L-W (Enforcement and Committal: Contact)*,[597] were such that in order to avoid the risk of a case losing focus, there needed to be four points of approach adopted by the courts and presiding judges, namely:

(1) Judicial continuity
(2) Judicial case management including effective timetabling
(3) A judicially set strategy for the case; and
(4) Consistency of judicial approach

It was thus evident to the Court, that from the protracted and unstable manner in which the case had been heard, none of these virtues were visible, and that as all court orders are enforceable under s.11N of the Children Act 1989, there had been a gross departure from judicial obligation by the now retired judge.

Looking again at the ECHR violations cited, it was held that there were obvious contradictions between the expressed wishes of the child, and her positive commentary of time spent with her father over the course of litigation; many of which were traceable to the overt hostility shown by the mother toward the appellant, and the naturally arising sense of loyalty by the daughter; although none of these were given proper analysis prior to the judgment awarded. This concluded that both arts.6 and 8 of the ECHR were breached, both in terms of fairness, and with regards to quality time shared between the appellant and his daughter; whereupon the Court upheld the appeal, before ordering the expansive court transcripts to be sent to the President of the Family Division and Chairman of the Family Justice Board for urgent review.

---

[597] [2010] EWCA Civ 1253 [96]-[98].

Key Citations

"The conduct of human relationships, particularly following the breakdown in the relationship between the parents of a child, are not readily conducive to organisation and dictat by court order; nor are they the responsibility of the courts or the judges."[598]

"There may be many cases where the wronged parent may be reluctant to push, or be seen to push, for enforcement proceedings against the other parent for breach of court orders; that circumstance does not, of itself, relieve the court of the responsibility for enforcing its own orders."[599]

"[O]rders for contact are orders of the court and, as such, consideration of the rule of law is directly engaged both when the court is considering making such an order and, crucially, when considering the consequences of any subsequent breach."[600]

"[T]he judge must, in the absence of good reason for any failure, support the order that he or she has made by considering enforcement, either under the enforcement provisions in CA 1989, ss 11J-11N or by contempt proceedings."[601]

"The first time that a judge should give serious consideration to whether or not he or she will, if called upon, be prepared to enforce a contact order should be before the order is made and not only after a breach has occurred."[602]

"If a directive contact order is called for, then, on making it, the judge should be clear, at least in his or her own mind, that, upon breach, enforcement may well follow. If, on the facts of the case, enforcement is not to be contemplated, then an alternative judicial strategy not involving a directive court order (and which might in an extreme case include a change of residence or, at the other extreme, dismissing the application for contact) must be developed."[603]

"It is plainly right for judges to make their evaluation of a child's welfare based upon the current situation, but in analysing that situation they must bring to bear such evidence that may be relevant from what has transpired in the past."[604]

---

[598] *A (A Child), Re* [2013] EWCA Civ 1104 [53] (McFarlane LJ).

[599] *A (A Child), Re* [2013] EWCA Civ 1104 [56] (McFarlane LJ).

[600] *A (A Child), Re* [2013] EWCA Civ 1104 [58] (McFarlane LJ).

[601] *A (A Child), Re* [2013] EWCA Civ 1104 [60] (McFarlane LJ).

[602] *A (A Child), Re* [2013] EWCA Civ 1104 [61] (McFarlane LJ).

[603] *A (A Child), Re* [2013] EWCA Civ 1104 [61] (McFarlane LJ).

[604] *A (A Child), Re* [2013] EWCA Civ 1104 [74] (McFarlane LJ).

9. *Re* G (Education: Religious Upbringing)

The needs of the child and the heritage of religious conformity are bound to reach an impasse when the parents share opposing views of life, and so it is that a divorced couple are forced to litigate when their five children are at risk of emotional and intellectual harm.

Born into families following the ultra orthodox principle of Judaism, it was by arranged marriage that the appellant and respondent were mutually bound before starting a family. Having raised five children aged between three and eleven, the marriage broke down, resulting in the father leaving home and returning to his religious community, while the mother immersed herself into a less demanding way of life, yet remaining faithful to the principles of her faith.

Under Chassidic (Hasidic) or Chareidi rules, a persons life is subject to strict controls covering their dietary intake, dress, education, speech, community responsibility, respect for elders, religious education and cultural heritage, as was embraced by the father, and in whose words it was made clear that:

> "Strict Chareidi parents will not allow their children to mix with children who are using the internet or watching television for fear that their own children will become corrupted."

Contrastingly, the mother had since abandoned herself of such restraints in favour of a more mainstream and unorthodox lifestyle, including obtainment of higher education and a prominent teaching position within an established school. It was for those reasons that the mother had made plans for the children to attend new schools, in order to gain greater access to both educational and professional advantages while growing up.

Having then applied for a shared residence order, the father had argued against the children being moved from their existing schools, on grounds that their change of lifestyle would cause long-term harm to both their wellbeing and standing within the Chareidi community and extended family; whereupon the court awarded residency in favour of the mother, while allowing extensive contact by the father. Tentatively granted leave to appeal, the father took issue with two elements of the hearing, namely (i) that the judge had erred in not granting the requested shared residence order and (ii) that he was wrong to have adopted the views of the mother.

As far back as the eighteenth century, men were assigned sole discretion as to how best their offspring were to be educated, and so remained beyond the powers of the court to interfere; however in light of the decision taken in *Ward v Laverty*,[605] the welfare of the child quickly became statutory principle, as found in s.1 of the Guardianship of Infants Act 1925, which reads:

> "When a court determines any question with respect to ... the upbringing of a child... the child's welfare shall be the court's paramount consideration."[606]

---

[605] [1925] AC 101.

[606] Guardianship of Infants Act 1925, s.1

This was further supported by s.1(2) of the 1925 Act, which explains that:

> "The court ... *shall not take into consideration whether from any other point of view the claim of the father, or any right at common law possessed by the father, ... is superior to that of the mother, or the claim of the mother is superior to that of the father.*"[607]

This allowed men and women the right to equal measure in the eyes of the law, particularly in matters such as these. It was thus held by the Court of Appeal that while the welfare of the children was integral to the decision making process, it was equally important to remain focussed on the bigger picture, as noted by Lord Bingham MR in *Re O (Contact: Imposition of Conditions)*, who said:

> "The court should take a medium-term and long-term view of the child's development and not accord excessive weight to what appear likely to be short-term or transient problems."[608]

Given the limitations of the Chareidi education system, which offered little beyond GCSE standards, it was noted that while art.9(1) of the European Convention on Human Rights (Freedom of thought, conscience and religion) allowed for the general traditions of religious practice, art.9(2) does stress that:

> "Freedom to manifest one's religion or beliefs shall be subject only to such limitations as are prescribed by law and are necessary in a democratic society in the interests of public safety, for the protection of public order, health or morals, or *for the protection of the rights and freedoms of others.*"[609]

And that when considering the long-term welfare needs of the children, it was vital to embrace the opportunities available to those living in a democracy, while addressing the innate need for progressive learning in a twenty-first century society. With further appreciation of the fact that the children had, for over two years, forgone their previously strict upbringing in lieu of a more liberal existence, it was finally concluded by the Court that the appeal for a reversal of fortune was now after the fact, and therefore unsustainable to the point of dismissal.

---

[607] Guardianship of Infants Ac 1925, s.1(2) (emphasis added).

[608] *Re O (Contact: Imposition of Conditions)* [1995] 2 FLR 124 (CA) 129 (Lord Bingham MR).

[609] European Convention on Human Rights 1950, art.9(2) (emphasis added).

Key Citations

"The voice of the father carries no more weight because he is the father, nor does the mother's because she is the mother. The weight to be attached to their views, if opposed, is to be determined on the basis of the merits or otherwise of the views being expressed, not on the basis of the gender of the person propounding them."[610]

"Evaluating a child's best interests involves a welfare appraisal in the widest sense, taking into account, where appropriate, a wide range of ethical, social, moral, religious, cultural, emotional and welfare considerations."[611]

"Our characters and understandings of ourselves from the earliest days are charted by reference to our relationships with others. It is only by considering the child's network of relationships that their well-being can be properly considered."[612]

"A child's best interests have to be assessed by reference to general community standards, making due allowance for the entitlement of people, within the limits of what is permissible in accordance with those standards, to entertain very divergent views about the religious, moral, social and secular objectives they wish to pursue for themselves and for their children."[613]

---

[610] *G (Education: Religious Upbringing), Re* [2012] EWCA Civ 1233 [24] (Munby LJ).

[611] *G (Education: Religious Upbringing), Re* [2012] EWCA Civ 1233 [27] (Munby LJ).

[612] *G (Education: Religious Upbringing), Re* [2012] EWCA Civ 1233 [30] (Munby LJ).

[613] *G (Education: Religious Upbringing), Re* [2012] EWCA Civ 1233 [39] (Munby LJ).

10. *Re* M (Parental Responsibilities Order)

Becoming a father and appreciating the weight of parental responsibility (PR) are two distinctly separate issues, and the courts are slow to grant such rights to unmarried fathers when the nature of their relationship to the child(ren) proves routinely disruptive and damaging to the sanctity of 'family', whether intact or fractured.

On this occasion, the appellant was father to a son aged eleven, who at the time of his birth, was declared fatherless on grounds that while the appellant's name was visible on the birth certificate, it was at a time before legislative changes granted parental rights to unmarried or estranged fathers under s.111 of the Adoption and Children Act 2002. The parents separated after seven years together, whereupon the appellant applied for a contact order, despite protestations that he had exhausted himself as a parent, and that he no longer wished to stay in his son's life. This was followed by his unexpected removal of their son from school, before disappearing for a number of days without any communication to both the mother, or the local police. After returning with his son, the appellant further refused welfare visits, before releasing him back into his school unharmed.

In response, the respondent mother applied for a residence order, while declaring that the appellant should be subjected to no contact, and a prohibited steps order. During the hearing, the father agreed to supervised contact, and things remained that way for the next two years, until the appellant applied for both PR and for direct contact with their son. During this hearing, the appellant requested to remove his application, before departing the court unexpectedly; at which point the judge awarded residency to the respondent, before issuing a two-year disposal order under s.91(14) of the Children Act 1989, thereby preventing any further orders of that kind from the appellant.

Despite total opposition from the respondent and their son, the appellant argued before the Court of Appeal that on a number of points, the judge had either overlooked, or under appreciated, the status rights afforded him, and that his commitment to his relationship with his son was beyond reproach. Contrastingly, the attending doctor's report told quite a different story, when outlining that:

> "It appears that when faced with rejection [father] will engage in varying behaviours, including cajoling, begging and threatening in order to manipulate others into meeting his needs and that when others do not meet his expectations he may become increasingly controlling, including expressing anger to manipulate them, transgressing boundaries in an effort to resume control of situations ... the prognosis for significant behaviour change is poor due to excessive denial ... it is possible that [father] will attempt to use his relationship with his son in an attempt to manipulate or denigrate [mother]."

This evidence ran counter to the nature of the appellants' appeal, and while fully appreciative of the arguments adopted, careful examination of the previous judgment revealed that far from neglecting to consider the needs of the appellant, the court had been explicit in its reasoning, and that when issuing the s.91(14) order, welfare, existing authority and proportion of risk had all been calculated, so as to justify both the dismissal of the claim for PR and the appeal itself.

Key Citations

"[W]here a father has shown commitment to a child, has a good relationship with the child and has sound and genuine reasons for wanting parental responsibility, an order granting him that status will not usually be refused simply because, through hostility to the child's mother or an excess of zeal, he may seek to exercise parental responsibility inappropriately."[614]

---

[614] *M (Parental Responsibility Order), Re* [2013] EWCA 969 [17] (Ryder LJ).

11. *Re* S (Care Order: Implementation of Care Plan)

In this conjoined appeal case, there were two matters in need of address and both involved a local authority and the issuing of final care orders for families in need of reunion. The first is *re S (Minors) (Care Order: Implementation of Care Plan)* and the second *re W (Minors) (Care Order: Adequacy of Care Plan)* as shown below:

Re S (Minors) (Care Order: Implementation of Care Plan)

As the mother of three children aged fourteen, eleven and ten, to two fathers, the oldest of them was raised by the father of his younger siblings, and over a course of almost a decade became subject to both emotional, physical and sexual abuse on an almost routine basis. Having run away from his home, the victim explained his suffering and was subsequently placed into foster care. The stepfather denied all allegations with the full support of the victim's mother, yet when challenged, displayed threatening behaviour before the local authority and was sentenced to community service.

In light of those events, the two younger children were also placed into foster care, while the parents separated in order to obtain their return to the family home, despite recommendations by professional experts that the father remained an unacceptable risk to the children. Following a hearing in the local court, the father was found guilty of sexually abusing the eldest child, while both parents were held to have been physically and emotionally abusive towards all three children, with particular regard to the eldest sibling.

The local authority responded by seeking care orders for the three children, and while it was agreed that the eldest was to remain in foster care, the younger children were designated a care plan involving their return to the mother. However, there was a degree of anxiety surrounding the absolute power of local authority decisions in such circumstances, and mention was made of the potential human rights violation should the mother and children not retain a tenable relationship, along with the proposal of interim care orders so as to provide assurances to the family. At the hearing, the judge granted final care orders for all three children, and yet over time, the promises of the social workers and appointed guardians dissolved into disappointment, after none of the proposed programmes materialised.

Having been presented to the Court of Appeal, it was held that the local authority had abjectly failed on its promise to provide care, but was acquitted under arguments of monetary cuts and a reduction in public resources; whereupon the mother contended that the court had erred in not considering her suggestions for interim care orders, while the children's guardian sought relief under ss.6 (Acts of public authorities) and 7 (Proceedings) of the Human Rights Act 1998 (HRA), both of which were dismissed.

Re W (Minors) (Care Order: Adequacy of Care Plan)

In this instance, the welfare of two boys aged ten and twelve years of age rested upon the intervention of the mothers grandparents, who themselves resided in the United States of America. Having met overseas, the parents returned to live in the United Kingdom in order to marry, before starting a family. During the course of their childhood, the boys had been subjected to numerous separations and reconciliations, and also spent considerable time living apart from one another, while remaining in contact with both parents. This chaotic existence had given rise to questions concerning the ability of the parents to meet the needs of the children, in large part due to the deteriorating mental health of the mother, who had made insubstantial allegations against the father, prior to the local authority applying for an emergency protection and interim care order.

Having established a care plan, it was agreed by the County Court that the two boys would be placed into foster care before the arrival of the American grandparents, who planned to live with them in the United Kingdom, despite reservations by the judge that their migration would materialise, and that the proposed therapy and marital management programmes would succeed; with particular emphasis on the mother's diagnosed imbalances.

Upon challenge by the local authority in the Court of Appeal, it was held that the care plan had been prematurely executed, and so the final care order was replaced with an interim order, while referring the case back to the awarding judge; an alteration which instigated reluctance by the grandparents to assume care of the boys unless under definite conditions. This prompted the reissue of a final care order with the full support of the parents, albeit in argument that they would apply to have the order discharged if their reunion was not provided in due course.

Under s.33 of the Children Act 1989, an acting local authority is granted parental responsibility (PR) for the duration of the assigned care order and can therefore determine the rights of the parents in relation to their children, while under s.100, the courts are expressly denied interference with those powers. However, s.6 of the HRA 1998 prevents a public authority from acting in a way that proves incompatible with a Convention right, while s.7 allows those victim of such actions, to brings proceedings against them. S.8 (Judicial remedies) further enables the court to decide how best to provide legal remedy, or issue powers appropriate to its jurisdiction. This translates that where a local authority infringes art.8 of the HRA 1998 (Right to respect for private and family life), the deciding court can lawfully grant relief to those affected.

More interestingly, under the Review of Children's Cases Regulations 1991,[615] a local authority is required to consider the possible discharge of a care order on a six-monthly basis, subject to the views and consideration of the child(ren) and parents, while s.3(1) of the Children Act 1989 provides that parents retain the same rights, duties, powers and parental responsibilities as before an order was made; therefore their civil rights are affected, but not wholly compromised. Finally, s.38 of the Children Act 1989 provides the court with powers to issue interim care orders, so as to provide safety and security for vulnerable children for a determined period.

With both cases put before the House of Lords, it was evident that in the first case, the Court of Appeal had introduced a 'starring' mechanism as a means of preventing failure to implement care plans, whereby each plan was marked with progressive indicators that when not reached in the agreed period, triggered automatic rights to reactivate the consultation process, in order to avoid missed or overlooked public body requirements; whereas in the second case no such mechanism had been used. This had prompted

---

[615] Review of Children's Cases Regulations 1991, SI 1991/895

intervention by the Secretary of State for Health, who received claims that ss.31, 33(3), 38 and 100 of the Children Act 1989 were incompatible with existing Convention rights, while in the second case, the local authority had appealed against the alteration of the care order and the broadening of judicial powers to award interim orders.

Examination of the Children Act 1989 and suggested incompatibility with Convention rights after the introduction of 'starring', drew immediate reference to the overlapping rights of courts when care orders are in effect, and while the House appreciated that the inventive use of rudimentary measures was a decision privy to Parliament, and that while there was stark evidence to support legislative reform, it was simply ultra vires for the Appeal Court to act without restraint.

With regard to the overextension of the interim care orders, when faced with an ill-prepared care plan, it was held that once powers are conferred to the local authority, it was unlawful for a court to restrict that control in favour of jurisdictional oversight. Therefore, the appeals bought by both a ministerial and public body were upheld, with notice that the powers of courts in such circumstances, were now in need of expansion if future lapses were to be addressed correctly.

Key Citations

"Where a care order is made the responsibility for the child's care is with the authority rather than the court. The court retains no supervisory role, monitoring the authority's discharge of its responsibilities. That was the intention of Parliament."[616]

"The Human Rights Act reserves the amendment of primary legislation to Parliament. By this means the Act seeks to preserve parliamentary sovereignty. The Act maintains the constitutional boundary. Interpretation of statutes is a matter for the courts; the enactment of statutes, and the amendment of statutes, are matters for Parliament."[617]

"A care order which keeps a child away from his family for purposes which, as time goes by, are not being realised will sooner or later become a disproportionate interference with the child's primary article 8 rights…"[618]

"[A]rticle 13 is not a Convention right as defined in section 1(1) of the Human Rights Act 1998. So legislation which fails to provide an effective remedy for infringement of article 8 is not, for that reason, incompatible with a Convention right within the meaning of the Human Rights Act."[619]

"By virtue of the Human Rights Act article 8 rights are now part of the civil rights of parents and children for the purposes of article 6(1). This is because now, under section 6 of the Act, it is unlawful for a public authority to act inconsistently with article 8."[620]

---

[616] S (Care Order: Implementation of Care Plan), re [2002] 2 AC 291 [25] (Nicholls LJ).

[617] S (Care Order: Implementation of Care Plan), re [2002] 2 AC 291 [39] (Nicholls LJ).

[618] S (Care Order: Implementation of Care Plan), re [2002] 2 AC 291 [54] (Nicholls LJ).

[619] S (Care Order: Implementation of Care Plan), re [2002] 2 AC 291 [60] (Nicholls LJ).

[620] S (Care Order: Implementation of Care Plan), re [2002] 2 AC 291 [71] (Nicholls LJ).

12. Thorner v Major

While of a strictly familial nature, this case relies upon elements of land law and principles of equity for its proximation of fact. After a decade-spanning relationship of trust and obligation observed by the appellant, it falls to the House of Lords to clarify the true meaning behind the time shared between two cousins.

The core of this dispute rests within the subjective disparity of those seeking claim to the estate of a private farmer, and the man who knew him probably better than anybody. After growing up and working on his father's farm, the appellant found himself extending his energies to his older cousin, after witnessing him suffer through death and divorce. Having no children of his own, the cousin had continued to toil the land left him, and in turn looked to the appellant to help manage the considerably extensive freehold.

For one reason or another, the arrangement required no payment exchange, and so it was that until the death of the landowner, the two men worked the farm, developing it further through an intimate relationship based upon the appellant's unique ability to understand the emotion and intentions of a man renowned for his narrow vocabulary and deep introspection.

When upon his death, the appellant followed up on his understanding that the farm had been bequeathed him, the claim of succession was contested on grounds of proprietary estoppel, along with the ambiguity of true intention displayed by the deceased. There were principally two events that triggered the assumption of entitlement, namely (i) a gesture that indirectly disclosed the plans of the elder cousin in relation to death duties and (ii) the inherent nature of their close friendship, and the disappearance and subsequent implied revocation of a will drawn up eight years prior to his passing.

Needless to say, the appellant had over the passage of time, made numerous adjustments to his own circumstances, in order that the relationship could sustain the changes discussed and the alterations incorporated into the estate; while there were a number of other minor events that further supported his interpretation that he would be the sole successor of his cousin's farm.

Having had his claim dismissed in the lower courts, it became fatal to the respondents in the House of Lords, that the principle of proprietary estoppel relies upon an inability to identify the land in contention, therefore the challenge brought against the appellant was fundamentally flawed and the House thus upheld the appeal. When summarising the power of promised succession, the words of Hoffman LJ in *Walton v Walton* reminded that:

> "The promise must be unambiguous and must appear to have been intended to be taken seriously. Taken in its context, it must have been a promise which one might reasonably expect to be relied upon by the person to whom it was made."[621]

---

[621] *Walton v Walton* (unreported) 14 April 1994 [16] (Hoffman LJ).

Key Citations

"If it is reasonable for a representee to whom representations have been made to take the representations at their face value and rely on them, it would not in general be open to the representor to say that he or she had not intended the representee to rely upon them."[622]

"Peter's representation that David would inherit Steart Farm speaks, at least where Peter remained the owner of an agricultural entity known as Steart Farm, as from his death and if, at that time, evidence were available to identify Steart Farm with certainty, David's claim to be entitled in equity to Steart Farm cannot, in my opinion, be rejected for want of certainty of subject matter."[623]

"[T]his case would, on the factual findings made by the judge and accepted by the Court of Appeal have justified a remedial constructive trust under which David would have obtained the relief awarded him by the judge."[624]

"[H]owever clear and unequivocal his intention to assure David that he was to have the farm after his death, Peter was always like to have expressed it in oblique language."[625]

"[I]t is unprofitable, in view of the retrospective nature of the assessment which the doctrine of proprietary estoppel requires, to speculate on what might have been."[626]

---

[622] *Thorner v Major* [2009] UKHL 18 [17] (Scott LJ).

[623] *Thorner v Major* [2009] UKHL 18 [18] (Scott LJ).

[624] *Thorner v Major* [2009] UKHL 18 [21] (Scott LJ).

[625] *Thorner v Major* [2009] UKHL 18 [26] (Rodger LJ).

[626] *Thorner v Major* [2009] UKHL 18 [65] (Walker LJ).

13. White v White

When a committed marriage runs its course, and the two parties responsible have amassed an estate of significant worth, should the 'Duxbury paradox' find just approval, or will the virtue of equality prevail?

After spending over three decades together as husband and wife, business partners and parents, the cross-appellants not only invested exorbitant amounts of money into what was termed a 'clean break' divorce, but wound up fighting over percentages, whilst losing sight of the objective first presented to the courts.

Having contributed roughly equal amounts of time and capital into a successful farming business, it was felt by the wife that she needed to end the marriage and strike out alone in a similar field. While on paper the division of assets appeared straightforward, there were anomalies in the form of individual benefit to inheritance by the husband, through valuable farming estate, and his decision to continue operating the business shared by the two parties, as opposed to liquidation in the wake of annulment.

During the original hearing, the judgment passed disproportionately in favour of the husband, leaving the wife with less than one-fifth of the estate value. This was calculated through the application of the Duxbury fund principle, as first described in *Duxbury v Duxbury*.[627] This antiquated approach to approximation of required financial assets, is based upon the idea that in order to establish the requisite level of income for the wife in a divorce, the phrase 'the longer the marriage and hence older the wife, the less the capital sum required for a Duxbury Fund' will suffice.

Following an unsurprisingly swift challenge, the Court of Appeal sensibly reconsidered the previous judgment, increasing her award to two-fifths of the estate upon grounds of equality, and on principle that the increased award now provided sufficient funds (£1.5m) for the wife to not only start her new venture, but have enough to live on without the burden of stress or discomfort. Similarly, the remaining estate was healthy enough for the husband to continue working, albeit with short-term financial help from his extended family.

While taken on its weighting, the outcome would appear at risk of bias, however the ethos that divorcing parties should take steps to help each other start afresh, is clearly present where the dissolution of the joint enterprise could have placed the husband at risk of suffering while the wife enjoyed the benefit of excessive capital for the purposes of need, despite making the choice to depart from a thriving and well-established business.

---

[627] [1992] Fam 62.

Key Citations

"In seeking to achieve a fair outcome, there is no place for discrimination between husband and wife in their respective roles."[628]

"It by no means follows that, in a case where resources exceed the parties' financial needs, the older wife's award will be less than the younger wife's. Indeed, the older wife's award may be substantially larger."[629]

"[E]quality should be departed from only if, and to the extent that, there is good reasons for doing so."[630]

"[T]he only plausible reason for departing from equality can be the financial help given by the husband's father. I agree, however, that the significance of this is diminished because over a long marriage the parties jointly made the most of that help and because it was apparently intended at least partly for the benefit of both."[631]

---

[628] *White v White* [2001] 1 AC 596 (HL) 605 (Nicholls LJ).

[629] *White v White* [2001] 1 AC 596 (HL) 609 (Nicholls LJ).

[630] *White v White* [2001] 1 AC 596 (HL) 615 (Cooke LJ).

[631] *White v White* [2001] 1 AC 596 (HL) 615 (Cooke LJ).

7. Medical Law

1. A Local Authority v E

The struggle for autonomy amidst the pain of abuse, is central to a case involving the wishes of a patient with a debilitating illness and the requisite obligations of the State. By balancing the safeguarding nature of the Mental Capacity Act 2005 with Convention rights, it is left to the courts to determine which argument brings the greatest reasoning.

After experiencing years of intense sexual abuse during the formative years of her childhood, the patient in question became prisoner to her manifestations of trauma through increased dependency on alcohol and medically prescribed opiates. The prologue is one of repeated lapses of overall function, underpinned by contrasting highs of academic achievement that defied her emotional scars; but through time, the former overshadowed the applicants deliberate plans for happiness in the form of chronic *Anorexia Nervosa.*

Following hospitalisation on numerous occasions, through dangerously low body weight, and when resulting variations of therapy proved collectively unsuccessful, it was taken by the applicant to submit advanced decisions surrounding life sustaining procedures where her health suffered to the point of imminent death; only to then provide paradoxical statements portraying her deep conviction to regain a life of meaning that had once been enjoyed. This cyclical existence placed prolonged stress upon the applicant's health and that of her parents and appointed specialists, who had all extended themselves beyond any obligation to keep what was considered an engaging and yet tormented woman alive.

Several years of medical intervention provided little to no lasting results, and so it was largely accepted that after a year of no real calorific ingestion, the patient had made clear her decision to refuse food, and that in light of her last advanced decision, she wished to remain in palliative care until the date of her impending death. When her body mass index (BMI) then reached a potentially fatal level, it was with the concerns of those assigned her care, that the matter went before the Court of Protection, in the aim of determining (i) if the patient lacked mental capacity at the time her last advanced decision was made, and (ii) whether it was in her best interests to cease intervention and leave her to die with dignity, or resort to long-term invasive nasogastric treatment to restore her BMI to that where therapeutic rehabilitation could again recommence.

Art.2 of the Human Rights Act 1998 (Right to life) determines that the State is under a duty to protect the individual right to life, and yet art.3 (Prohibition of torture) serves to prevent any inhuman or degrading treatment. In this case, the proposed medical programme would by all accounts place unreasonably high levels of physical and emotional stress upon the patient; in part as the result of years of previous treatments producing a ravaged immune system with weakened bones mass. However, arts.5 (Right to liberty and security) and 8 (Right to respect for private and family life) both enforced the applicant's right to die with dignity, while in a manner that suited both herself and her family.

In light of her advanced decision, the contradiction of mental capacity while suffering from an eating disorder allowed s.3(1) of the Mental Capacity Act 2005 to question if the cessation of ingestion can validate the supposition that a person can understand and evaluate, information as part of a decision making process when they are consciously killing themselves, despite knowing the consequences of that action. For that reason, it was argued that any suggestion that the advanced decision was undertaken while *compos mentis*, failed when an irrational request serves only to end a life and not preserve it.

With full appreciation of the medical evidence and lengthy testimony of all parties (aside from the patient, whose heath was too critical for an appearance), it was concluded that in spite of the discouraging background to both the applicant's childhood experiences and the endemic frustrations of anorexia, there remained a concept and hope, that at the age of thirty-two, it was not too late to rule out any meaningful recovery, nor the chance for the applicant to resume the full life she had once, if only briefly, created.

For those reasons, the applicant was deemed lacking mental capacity at the execution of her advanced decision, therefore forcible recovery was in her best interests, and that such action failed to interfere with the Convention rights presented.

Key Citations

"[I]t is artificial to treat the various forms of intervention involved in forcible feeding individually. They are all central to or supportive of a single purpose. I therefore find that E lacks capacity to accept or refuse treatment in relation to any interventions that are necessary in conjunction with forcible feeding."[632]

"E's actual behaviour in refusing food has been entirely consistent with her decision and I would have been reluctant to conclude that her decision was undermined by trusting statements about what are bound to be deeply mixed feelings."[633]

"For present purposes, I find nothing in E's statements to indicate a belief that, if she were well, she would not want efforts to be made to save her."[634]

"[T]he balance to be struck places the value of E's life in one scale and the value of her personal independence in the other, with these transcendent factors being weighed in the light of the reality of her actual situation."[635]

"If taken too far, the argument that everything that can be done must be done carries the risk of discrimination against incapacitated persons by depriving them of options that are available to the capacitous…"[636]

---

[632] *A Local Authority v E* [2012] EWHC 1639 (COP) [67] (Jackson J).

[633] *A Local Authority v E* [2012] EWHC 1639 (COP) [69] (Jackson J).

[634] *A Local Authority v E* [2012] EWHC 1639 (COP) [79] (Jackson J).

[635] *A Local Authority v E* [2012] EWHC 1639 (COP) [118] (Jackson J).

[636] *A Local Authority v E* [2012] EWHC 1639 (COP) [134] (Jackson J).

2. A Local Authority v Mrs A and Mr A

When two mentally challenged adults elect to cohabit and then marry, the nature of their relationship is brought into question, after a pattern of domestic abuse overshadows any informed choice to start a family. It is then that the local authority seeks forced contraception, in order to prevent the continuation of suffering, and the potential loss of children through predicted adoption.

With diagnosed *Atypical Autism*, the applicant in this Court of Protection case found herself at an emotional impasse, when trying remain in her marriage and evaluate the sensibility of motherhood under the suffocating grasp of a controlling partner. The two parties involved, met when working as community volunteers and while the husband had enjoyed the security of a close family relationship, the wife had been fatherless from a young age, before being forced to live alone (albeit with community support) when her mother emigrated a number of years later.

Through a series of dysfunctional relationships, the applicant had also found herself pregnant on two separate occasions, both of which resulted in her surrendering the child to the care system, on grounds that her limited intelligence and reasoning skills fell far short of those required to provide a safe parenting environment. In fact, it was only after having met her now husband, that the couple were given the freedom to live together under the regular supervision of the local authority; while in order to prevent further unwanted pregnancies, the applicant was asked to undergo routine depot injections under the terms of her Guardianship order, as enacted under the Mental Health Act 1983.

During the course of their time together, the husband, who himself suffered from low intelligence, began to exhibit domineering behaviour over the applicant, often obstructing access to those assigned her monitoring, until reaching a level that her social activity was virtually non-existent, and when seen by her case managers, she displayed minor bruising, and complained that she was both unhappy and afraid of her partner.

It was also disclosed that in recent months, they had decided to start a family, and that she no longer wished to receive the injections; although when given the freedom to respond alone, the applicant often expressed her reservations, but that unless complied with, she feared becoming homeless, as the property shared was beneficially his. Despite making concerted attempts to maintain regular contact, the aggressive manner in which her husband denied them access left the council unable to assess both her personal safety and the risks of her falling pregnant, while under the pervasive influence of a man lacking any cogent understanding of her fragility and fear of reprisal.

Having exhausted all options surrounding the management of the applicant's social care, it was left to the Court of Protection to address whether the applicant could prove her capacity to determine (i) that she understood the concept of motherhood, (ii) that she could likewise make a measured decision as to her cessation of contraception, and (iii) whether an injunction should be applied to her husband, to prevent future interference in her autonomous rights. What distinguished this matter from many before, was that the issue of contraception had not been properly considered when assessing mental capacity, so the validity of applying a judicial test raised genuine doubts as to the widening of qualifying criteria over and above that of a State medical clinic.

While it was also considered that the applicant had undergone a number of interviews concerning parental responsibility and contraception, her answers often ran risk of appearing scripted, therefore the balance hung in equal measure regards any certainty of mind when entering into pregnancy, or likewise preventing it. It was on this additional evidence, that the court found a test of mental capacity was by extension, unfair when her freedom to choose was strangulated by external persuasions.

It was then decided that the best way forward, was through deliberate post-natal education and greater inclusion of the husband into the decision making process, which would not only show support of arts.8 (Right to respect for private and family life) and 12 (Founding a family) of the European Convention on Human Rights, but preclude the need for State intervention, where mediation and continued encouragement for capacitous thinking would hopefully give rise to the best possible outcome for all.

Key Citations

"[T]he administration of contraception is different from any other medical procedure, since (leaving aside sterilisation) no other medical procedure, or the refusal of it, produces such significant social consequence as the potential creation of a child."[637]

"Although in theory the 'reasonably foreseeable consequences' of not taking contraception involve possible conception, a birth and the parenting of a child, there should be some limit in practice on what needs to be envisaged, if only for public policy reasons."[638]

"To apply the wider test would be to 'set the bar too high' and would risk a move away from personal autonomy in the direction of social engineering. Further, if one were to admit of a requirement to be able to foresee things beyond a child's birth, then drawing a line on into the child's life would be nigh impossible."[639]

"In view of what I find to be the completely unequal dynamic in the relationship between Mr and Mrs A, I am satisfied that her decision not to continue taking contraception is not the product of her own free will."[640]

"[A]ny step towards long-term court imposed contraception by way of physical coercion, with its affinity to enforced sterilisation and shades of social engineering, would raise profound questions about State intervention in private and family life."[641]

---

[637] *A Local Authority v Mrs A and Mr A* [2010] EWHC 1549 (Fam) [59] (Bodey J).

[638] *A Local Authority v Mrs A and Mr A* [2010] EWHC 1549 (Fam) [63] (Bodey J).

[639] *A Local Authority v Mrs A and Mr A* [2010] EWHC 1549 (Fam) [63] (Bodey J).

[640] *A Local Authority v Mrs A and Mr A* [2010] EWHC 1549 (Fam) [73] (Bodey J).

[641] *A Local Authority v Mrs A and Mr A* [2010] EWHC 1549 (Fam) [77] (Bodey J).

3. Chester v Afshar

'But for' causation and the principles of tort, while reminiscent of criminal procedure, can fall foul to policy loopholes when a duty of care is involved. In this matter, the actions (or inactions) of a neurosurgeon left a patient paralysed and angry after full disclosure had not been established prior to her operation.

After suffering for a number of years with lower back pain, the respondent had reached the point that regular injections were no longer of relief, and had now given serious thought to surgical intervention, despite long standing fears around the field of operative medicine. Having consulted her rheumatologist at length, she was confidently advised to procure the services of a Harley Street practitioner with a solid reputation for the proposed kind of operation.

The recommended procedure involved delicate removal of a number of vertebrae that would by extension, bring an end to her pain, but not without associated risks inherent to the work. Upon her first visit with the appellant, the two individuals took time to discuss the course of action, along with known side-effects and possible nerve damage. Having consented to undergo the surgery, the respondent was treated a few days following the meeting; after which her recovery was less positive than had been anticipated, and which had in fact, left the respondent immobile and diagnosed with *Cauda Equine Syndrome*.

Having sought damages for what the respondent considered to be negligence through a breach of duty to inform her of the known (and well documented) risks associated with the operation, the first judge found that in order to reach a balanced decision, it was important to address both the breach of duty to fully disclose, and the liability for the subsequent injury arising from the procedure. On this occasion, and relying upon the evidence presented, the court took time to debate the principal function of causation, in which the defendant is not required to establish exemption, but rather that the claimant must take the necessary steps to demonstrate how their breach caused either injury or loss, and that where adherence to policy and procedure had occurred, the resulting facts would have prevented any need for remedy.

With judgment found in favour of the respondent in the first hearing, the surgeon moved to appeal, before finding his challenge dismissed for the same reasons. It was then, after granting permission to appeal to the House of Lords, that the finer details of causation and right to damages became of greater significance.

While the discussion revolved around similar medical cases applying tortious doctrines of causality, the named risk attached to lumbar stenosis removal ran within a very narrow margin of around one to two percent; and it had been proven, as well as agreed, that irrespective of the performing surgeon, the potential for the syndrome remained equally viable. This translated that a lack of absolute disclosure by the appellant, while disconcerting in the immediate sense, could not be held as contributory to the injurious outcome experienced by the respondent. However, the division between the House was such that enough case material had amassed to instigate a reconsideration of the logic of causality; and that when embracing the autonomous rights of the patient, it was simply unethical to allow minimal disclosure and a weakness of causative proximity, to remove access to knowledge; which on this occasion, might have led to alternative solutions to pain and discomfort. By mindfully broadening the duty of care principle, the House found in favour of the respondent and thus awarded accordingly.

Key Citations

"In modern law medical paternalism no longer rules and a patient has a prima facie right to be informed by a surgeon of a small, but well established, risk of serious injury as a result of surgery."[642]

"In this case there is no dispute that Mr Afshar owed a duty to Miss Chester to inform her of the risks that were inherent in the proposed surgery, including the risk of paralysis."[643]

"It was his duty to warn her of the risks of the operation that he was proposing to perform, and it was in the course of that same operation that she sustained the very kind of injury that he ought to have warned her about."[644]

"To leave the patient who would find the decision difficult without a remedy, as the normal approach to causation would indicate, would render the duty useless in the cases where it may be needed most."[645]

"The function of the law is to enable rights to be vindicated and to provide remedies when duties have been breached. Unless this is done the duty is a hollow one, stripped of all practical force and devoid of all content."[646]

---

[642] *Chester v Afshar* [2004] UKHL 41 [16] (Bingham LJ).

[643] *Chester v Afshar* [2004] UKHL 41 [55] (Hope LJ).

[644] *Chester v Afshar* [2004] UKHL 41 [62] (Hope LJ).

[645] *Chester v Afshar* [2004] UKHL 41 [87] (Hope LJ).

[646] *Chester v Afshar* [2004] UKHL 41 [87] (Hope LJ).

4. H v Associated Newspapers Ltd and N (A Health Authority)

Balancing the need to protect individual privacy against those of public interest, is both difficult and often painful for the party that loses. When a healthcare worker retires through ill-health, it is under a truth that HIV infection was the primary cause for departure.

The employer concerned, followed procedural rules during the ending of the relationship, but later found themselves torn between performing an obligatory 'look back' exercise, which required contact with patients that had been assigned the retirees care when carrying our their duties, and assisting with the request that the former healthcare worker's privacy be respected. (It must be noted that at the point of litigation, the former element was still uncertain due to a change of guidelines, and therefore such actions may have proven unnecessary pending the revised policy).

The escalating factor in this appeal case, was the knowledge that while the infected worker was contractually obliged to submit the medical records of those treated under the National Health Service, a reasonable percentage of the remaining patients had been seen privately, and were therefore liable for protection against disclosure under the Data Protection Act 1998.

Shortly after the 'look back' request was made, the former employee secured a court order preventing any publication of patient records that might allow for disclosure of the infected party, on grounds of unlawfulness and a fundamental right to individual privacy. After a newspaper learned of the matter, it published an article on grounds of public interest, although in breach of a previously issued restraining order, and aware that disclosure of the Health Authority at least, would soon allow readers to make educated guesses as to the identity of the infected party.

This led to action being taken against the newspaper, on the footing that the previously published article had indirectly disclosed the identity of the healthcare worker through disclosure of the gagging order, and the subject to which it applied. There were of course a number of other factors that required diligence from the courts, but the essence of the argument also addressed very sensitive and fear-laden concerns, that threatened disproportionate cost implications upon the State, along with a risk of flagrant sensationalism.

On this occasion, the court ruled that until such time as the new guidelines were issued, the newspaper must reduce the identities of both the employer and employee to initials, which would allow the nature of the matter to become publicly accessible, while concealing the names of the two parties involved; and that should the new guidelines require absolute disclosure of medical records private or otherwise, the infected party must comply.

Key Citations

"[I]f healthcare workers are not to be discouraged from reporting that they are HIV positive, it is essential that all possible steps are taken to preserve the confidentiality of such reports."[647]

"We would view with concern any attempt to invoke the power of the Court to grant an injunction restraining freedom of expression merely on the ground that release of the information would give rise to administrative problems and a drain on resources. Such consequences are the price which has to be paid, from time to time, for freedom of expression in a democratic society."[648]

"If an investigative journalist were to put two and two together, the injunction would still restrain any publication of material that would lead to the deduction of H's speciality or of when he was diagnosed as HIV positive."[649]

---

[647] *H (A Healthcare Worker) v Associated Newspapers Ltd and N (A Health Authority)* [2002] EWCA Civ 195 [27] (Lord Phillips MR).

[648] *H (A Healthcare Worker) v Associated Newspapers Ltd and N (A Health Authority)* [2002] EWCA Civ 195 [41] (Lord Phillips MR).

[649] *H (A Healthcare Worker) v Associated Newspapers Ltd and N (A Health Authority)* [2002] EWCA Civ 195 [47] (Lord Phillips MR).

5. Hotson v East Berkshire Area Health Authority

Causation before assessment of damages, are two requisite elements of tort liability, so when in a medically related case, the claimants elect to rely upon contract law doctrine to extend the culpability of a local Health Authority, the facts not only become confusing, but the victim's scope of remedy is lost in the shuffle.

While playing as a thirteen year-old boy, the respondent in this matter fell from a tree and suffered serious injury to his hip. Undiagnosed at the first point of contact with the serving hospital, the minor was instead treated for damages to his knee, duly returning home to recover.

Within a five day period, the patient's father complained to his local doctor, and requested that the hospital reexamine his injuries, as his son had been left struggling to walk or stand, and unable to cope with the pain resulting from the fall. Upon x-ray of his pelvic region, it was then discovered that the respondent had in fact, suffered a displacement of the left epiphysis, a condition known to lead to immobility and deformity of the affected limb through *Avascular Necrosis* if left untreated for the briefest of time.

Two years after the incident a writ was issued, claiming the doctors and local authority had collectively acted in breach of their professional duties, and that such negligence had given cause to claim damages for (i) the five days during which the son had been left in pain and improperly treated, and (ii) the loss and damages arising from a life of disability stemming from the disease itself.

In the first hearing, the judge awarded damages for the pain suffered during the period of misdiagnosis, following the local authority's willingness to account for the gross error of judgment; while secondary to the claim, and holding the greatest financial reward for the respondents, was the contention that the hospital's inability to diagnose and treat the initial symptoms, was tantamount to a loss of benefit to both timely treatment, and possible avoidance of the necrosis.

Using expert witness statements and surrounding medical knowledge, it was contested that either the extent of the fall itself could have proven severe enough to allow for the disease to flourish, or that the time lost between the accident and the correct diagnosis was sufficient enough to do much the same. Relying upon the principle of 'chance' in contract law, it was argued that unlike the tortious balance of probabilities (which turn upon strict percentages), the respondent ought to be entitled to damages where *any* percentage could be established.

In conclusion, it was found by the judge that the uncertainty of the evidence presented, left him in such a position as to use judicial discretion when averaging out the likelihood that either of those points raised could apply. Basing the outcome on his own limited knowledge, the judge concurred that had the injury been acknowledged and duly treated, there was a seventy-five percent chance the respondent would have made a full recovery; therefore by calculating down the predetermined damages figure, a sum of £11,500 plus £150 for pain and suffering caused by the breach was awarded in favour of the patient.

When taken to appeal, the Court upheld the previous decision, but granted leave to appeal to the House of Lords; where the concept of contract law approaches to tort related matters were given a degree of consideration, but never wholly ruled out. Rather it was the nature of this particular case that gave cause for concern, as where, upon the balance of probabilities, the cause of the damages could not be fully established, there could be no presumption of liability for extenuating injuries, unless proven to be beyond at least a fifty-precent margin. It was therefore agreed, that while the damages for pain and suffering resulting from the breach were free from debate, the additional settlement had been unjustly granted, and was subsequently owed back to the appellants with interest.

Key Citations

"I see no reason why the loss of a chance which is capable of being valued should not be capable of being damage in a tort case just as much as in a contract case."[650]

"Unless the plaintiff proved on a balance of probabilities that the delayed treatment was at least a material contributory cause of the avascular necrosis he failed on the issue of causation and no question of quantification could arise."[651]

"[I]f the plaintiff had proved on a balance of probabilities that the authority's negligent failure to diagnose and treat his injury promptly had materially contributed to the development of avascular necrosis, I know of no principle of English law which would have entitled the authority to a discount from the full measure of damage to reflect the chance that, even given prompt treatment, avascular necrosis might well still have developed."[652]

"The debate on the loss of a chance cannot arise where there has been a positive finding that before the duty arose the damage complained of had already been sustained or had become inevitable."[653]

"Once liability is established, on the balance of probabilities, the loss which the plaintiff has sustained is payable in full. It is not discounted by reducing his claim by the extent to which he has failed to prove his case with 100 per cent certainty."[654]

---

[650] *Hotson v East Berkshire Area Health Authority* [1987] AC 750 (HL) 764 (Dillon LJ).

[651] *Hotson v East Berkshire Area Health Authority* [1987] AC 750 (HL) 782 (Bridge LJ).

[652] *Hotson v East Berkshire Area Health Authority* [1987] AC 750 (HL) 783 (Bridge LJ).

[653] *Hotson v East Berkshire Area Health Authority* [1987] AC 750 (HL) 792 (Ackner LJ).

[654] *Hotson v East Berkshire Area Health Authority* [1987] AC 750 (HL) 793 (Ackner LJ).

6. Gregg v Scott

Loss of chance, the balance of probabilities, and legislative reform, become the focus of discussion in a matter bearing the superficial hallmarks of a linear tort claim, but that upon closer inspection, was approached in all the wrong ways.

Having consulted his local GP with concerns over a swollen lump beneath his armpit, the appellant was told that it represented little more than a lipoma (soft fatty lumps), and that no further investigation was needed. Roughly a year afterwards, the appellant relocated, after which he presented the same symptoms to his new doctor, who despite reaching the same conclusion, took the step of referring him to submit a biopsy for examination. Upon inspection of the sample, it was quickly established that far from being harmless, the appellant was in fact suffering from *Anaplastic Lymphoma Kinase Negative,* the more aggressive of two types of non-Hodgkin's lymphoma.

The typical prognosis for this complex form of cancer is one that offers a life expectancy of little more than ten years, following successful observation and established treatment. To the appellant's detriment, he had missed any opportunity to undergo preliminary and less invasive therapies, as a period of nine months had elapsed without knowledge of the disease, and that during this time, the infection had spread across his chest. This resulted in increased pain and suffering, along with the inability to continue working, or having any reasonable quality of daily life, without a constant fear of death and dramatically reduced energy levels.

When seeking remedy for the negligent breach of his original doctor, the appellant argued that while his initial chances of a relapse-free ten years were estimated as resting between forty-two to forty-five percent, the abject failure to properly diagnose, or even refer the appellant for examination, had reduced that figure to around twenty-five percent, along with the increased levels of pain and discomfort suffered during the time between healthcare professionals.

Relying upon the maxim 'damages are the gist of negligence', the appellant chose an unorthodox approach that sought recovery upon his loss of chance of recovery, as opposed to a straightforward claim for full damages in direct relation to the injurious nature of the tumour growth and accompanying pain, arguing that had the disease been correctly identified, it might not perhaps have occurred. Using expert testimony and statistical data to contest the degree to which the appellant was entitled to damages, it was ultimately found by the first judge that there was inconclusive evidence to suggest that the delay in diagnosis would have made any lasting impact upon the progression of the cancer, and so no greater an outcome could be found to exist, other than the one faced by the appellant during trial.

Upon appeal, the Court judged by a majority in favour of the previous decision, and so it was left again to the House of Lords for a conclusive finding. By examining the facts surrounding *Hotson v East Berkshire Area Health Authority,*[655] the House was by a close margin, able to distinguish the nature of this particular medical error, and thus evaluate the argument that the grievousness of miscalculation around terminal illness, ought not to rely upon the balance of probabilities, but should instead rest upon any dramatic

---

[655] [1987] AC 750.

reduction in life expectancy, where such an oversight was wholly avoidable through proper conduct and rigorous application of research.

By close scrutiny of the statistical data, it was also discovered that despite the forecasted levels of survival cited by academic assistance, the patient had since confounded the figures through his continued lifespan in the aftermath of intense chemotherapy; which by extension, served to defeat his theory that had the treatment been undertaken earlier than was found, he would have been alive longer than expected. Given that causation could no longer be proved, it was only natural that the appeal was dismissed, while some harsh lessons in choice of legal representation were learned.

Key Citations

"It is always likely to be much easier to resolve issues of causation on balance of probabilities than to identify in terms of percentage the effect that clinical negligence had on the chances of a favourable outcome."[656]

"[I]t seems to me that there is a danger, if special tests of causation are developed piecemeal to deal with perceived injustices in particular factual situations, that the coherence of our common law will be destroyed."[657]

"Doctors do not cause the presenting disease. If they negligently fail to diagnose and treat it, it is not enough to show that a claimant's disease has got worse during the period of delay. It has to be shown that treating it earlier would have prevented that happening, at least for the time being."[658]

"[I]t cannot be said that the later pain, suffering and loss of amenity caused by the need for further treatment, and the associated loss of earnings and costs of care, were consequential on the injury caused by the negligence. Even if the initial treatment had led to remission, the need for further treatment and the relapses would have happened anyway because of the disease."[659]

"Some wrongs are actionable whether or not the claimant has been damaged. But damage is the gist of negligence. So it can never be enough to show that the defendant has been negligent."[660]

---

[656] *Gregg v Scott* [2005] UKHL 2 [170] (Phillips LJ).

[657] *Gregg v Scott* [2005] UKHL 2 [172] (Phillips LJ).

[658] *Gregg v Scott* [2005] UKHL 2 [203] (Baroness Hale).

[659] *Gregg v Scott* [2005] UKHL 2 [205] (Baroness Hale).

[660] *Gregg v Scott* [2005] UKHL 2 [217] (Baroness Hale).

7. PC v City of York Council

As is the nature of the human condition and subjective reasoning, the guidance of the Mental Capacity Act 2005 (MCA) and decisions made by those subject to its limitations, are sometimes in direct conflict. In this particular case, the issues in hand revolved around the interpretation of statute, and differing circumstances upon which those rules applied.

From a young age, the appellant had been legally defined as suffering from mild to moderate learning disabilities, and now as a forty-eight year-old woman, she had chosen to enter into a marriage with a known, and recently convicted sex offender, prior to his incarceration. Having previously endured complex and dysfunctional relationships with men of a similar ilk, there had also been abortive pregnancies, and a child that was since put into care to avoid any risk of sexual abuse.

At the point of the original hearing, the time had come for the husband's release, and so it was with grave concern for the appellant, and any potential offspring, that the local authority sought to use the power of the Court of Protection as a means of removing any prospect that the two parties might resume cohabiting, in order that the husband would proceed to groom her into acquiescing to pregnancy, and his subsequent sexual abuse of the resulting child(ren).

The problem faced by the council was that under s.27(1) of the MCA 2005, it provides that those found to lack mental capacity cannot be denied the right to determine whether they choose to consent to (i) enter a marriage or civil partnership, (ii) have sexual relations, or (iii) divorce after a two-year period of separation. In a similar way, s.3(1) explains that any person agreed to lack capacity is deemed unable to make a decision for themselves if they cannot (i) understand the information pertaining to the decision, or (ii) evaluate and apply that information as part of the decision process.

While it was agreed in the first hearing that the appellant failed to meet the determinant criteria for her ability to make an informed decision regards personal safety and vulnerability to her husband's predatory behaviour, the verdict was immediately challenged before the Court of Appeal.

Here, the line taken was that where the interpretation of the MCA 2005 clearly provided that certain decisions were beyond the remit of those falling under its scope, the courts and common law system had already granted by its own principles, a right for an individual suffering from a lack of mental capacity to enter without consultation, into acts that were by extension, inherent to serious consequences and purposeful deliberation; examples of which included the contract of marriage and intimate, yet risky, acts of sex.

It was argued that this raised questions as to whether the statute was contradictory when treating one act as generic and the other as context specific; especially as it was contested that while entering into marriage was not considered central to the choice of partner, the courts had at times, espoused that sexual activity was subject to the form in which those behaviours took, and that perhaps under certain conditions, judicial protection might then be applied, even if contrary to the choice of the individual concerned.

Acknowledging the irony of that statement, the Court examined further the suggested flaws, but maintained that the design of the 2005 Act was one of flexibility, and that the issues presented, determined their relevance inasmuch where the appellant had the competence to undertake her vows of marriage, so it must be considered that she was aware enough to communicate effectively with the local authority when, and if, the time came to intervene; and that on reliance of s.1(4) of the MCA 2005, it was important for the parties present to observe that a person is not to be treated as unable to make a decision, merely because they make an unwise one.

Key Citations

"The subsequent implementation of the MCA 2005 does not establish any basis for questioning the continued applicability of a general and non-specific approach to capacity to marry in proceedings under the Act."[661]

"[A]ll decisions, whatever their nature, fall to be evaluated within the straightforward and clear structure of "MCA 2005, ss 1 to 3 which requires the court to have regard to 'a matter' requiring 'a decision'. There is neither need nor justification for the plain words of the statute to be embellished."[662]

"The central provisions of the MCA 2005 have been widely welcomed as an example of plain and clear statutory language. I would therefore deprecate any attempt to add any embellishment or gloss to the statutory wording unless to do so is plainly necessary."[663]

"[C]apacity to marry, involves understanding matters of status, obligation and rights, the other, contact and residence, may well be grounded in a specific factual context. The process of evaluation of the capacity to make the decision must be the same, but the factors to be taken into account will differ."[664]

"The Court of Protection does not have jurisdiction to act to 'protect' these women if they do not lack the mental capacity to decide whether or not to be, or continue to be, in such a relationship."[665]

"I well understand that all the responsible professionals take the view that it would be extremely unwise for PC to cohabit with her husband. But adult autonomy is such that people are free to make unwise decisions, provided that they have the capacity to decide."[666]

---

[661] *PC v City of York Council* [2013] EWCA Civ 478 [23] (Hedley LJ).

[662] *PC v City of York Council* [2013] EWCA Civ 478 [35] (Hedley LJ).

[663] *PC v City of York Council* [2013] EWCA Civ 478 [37] (Hedley LJ).

[664] *PC v City of York Council* [2013] EWCA Civ 478 [38] (Hedley LJ).

[665] *PC v City of York Council* [2013] EWCA Civ 478 [53] (Hedley LJ).

[666] *PC v City of York Council* [2013] EWCA Civ 478 [64] (Lewison LJ).

8. R (C) v Berkshire Primary Care Trust

Psychological dependence upon a surgical procedure to establish a definite sense of identity lies within the heart of this matter, when a transgender patient experiences disappointment with the outcome of hormone treatment, and seeks remedy from the National Health Service (NHS).

Having experienced a life of emotional turmoil and unrelenting conflict with the gender nature afforded him, a man takes the steps required to adjust his gender to that of a woman, inasmuch as reassignment procedures will allow. While not yet at the point of invasive surgery, the appellant elected to follow course of therapy, that by its own methodology, would increase his existing breast tissue to that of an average woman, thereby removing any anxieties that society would (on a superficial level) ever confuse him with a man.

At the conclusion of the programme, the appellant was left with only a minimal increase in growth, and so the inadequacy felt, lingered to the point of mild depression and disillusionment with both himself and the future. Following consultation with his consultant psychiatrist, his case was put forward to the relevant Primary Care Trust, in the hope that both the poor outcome of the biological intervention, and the circumstantial criteria of the Gender Dysphoria and Cosmetic Breast Surgery Policies, would allow funding for breast augmentation (*Augmentation Mammoplasty*) to redress the balance.

Having had prior experience of transgender applications for the mammoplasty, and in the knowledge that current policy considers the procedure to be low priority, the Primary Care Trust conducted independent research to establish if there was sufficient data to support the claim that breast augmentation was important enough to have a positive impact upon a patient's life and mental health, in claims where such surgical adjustments are compellingly argued.

Despite previous case discussions around the subject, the results of the investigative report concluded that there remained insufficient justification to amend the policy, and so with the exception of extreme cases, the funding would not be provided, therefore the patients would need to seek their own source of revenue. Having first been refused, and in consideration of two complaints from the Health Commission, the second application failed again. before a request for judicial review was submitted. On this occasion, the application for review was dismissed, before the appellant moved to argue for funding on grounds of human rights violations and discrimination.

Citing arts.8 (Right to respect for private and family life) and 14 (Prohibition of discrimination) of the Human Rights Act 1998, it was contested that denial of surgery was a breach of that right, thus excessively demanding an emotionally distressed transgender man to suffer beyond that of an equally unhappy natural woman when determining eligibility for funding; and that such a distinction resulted in nothing less than discrimination between the two types of patient.

Having evaluated the history behind the matter, and the recent investigatory methods used by the NHS, it was concluded that great attention had been placed upon the equality of patients emotional well-being, and that unilateral guidelines were exacting enough to determine when funding was appropriate. This was explained in the decisive notes which read that any patient seeking to obtain funding for policy procedures must demonstrate:

(1) That the patient's case constitutes exceptional circumstances
(2) That there is evidence of significant health benefit from the requested treatment, and
(3) There is evidence of the intervention improving health status

On this occasion, the court agreed that despite evidence of 'chronic mild to moderate distress' conveyed by the patient's doctor, there was simply nothing to suggest that his situation was any more exceptional than a patient denied the resources, or that his symptoms were similar to those qualifying, transgender or otherwise.

Key Citations

"The claimant's point of view is that she is different from and more needy than a natal woman with a similar problem matters; but it is a point of view which has to take its place within both legal and clinical criteria."[667]

---

[667] *R (C) v Berkshire Primary Care Trust* [2011] EWCA Civ 247 [56] (Hooper LJ).

9. R (Condliff) v North Staffordshire Primary Care Trust

Accusations of human rights violations and irrationality of policy, lay behind this failed judicial review hearing, after denied Care Trust funding of laparoscopic gastric surgery for a morbidly obese patient.

While often difficult to draw absolute clarity from National Health Service guidelines and framework policies, the matter dealt with here, stems from a number of misapplications, breakdowns in communication and unwillingness to pursue a claim through the accorded channels. As is perhaps not common knowledge, it is operationally agreed that the associated Primary Care Trusts of the United Kingdom, are given the freedoms to set (within reason) their own thresholds and qualifying criteria for certain procedures, one of which includes preventative gastric surgeries to patients seen as most in need.

Unfortunately on this occasion, the patient's Body Mass Index (BMI) fell short of the required level, despite neighbouring counties demonstrating more lenient grading for the same treatment. Subsequently, when his application for an individual funding request was refused on grounds that his condition failed to meet the prescribed eligibility, the call for judicial review commenced.

Resting upon four reasons for review, the claimant cited (i) that the policy guidelines set by the issuing body were discriminatory, in that they precluded social factors relevant to a claim for exclusivity, (ii) that as a result of such prohibition, art.8 of the Human Rights Act 1998 (HRA) (Right to respect for private and family life) was in contravention, (iii) that the same breach impacted upon art.6 of the HRA 1998 (Right to a fair trial), and (iv) that the conclusive argument against funding, lacked clarity enough to satisfy the patient and acting representatives.

Upon close examination of the facts, it was agreed that while no such interferences of human rights could be seen to exist in the former article, the resulting decision of the latter would have remained the same regardless. This position was supported by the observation that social factors were immaterial when deciding the award of funds, and that the prerequisite medical evidence for exception was balanced enough to remain within the two articles presented. In closing, it was also found that the written opinion of the key adjudicating panel consultant was determinable enough to uphold their decision to reject the application, and that in light of those collective arguments, a judicial review could not stand.

Key Citations

"It seems to me a legitimate point to say that for the PCT, essentially concerned with clinical matters, it will be difficult to make an objective assessment of individuals' differing non-clinical factors, even if not impossible."[668]

"It is hard to see how non-clinical social factors are to be treated other than by generally ruling them in or ruling them out. Any other policy would be very complex and time consuming."[669]

"There is the further point that if social factors were permitted there would be many more applications which would take longer to process with inevitable consequences for resources which would otherwise be available for others."[670]

"If the Social Factors Exclusion, as a policy, does not violate A8 (in other words there is no need to consider non-clinical social factors insofar as they would not be considered anyway and insofar a they touched upon A8 rights) I fail to see how any decision which applied it is subject to some yet further A8 scrutiny."[671]

"If my primary analysis of the A8 position is correct, there is no scope for A6 to operate with reference to A8 because no A8 obligations rose at all."[672]

"The decision of the PCT was an administrative one, allocating or not allocating medical resources on the basis of evaluative judgements where there is no underlying "right" to any particular medical treatment, only target duty on the PCT to provide it."[673]

---

[668] *R (Condliff) v North Staffordshire Primary Care Trust* [2011] 872 (Admin) [65] (Waksman J).

[669] *R (Condliff) v North Staffordshire Primary Care Trust* [2011] 872 (Admin) [65] (Waksman J).

[670] *R (Condliff) v North Staffordshire Primary Care Trust* [2011] 872 (Admin) [66] (Waksman J).

[671] *R (Condliff) v North Staffordshire Primary Care Trust* [2011] 872 (Admin) [71] (Waksman J).

[672] *R (Condliff) v North Staffordshire Primary Care Trust* [2011] 872 (Admin) [75] (Waksman J).

[673] *R (Condliff) v North Staffordshire Primary Care Trust* [2011] 872 (Admin) [78] (Waksman J).

10. R (Rogers) v Swindon NHS Primary Care Trust

Irrationality and subsequent weakness of policy are the key ingredients of this appeal case. When a breast cancer patient is diagnosed with a particular form of metastasis, the consultant responsible for their treatment, prescribes a medicine that while proven to significantly prevent the progression of this specific virus, is a brand still yet to undergo full inclusion within the regulatory core of acceptable National Health Service medicines.

After the patient volunteered to self-fund her course of treatment, the spiralling costs quickly proved overwhelming, at which point she applied to her regional Primary Care Trust to request funding (action not frowned upon in certain circumstances). When the trust refused to provide any financial assistance on grounds that the drug used was not officially recognised and therefore subject to certain qualifying criteria, the appellant sought appeal through judicial review, citing an inherent failure to properly establish sound reasons for non-funding, despite statistical supportive evidence, first-hand testimony and a general position of endorsement by the Secretary of State for Health.

When examined in the Court of Appeal, the emerging facts showed a lack of collective agreement as to exactly why funding for this specific treatment would be prohibited, along with an erring of caution to offer those funds. This proved a baseless hesitation when held against the 'ethical over monetary' line taken by the Health Secretary (and regulatory bodies) and their drive for swift inclusion of this new weapon in the fight against breast cancer.

Upon ruling in favour of the patient, it was advised by the Court that far from being in any position to 'rubber stamp' the uninterrupted sponsoring of the appellant's course of treatment, it was left to the Primary Care Trust and ruling bodies to further refine their criteria for approved patient administration, in order that future prescriptions would avoid undue objections during the uptake of other medicines such as the one under review.

Key Citations

"[A] trust which complies with the guidance (as the PCT sought to do) cannot refuse to fund treatment simply on the basis that Herceptin is unlicensed and unapproved by the NICE."[674]

"The non-medical personal situation of a particular patient cannot in these circumstances be relevant to the question whether Herceptin prescribed by the patients' clinician should be funded for the benefit of the patient."[675]

"In these circumstances there is no rational basis for distinguishing between patients within the eligible group on the basis of exceptional clinical circumstances any more than on the basis of personal, let alone social circumstances."[676]

---

[674] *R (Rogers) v Swindon Primary Care Trust* [2006] 1 WLR 2649 [74] (Lord Clarke MR).

[675] *R (Rogers) v Swindon Primary Care Trust* [2006] 1 WLR 2649 [79] (Lord Clarke MR).

[676] *R (Rogers) v Swindon Primary Care Trust* [2006] 1 WLR 2649 [81] (Lord Clarke MR).

11. R (Watts) v Bedford Primary Care Trust and Secretary of State for Health

Finally decided within the European Court of Justice, this protracted and game-changing case determines well the principle of unreasonableness, whether individually, or in this instance, as exercised through the actions (or inactions) of the National Health Service (NHS) of Great Britain.

When diagnosed as having severe osteoarthritis in both hips, an elderly lady was duly assigned a slot in a typically lengthy waiting list, on the proviso that her operation would at least begin inside a twelve-month period, but that no other adjustments could be made under the existing policy framework.

Clearly distressed and left in constant pain, the patient took it upon herself to request a permission form which under Regulation 1408/71, enabled her to seek medical treatment in another EU Member State at cost to herself, before claiming back those costs under the umbrella of art.49 EC. When authorisation for her application was refused on the grounds that the inherently free infrastructure of the NHS prevented such claims as a matter of course, the applicant went ahead and secured an operation in France regardless.

During the period between the successful operation and her application for authorisation, the patient's condition worsened, to the degree that her consultant elevated her need for surgery. This action reduced the waiting time from twelve months to three or four months, but unfortunately left her unable the receive the care (and ultimately adequate pain relief) she needed, and so her paid surgery went ahead two months before any provisional opening was made available to her in the United Kingdom.

When pursuing the right to seek judicial review in order to recoup her costs under her individual EU rights, the High Court dismissed her claim under constitutional grounds, while her subsequent appeal against such immediate objection escalated matters to the Court of Appeal, who themselves referred it to the European Court of Justice for a preliminary ruling under art.177 EC.

After much scrutiny and comparison with similar EU cases, it was held by the Court that any refund issued in respect of treatment sought in another Member State, did not contravene art.152(5) EC which provides that "Community action in the field of public health shall fully respect the responsibilities of the Member States for the organisation and delivery of health services and medical care", while any excuse offered with regard to waiting times and the limitations of such healthcare provision, failed to satisfy the individual rights offered under art.49 EC.

Key Citations

"[T]he national authorities are required to have regard to all the circumstances of each specific case and to take due account not only of the patient's medical condition at the time when authorisation is sought and, where appropriate, of the degree of pain or the nature of the patient's disability, which might, for example, make it impossible or extremely difficult for him to carry out a professional activity, but also of his medical history…"[677]

"Considerations relating to the management of waiting lists can only justify a refusal to receive hospital treatment in another Member State if those waiting lists are managed in such a way that they take the individual medical needs of patients sufficiently into account and do not prevent treatment being provided in another Member State in case of urgency."[678]

"The fact that, because the hospital treatment in the National Health Service in question is free of charge, the legislation of the competent Member State does not include a tariff for reimbursement, does not preclude the application of the provisions of articles 22(1)(c)(i) and 36 of Regulation No.1408/71."[679]

"[A] patient who was authorised to go to another Member State to receive there hospital treatment or who received a refusal to authorise subsequently held to be unfounded is entitled to seek from the competent institution reimbursement of the ancillary costs associated with that cross-border movement for medical purposes provided that the legislation of the competent Member State imposes a corresponding obligation on the national system to reimburse in respect of treatment provided in a local hospital covered by that system."[680]

---

[677] *R (Watts) v Bedford Primary Care Trust and Secretary of State for Health* [2003] EWHC 2228, Opinion of AG Geelhoed, para 98.

[678] *R (Watts) v Bedford Primary Care Trust and Secretary of State for Health* [2003] EWHC 2228, Opinion of AG Geelhoed, para 129.

[679] *R (Watts) v Bedford Primary Care Trust and Secretary of State for Health* [2003] EWHC 2228, para 127 (ECJ).

[680] *R (Watts) v Bedford Primary Care Trust and Secretary of State for Health* [2003] EWHC 2228, para 149 (ECJ).

12. R v Cambridge Health Authority *ex p* B

This appeal case explores the difficulties faced by medical professionals, governing bodies and courts, when upon the balance of probabilities (and irrespective of costs or arguments against their application), the cessation of medically prescribed treatment is the only viable solution for all parties.

When the family of young girl with advanced *Myeloid Leukaemia* is told that their hopes of beating the disease are beyond that of any real success, the father is compelled to seek overseas opinion, in order that he might seek to procure the funds from the National Health Service. His reasoning, is that despite a likely remission percentage of between ten and twenty percent (along with a repeated bombardment of chemotherapy and further transplantation of bone marrow), he has been convinced by private medical doctors in the United States of America, that his daughter can, and most likely would, survive.

Unfortunately, as had already been agreed by the consultants involved, the only method open to possibility would in fact be the previously described two-step process; and which if taken together, would require not only tremendous physical, mental and emotional turmoil on the part of the child, but also at a cost that defied provision, on the very low chance that a patient would be alive upon completion. After seeking judicial review of the Health Authority's rejection to fund further treatment, the presiding judge rescinded their decision, and requested reconsideration in light of the wishes of the child's family.

This ruling was appealed against, and when dealt with by the Court of Appeal, it was found after balancing both the needs of the parents and those of the care providers, that when such bleak rates of recovery were evident, it served no cause for the child's best interests when the prognosis was a period of prolonged suffering and no probable chance of success. The Court also felt that their decision would have remained consistent if funding concerns were not subject to the debate, and that while the judges felt tremendous sympathy for the predicament faced by both parent and child, theirs was not one of medical wisdom, but the ruling of lawfulness within State department practice and application of policy.

Key Citations

"Difficult and agonising judgments have to be made as to how a limited budget is best allocated to the maximum advantage of the maximum number of patients. That is not a judgment which the court can make."[681]

"The powers of this court are not such as to enable it to substitute its own decision in a matter of this kind for that of the authority which is legally charged with making the decision."[682]

---

[681] *R v Cambridge Health Authority ex parte B* [1995] AII ER 129 (CA) 906 (Lord Bingham MR).

[682] *R v Cambridge Health Authority ex parte B* [1995] AII ER 129 (CA) 907 (Brown P).

13. *Re* C (Adult: Refusal of Treatment)

Drawing reference again from s.3(1) of the Mental Capacity Act 2005, the imposition of State authority where a patient has argued to the contrary, is placed before the courts when prevention of irreversible surgery is contended through a diagnosed psychiatric illness.

After the violent stabbing of his former girlfriend, a man is tried and convicted, before later being diagnosed as a chronic paranoid schizophrenic. Roughly twenty years on, while serving as a patient in Broadmoor Hospital, the resident surgeon concluded that following an accident in the showers, where the patient had injured his ankle, evidence of a necrotic ulcer had formed. Basing his medical judgment on procedural policy, it was proposed that in order to prevent further infection and possible death, it would be best to have the leg amputated below the knee as soon as possible. This was also resting upon the presumption that the patient's injury amounted to *Peripheral Vascular Disease* with the small vessel variant, a condition non-receptive to bypass surgery.

Upon this prognosis, the patient immediately refused to consent to any surgical removal of the lower portion of his leg, proclaiming he would prefer to die with both legs than continue living with one. It was however known that despite the risk of death if left unaddressed, the amputation itself carried a fifteen percent risk of mortality; whereas there were other options available, including antibiotics and skin grafts where dead tissue removal was successful.

With consideration of the destructive nature of paranoid schizophrenia, the consultant vascular surgeon took it upon himself to make a provisional booking for surgery despite the refusal of the patient, after which the resident medical officer and consultant forensic psychiatrist sought advice from an independent solicitor with regard to the legal ramifications of overriding the will of the patient, where his lack of consensual ability was perceived to exist. Having reached a deadlock, it was then agreed that litigation was the only course of option; whereupon the patient applied for an injunction to (i) prevent the proposed operation on grounds of conflict of interest, and (ii) to deny those who may try at a later date, to perform the same surgery without his written consent.

Using a combination of the debilitating effect of mental illness and the prerequisite test for establishing capable reasoning, the hospital argued that delusions of grandeur and fantasies of having practiced as a doctor were sufficient reasons to deny the patient any right to determine what was in his best interests, and that the inability to understand the gravity of the infection could not uphold any petition for injunctive measures, despite the fact that alternative treatments had already shown themselves to be effective upon the date of the hearing.

By careful means of observation around the patient's conduct and logic before the judge, it was deemed that while the hospital established a strong case for intervention, it was still within the jurisdiction of the courts to determine if, and when, the granting of an injunction was both fair and conjunctive to the preservation of individual rights and the autonomy of the patient, before issuing the very same.

Key Citations

"If the patient's capacity to decide is unimpaired, autonomy weighs heavier, but the further capacity is reduced, the lighter autonomy weighs."[683]

"[I]t was clear to me that C was quite content to follow medical advice and to co-operate in treatment appropriately as a patient as long as his rejection of amputation was respected."[684]

"C himself throughout the hours that he spent in the proceedings seemed ordinarily engaged and concerned. His answers to questions seemed measured and generally sensible. He was not always easy to understand and the grandiose delusions were manifest, but there was no sign of inappropriate emotional expression."[685]

"I think that the question to be decided is whether it has been established that C's capacity is so reduced by his chronic mental illness that he does not sufficiently understand the nature, purpose and effects of the proffered amputation."[686]

"[T]he presumption that C has the right of self-determination has not been displaced. Although his general capacity is impaired by schizophrenia, it has not been established that he does not sufficiently understand the nature, purpose and effects of the treatment he refuses."[687]

"I consider that an individual should have the same ready access to judicial determinations in extreme circumstances. Equally, since the same authorities recognise the right to frame a refusal as a declaration extending beyond present to future circumstances, I see no reason why injunctive or declaratory relief should not be equally extensive."[688]

---

[683] *C (Adult: Refusal of Treatment), re* [1994] 1 WLR 290 (Fam) 292 (Thorpe J).

[684] *C (Adult: Refusal of Treatment), re* [1994] 1 WLR 290 (Fam) 293 (Thorpe J).

[685] *C (Adult: Refusal of Treatment), re* [1994] 1 WLR 290 (Fam) 294 (Thorpe J).

[686] *C (Adult: Refusal of Treatment), re* [1994] 1 WLR 295 (Fam) 292 (Thorpe J).

[687] *C (Adult: Refusal of Treatment), re* [1994] 1 WLR 295 (Fam) 292 (Thorpe J).

[688] *C (Adult: Refusal of Treatment), re* [1994] 1 WLR 296 (Fam) 292 (Thorpe J).

14. *Re* SB (A patient: capacity to consent to termination)

Long-standing mental illness and an unwanted pregnancy in an unhappy marriage, are the ingredients for unpredictable behaviour pending a life no child should endure. When a choice to terminate is made by the party afflicted with emotional instability, it is left to the Court of Protection to ensure that the final decision is both within the law and the interests of those at risk.

In an *ex tempore* judgment, the court was presented with the facts surrounding a bi-polar mother-to-be, who at twenty-three weeks, stood upon the threshold of legal abortion under the Abortion Act 1967. With a history of continuous medication for a condition known to cause paranoia, depression and manic or exaggerated behaviours for indeterminable periods, the applicant had become involved in a relationship that was once seemingly happy, but had since descended into one of physical distance and non-communication.

During the early stages of their courtship, the applicant had fallen pregnant, before quickly resorting to a medical abortion on grounds that the level of her ongoing medication would significantly impair foetal development and risk further complications for both her and the baby. It was only after marrying and relocating to the United Kingdom, that the applicant later became pregnant again, and thus elected to cease taking her medication in order to enjoy a healthy antenatal experience, while protecting the needs of the unborn child.

However, as is common to those suffering bi-polar disorder, the risk of relapse through non-medication and the stresses of pregnancy, are both magnified in comparison to non sufferers, therefore it is only in the most secure of relationships that one might consider such a dramatic change in circumstances. On this occasion, the applicant began to exhibit patterns of erratic behaviour, stemming from a belief that both her husband and mother were to some degree, conspiring against her, and that should the child be born, there would be little to no support from either party. This sense of isolation compounded her conviction that an abortion was the only viable solution, and so she took steps to have it removed privately.

In light of her dramatic change of heart, and following a number of violent actions towards her husband, she was detained under s.2 of the Mental Health Act 1983, while continuing to demand that the pregnancy be terminated. It was for that reason, that the matter was brought before the Court of Protection. Under the weight of collective professional opinion, and the relevant sections of the Mental Capacity Act 2005, it was argued by the husband and mother, that by virtue of the fact that the applicant suffered from a mental disorder, and that s. 2(1) of the 2005 Act provided how:

> "[A] person lacks capacity in relation to a matter if at the material time he is unable to make a decision for himself in relation to the matter, because of an impairment of, or a disturbance in the functioning of, the mind or brain."[689]

It was irrational for the applicant to determine, or appreciate, the consequences attached to a surgical abortion, as outlined in s.3(1) of the 2005 Act. In contrast, the applicant

---

[689] Mental Capacity Act 2005, s.2(1)

gave many salient reasons as to why she felt there was no possibility of continuing to full term, particularly the unethical concept of giving birth while detained, only to offer the child out for adoption, along with her willingness to commit suicide should her wishes not be respected.

With diligent consideration of the needs of all parties involved, and with appreciation of the diminishing time remaining before termination became illegal, the judge reviewed the past actions and statements of the applicant, before summarising that despite illusory fears and deep seated suspicions towards her husband and mother, there was little doubt as to the reasons why his wife believed her decision should be upheld, and that it was beyond the courts to deny her full exercise of her individual freedom to choose, regardless of whether others agreed or disagreed. For those reasons, she was considered capable of expeditiously pursuing a termination in the means medically agreed.

Key Citations

"I had and have no doubt whatsoever that this lady has ample capacity and autonomy directly to instruct her own lawyers to effectively protect and pursue her own position and interests in the case."[690]

"There is absolutely no doubt whatsoever that this lady has, many weeks ago, made a decision. She persists in it, and she very, very strongly urges it upon me today. So there is no doubt that she has a capacity to "make" a decision and she has made one."[691]

"[I]t is important to emphasise her evidence, which I accept, that she has not experienced a sense of regret about her previous termination. She was very clear that she regrets that she became pregnant that time, but not the termination."[692]

"[E]ven if the patient has some skewed thoughts and paranoid or delusional views with regard to her husband and his attitude towards her and his behaviour, she gives many other reasons for desiring a termination."[693]

"She said she is very worried about her ability to bring up a child. Since it is so strongly said that she has for 8 years suffered from a lifelong, relapsing bi-polar disorder, it is entirely rational that she has that worry."[694]

---

[690] *Re SB (A Patient: capacity to consent to termination)* [2013] EWHC 1417 (COP) [30] (Holman J).

[691] *Re SB (A Patient: capacity to consent to termination)* [2013] EWHC 1417 (COP) [38] (Holman J).

[692] *Re SB (A Patient: capacity to consent to termination)* [2013] EWHC 1417 (COP) [39] (Holman J).

[693] *Re SB (A Patient: capacity to consent to termination)* [2013] EWHC 1417 (COP) [41] (Holman J).

[694] *Re SB (A Patient: capacity to consent to termination)* [2013] EWHC 1417 (COP) [42] (Holman J).

8. Property Law

1. AG Securities v Vaughan

As later discussed in *Aslan v Murphy*,[695] the protection of exclusive possession under the Rent Act 1977 is under scrutiny when another two cases are subject to judicial wisdom. In the first instance, the collective arguments of four individuals rally against the wishes of a landlord looking to remove them in favour of longer-term arrangements; while in the second case, the needs of two cohabiting parties are contested before a landlord seeking their departures for similar reasons.

AG Securities v Vaughan

Situated near the very popular West End of London, the building in question was a four-bedroom flat that had been apportioned to accommodate four individual residents at any one time. The nature of the arrangements were unique to each party, so subsequently there were four separate contracts precluding the right to exclusive possession on grounds that each licence was for a six-month period, before commencing as a rolling one month contract, prior to predetermined notices to quit from either landlord or licensee.

Over a period of around three years, the appellants had by grant of the respondent, enjoyed intrusion free use of the flat, and were eventually left to determine through interviews and group discussion, who would replace those vacating their rooms during the passage of time. Each party also paid differing amounts of rent, and had acquiesced to the terms of their agreements when becoming part of the group in occupation.

When the time came for the landlord to reassess how he wished to lease the flat, it was decided that long-term sub-leases were preferred, at which point notice to quit was served upon the four remaining occupiers. This prompted the local authority to establish through the rent officer, whether the appellants were in fact considered tenants under s. 68 of the Rent Act 1977, and not licensees (as suggested by the respondent and indicated in the terms of their individual contracts), and thus how best to determine a fair market rent.

The landlord contested the application, and sought to apply an injunction against the local authority, while seeking payment of rent arrears by the appellants. On this occasion, the judge found in favour of the respondent, and declared the appellants licensees. Upon appeal, three of the appellants were successful in reversing the previous decision by the court, thereby granting the appellants powers of joint tenancy, whereupon the respondent appealed.

With a verdict of two to one for the now appellants, the principles of exclusive possession and joint tenancy were examined, within which the rights determined in *Street v Mountford*[696] require exclusive possession in lieu of payable rents for a

---

[695] [1990] 1 WLR 766.

[696] [1985] AC 809.

determinable period. On this occasion, although the contract contradicted the nature of the living arrangements, the four appellants had enjoyed uninterrupted possession of the flat, and were subject to finite durations of contract prior to the respondent's remuneration for privilege of occupancy.

With regard to joint tenancy and the principles of unity of possession, interest, title and time, it was held that at one point, the four appellants were equal in their period of residency, and while each resident held separate contracts, their duration was of the same length, therefore unity of term applied, despite disparate cessation of each agreement. While title must be held under the same Act, there was by implication, a single agreement that bound each resident to the same conditions; and although the contractual periods overlapped, each was determinable in duration, and therefore valid in terms of ascertainment. This somewhat overreaching of the principles of tenancy, amounted to judgment in favour of the appellants and award of costs.

Appealed again in the House of Lords, it was quickly concluded that to allow a joint tenancy to exist would be an affront to the four unities, when no one person was granted exclusive interest in the property but instead, were merely sharing a right to occupancy under licence; and that when compelled to enforce their legal rights, the technicalities of the contracts denied them tenancy powers, regardless of how hard they tried to collaborate.

Antoniades v Villiers

In this matter, an experienced property manager took the steps to observe the legal principles held in *Somma v Hazelhurst*,[697] where it was held that two parties sharing the same room while under separate contracts, can enjoy the rights of exclusive possession, and thus those of the Rent Act 1977, despite signing licence agreements. It was after openly discussing the respondent's preference to licence agreements, that the appellants willingly co-signed separate, yet identical agreements on the same day, before commencing their occupancy as contracted.

Part of the agreement stipulated that at the luxury of the respondent, there was a possibility that additional residents may be added to the house, and that until such time, the appellants were to cohabit as husband and wife (even though they were just boyfriend and girlfriend). Little over a year later, the respondent issued them with a month's notice to vacate the property, following disputes over non-payment of rent. It was then that the appellants' asserted themselves as tenants and not licensees, after which the rent officer upheld their claim and registered a lower rent than had been previously agreed.

Having taken them to court, it was found by the judge that while the terms of the agreement were reflective of the outcome of *Somma*, the recent decision taken by the House of Lords in *Street* had in essence, reversed that position back in favour of the appellants, when Templeman LJ said:

"Although the Rent Acts must not be allowed to alter or influence the construction of an agreement, the court should, in my opinion, be astute to detect

---

[697] [1978] 1 WLR 1014.

and frustrate sham devices and artificial transactions whose only object is to disguise the grant of a tenancy and to evade the Rent Acts."[698]

This translated that those once considered licensees under similar circumstances to the one created by the respondent's draft, were now deemed tenants under protection of the Rent Act 1977. By following verbatim the minds of the judges, the court found in favour of the appellants, and dismissed the possession order.

In the Court of Appeal, the two judges agreed that great lengths had been taken by the respondent to act inside the legalities of occupancy rights, and that the transparent nature of the relationship both before and after the signing of the agreements, dictated how no efforts were made to conceal the limitation of rights ascribed the two parties. For this reason, the appeal was upheld and possession procedures left to recommence.

Further appealed and evaluated in the House of Lords, the meaning of the agreements while appearing legitimate, were now held to be nothing short of manipulative and misleading. It was also agreed that by the two appellants signing mirroring contracts and paying the same amounts each calendar month, they had by extension, been afforded the same rights and freedoms provided for tenants under the very Act the respondent had looked to avoid. It was also agreed that aside from clause 16, which allowed the respondent to reside himself, or introduce another occupier, there was nothing to suggest that a joint tenancy based upon interdependence did not exist, and for those reasons the appeal was allowed.

Key Citations

"The four respondents acquired their contractual rights to occupy the flat in question and undertook their relevant obligations by separate agreements with the appellants made at different times and on different terms. These rights and obligations having initially been several, I do not understand by what legal alchemy they could ever become joint."[699]

"Having no estate in land, they could not sue in trespass. Their remedy against intruders would have been to persuade the appellants to sue as plaintiffs or to join the appellants as defendants by way of enforcement of their contractual rights."[700]

"[I]t seems to me, with respect to the majority of the Court of Appeal, to require the highest degree of artificiality to force these contracts into the mould of a joint tenancy."[701]

"[T]he provisions of the joint agreement purporting to retain the right in the respondent to share the occupation of the flat with the young couple himself or to introduce an

---

[698] *Street v Mountford* [1985] AC 809 [825] (Templeman LJ).

[699] *AG Securities v Vaughan* [1990] 1 AC 417 (HL) 453 (Bridge LJ).

[700] *AG Securities v Vaughan* [1990] 1 AC 417 (HL) 454 (Bridge LJ).

[701] *AG Securities v Vaughan* [1990] 1 AC 417 (HL) 454 (Bridge LJ).

indefinite number of third parties to do so could be seen, in all the relevant circumstances, to be repugnant to the true purpose of the agreement."[702]

"They were introduced into the agreement for no other purpose than as an attempt to disguise the true character of the agreement which it was hoped would deceive the court and prevent the appellants enjoying the protection of the Rent Acts."[703]

"Since parties to an agreement cannot contract out of the Rent Acts, a document which expresses the intention, genuine or bogus, of both parties or of one party to create a licence will nevertheless create a tenancy if the rights and obligations enjoyed and imposed satisfy the legal requirements of a tenancy."[704]

"[T]he grant of a tenancy to two persons jointly cannot be concealed, accidentally or by design, by the creation of two documents in the form of licences."[705]

"[I]t is clear from the negotiations which had taken place, from the surrounding circumstances, and from subsequent events, that Mr. Antoniades did not intend in February 1985, immediately or contemporaneously, to share occupation or to authorise any other person to deprive Mr. Villiers and Miss Bridger of exclusive occupation of the flat."[706]

"The Rent Acts prevent the exercise of a power which would destroy the tenancy of Mr. Villiers and Miss Bridger and would deprive them of the exclusive occupation of the flat which they are now enjoying. Clause 16 is inconsistent with the provisions of the Rent Acts."[707]

"These clauses cannot be considered as seriously intended to have any practical operation or to serve any purpose apart from the purely technical one of seeking to avoid the ordinary legal consequences attendant upon letting the appellants into possession at a monthly rent."[708]

"If the real transaction was, as the judge found, one under which the appellants became joint tenants with exclusive possession, on the footing that the two agreements are to be construed together, then it would follow that they were together jointly and severally responsible for the whole rent. It would equally follow that they could effectively exclude the respondent and his nominees."[709]

---

[702] *AG Securities v Vaughan* [1990] 1 AC 417 (HL) 454 (Bridge LJ).

[703] *AG Securities v Vaughan* [1990] 1 AC 417 (HL) 454 (Bridge LJ).

[704] *AG Securities v Vaughan* [1990] 1 AC 417 (HL) 458 (Templeman LJ).

[705] *AG Securities v Vaughan* [1990] 1 AC 417 (HL) 458 (Templeman LJ).

[706] *AG Securities v Vaughan* [1990] 1 AC 417 (HL) 461 (Templeman LJ).

[707] *AG Securities v Vaughan* [1990] 1 AC 417 (HL) 462 (Templeman LJ).

[708] *AG Securities v Vaughan* [1990] 1 AC 417 (HL) 468 (Oliver LJ).

[709] *AG Securities v Vaughan* [1990] 1 AC 417 (HL) 469 (Oliver LJ).

2. Aslan v Murphy

In order to enjoy the protective nature of exclusive possession from the powers of the Rent Act 1977, it must first be established what type of contractual arrangement has been agreed. In this instance, the Court of Appeal decided upon two cases where landlords seeking possession were subject to examination.

Aslan v Murphy (No 1 and No 2)

Having entered into a living arrangement with the landlord of a hotel, the appellant was granted use of a basement room, while deprived of many freedoms in lieu of strict usage controls. The extent of those restrictions included a ninety-minute window where the appellant was denied access to the room, as well as having to surrender the room keys to the respondent when leaving the room. It was thus argued that the contract was between a licensor and licensee, as opposed to that of landlord and tenant. This alteration of rights prevented the appellant from retention of occupancy under the Rent Act 1977, and so having sought repossession of the room, the matter went to court, whereupon the necessary order was granted prior to an appeal, where the Court found that tenancy rights did exist.

Around the same time, the local authority served a closing order against the respondent upon grounds that the room was unfit for human occupancy, and therefore unable to stand as chargeable for rents, as per s.266 of the Housing Act 1985. This led to a second possession order in favour of the respondent. However, in order to secure alternative accommodation through the local authority, the appellant requested that the courts declared the actual nature of the contract, as no notice to quit had been served, and that the appellant was now protected through exclusive possession until such time as notice was given. Relying upon s.276 of the 1985 Act, the respondent countered that the power of the closing order negated any right to exclusive protection, while under s.277 of the same Act, it was further contended that any continued occupancy by the appellant constituted a criminal offence, subject to occupancy penalties.

Put before the Court of Appeal, it was held that until clarification of the contract could be ascertained, there could be no effect to the possession order, despite the powers claimed under the Housing Act 1985, and that until such time, neither party could pursue their own ends.

Duke v Wynne

In this case, the relationship was that between a homeowner and a family in need of accommodation, while the contract entered into, was one where the respondent reserved the right to terminate the arrangement on, or around, a two-year period. Due to the generous size of the property, there was also express denial of exclusive possession within the terms of the contract, due to a provision for additional parties to share the home at the privilege of the respondent.

During the two years in which they remained in occupancy, the appellants used the whole of the house, and at no point did any new occupiers enter the property, despite such prohibition. At the point in which the respondent sought possession following her decision to emigrate, it was contested by the appellants that with no alternate means of accommodation, and having had free reign of the house, they were now entitled to remain in occupancy under the terms of the Rent Act 1977, and through the protection of exclusive possession.

Having considered the wording of the contract and the manner in which the appellants had been allowed to reside, it was held by the Court that without any evidence of shared occupancy, the appellants had by virtue of their liberties, enjoyed exclusive possession of the home for the duration of the time passed, and that vacant possession was not legally enforceable, failing any notice to quit.

Key Citations

"[T]here are materials from which it is possible to infer that the occupier is a lodger rather than a tenant. But the inference arises not from the provisions as to keys, but from the reason why those provisions formed part of the bargain."[710]

"[I]t is quite clear that the true bargain was that the Wynnes should be entitled to exclusive occupation unless and until Mrs. Duke wanted to exercise her right to authorise someone else to move in as a lodger and she never suggested that this was a serious possibility."[711]

"[H]er wish to have a key was not dictated by any obligation to provide services or anything else from which it could be inferred that she was herself occupying the house as well as the defendants."[712]

"[T]he tenant only commits an offence if he continues to occupy the premises as a place in which he lives, he may use it for other purposes, such as storing furniture, which would not involve the commission of a criminal offence. And in the present case Mr. Murphy has ceased to live in the room."[713]

"In our judgment before the respondent can claim possession she must determine the contractual tenancy."[714]

"If the tenant wishes to continue to be liable for the rent, notwithstanding that he cannot live in the room, he is entitled to maintain that his tenancy has never been determined."[715]

---

[710] *Aslan v Murphy* [1990] 1 WLR 766 (CA) 773 (Lord Donaldson MR).

[711] *Aslan v Murphy* [1990] 1 WLR 766 (CA) 775 (Lord Donaldson MR).

[712] *Aslan v Murphy* [1990] 1 WLR 766 (CA) 776 (Lord Donaldson MR).

[713] *Aslan v Murphy* [1990] 1 WLR 766 (CA) 777 (Lord Donaldson MR).

[714] *Aslan v Murphy* [1990] 1 WLR 766 (CA) 777 (Lord Donaldson MR).

[715] *Aslan v Murphy* [1990] 1 WLR 766 (CA) 777 (Lord Donaldson MR).

3. Barrett v Barrett

Resting upon the equitable maxim 'he who comes to equity must come with clean hands', the clandestine collusion between two brothers falls foul, when the agreement dissolves in favour of the abetting sibling.

After lapsing into bankruptcy, a business owner tries to circumvent the dissolution process in an attempt to save his home from repossession. In order to achieve this, he asks that his brother purchase the property from the bankruptcy trustees, before holding the house on trust until such time that the now appellant is able to regain legal title.

While agreeing to this proposition, the respondent approaches the trustee, before securing the property through cash downpayment and mortgage redemption, prior to allowing the appellant to regain occupancy. A second agreement followed that enabled the appellant to make contributions to the mortgage repayments, as well as investing money into the maintenance of the home; again under the pretence that the respondent held the property on trust and nothing more.

Fifteen years after the repurchase, the respondent sold the property for significant profit, placing roughly half the proceeds in trust with his sister, who then refused to pay the money back, on grounds that the respondent had breached his agreement and duty as a trustee to his brother. At this point, the appellant issued proceedings for its recovery, before the sister part-paid the appellant and placed the remainder in the hands of the court. This resulted in the appellant issuing proceedings for the balance held, while the respondent counter claimed to defend his position .

Relying upon the argument of numerous trusts (express, constructive, common intention and resulting) with which to recover the sale proceeds, it was argued that by selling the home, the respondent had unlawfully profited from his position as a trustee, and that as such, the money was now owed to the appellant and enforceable through equity. This claim was struck out in the first instance, on grounds that equity will not allow a trust created through illegality to stand, and therefore no remedy in law could exist when the appellant had requested that the respondent purchase the home in order to avoid duties brought about under s.333(2) of the Insolvency Act 1986.

When heard in the Court of Appeal, the facts were revisited with little to no effect for the appellant, despite continued multiple arguments from his representative. While the appellant accepted that the original agreement served two aims (retention of the home and avoidance of creditor payments), the Court would not ignore the reality that the same person seeking equitable remedy, was behind the illegal concept and undertaking of, a property purchase designed to undermine and breach the legal duty owed when winding down a business. It was then, for that very simple and yet unmistakeable reason, that the judge upheld the previous findings and flatly dismissed the appeal.

Key Citations

"[T]he pleaded agreement or arrangement involved the creation of a new interest in favour of Thomas, his original interest in the property having vested in his trustee in bankruptcy. The creation of such an interest was not of itself unlawful. The illegality lay in the failure to disclose the acquisition of this new interest to his trustee in bankruptcy."[716]

"Even if I accept the premise of a dual purpose, it would not assist Thomas but in any event the only purpose of the trust arrangement, as opposed to the purchase from the trustee in bankruptcy, can have been to conceal Thomas's interest from the trustee in bankruptcy."[717]

"[E]quitable proprietary rights are to be treated in essentially the same way as legal proprietary rights and will be enforced provided that the claimant does not plead or lead evidence of the illegality."[718]

"Contributions to mortgage instalments do not stand in the same position as direct contributions to the purchase price. They may be intended to confer a beneficial interest on the payer, but equally they may be intended as an advance to the mortgagor…"[719]

"[T]he purpose of purchasing the property in the name of John was "to avoid its being repossessed by the Trustee in Bankruptcy". Without that purpose, the agreement or arrangement has no rational explanation."[720]

"[W]here the existence of the trust and of the claimant's alleged beneficial interest under it depends on no more than an agreement entered into for the illegal purpose of deceiving third persons, the beneficial interest will not be recognised or enforced…"[721]

---

[716] *Barrett v Barrett* [2008] EWHC 1061 (Ch) [12] (Richards J).

[717] *Barrett v Barrett* [2008] EWHC 1061 (Ch) [14] (Richards J).

[718] *Barrett v Barrett* [2008] EWHC 1061 (Ch) [17] (Richards J).

[719] *Barrett v Barrett* [2008] EWHC 1061 (Ch) [24] (Richards J).

[720] *Barrett v Barrett* [2008] EWHC 1061 (Ch) [25] (Richards J).

[721] *Barrett v Barrett* [2008] EWHC 1061 (Ch) [26] (Richards J).

4. Borman v Griffith

Implication by way of contract, is argued in a case involving the conflict of interests between two tenants, and a perhaps disorganised and rushed grant of occupancy by the landlord.

In a time immediately before the Law of Property Act 1925, a landowner sought to let out a part of his estate for a determined period. Under the terms of the lease there was at the time, a gravelled road that passed by the tenant's rented property named 'The Gardens', while leading to the door of the main estate property named 'The Hall'.

At the time the tenant began his residence, there was also an unfinished bridleway that allowed for access to the rear of the Gardens, albeit given no mention within the contract, nor any reliable evidence that use of the drive had been orally agreed between the two parties. During this period, and shortly after taking occupancy of the Gardens, the Hall was leased to another occupier, with no subsequent issues arising between them.

A few years afterwards, this same tenant vacated the Hall, and so the landowner let it out to another party for a fixed period, after which the occupier of the Gardens continued to use the gravelled drive as a means of access to the front of his property, as he had since his lease began. Two years after taking up residency, the defendant in this case erected a wire fence to prevent the claimant and tenant of the Gardens from using the gravelled drive as a means of access, hence resulting in litigation.

Relying upon the wording of s.62(1) of the Law of Property Act 1925, and the fact that there had never been any other suitable means of access to his home, the claimant argued that an easement by way of implication had been granted by the landlord. When considered by the court, the facts determined that there was a clear difference between the granting of a lease and the conveyance of interest in land or property; and that in this instance the former applied.

There was however, the principle that under the terms of the contract, there could be argued, an obligation to undertake full performance of the rights bestowed the claimant, where unless the contract provides specific exclusion of a right of way between two sharing tenants, the gravelled drive afforded both users equal powers to enforce their rights. It was on these grounds that the judge endorsed the action and awarded accordingly.

Key Citations

"[T]he definition of "conveyance" in the Conveyancing Act, 1881, is limited to documents made by deed, and the contract in the present case is not by deed."[722]

"[A] lease for any term of more than three years must be by deed, and it is well known that, under s.3 of the Real Property Act, 1845, "…a lease, required by law to be in writing, of any tenements or hereditaments…. shall…be void at law unless made by deed.""[723]

"[W]here, as in the present case, two properties belonging to a single owner and about to be granted are separated by a common road, or where a plainly visible road exists over the one for the apparent use of the other, and that road is necessary for the reasonable enjoyment of the property, a right to use the road will pass with the quasi-dominant tenement, unless by the terms of the contract that right is excluded…"[724]

"[A] grantor of property, in circumstances where an obvious, i.e., visible and made road is necessary for the reasonable enjoyment of the property by the grantee, must be taken prima facie to have intended to grant a right to use it."[725]

---

[722] *Borman v Griffith* [1930] 1 Ch 493 (Ch D) (Ch) 497 (Maugham J).

[723] *Borman v Griffith* [1930] 1 Ch 493 (Ch D) (Ch) 498 (Maugham J).

[724] *Borman v Griffith* [1930] 1 Ch 493 (Ch D) (Ch) 499 (Maugham J).

[725] *Borman v Griffith* [1930] 1 Ch 493 (Ch D) (Ch) 499 (Maugham J).

5. Browne v Flower

Derogation from grant by way of illegal easement, and the right to peaceful enjoyment of property, make for a brief and yet divisive matter, when two leaseholders seek to enforce their own entitlements in the courts.

Having recently acquired tenancy in a shared building, the respondent took steps to reduce her portion of the property, in exchange for subletting to an additional tenant. In order for this to work, it was proposed by the leaseholder to the landlord, that an iron external staircase would allow for access when the using the room created. The landlord raised no objections, and so the work went ahead as planned.

Having rented the ground floor of the same building, the claimant's privacy was impinged upon, as the staircase was erected between two of her bedroom windows. This translated that the sub-tenant using the stairs was now afforded a clear view into those rooms.

Under the terms of the lease, the landlord was under obligation not to derogate from the arrangement, which included an agreement that no tenant would suffer, or cause to suffer, another tenant any nuisance or reduction of the view to the outside gardens while in occupancy. As was clear from the location and purpose of the staircase, the claimant was now placed into a position where she either installed blinds or curtains to restrict the view, or argued that the imposition and loss of light resulting from them had constituted a breach of agreement on the part of the landlord.

Upon litigation, the court heard about, and fully appreciated, the invasive nature of the staircase, but when relying upon similar case precedent, there was insufficient evidence to suggest that the invasion of privacy amounted to total loss of the views provided for by the outside gardens, or any enjoyment of natural light. It was held instead, that the change in circumstances proved mere inconvenience at particular times of the day and little more. It was also held that while the terms of the lease prevented any use of the property beyond that of private tenants, the staircase had been built upon adjoining land, and not that used and paid for by the tenants, therefore it fell beyond the scope of claim.

In closing, the judge awarded in favour of the respondents, before noting that the landlord had only consented with the erection of the staircase on the respondent's assurances that the claimant had raised no objections, therefore there had been misrepresentation as to any disagreement prior to their installation, and so no order for her costs were made.

Key Citations

"[I]f the grant or demise be made for a particular purpose, the grantor or lessor comes under an obligation not to use the land retained by him in such a way as to render the land granted or demised unfit or materially less fit for the particular purpose for which the grant or demise was made."[726]

"[T]hough possibly there may not be known to the law any easement of light for special purposes, still the lease of a building to be used for a special purpose requiring an extraordinary amount of light might well be held to preclude the grantor from diminishing the light passing to the grantee's windows, even in cases where the diminution would not be such as to create a nuisance…"[727]

"Much as I sympathize with the plaintiffs, it would, in my opinion, be extending the implications based on the maxim that no one can derogate from his own grant to an unreasonable extent if it were held that what has been done in this case was a breach of an implied obligation."[728]

"[T]o constitute a breach of such a covenant there must be some physical interference with the enjoyment of the demised premises, and that a mere interference with the comfort of persons using the demised premises by the creation of a personal annoyance such as might arise from noise, invasion of privacy, or otherwise is not enough."[729]

---

[726] *Browne v Flower* [1911] 1 Ch 219 (Ch) 226 (Parker J).

[727] *Browne v Flower* [1911] 1 Ch 219 (Ch) 226 (Parker J).

[728] *Browne v Flower* [1911] 1 Ch 219 (Ch) 227 (Parker J).

[729] *Browne v Flower* [1911] 1 Ch 219 (Ch) 228 (Parker J).

6. Cheltenham and Gloucester Building Society v Norgan

When a mortgagor falls into financial difficulty, the courts are often the final voice of reason, particularly in instances where repossession is the preferred solution and negotiations have been strained beyond benefit.

Having occupied the family home for a well over twenty years, it was decided by the husband that in order to retain the security of his business, he would sell his equal share of the property to his wife in exchange for much needed capital. Under the conditions of the new mortgage, the wife was expected to meet the full term of the balance inside a twenty-two year period; this was achieved through clearing the interest before tackling the principle sum borrowed.

After four years of regular payments, the business ran into potential ruin, and so it became untenable for the wife to meet her requirements. Around this time, the original lender had been acquired by another much larger firm, and so the interest rates had seen a significant increase, thereby exacerbating an issue that was at first glance, addressable. When the lender sought to repossess, the courts suspended the order, while renewed payment terms were attempted between the parties. After further payment gaps, the arrears reached unmanageable levels, at which point both a possession warrant and two additional suspensions were granted, until the case was decided in favour of a four-year 'catch up' period and a right to seek repossession, should the mortgagors default under the renewed terms.

When challenged before the Court of Appeal, the debate surrounding 'reasonable periods' in which a borrower could readjust payments in lieu of spiralling arrears was laid bare, with consideration of both the needs of the lender and the realities of mortgage arrangements. With detailed reference to the industry guidelines as well as the mortgagees company policy, it was found that while an ethos of working partnership and customer support was commercially indicative, the actions taken to secure repossession, despite evident attempts to redress the shortfalls, displayed a more mercenary approach to common repayment issues, and one found wanting when proposed workable solutions were presented in court by the appellant.

Having again looked at the judicial adage that a reasonable period could in fact be the terms of the original mortgage, and that under those circumstances the lender stood to profit as was initially agreed, it was held that restrictive periods of between two and five years typically resulted in nothing more than repeated appeals and a flagrant misuse of court time. With note of this obvious disparity, the judges upheld the mortgagor's appeal, and requested that greater consideration was required of the mortgagees when assessing the validity and proper use of repossession under similar circumstances.

Key Citations

"The statement of practice of the Council of Mortgage Lenders does not bind the plaintiffs to a particular course of action."[730]

"[M]y finding that only a far shorter period would be reasonable makes it impossible for the court's power under section 36 to be exercised in the defendant's favour."[731]

"It does seem to me that the logic and spirit of the legislation require, especially in cases where the parties are proceeding under arrangements such as those reflected in the CML statement, that the court should take as it's starting point the full term of the mortgage."[732]

"I am unable myself to see why two years rather than one, or four rather than five, should be regarded as the correct starting point, or how it is possible to establish any period without taking into account how long the original period was."[733]

"When the borrower is likely to be able to make regular payments, of whatever amount, then in general it can be said that the longer the period then the more "reasonable" it will be for him."[734]

"[I]t cannot be wrong or unreasonable to consider what the prospects are of the borrower paying the arrears of interest in full by the end of the term."[735]

"[T]hey cannot claim they are losing interest by reason of their inability to recover the amount of their loan to the mortgagor and then re-lend it, at a lower rate, to a customer of their own."[736]

---

[730] *Cheltenham and Gloucester Building Society v Norgan* [1996] 1 WLR 343 (CA) 351 (Waite LJ).

[731] *Cheltenham and Gloucester Building Society v Norgan* [1996] 1 WLR 343 (CA) 351 (Waite LJ).

[732] *Cheltenham and Gloucester Building Society v Norgan* [1996] 1 WLR 343 (CA) 353 (Waite LJ).

[733] *Cheltenham and Gloucester Building Society v Norgan* [1996] 1 WLR 343 (CA) 356 (Evans LJ).

[734] *Cheltenham and Gloucester Building Society v Norgan* [1996] 1 WLR 343 (CA) 356 (Evans LJ).

[735] *Cheltenham and Gloucester Building Society v Norgan* [1996] 1 WLR 343 (CA) 357 (Evans LJ).

[736] *Cheltenham and Gloucester Building Society v Norgan* [1996] 1 WLR 343 (CA) 357 (Evans LJ).

7. Cobbe v Yeoman's Row Management Ltd

With a full appreciation of the restraints of their relationship, two commercial agents chose to enter into a project, that while theoretically profitable, was fraught with uneven rights and a potential to devolve. It was this fundamental oversight of arms-length protection, that brought the parties to a court faced with a number of overlapping claims.

After enjoying residence within an enviable plot, the owner and a well known property developer entered into a working arrangement which stood to produce significant gain to both parties, should their plans come to fruition. The caveat in this joint enterprise, was that the developer was to commit considerable financial outlay and time in order for the end result to manifest. This entailed the pursuance of planning permission, along with demolition of the landowner's current property, before drafting a written contract around the construction of a number of high-end town houses that were later to be sold for a pre-agreed figure, which when combined, could achieve a collective value that once surpassed, amounted to equal profit sharing between the two investors.

Unfortunately, in addition to the initial costs, the developer was also expected to furnish them with a lump sum payment of around £12m prior to the construction and sale of the new homes. This additional burden increased the obligations of the respondent in the knowledge that a verbal agreement was all that reinforced their individual (and contractual) rights. After securing planning permission, the appellant then sought to increase her share of the threshold profits, despite her previous assurances that an equal split was agreeable. This led to proceedings under contractual breach; however the judge moved to consider the case within a number of other principles, including proprietary estoppel, constructive trust, unjust enrichment, *quantum meruit* and a consideration of tortious deceit.

Following reasoned evaluation, it was agreed that a claim for proprietary estoppel could hold, while remedy under a constructive trust would also prove advantageous. During appeal at the House of Lords, it was then properly established that despite close examination of the parameters of estoppel, there was insufficient certainty to warrant grant of interruption, and that while almost within the vein of constructive trusts, the prior ownership of land ruled out the prerequisite of a joint purchase, and relied more upon the reversal of the appellant's acquiescence.

The denial of those rights drew the cause of claim toward a more personal infraction, that while dishonourable in appearance, fell within the legalities of commercial dealings, but not without casualty. This inequality then led to dismissal of the appeal, in view of a settlement for *quantum meruit*, albeit subject to the terms first set down in the original judgment.

Key Citations

"[U]nconscionability of conduct may well lead to a remedy but, in my opinion, proprietary estoppel cannot be the route to it unless the ingredients for a proprietary estoppel are present."[737]

"It would be an unusually unsophisticated negotiator who was not well aware that oral agreements relating to such an acquisition are by statute unenforceable and that no express reservation to make them so is needed."[738]

"[P]roprietary estoppel cannot be prayed in aid in order to render enforceable an agreement that statute has declared void."[739]

"She knew he was providing his services in the expectation of becoming the purchaser of the property under an enforceable contract. So no fee was agreed. In the event the expected contract did not materialise but a *quantum meruit* for his services is a common law remedy to which Mr Cobbe is entitled."[740]

"Where an agreement is reached under which an individual provides money and services in return for a legal but unenforceable promise which the promissor, after the money has been paid and the services provided, refuses to carry out, the individual would be entitled in my opinion, to restitutionary remedy."[741]

"It is not enough to hope, or even have a confident expectation, that the person who has given assurances will eventually do the right thing."[742]

"[A]s persons experienced in the property world, both parties knew that there was no legally binding contract, and that either was therefore free to discontinue the negotiations without legal liability."[743]

---

[737] *Cobbe v Yeoman's Row Management Ltd* [2008] UKHL 55 [16] (Scott LJ).

[738] *Cobbe v Yeoman's Row Management Ltd* [2008] UKHL 55 [27] (Scott LJ).

[739] *Cobbe v Yeoman's Row Management Ltd* [2008] UKHL 55 [29] (Scott LJ).

[740] *Cobbe v Yeoman's Row Management Ltd* [2008] UKHL 55 [42] (Scott LJ).

[741] *Cobbe v Yeoman's Row Management Ltd* [2008] UKHL 55 [43] (Scott LJ).

[742] *Cobbe v Yeoman's Row Management Ltd* [2008] UKHL 55 [65] (Walker LJ).

[743] *Cobbe v Yeoman's Row Management Ltd* [2008] UKHL 55 [91] (Walker LJ).

8. Copeland v Greenhalf

The definition of an easement is one that runs with and benefits the land, when recognised under common law. In this instance, the proclamation of easement by prescription, belied what may be equally construed as adverse possession, while defying the traditional purpose of rights of way over adjoining land.

When an estate comprising fields and a private orchard was sold to a new owner, a neighbouring property owner found themselves subject to complaint and mandatory injunction, when their use of a strip of the newly acquired land amounted to little more than exclusive possession under the pretence of an easement.

The defendant in this matter occupied and operated, a wheelwright business that had enjoyed the benefit of storing carriages, and now, commercial and agricultural vehicles awaiting repair on the strip in question. While the manner in which these items were left allowed for entrance and exit to the owner's house, there had on occasion, been disruption to the use of the strip beyond that which was held as reasonable.

Having then taken the defendant to court in order for the vehicles to be removed, the argument was put before the judge that prior to the recent purchase, an agreement had been made between the former owners and the defendant, thus allowing him and his father to store carriages and spare parts until such time that they could be serviced and returned to their customers. This arrangement dated back half a century, and so when the home had been leased to tenants, no complaints had been made regards the defendants use of the land. This amounted to a claim that the existence of an easement was valid under the Prescription Act 1832.

While easements can be enforced by prescription, the court was indifferent to the manner in which the defendants had used the land, inasmuch as far from using the strip as a means of access, they had simply left a number of objects in situ, with the luxury of knowing they may, or may not, be used and removed. Furthermore, the defendant's land was adjacent to the strip and so did not touch the property in question, therefore it fell outside the scope of easement rights, and thus failed to determine the arrangement as one comprising a right of way.

With the defendant relying upon the far-reaching *Attorney-General of Southern Nigeria v John Holt & Co (Liverpool) Ltd*[744] to distinguish the claim, it was agreed that while no immediate objections had been raised by the previous owners, the occupying tenants or the new owners, it was not possible to consider the manner in which the land was used as a means of access but one of possession, therefore no claim for the former could be upheld.

---

[744] [1915] AC 599.

Key Citations

"[T]he right claimed goes wholly outside any normal idea of an easement, that is, the right of the owner or the occupier of a dominant tenement over a servient tenement. This claim (to which no closely related authority has been referred to me) really amounts to a claim to a joint user of the land by the defendant."[745]

"It is virtually a claim to possession of the servient tenement, if necessary to the exclusion of the owner; or, at any rate, to a joint user, and no authority has been cited to me which would justify the conclusion that a right of this wide and undefined nature can be the proper subject-matter of an easement."[746]

---

[745] *Copeland v Greenhalf* [1952] Ch 488 (Ch) 498 (Upjohn J).

[746] *Copeland v Greenhalf* [1952] Ch 488 (Ch) 498 (Upjohn J).

9. Edwards v Lloyds TSB Bank Plc

Joint legal title to a shared property is designed to protect the interests of those involved, and yet when a divorcee falsely enters into contract with a bank for company reasons, the outcome almost costs the remaining party their home.

After purchasing the house in joint names, and spending almost a decade together raising their children, the wife petitioned for a divorce after the husband left the home, before disappearing from the family unit altogether. It was during this time, that he approached his bank to significantly extend his company overdraft.

As part of this arrangement, the lender sought insurance for the debt, choosing to allow a second mortgage charge to be held in favour of the husband, without making enquiries as to the exact nature of the existing mortgage. Unbeknownst to his wife (the claimant in this matter), he also used another person to forge her signature, while claiming that he held sole legal title to the property.

Four years after his departure, and the newly agreed contract with the counter-claimants, the county court finalised the divorce on the proviso that the former husband relinquished his legal and beneficial interest in the home to the claimant; stipulating that his failure to do so, would result in a District Judge executing his agreement in deed to complete the transaction.

Unfortunately, neither of those requisites were performed, therefore his legal and beneficial title remained unchanged at the date the bank claimed recovery of the fifty percent share, following his company insolvency and non-payment of the accrued debt.

The cause of action, was that the claimant was now requesting the bank remove its notice of caution from the Land Registry, on grounds that it held no legal rights, nor beneficial interest, as it had failed to register its interest as per s.2 of the Law of Property (Miscellaneous Provisions) Act 1989, and that the re-mortgage was made under false pretences without knowing consent from the claimant. The bank had countered that under ss.14 and 15 of the Trusts and Appointment of Trustees Act 1996, they had a right to require sale of the property in order to obtain the debt and outstanding interest.

While the court agreed that the contract between the bank and the former husband was made under illegal means, s.63 of the Law of Property Act 1925 allowed that any signature to a legal conveyance was enforceable under law where the intention was expressed and executed as required. On this occasion, the deed signed with the bank was enforceable to the extent that the ex-husband had the power to submit his portion of the home for collateral; and so for that reason alone, the bank was now holder of both legal and equitable title to the house, until such time as the debt was repaid.

However, the terms of s.15 Trusts and Appointment of Trustees Act 1996 require that the court must take into account a number of preventative factors when faced with these situations. These include consideration for the needs and intentions of the occupiers (where the house is now held on trust), those of the minors (who are by default reliant upon the safety of the home) and those of secured creditors such as the bank.

With those caveats in mind, the court ruled that there would be (i) no immediate sale of the house, (ii) an order for postponement for a period of five years, and (iii) ongoing communications between the bank and the claimant, during which she was afforded the option to repay some of the ongoing interest of the debt outstanding, or wait until the sale is completed, as there was sufficient equity in the home to absorb the total debt value when the five years expired.

Key Citations

"[A]lthough the deed did not create a legal mortgage of the entire ownership interest in the house, it did create an equitable mortgage of the husband's 50% beneficial (or equitable) interest in the house."[747]

"[T]he deed would not bind any person whose signature to it had been forged (that is in this case, Mrs Edwards), but it would continue to bind the person who had forged it, in so far as it affected any property interest which that person owned."[748]

"Section 2 renders certain contracts unenforceable. it does not render ineffective an instrument which, s.2 apart, is effective to create an immediate legal or equitable property interest of some kind."[749]

"The husband's beneficial interest became Mrs Edwards beneficial interest, but, as respects that beneficial interest, Mrs Edwards held it subject to the bank's equitable charge."[750]

"The equitable charge which the bank had at the time of the court order was an equitable interest which did not affect the legal interest in the house: it affected only the husband's beneficial interest, which was an equitable interest, not a legal interest."[751]

---

[747] *Edwards v Lloyds TSB Bank Plc* [2004] EWHC 1745 [16] (Park J).

[748] *Edwards v Lloyds TSB Bank Plc* [2004] EWHC 1745 [18] (Park J).

[749] *Edwards v Lloyds TSB Bank Plc* [2004] EWHC 1745 [21] (Park J).

[750] *Edwards v Lloyds TSB Bank Plc* [2004] EWHC 1745 [22] (Park J).

[751] *Edwards v Lloyds TSB Bank Plc* [2004] EWHC 1745 [25] (Park J).

10. Gillett v Holt

The notorious ambiguity of estoppel is explored here, through the unexpected end of a lifelong working relationship built upon trust, duty and a faith of spirit; and as is so often found in matters such as these, it appears that a man's word is not always his bond.

After investing the best part of forty years into a farming alliance that created an almost familial structure, the arrival of a divisive party, witnessed the destructive end of a mutually prosperous and seemingly concrete friendship. When a younger man forged a meaningful relationship with an older farmer, the two men became almost father and son, with the former relying upon, and often following, the wisdom of the latter, in accordance with domestic arrangements, career aspirations and even parenting decisions; all while sustaining and enriching the estate's financial footing through the course of his duties.

This interdependence became the foundation of a commercial enterprise, that by definition, became more complex and so required increased investment from both the employer's paid advisers and the younger man's wife as a co-contributor. During the many years spent together, there had been a significant number of verbal declarations as to the intentions of the elder man when it came time to choose a successor to his sprawling estates, and it was these quasi-promises, along with multiple wills, that coloured the appellants choice-making and calculated reluctance to set aside the type of financial provisions one might ordinarily expect.

The mechanics of the business, and associated friendship, continued to flourish until the arrival of a trained solicitor, who, for one reason of another, began making spurious claims that the appellant and his wife were defrauding the business, and that legal intervention was ultimately necessary. This course of action and influential advice also led to the couple's removal from the existing will and sole beneficial rights, which were instead passed to the now co-defendant.

After an exhaustive cross-examination in the original hearing, the deciding judge awarded against the appellant, despite his claim of proprietary estoppel, following the removal of his presence in the will and inherent reliance upon the goodwill of the defendant during the passage of time.

At appeal, the fluid and therefore often misinterpreted principle of estoppel, was held to close scrutiny, along with the previous findings of the judge; whereupon it became clear that while a degree of effort had been put into the relevance of estoppel, the obvious right to claim had been lost to principles attributable to succession law. Through the delicate use of equity, the court then agreed that there was ample evidence to show a detriment under continued reliance, and that in order for a clean break to exist, there needed to be a reversal of fortune on the part of the co-defendant, and a 'coming good' on the word of the older man.

Key Citations

"[T]here must be a sufficient link between the promises relied on and the conduct which constitutes the detriment."[752]

"The detriment need not consist of the expenditure of money or other quantifiable financial detriment, so long as it is something substantial."[753]

"[F]or thirty years Mr and Mrs Gillett and their sons provided Mr Holt with a sort of surrogate family."[754]

"[T]hey relied on Mr Holt's assurance, because they thought he was a man of his word, and so they deprived themselves of the opportunity of trying to better themselves in other ways."[755]

---

[752] *Gillett v Holt* [2001] Ch 210 (CA) 230 (Walker LJ).

[753] *Gillett v Holt* [2001] Ch 210 (CA) 232 (Walker LJ).

[754] *Gillett v Holt* [2001] Ch 210 (CA) 234 (Walker LJ).

[755] *Gillett v Holt* [2001] Ch 210 (CA) 235 (Walker LJ).

11. Marcou v Da Silvaesa

Due to similarity of circumstance and the nature of the positions argued, this appeal hearing involved two separate, but inextricably linked, claims for tenancy under the pretence of sham agreements. While both sharing the same fundamental contracts, there were deviations both within and without the documents, that deserved enquiry, if at least to clarify the terms of occupancy.

Markou v Da Silvaesa

Having entered into an agreement displaying the hallmarks of a licenced residency, it was argued that after being requested to leave the premises following a change in property ownership, the two parties in occupancy were legally entitled to remain so under the assumption of a tenancy. This was largely reliant upon the poorly worded contract, insomuch as clauses 1 and 2 were at no point enforced, and where the latter clause defied logic and reason when providing for a practical living arrangement.

Clause 1 required that each day, the appellants were expected to vacate the premises between 10.30am and noon for the duration of the contract, while clause 2 reserved a right for the landlord to remove and/or substitute items of furniture as deemed necessary. What became of concern, was that the contract also required that the claimants not only vacated the property, but took their personal possessions too; a stipulation that by all accounts, was impossible to execute. Likewise, the right to remove furniture rendered the appellants powerless to prevent beds or other essential items, from being taken away should the respondent see fit to do so.

Upon the respondent's application for possession under Order 113 of the Rules of the Supreme Court (RSC), the appellants challenged its validity, on grounds that the agreement signed was nothing less than a sham, and that when applying the principles of *Street v Mountford*,[756] there could be no right to remove them. In the first hearing, the judge ruled that despite vagaries in the terms of the contract, there was insufficient evidence to suggest sham intentions, particularly when the majority of the terms were clear and concise as to the engaging parties occupancy as licensees; and when later asked for the matter to be dealt with in the County Courts for the purposes of trial rather than summary judgment, the option was also dismissed.

When presented to the Court of Appeal, any contention that the agreement constituted a sham was, despite clearer presentation of the facts, further dismissed on grounds that echoed the previous judge. However, the complications arising from the oddly drafted clauses raised significant issue around the right to allow possession when so much certainty lingered as to the exactness of the relationship shared between landlord and licensees. This concern sustained the appeal in favour of new proceedings under trial, before any conclusive findings could be reached.

Crancour Ltd v Merola

Operating under identical contracts, the appellants relied upon oral agreements between themselves and the resident housekeeper, when challenging the presumption of licensee

---

[756] [1985] AC 809.

over what they believed to be exclusive possession leading to tenancy. Prior to the change in ownership, the appellants had engaged in conversation with the domestic help, whereupon the offer to clean the room in accordance with the contract was turned down in favour of privacy while in occupancy. Alternately, the appellants left their bed linen and waste outside the door in order to benefit from the services provided by the landlord. It was for this reason, that the claim for tenancy was argued, along with the issues raised in the first case.

As was agreed above, the lack of certainty for clauses 1 and 2, coupled with a need for witness testimony with regard to the orally agreed terms, meant that just as before, the issue of possession orders could not be sustained without renewed appreciation of the full facts, and so the appeal was upheld in conjunction with the directions cited.

Key Citations

"The learned judge, in my opinion, was right in reaching the conclusion that, if the written agreement represented the agreement between the parties, then, upon its true construction, these appellants were lodgers and not tenants."[757]

"[I]t is not open to the court to dismiss as "sham" a term in an agreement merely because it is either effective in demonstrating that the agreement does not grant exclusive occupation or, taken with other terms, contributes to that result."[758]

"The presence of such a term, in the absence of an allegation of an intent to deceive or deliberately to take unfair advantage of the occupier—and none is made—does not, in my opinion, by any process of infection spread some debilitating weakness to other terms of which the genuineness is not in doubt, either on the face of the agreement or according to evidence available or sought to be tendered."[759]

"[I]t would be unsatisfactory for summary judgment to be given in favour of a landlord on the strength of a form of written agreement when prima facie the basic clause in that agreement is an artificial contrivance intended to mislead and thereby to create or strengthen a claim by the landlord that the agreement was outside the Rent Acts."[760]

"[T]he use of the words such as licence or lease in the agreement is not definitive, nor indeed is the de facto intention of either or both of the parties. Subject to the agreement on its face appearing to be a sham, the effect in law of the agreement must depend upon its construction in accordance with the normal rules in the context of its factual matrix and genesis."[761]

---

[757] *Marcou v Da Silvaesa* [1986] 52 P & CR 204 (CA) 212 (Gibson LJ).

[758] *Marcou v Da Silvaesa* [1986] 52 P & CR 204 (CA) 215 (Gibson LJ).

[759] *Marcou v Da Silvaesa* [1986] 52 P & CR 204 (CA) 216 (Gibson LJ).

[760] *Marcou v Da Silvaesa* [1986] 52 P & CR 204 (CA) 226 (Nicholls LJ).

[761] *Marcou v Da Silvaesa* [1986] 52 P & CR 204 (CA) 229 (Purchas LJ).

12. Midland Bank Plc v Cooke

When two first-time homebuyers rely upon a financial donation from family members, the equality of shared ownership becomes displaced, despite individual perceptions of common intention and the partnership of marriage.

When two young newlyweds entered into a mortgage of their family home, it was not without a significant cash contribution from the groom's parents. This gift was bestowed upon the couple after the bride's parents covered the costs of the wedding, which therefore implied equal investment into their committed relationship. At the time of conveyance, the deeds fell under sole title in favour of the groom and no assumptions were otherwise made than it was their home, and that both parties were joint occupants, and thus entitled to equal benefits.

A few years after the purchase, the nature of the mortgage altered, and was now liable under the terms of an acquiring bank; at which point the wife was asked to sign away any beneficial interest she held in favour of the new mortgagee. Her agreement to this request was given (albeit under visible duress) so as to enable her husband's continued business operation, and so the family (now with three children) could remain in secure occupation.

After re-mortgaging the property a number of years later, the wife took the opportunity to have her name included within the title, and thus became a legal tenant-in-common. When the business began to fail and the mortgage fell into unrecoverable default, the bank sought to repossess, at which point the wife challenged the order, on grounds that any relinquishing of interest had not been of her volition; rather that her now estranged husband's undue influence had led her to act against her will while under marital obligation.

In the first hearing, the judge found in favour of the wife on the grounds described, before going further to explain that while her collective time and monies invested into the home during the course of their marriage could not translate into an equal half-share of the property, it did result in a six percent stake-holding, arising from her half-share entitlement of the cash gifted by the groom's parents at the point of purchase; and therefore under those circumstances any repossession order could not stand.

When challenged by the bank and the wife in the Court of Appeal, the principle of shared equity was given greater consideration, along with the equitable maxim 'equality is equity', which on this occasion was not relied upon. Instead, it was agreed that the wife's actions first dismissed as non-contributory, were now embraced as wholly acceptable, despite no verbal agreements between the couple as to whether or not the home was equally divisible to begin with.

Key Citations

"[I]t would not only be sensible to draw the inference that the bridegroom's parents intended to make a present to them both of the money's which were to be applied in the purchase, but highly artificial to draw any other inference."[762]

"[T]he court in the exercise of its equitable jurisdiction would not permit the husband in whom the legal estate was vested and who had accepted the benefit of the contributions to take the whole beneficial interest merely because at the time the wife made her contributions there had been no express agreement as to how her share in it was to be quantified."[763]

"[I]t would be anomalous, against that background, to create a range of homebuyers who were beyond the pail of equity's assistance in formulating a fair presumed basis for the sharing of beneficial title, simply because they had been honest enough to admit that they never gave ownership a thought or reached any agreement about it."[764]

"[P]ositive evidence that the parties neither discussed nor intended any agreement as to the proportions of their beneficial interest does not preclude the court, on general equitable principles, from inferring one."[765]

"[T]hat this was a couple that had chosen to introduce into their relationship the additional commitment which marriage involves, the conclusion becomes inescapable that their presumed intention was to share the beneficial interest in the property in equal shares."[766]

---

[762] *Midland Bank Plc v Cooke* [1995] 4 All ER 562 (CA) 741 (Waite LJ).

[763] *Midland Bank Plc v Cooke* [1995] 4 All ER 562 (CA) 743 (Waite LJ).

[764] *Midland Bank Plc v Cooke* [1995] 4 All ER 562 (CA) 746 (Waite LJ).

[765] *Midland Bank Plc v Cooke* [1995] 4 All ER 562 (CA) 746 (Waite LJ).

[766] *Midland Bank Plc v Cooke* [1995] 4 All ER 562 (CA) 747 (Waite LJ).

13. Moncrieff v Jamieson

Vehicular access through the granting of a servitude (or easement), is something that when not considered at the date of grant, can also fail to appreciate the need to park within the allotted space over the course of time. In this matter, the presence of land-locking and the limitations of geography, presented the respondents with no real means to enjoy their occupation as freeholders, when the parking of their car(s) was to be restricted to a public road, literally hundreds of metres away from the family home.

Situated in the village of Sandsound in the Shetland Islands, the cause of action rested upon the estranged living arrangements between three parties. The respondents were owners of a property first purchased from one of the appellants in 1973, and which was built on a coastal plot allowing access via a stone stepped path across the vendor's land, or equally by boat; while due to the formation of the land, it was impossible to park cars on the land owned by the respondents. The appellants were the vendor (third appellant) and his son and wife (first and second appellants), who owned a neighbouring property situated in the same of land as the respondents.

At the time of conveyance, the deed included a clause granting "a right of access from the branch public road through Sandsound". This public route terminated short of a gate set at the top of the steps, and during the preceding ten to fifteen years, the respondents used the land around the gate for parking, unloading and reloading purposes, and to provide subcontractors with parking space while undertaking work on their house.

This regular use of land was never objected to by the vendor, and so continued without interruption, until such time that the second appellant and the respondent constructed a new section of road that allowed the respondents dual parking and turning space. Having both enjoyed the space provided, it was later decided by the second appellant that he would extend his garden and use the parking area to accomplish it. This resulted in the respondents being forced to park on the vendor's land, which was some distance away.

When put before the courts, it was argued that the terms of the servitude implied that a right to park formed part of the covenant, and so denying them such rights was a breach of the obligation carried within the terms of the disposition. After considering volumes of testimony and associated evidence, the court employed the services of the local sheriff who, after a laboured inspection, decided by interlocutory judgment that the respondents were entitled to exercise their right to park, and that any interference by the three appellants would result in legal action by the court.

Upon appeal, the Court found disagreement with the mechanics of the injunctive measure, and amended the declaration to provide a legal right to park within the area determined by the servitude, so as to allow freedom to enjoy the rights contained within it.

When presented before the House of Lords, the principles of easements and rights to park, were carefully balanced when assessing both the needs of the dominant tenement and the servient tenement. While use of the land permits freedom to pursue access, it must also continue to the serve the needs of the servient tenement, when equally enjoying use of the remaining land. This formed the premise of debate, and so it was decided that implication can be relied upon when embracing the entirety of the servitude, insofar as enjoyment of the grant must be provided for in full, so as to defeat anything that runs counter to its effect. This translated that the right to park in the area previously used, remained free of obstruction and the appeal was uniformly dismissed.

Key Citations

"[T]he fact that very little, if any, use was being made of the servient tenement at that time for the parking of vehicles cannot be taken as an indication that the need to park vehicles there when Da Store became habitable cannot have been in contemplation."[767]

"While a servitude right must be construed in such a way as to minimise the burden on the servient proprietor, it must not be construed so strictly as to defeat the right granted to the dominant proprietor."[768]

"[I]n view of its particular and unusual circumstances, the rights ancillary to the express grant of a right of access in favour of the dominant tenement include a right to park vehicles on the servient tenement, in so far as this is reasonably incidental to the enjoyment of the dominant tenement."[769]

"I can see no reason in principle, subject to a few qualifications, why any right of limited use of the land of a neighbour that is of its nature of benefit to the dominant land and its owners from time to time should not be capable of being created as a servitudal right in rem appurtenant to the dominant land…"[770]

"[I]f the suggested test for the acquisition of a parking right ancillary to the servitudal right of access is satisfied, then, for the same reason, the express grant of that servitudal right would in my opinion justify the implication of a servitudal right to park."[771]

"Arrangements consensually made as to the manner of exercise of servitudes can, of course, be consensually varied, but once made, and particularly if the dominant owner has incurred expenditure pursuant to the arrangements, ought not, in my opinion, to be capable of unilateral variation by the servient owner."[772]

"Every servitude prevents any use of the servient land, whether ordinary or otherwise, that would interfere with the reasonable exercise of the servitude."[773]

---

[767] *Moncrieff v Jamieson* [2007] UKHL 42 [30] (Hope LJ).

[768] *Moncrieff v Jamieson* [2007] UKHL 42 [34] (Hope LJ).

[769] *Moncrieff v Jamieson* [2007] UKHL 42 [36] (Hope LJ).

[770] *Moncrieff v Jamieson* [2007] UKHL 42 [47] (Scott LJ).

[771] *Moncrieff v Jamieson* [2007] UKHL 42 [52] (Scott LJ).

[772] *Moncrieff v Jamieson* [2007] UKHL 42 [53] (Scott LJ).

[773] *Moncrieff v Jamieson* [2007] UKHL 42 [54] (Scott LJ).

14. Parker v British Airways Board

Under the breadth of property ownership, does the principle of occupier's rights supersede the entitlement of an authentic finder, or is the common law more complex than it appears?

While waiting to catch a flight, a qualified guest of an airport lounge discovered an abandoned men's gold bracelet on the seating area floor. By virtue of his own honesty, the respondent handed the jewellery to a member of staff, on the proviso that should the original owner not be found, the airline was to forward the item to his home address as provided.

After waiting almost a year, the appellants instead took it upon themselves to sell the bracelet, while directly profiting from the sale. Upon discovery of this, the respondent immediately sued for loss incurred from the deceit and conversion of assets. In the first hearing, the judge awarded in favour of the passenger, whereupon the airline appealed, and the matter was given greater thought.

When assessing the imputation that occupiers of land are privy to greater powers of ownership to lost property, distinctions were drawn in order to clarify where the exceptions to those assumptions lay. In common law, it has been largely agreed (through the progression of case law) that in many familiar circumstances, the rights to ownership of property construed as abandoned or lost, would fall to the landowner. However, in this case the airline took no steps to draw notice to that right when considering the frequency and nature of transient visitors to their lounge. In contrast, the only provisions made for matters involving lost property, entailed procedural guides for staff members and nothing more.

After careful evaluation of the two prevailing rights, and when comparing to the honest intentions of the passenger to an abject failure of the airline to express their position when handling lost property, the Appeal Court held that it would be unreasonable to deny the respondent his fundamental rights to ownership of property honestly acquired in the absence of the original owner.

Key Citations

"[I]f a finder is under a duty to take reasonable steps to reunite the true owner with his lost property, this will usually involve an obligation to inform the occupier of the land of the fact that the article has been found and where it is to be kept."[774]

"[A] finder of chattel, whilst not acquiring any absolute property or ownership in the chattel, acquires a right to keep it against all but the true owner or those in a position to claim it through the true owner or one who can assert a prior right to keep the chattel which was subsisting at the time when the finder took the chattel into his care and control."[775]

"The plaintiff was not a trespasser in the executive lounge and, in taking the bracelet into his care and control, he was acting with obvious honesty. Prima facie, therefore, he had a full finder's rights and obligations."[776]

"Evidence was given of staff instructions which govern the action to be taken by employees of the defendants of the defendants if they found lost articles or lost chattels were handed to them. But these instructions were not published to users of the lounge."[777]

"[O]n the evidence available, there was no sufficient manifestation of any intention to exercise control over lost property before it was found such as would give the defendants a right superior to that of the plaintiff or indeed any right over the bracelet."[778]

"Against all but the true owner a person in possession has the right to possess. It should follow therefore that an innocent handler of property who intends to take it for the purpose of discovering the owner and returning it to him should not be in dangers of infringing any right in a third party."[779]

---

[774] *Parker v British Airways Board* [1982] QB 1004 (CA) 1017 (Donaldson LJ).

[775] *Parker v British Airways Board* [1982] QB 1004 (CA) 1017 (Donaldson LJ).

[776] *Parker v British Airways Board* [1982] QB 1004 (CA) 1018 (Donaldson LJ).

[777] *Parker v British Airways Board* [1982] QB 1004 (CA) 1019 (Donaldson LJ).

[778] *Parker v British Airways Board* [1982] QB 1004 (CA) 1019 (Donaldson LJ).

[779] *Parker v British Airways Board* [1982] QB 1004 (CA) 1019 (Eveleigh LJ).

15. *Re* Ellenborough Park

As can be traced back through the historic case law surrounding easements, there has been much dispute as to exactly what constitutes such a privilege; and so in *Re Ellenborough Park*,[780] a generosity of scope was favourably agreed upon and the principle further refined.

When the considerate nature of the original owner of Ellenborough Park (itself no more than an expansive parcel of land) bestowed conditional rights upon the future freeholders of property encircling it, those privileges allowed exclusive enjoyment of the space and fresh air afforded them; yet the vendor had no idea that many years later, this same kindness of spirit would be challenged by those succeeding him.

For almost one hundred years, the owners of the chosen properties had enjoyed uninterrupted peaceful use, until World War II forced the temporary military occupation of both the park and the homes built around it. After returning the houses back to their current owners (along with suitable compensation for their use), it was decided by the trustees of Ellenborough Park, that continued access to the gardens would no longer be accepted, and that under the terms of the original conveyance, no such easements had ever been put into effect.

Under the general terms prescribed by common law, there are a number of criteria that need to be met for an easement to exist. These critical elements include the principles that those assigned the granting of an easement must take it on the understanding that use of such a covenant relies upon utility and benefit from the right, and that benefit of the easement must derive from the granting of such a right. Because Ellenborough Park was cosmetically different from most commonly prescribed easements, it was argued that the mere capacity to wander freely upon a large plot of land (albeit subject to expressly detailed maintenance contributions) amounted to nothing more than a '*jus spatiandi*', which is a phrase typically assigned to public parks and recreational areas requiring little more than careful observation of the rules associated with their use.

In the first hearing, the judge found in favour of the defendants, and so when further considered under appeal, an in-depth examination of the founding conveyance revealed very succinct terminology as to support, and endorse, the intentions of the estate owner; in that he had not only established by definition, the presence of easements to the freeholders, but that such consideration had been expressly granted by way of the deed's construction. This decision has since proven instrumental to the variances in the physical representation of easements, and the reinterpretation of covenants provided for by way of grant.

---

[780] [1956] Ch 131.

Key Citations

"Unless therefore, I am compelled by the state of the authorities I am not anxious to deprive the owners of the plots on the former White Cross Estate of the rights which the vendors' conveyances from 1855 to 1864 or thereabouts, attempted to give them."[781]

"[T]he conveyances of parts of the White Cross Estate conferred on the purchasers and their successors in title legal and effective easements to use the pleasure ground known as Ellenborough Park in the manner in which it was intended by the conveyances to be used."[782]

"[T]he language of the deed of 1864 is clearly to the effect that the right of enjoyment of the garden was intended to be annexed to the premises sold, rather than given as a privilege personal to their purchaser."[783]

"There is clear authority that, if such be the substantial effect of the covenant, its benefit and burden will run with the land."[784]

"[A]n easement must be appurtenant to an estate for the benefit of that estate and its owner and that it cannot at the same time lawfully be enjoyed by any other person."[785]

"We see nothing repugnant to a man's proprietorship or possession of a piece of land that he should decide to make it and maintain it as an ornamental garden, and should grant rights to a limited number of other persons to come into it for the enjoyment of its amenities."[786]

"No doubt a garden is a pleasure - on high authority it is the highest of pleasures - but in our judgement it is not a right having no quality either of utility or benefit as those words should be understood."[787]

---

[781] *Ellenborough Park, Re* [1956] Ch 131 (Ch) 150 (Danckwerts J).

[782] *Ellenborough Park, Re* [1956] Ch 131 (Ch) 151 (Danckwerts J).

[783] *Ellenborough Park, Re* [1956] Ch 131 (Ch) 167 (Lord Evershed MR).

[784] *Ellenborough Park, Re* [1956] Ch 131 (Ch) 168 (Lord Evershed MR).

[785] *Ellenborough Park, Re* [1956] Ch 131 (Ch) 172 (Lord Evershed MR).

[786] *Ellenborough Park, Re* [1956] Ch 131 (Ch) 176 (Lord Evershed MR).

[787] *Ellenborough Park, Re* [1956] Ch 131 (Ch) 179 (Lord Evershed MR).

16. Stack v Dowden

When a long-term relationship founded upon fierce independence to the exclusion of marriage reaches breaking point, the effects of separation are altered through the sale of the family home. Where domestic legislation lends assistance to the courts under the Married Women's Property Act 1882 and Matrimonial Causes Act 1973, there was, at the point of this hearing, no legal framework within which the division of proprietary rights could be easily established where no declaration of trust had been officiated.

Having met as a young couple before sharing a home together, the title of the first property was held for the respondent, after a sole purchase made with a considerable cash investment and the remainder by way of mortgage. During the next decade, the two parties created a family and began raising four children out of wedlock, while maintaining to all effects, separate financial accounts. Through the course of their time in residence, there were a number of improvements made to the property, and while the appellant laid claim to the majority of the work, it was proven undeterminable, and thus assumed as equally contributed to.

When the time came to sell the home, there had been a significant profit made in favour of the respondent, which was immediately reinvested in their second home; whereupon the couple entered into a joint purchase under secured borrowing for the remaining balance, before registering the new house under equal ownership. In the absence of any declaration of trust, the couple opted to include a survivorship declaration that provided for absolute ownership under the death of either party. During this period, the financial contributions were again favourable by some margin, to the respondent, although there was increased investment on the part of the appellant.

Less than ten years later, the couple decided to separate, and it was agreed that the appellant would leave the home and seek residence elsewhere, for the sake of the children and domestic stability. As part of this agreement, the two parties underwent civil proceedings, where it was settled that in consideration for his leaving, the respondent would make specified monthly payments to help subsidise the appellant's living costs under the terms of the Trusts of Land and Appointment of Trustees Act 1996, until such time as the sale of the house was complete.

It was after the failed renewal of the monthly payments, that the appellant sought claim for equal division of the sale proceeds, upon grounds that they had entered into the purchase of the second home as joint owners, and so under the principle of common intention and the legality of the conveyance, he was entitled to half the value of the sale, despite any claim to the contrary.

In the original hearing, the judge assessed the arguments through the essence of a working partnership, and chose to place greater weight upon the perceived intentions displayed when raising a family and managing their financial obligations; thereby ignoring the division of equitable wealth and awarding a fifty-fifty distribution of the sale funds to both parties.

Upon appeal, the Court took a wholly different view, and took pains to calculate the proportion of investment shown by the couple during their time in the home; ultimately arriving at a sixty-five to thirty-five percent division, along with the cessation of compensatory payments, in lieu of his premature departure and relocation of residence.

When bought before the House of Lords, the discussion revolved around the complexities of unmarried couples, and the often misleading nature of common intention when needing further detailed evidence as to the minds of those in contention. It was also agreed that while the appellant had enjoyed the security of monthly payments, his removal from the home was agreed under the terms of the Family Law Act 1996, and so any claim brought against his non-payment was fatal to observance of the applied statute.

With regard to the readjusted percentages, the House held that at best, the figure might be recalculated within a minor percentage, however the strength of the respondent's evidence as to her financial investment, remained as convincing as it was in the appeal, and so aside from any idea that a resulting trust could have been argued for in respect of beneficial interest, the outcome required no further interference.

Key Citations

"The formalities required for the transfer of registered land were designed to meet the concerns of the Land Registry rather than the parties. The Land Registry is not concerned with the equities. It is concerned with whether the registered proprietor or proprietors can give a good title to a later transferee."[788]

"It should only be expected that joint transferees would have spelt out their beneficial interests when they intended them to be different from their legal interests. Otherwise, it should be assumed that equity follows the law and that the beneficial interests reflect the legal interests in the property."[789]

"The law has indeed moved on in response to changing social and economic conditions. The search is to ascertain the parties' shared intentions, actual, inferred or imputed, with respect to the property in the light of their whole course of conduct in relation to it."[790]

"It cannot be the case that all the hundreds of thousands, if not millions, of transfers into joint names using the old forms are vulnerable to challenge in the courts simply because it is likely that the owners contributed unequally to their purchase."[791]

"When a couple are joint owners of the home and jointly liable for the mortgage, the inferences to be drawn from who pays for what may be very different from the inferences to be drawn when only one is owner of the home."[792]

---

[788] *Stack v Dowden* [2007] UKHL 17 [50] (Baroness Hale).

[789] *Stack v Dowden* [2007] UKHL 17 [54] (Baroness Hale).

[790] *Stack v Dowden* [2007] UKHL 17 [60] (Baroness Hale).

[791] *Stack v Dowden* [2007] UKHL 17 [68] (Baroness Hale).

[792] *Stack v Dowden* [2007] UKHL 17 [69] (Baroness Hale).

17. **Wheeldon v Burrows**

Derogation from grant and the conclusive nature of conveyances, were judicially clarified when a landowner chose to divide his estate into two distinct plots. When individually sold at auction, the design was that each sale stood on its own merits, but were subject to identical contracts. Unfortunately once sold, the purchasers crossed swords over their right to enjoy both privacy and right to light and the terms of the conveyance became lost in translation.

With a year between each sale, the first conveyance contained a portion of land that stood separate from the second by the existence of a brick wall. The second conveyance included a brick building that had been erected fairly close to the wall, and had been previously modified to stand as a workshop. This refurbishment included the installation of three windows that faced the first plot, and which allowed for natural light to pass through them.

Both contracts for sale were identical, and neither included any express reservations by the previous owner, aside from a stipulation that the first lot was subject to a favourable right for the purchasers and occupiers of the second plot for a indeterminable period. However, this was non-specific in context and therefore difficult to establish or enforce.

Around five years after the sale of both parcels of land, the claimant in the original hearing erected a fence that ran along the border of her land, but which then obscured the view of the defendant when using his workshop. This resulted in the defendant demolishing the fencing, under the assertion that when taking ownership of the property, it was under the implication of an easement, that while not expressed within the deed, was inherited from the vendor and therefore enforceable at law.

This reaction resulted in litigation, and one in which the court came under a deluge of cases that while relevant to property and the rules of easements and grants, failed to overturn the principle that when under contract to a disposition of land, the vendor cannot derogate from the express terms of the sale, unless under exceptional circumstances involving the necessary preservation of an easement for the mutual benefit of the contracting parties.

It was also evident that at no point had the vendor taken steps to include any express reservation to the two parties, and that failure to do so, could only result in a derogation to induce a remedy, which the courts could not, and would not, entertain. In conclusion, the court awarded in favour of the claimant, and ordered an injunction to prevent further trespass.

Upon appeal, the Court reassessed the cases used in argument for the implied right to light, and again concluded that should the law adopt a view that implication of rights and reservations were automatic to a conveyance, the principles upheld for the rights of ownership and peaceful use and enjoyment of land would be violated beyond reason. And so for those impenetrable virtues to remain in effect, the appeal was dismissed and the previous decision upheld.

Key Citations

"[N]o implication can be made of a reservation of an easement to the grantor, although there may be an implication of a grant to the grantee."[793]

"It appears to me to be an immaterial circumstance that the easement should be apparent and continuous, for non constat that the grantor does not intend to relinquish it unless he shews the contrary by expressly reserving it."[794]

---

[793] *Wheeldon v Burrows* (1879) LR 12 Ch D 31 (Ch) 55 (Thesiger LJ).

[794] *Wheeldon v Burrows* (1879) LR 12 Ch D 31 (Ch) 56 (Thesiger LJ).

18. Williams & Glyn's Bank Ltd v Boland

'Persons in actual occupation', 'overriding interests', and the repossession of two matrimonial homes (see also *Williams & Glyn's Bank Ltd v Brown*[795] in this hearing) from defaulting husbands, gave the wives involved, their first real chance of preventing injustice through the exercise of equitable rights.

The aim of this appeal hearing was to establish whether actual occupation of land (or property therein), was considerable enough to constitute an overriding interest, both under repossession of the land, or through the proceeds of sale. The archaic history behind property law is sadly one that until the decade prior to this appeal, denied women the fundamental right to declare equitable interest in the marital home they both shared, and increasingly invested in.

On this occasion, there were two similar matters involving the indiscretions of the men, who, while acting under individually assigned companies, took it upon themselves to remortgage the family home in order to expand their business interests. While this may not seem particularly unusual, what removed them from average expectation was that in both instances, the appellants held sole legal title to the properties, and withheld knowledge from their spouses that the additional charges had been agreed with the lenders.

In *Boland*, the husband had chosen to borrow in order to secure storage space for his construction partnership, while in *Brown*, the objective was that of additional investment into a developing film production company. Both of these men used the same bank, and on both occasions, the bank themselves failed to make adequate enquiries as to who else shared the homes, and to what extent their interests might affect the bank's ability to repossess under default.

When both parties became unable to meet the increased repayments, separate proceedings were started against them for recovery of the capital, at which point the judges awarded in favour of the bank, before the appellants sought relief on grounds that the wives were unwitting casualties of the contractual arrangements between the bank and businessmen; and that on consideration of their collective financial contributions to the properties, the bank had no footing upon which to seek repossession without court order support.

With laboured consideration of the changes in statute, and the arguments presented against the rights of the women, it was unanimously found that despite previously (and outmoded) held views of the roles women play within property ownership, the world was now a very different place, and that without the enduring commitment of hardworking wives and mothers, it was often impossible for many homes to remain free of reclaim.

Furthermore, the bank in the former case had every opportunity to sell the storage space for a considerable sum, and yet opted to sell for a figure grossly below market value, before trying in vain to convert the mortgagees home into recoverable assets, while

---

[795] [1981] AC 487.

overlooking its own professional obligation to observe lending policy and make sufficiently exhaustive enquiries at the outset.

Key Citations

"I would only say that occupation need not be in one single person. Two persons can be in actual occupation, by themselves jointly or each of them severally."[796]

"Once it is found that a wife is in actual occupation, then it is clear that in the case of registered land, a purchaser or lender would be well advised to make inquiry of the wife."[797]

"If a bank is to do its duty, in the society in which we live, it should recognise the integrity of the matrimonial home."[798]

"In my opinion each of the wives, Mrs Brown and Mrs Boland is entitled to be protected in her occupation of the matrimonial home. The bank is not entitled to throw these families out into into the street…"[799]

"They are co-owners in equity with the persons holding the legal estate and at all material times were sharing the property, in the sense of living in the house with the co-owner, and physically, at least, occupying it."[800]

"[I]n consequence of the financial contributions made by the wives, the husbands in whom the legal estate is vested hold the property in trust for themselves and their wives as tenants in common in shares proportionate to the contributions each has made."[801]

"[T]he interests in persons in the positions of the wives ought not to be dismissed as a mere interest in the proceeds of sale except where it is essential to the working of the scheme to do so."[802]

"[T]he wives' interests have not been overreached and are not capable of being overreached because in each case the land was held by a sole trustee who has no overreaching powers."[803]

---

[796] *Williams & Glyn's Bank Ltd v Boland* [1981] AC 487 (CA) 331 (Lord Denning MR).

[797] *Williams & Glyn's Bank Ltd v Boland* [1981] AC 487 (CA) 332 (Lord Denning MR).

[798] *Williams & Glyn's Bank Ltd v Boland* [1981] AC 487 (CA) 332 (Lord Denning MR).

[799] *Williams & Glyn's Bank Ltd v Boland* [1981] AC 487 (CA) 333 (Lord Denning MR).

[800] *Williams & Glyn's Bank Ltd v Boland* [1981] AC 487 (CA) 333 (Ormrod LJ).

[801] *Williams & Glyn's Bank Ltd v Boland* [1981] AC 487 (CA) 333 (Ormrod LJ).

[802] *Williams & Glyn's Bank Ltd v Boland* [1981] AC 487 (CA) 336 (Ormrod LJ).

[803] *Williams & Glyn's Bank Ltd v Boland* [1981] AC 487 (CA) 337 (Ormrod LJ).

9. Tort Law

1. Bolam v Friern Hospital Management Committee

Medical negligence and the values of medical community views, run counter to one another unless such disparity can be reasonably justified. On this occasion, the rather outlandish practice of electro-convulsive therapy (ECT) resulted in serious injury, when the patient was left partially restrained and therefore vulnerable to harm.

Having attended the Friern Mental Hospital as a voluntary patient, the claimant was left suffering a double fracture of the *Acetabulum* (pelvic cup) resulting from impact of the head of the femur, when the use of full restraints had been spared. The use of ECT had been around for a number of years, and while accidents were rare, they were not without incident. Yet it was contended by the defendants that in over 50,000 applications, there had only been one case of acetabular fracture reported.

At the point of litigation, the claimant argued that when discussing the procedure with his consultant, there had been (i) no explanation of the risks attached, (ii) no mention given as to the possible use of muscle relaxants, and (iii) little the use of restraint, aside from two nurses holding his chin and shoulders, so as to avoid him falling from the sofa used; and so it was for these reasons, that a claim for negligence was put before the court.

In their defence, the defendants contended that the nature of ECT was one that both divided the medical industry, while allowing a discretionary approach to the use of restraints and relaxants; both of which drew strong argument to the contrary, as with those who conversely promoted them. It was also argued that depending on the circumstances, many practitioners elected to withhold any discussion of risk, as it could exacerbate the patient's fears, thereby discouraging any opportunity to undergo the treatment.

Relying upon expert evidence from a consultant psychiatrist, the court had agreed that in most negligence cases, the objective view of the everyday man was sufficient to establish negligence. However in matters such these, the test required greater professional knowledge, so as to mirror the complexities of ECT, while in *Hunter v Hanley* it had recently been remarked by Lord President Clyde that:

> "In the realm of diagnosis and treatment there is ample scope for genuine difference of opinion and one man clearly is not negligent merely because his conclusion differs from that of other professional men, nor because he has displayed less skill or knowledge than others would have shown. The true test for establishing negligence in diagnosis or treatment on the part of a doctor is whether he has been proved to be guilty of such failure as no doctor of ordinary skill would be guilty of, if acting with ordinary care."[804]

It was then explained by the expert witness, that whilst the avoidance of risk disclosure was one subject to the individual requirements of the case, there was little to endorse

---

[804] *Hunter v Hanley* [1955] SLT 213 (SC) 204 (Clyde LP).

withholding the information when the risks were considered so small, and that the use of relaxants was a virtual prerequisite.

Where restraint was used, there had been instances where the patients were placed into a made bed to avoid excessive limb flailing; however, general medical consensus was that restraint of the feet could result in serious injury when the body was treated like a 'rigid stick', and so the approach used by the defendants was not considered unusual nor frowned upon.

With the facts explained to a discerning jury, the point was made that mere negligence was not one of simple black-and-white thinking, but a cumulative process that began with ignorance of the patient and the attached dangers, and ended with even less consideration of the outcome, or the injuries sustained. It was also stressed that the incident itself had occurred nearly four years prior to the hearing, and so knowledge of ECT had grown beyond that which was known at the time; after which a lengthy deliberation found the jury returning a verdict in favour of the defendants.

Key Citations

"In the ordinary case which does not involve any special skill, negligence in law means a failure to do some act which a reasonable man in the circumstances would do, or the doing of some act which a reasonable man in the circumstances would not do; and if that failure or the doing of that act results in injury, then there is a cause of action."[805]

"[I]n the case of a medical man, negligence means failure to act in accordance with the standards of reasonably competent medical men at the time."[806]

"[A] mere personal belief that a particular technique is best is no defence unless that belief is based on reasonable grounds."[807]

---

[805] *Bolam v Friern Hospital Management Committee* [1957] 1 WLR 582 (QB) 586 (McNair J).

[806] *Bolam v Friern Hospital Management Committee* [1957] 1 WLR 582 (QB) 586 (McNair J).

[807] *Bolam v Friern Hospital Management Committee* [1957] 1 WLR 582 (QB) 587 (McNair J).

2. Cambridge Water Co v Eastern Counties Leather Plc

Foreseeability within the tort of negligence and nuisance has over time, become an integral element of the decision making process, yet there was a period when mere acts were suffice to claim damages. In this matter, the actions of a manufacturer that while deemed harmless at the time, became key to a claim for substantial costs, and one in which existing precedent was brought into question on the principles of natural justice.

Founded in 1879, the appellant company Eastern Counties Leather (ECL), were a leather goods manufacturer that relied upon particular treatment processes in order to soften the pelts used. Since the early 1950s, the firm used trichloroethene (TCE), until around 1973, when they switched to perchloroethene (PCE), as was then considered the industry standard.

Around 1976, the respondent company Cambridge Water Company (CWC), purchased an industrial site containing a borehole, situated roughly one to three miles north west of the village in which the ECL operated, and began using the hole as a source of public drinking water. Prior to its implementation within the regional water supply, a number of test were carried out to ensure contamination levels were below the prescribed limits set under the Water Resources Act 1963.

In 1980, both the World Health Organisation and Council of the European Communities drafted Directive 80/778/EEC, in relation to the safe human consumption of drinking water, which was later transposed into the Water Industry Act 1991 under secondary legislation.[808] Under this Act, it was stated that the maximum admissible concentration of PCE was 10µg per litre of water. Subsequent borehole tests carried out in the early 1980s, showed PCE concentration levels of between 70 and 170µ per litre, which prompted investigation by the respondents as to the source of the contaminant.

As was evident, ECL had continued to use PCE until 1991, while it was common for the appellants to store roughly 25,000 litres in drums at any one time. During the application stage, these drums were driven by forklift to the degreasing machines, whereupon the PCE was poured directly into their reservoirs. It was not uncommon for spillages to occur, after which the PCE would be quickly cleaned up, so as to avoid accidents or inhalation of fumes, and as the floors themselves were concrete, it would not have seemed possible that any residual liquid could seep into the soil below.

After commissioning independent research into the presence of PCE in the borehole, it was established that trace elements of PCE had in fact passed through the sub-structure of ECL over a course of nearly twenty years, eventually joining the water supply used by the appellants; and while the individual amounts were insufficient to cause harm, they had amassed over time so as to push the levels found far beyond that allowed. This in turn led to the decommissioning of the borehole and inevitable litigation.

In the first hearing, the respondents claimed for substantial damages of around £1m for the cost of a new pumping station, following the borehole closure and cited negligence, nuisance and non-natural use of the land provided under the principles espoused in

---

[808] The Water Supply (Water Quality) Regulations 1989, SI 1989/1147

Rylands v Fletcher,[809] upon which the claim was summarily dismissed. Presented to the Court of Appeal, the respondents argued that the judge had erred in law, while the appellants contended that they were not liable for the lost PCE, on grounds of foreseeability, that the burden of proof was that of the respondents and not the appellants, and that the evidence submitted was inadequate.

Turning to the outcome in *Ballard and Tomlinson*, the Court held that Pearson J, who remarked:

> "[I]t seems to me that although nobody has any property in the common source, yet everybody has a right to appropriate it, and to appropriate it in its natural state, and no one of those who have a right to appropriate it has a right to contaminate that source so as to prevent his neighbour from having the full value of his right of appropriation. . . . Neither does it matter whether the parties are or not contiguous neighbours. *If it can be shown in fact that the defendants have adulterated or fouled the common source, it signifies not how far the plaintiffs land is from their land.*"[810]

Encapsulated the very essence of nuisance, and that in failing apply the principle, the previous judge had overlooked the strictness of the nuisance doctrine and thus denied the right to damages. Thus for that fundamental reason, the appeal was upheld and almost £1.7m awarded in favour of the respondents.

Presented before the House of Lords, the dicta of Blackburn J in *Rylands* explained well that:

> "We think that the true rule of law is, that the person who for his own purposes brings on his lands and collects and keeps there anything likely to do mischief if it escapes, must keep it in at his peril, and, *if he does not do so, is prima facie answerable for all the damage which is the natural consequence of its escape.*"[811]

Yet the House held that while nuisance in its singular use brings certainty to the liability of those found answerable, it precludes the necessary factor of foreseeability, which on this occasion was starkly evident inasmuch as it had taken almost twenty years for the PCE levels to reach significant risk, and that there was insufficient knowledge on the part of the appellants to even begin to appreciate that liquids could permeate concrete before navigating through numerous other substratum, prior to joining a stream more than thirty metres below ground. For this reason it was held that the previous decisions were unsustainable, and that rather than a matter for negligence or nuisance, it was at best, an example of historic pollution which was not subject to legislative effects at the time, thus the appeal was allowed.

---

[809] (1866) LR 1 Ex 265.

[810] *Ballard v Tomlinson* (1885) 29 Ch D 115 (Ch) 121 (Pearson J) (emphasis added).

[811] *Rylands v Fletcher* (1866) LR 1 Ex 265 (Exch Ch) 279 (Blackburn J) (emphasis added).

Key Citations

"[I]t is still the law that the fact that the defendant has taken all reasonable care will not of itself exonerate him from liability, the relevant control mechanism being found within the principle of reasonable user. But it by no means follows that the defendant should be held liable for damage of a type which he could not reasonably foresee…"[812]

"[I]f a plaintiff is in ordinary circumstances only able to claim damages in respect of personal injuries where he can prove such foreseeability on the part of the defendant, it is difficult to see why, in common justice, he should be in a stronger position to claim damages for interference with the enjoyment of his land where the defendant was unable to foresee such damage."[813]

"[K]nowledge, or at least foreseeability of the risk, is a prerequisite of the recovery of damages under the principle; but that the principle is one of strict liability in the sense that the defendant may be held liable notwithstanding that he has exercised all due care to prevent the escape from occurring."[814]

"I feel bound to say that the storage of substantial quantities of chemicals on industrial premises should be regarded as an almost classic case of non-natural use; and I find it very difficult to think that it should be thought objectionable to impose strict liability for damage caused in the event of their escape."[815]

---

[812] *Cambridge Water Co v Eastern Counties Leather plc* [1994] 2 AC 264 (HL) 300 (Goff LJ).

[813] *Cambridge Water Co v Eastern Counties Leather plc* [1994] 2 AC 264 (HL) 300 (Goff LJ).

[814] *Cambridge Water Co v Eastern Counties Leather plc* [1994] 2 AC 264 (HL) 302 (Goff LJ).

[815] *Cambridge Water Co v Eastern Counties Leather plc* [1994] 2 AC 264 (HL) 309 (Goff LJ).

3. Campbell v Mirror Group Newspapers (MGN)

Convention principles and the juxtaposition between public interest and individual privacy, are central to a clamant's case when sensitive information is rightly or wrongly disclosed. On this occasion, the needs of a known supermodel are considered secondary to the public knowledge of her drug addiction, thus sparking fierce debate as to where the lines of journalistic privilege and private health are to be drawn.

Following numerous televised interviews, in which the appellant denied any use of recreational drugs, she was rushed to hospital for emergency treatment in what was described as an allergic reaction to antibiotics. Some months later, the appellant was photographed outside a known Narcotics Anonymous in an unknown part of London, and those images were included in a multiple-paged newspaper article entitled 'Naomi: I am a drug addict'.

This publication revealed that despite her historic protestations, the appellant was a long-term user of drugs, and that in a battle to overcome addiction, she had enrolled into a self-help programme, as had been shown in the accompanying images. Unfortunately, contained within one of the pictures was the sign of a well-known café, which therefore made clear exactly where the venue was situated, thereby allowing readers to know where she may be found, while the article text revealed how often she might be attending. Prior to its release, the newspaper editor had contacted the appellant's agent to request some collaborative comments, upon which they were told that the images taken were a violation of the appellant's right to privacy and confidentiality in relation the anonymous nature of the therapy used.

Despite this express disapproval, the respondents ran the story, upon which litigation was immediately initiated. In the first hearing, the appellant claimed for breach of confidence and sought damages under the Data Protection Act 1998, whereupon she was awarded a total of £3,500 by the court. Taken to the Court of Appeal, the judgment was reversed and the award discharged. Presented to the House of Lords, the opposing nature of both arts.8 (Right to respect for private and family life) and 10 (Freedom of expression) of the Human Rights Act 1998 (HRA) were given equal consideration, with particular regard to the restrictive nature of arts.8(2) and 10(2), which both confer the the need to exercise restraint where the rights and protections of others are affected.

While *Wainwright v Home Office*[816] had decided there was no tortious right to claim invasion of privacy, there was due remedy where a breach of confidence was found to exist, as explained by Chieveley LJ in *Attorney-General v Guardian Newspapers Ltd (No 2)*, where he remarked:

> "[A] duty of confidence arises when confidential information comes to the knowledge of a person . . . in circumstances where he has notice, or is held to have agreed, that the information is confidential, with the effect that it would be

---

[816] [2003] UKHL 53.

just in all the circumstances that he should be precluded from disclosing the information to others."[817]

It was also pointed out that clause 3(i) of the Editors' Code of Practice of the Press Complaints Commission provides:

> "(iii) It is unacceptable to photograph individuals in private places without their consent. Note - Private places are public or private property where there is a reasonable expectation of privacy."

Which put the respondent in a difficult position when justifying the use of potentially harmful images in a story that may best have remained wholly textual. In cases similar to the one discussed, there had been reliance upon the objective test laid down in *Australian Broadcasting Corpn v Lenah Game Meats Pty Ltd*, in which Gleeson CJ had outlined:

> "The requirement that disclosure or observation of information or conduct would be highly offensive to a reasonable person of ordinary sensibilities is in many circumstances a useful practical test of what is private."[818]

However the House agreed that while many readers of tabloid newspapers would view the article with a degree of cynicism after the appellant had publicly lied about her drug use, it was only reasonable that the best person to determine the validity of such a publication would be one who walked in similar shoes as the appellant. This required the House to balance the needs of the newspaper with those of the appellant, as had been applied in *Bladet Tromsø and Stensaas v Norway*, where the court said:

> "Although the press must not overstep certain bounds, in particular in respect of the reputation and rights of others and the need to prevent the disclosure of confidential information, its duty is nevertheless to impart in a manner consistent with its obligations and responsibilities information and ideas on all matters of public interest."[819]

Which was a position concurrent with s.12(4) of the HRA 1998, which reads:

> "The court must have particular regard to the importance of the Convention right to freedom of expression and, where the proceedings relate to material which the respondent claims, or which appears to the court, to be journalistic, literary or artistic material (or to conduct connected with such material), to (a) the extent to which (i) the material has, or is about to, become available to the

---

[817] *Attorney-General v Guardian Newspapers Ltd* (No 2) [1990] 1 AC 109 (HL) 281 (Chieveley LJ).

[818] *Australian Broadcasting Corpn v Lenah Game Meats Pty Ltd* [2001] HCA 63 [42] (Gleeson CJ).

[819] *Bladet Tromsø and Stensaas v Norway* (1999) 29 EHRR 125 [59] (Commission Decision).

public; or (ii) it is, or would be, in the pubic interest for the material to be published; (b) any relevant privacy code."[820]

By embracing both elements to the argument, the House declared that while the respondents went to pains in order to run what they considered a 'sympathetic' piece, the very clandestine nature of Narcotics Anonymous was one that protected the needs and identities of those attending. And so when the respondents gained unauthorised insight of the appellant's treatment, they did so in the knowledge that it represented a violation of her art.8 rights, despite any previous misrepresentations on her part. And so it was for those fundamental reasons, that the House upheld the appeal and awarded accordingly.

Key Citations

"Any interference with the public interest in disclosure has to be balanced against the interference with the right of the individual to respect for their private life. The decisions that are then taken are open to review by the court."[821]

"Any restriction of the right to freedom of expression must be subjected to very close scrutiny. But so too must any restriction of the right to respect for private life."[822]

"A close examination of the factual justification for the restriction on the freedom of expression is needed if the fundamental right enshrined in article 10 is to remain practical and effective. The restrictions which the court imposes on the article 10 right must be rational, fair and not arbitrary, and they must impair the right no more than is necessary."[823]

---

[820] Human Rights Act 1998, s.12(4)

[821] *Campbell v Mirror Group Newspapers* [2004] UKHL 22 [113] (Hope LJ).

[822] *Campbell v Mirror Group Newspapers* [2004] UKHL 22 [113] (Hope LJ).

[823] *Campbell v Mirror Group Newspapers* [2004] UKHL 22 [115] (Hope LJ).

4. Caparo Industries Plc v Dickman

When predatory investors choose to act upon the advice or information given outside the remit of those assigned to prescribe it, they do so under risk of their own suffering, and within the rules of industry and commerce. On this occasion, the cross-appellants argued that their reliance upon the annual statement provided by a company's accountants led to increased investment, despite the fact that the statement turned out to be inaccurate.

When the appellants (a public limited company) fell victim to poor financial trading, their stock market share values began dropping, and were in turn, bought up in considerable number by the cross-appellants. While buying as outside investors, they secured an almost thirty percent share of the failing company, after which they became registered investors, and acted quickly to gain a majority controlling hold of the firm. These additional purchases were made after learning from the annual shareholder statement that the company was due a healthy pre-tax profit. However, after the purchases had been made, it became apparent that the accounts had been poorly prepared, showing instead a considerable loss of profit.

During the appeal, it was claimed that the accountants owed a duty of care to the now primary shareholders of the company when drafting the legally required statement, and that such care rendered them liable for the losses inherited by the investors. In this instance, a duty of care was determinable by the relationship between (or proximity to) both accountants and investors. Citing *Hedley Byrne & Co Ltd v Heller and Partners*,[824] the distinction was made between expert advice (albeit subjective) from a banker, and an annual submission from a firm of accountants, and that despite an implied culpability on the part of the accountants, an error was made, upon which a negative investment took place.

What distinguished the two activities, was that the former was expressly undertaken to prevent loss upon lending of monies, whereas at no point did the accountants have knowledge of a planned takeover bid (despite suggestions made by the investors during the hearing). This clear divide presented the notion that duty of care is always applicable, as the two events are less similar than might first appear. However, the accountants were only held liable for the losses made as shareholders and not those of outside investors.

The House of Lords concluded that if it were reasonable to place conscious liability upon all acts of certain parties, it would be impossible to distinguish responsibility from neglect, and in this instance there was clear frustration at an unforeseen outcome, but one requiring mindfulness that the very nature of financial investment is itself, riddled and prone to loss.

---

[824] [1963] 2 All ER 575.

Key Citations

"They owe the duty, of course, to their employer or client; and also I think to any third person to whom they themselves show the accounts, or to whom they know their employer is going to show the accounts, so as to induce him to invest money or take some other action on them. But I do not think the duty can be extended still further so as to include strangers…"[825]

"I do not think that such a relationship should be found to exist unless, at least, the maker of the statement was, or ought to have been, aware that his advice or information would in fact be made available to and be relied upon by a particular person or class of persons for the purposes of a particular transaction or type of transaction."[826]

"It is never sufficient to ask simply whether A owes B a duty of care. it is always necessary to determine the scope of duty by reference to the kind of damage from which A must take care to save B harmless."[827]

"As a purchaser of additional shares in reliance on the auditor's report, he stands in no different position from any other investing member of the public to whom the author owes no duty."[828]

"I find it difficult to believe, however, that the legislature, in enacting provisions clearly aimed primarily at the protection of the company and its informed control by the body of its proprietors, can have been inspired also by consideration for the public at large and investors in the market in particular."[829]

"To widen the scope of the duty to include loss caused to an individual by reliance upon the accounts for a purpose for which they were not supplied and were not intended would be to extend it beyond the limits which are so far deductible from the decisions of this House."[830]

---

[825] *Caparo Industries plc v Dickman* [1990] 2 AC 605 (HL) 622 (Bridge LJ).

[826] *Caparo Industries plc v Dickman* [1990] 2 AC 605 (HL) 624 (Bridge LJ).

[827] *Caparo Industries plc v Dickman* [1990] 2 AC 605 (HL) 627 (Bridge LJ).

[828] *Caparo Industries plc v Dickman* [1990] 2 AC 605 (HL) 627 (Bridge LJ).

[829] *Caparo Industries plc v Dickman* [1990] 2 AC 605 (HL) 632 (Oliver LJ).

[830] *Caparo Industries plc v Dickman* [1990] 2 AC 605 (HL) 654 (Oliver LJ).

5. Donoghue v Stevenson

In this case, the principle of negligence beyond the strictness of contractual duty becomes pivotal to a claim for damages, when a consumer becomes victim to sickness through the consumption of a contaminated beverage.

In 1928, two friends entered a café in central Scotland and proceeded to order some ice-cream and ginger beer. Unknown to the appellant, one of the bottles provided contained the decomposed remains of a snail, which when poured onto the ice-cream, left the appellant in a state of shock, and later subjected to gastro-enteritis, having partially drunk the ginger beer beforehand.

This resulted in litigation on grounds concerning (i) the manufacturer's inability to safely store the bottles prior to their filling, (ii) a lack of care when considering the potential for those drinks to be consumed by unwitting customers, (iii) failure to implement a suitable quality control/inspection system prior to distribution, and (iv) failure to use clear, as opposed to dark opaque bottles, to avoid such events.

Although the common law position was comparable between English and Scottish law, the claim was unique in that it circumvented the contractual obligations often found in negligence claims. The court in the first instance had allowed the claim, while the Second Divisional court dismissed it by a majority, before the appellant sought relief in the House of Lords.

Here, a number of recent cases were explored, so as to ascertain the extent of liability in matters where there are no contractual obligations. Erring on the side of restraint as to how far a claim such as this might extend, comments mades by Parke B in *Longmeid v Holliday* suggested that:

> "It would be going much too far to say, that so much care is required in the ordinary intercourse of life between one individual and another, that, if a machine not in its nature dangerous, ... but which might become so by a latent defect entirely unknown, although discoverable by the exercise of ordinary care, should be lent or given by one person, even by the person who manufactured it, to another, the former should be answerable to the latter for a subsequent damage accruing by the use of it."[831]

However in *George v Skivington*,[832] the sale of harmful shampoo, which had been used not by the purchaser but a third party, had allowed claim for negligence caused upon a duty of care by the manufacturer when mixing the ingredients; while in *Francis v Cockerell*,[833] a racecourse spectator injured through the collapse of a viewing stand, was able to recover not from the builder himself, but the agent of the venue.

---

[831] *Longmeid v Holliday* (1851) 6 EX 761, 768 (Parke B).

[832] (1869-70) LR 5 Ex 1.

[833] (1870) LR 5 QB 501.

On this occasion, the appellant relied upon the words of Lord Brett MR in *Heaven v Pender*, who clarified that:

> "[W]henever one person is by circumstances placed in such a position with regard to another that every one of ordinary sense who did think would at once recognize that if he did not use ordinary care and skill in his own conduct with regard to those circumstances he would cause danger of injury to the person or property of the other, a duty arises to use ordinary care and skill to avoid such danger..."[834]

Therefore it was argued that regardless of contractual elements, there was, by virtue of reasonableness and decency, an inherent encumbrance upon the respondent manufacturer to both evaluate and consider the position of the consumer when preparing and sealing his drinks, and that anything less than that consideration was tantamount to fundamental neglect and tortious liability.

Contrastingly, in *Pender* Esher LJ had also argued that:

> "The question of liability for negligence cannot arise at all until it is established that the man who has been negligent owed some duty to the person who seeks to make him liable for his negligence. What duty is there when there is no relation between the parties by contract? A man is entitled to be as negligent as he pleases towards the whole world if he owes no duty to them."[835]

While in *Bates v Batey & Co Ltd*,[836] the manufacturers of ginger beer were not deemed liable for an injury caused to an unsuspecting consumer from a defect unknown, and yet discoverable through reasonable investigation.

Having evaluated the reluctance of the courts to extend in some instances, while offering generous judgment in others, it was, albeit by a narrow margin, decided that despite no contractual duties to envisage the effects of a contaminated product upon an innocent purchaser, there was an almost ethical prerequisite to remain diligent in the preparation and storage of such substances. And so despite the abject refusal by the Second Division of the Court of Session in Scotland to acknowledge the appellant's rights, the House reversed the finding and restored the order of the first judge.

---

[834] *Heaven v Pender* (1883) 11 QBD 503 (QB) 509 (Lord Brett MR).

[835] *Heaven v Pender* (1883) 11 QBD 503 (QB) 509 (Esher LJ).

[836] [1913] 3 KB 351.

Key Citations

"[T]he omission to exercise reasonable care in the discovery of a defect in the manufacture of an article where the duty of examination exists is just as negligent as the negligent construction itself."[837]

"[T]he manufacturer, or indeed the repairer, of any article, apart entirely from contract, owes a duty to any person by whom the article is lawfully used to see that it has been carefully constructed."[838]

"[I]n order to support an action for damages for negligence the complainant has to show that he has been injured by the breach of a duty owed to him in the circumstances by the defendant to take reasonable care to avoid such injury."[839]

"The liability for negligence, whether you style it such or treat it as in other systems as a species of "culpa," is no doubt based upon a general public sentiment of moral wrongdoing for which the offender must pay. But acts or omissions which any moral code would censure cannot in a practical world be treated so as to give a right to every person injured by them to demand relief."[840]

"Who, then, in law is my neighbour? The answer seems to be persons who are so closely and directly affected by my act that I ought reasonably to have them in contemplation as being so affected when I am directing my mind to the acts or omissions which are called in question."[841]

"[A] manufacturer of products, which he sells in such a form as to show that he intends them to reach the ultimate consumer in the form in which they left him with no reasonable possibility of intermediate examination, and with the knowledge that the absence of reasonable care in the preparation or putting up of the products will result in an injury to the consumer's life or property, owes a duty to the consumer to take that reasonable care."[842]

"The cardinal principle of liability is that the party complained of should owe to the party complaining a duty to take care, and that the party complaining should be able to prove that he has suffered damage in consequence of a breach of that duty."[843]

---

[837] *Donoghue v Stevens* [1932] AC 562 (HL) 569 (Buckmaster LJ).

[838] *Donoghue v Stevens* [1932] AC 562 (HL) 577 (Buckmaster LJ).

[839] *Donoghue v Stevens* [1932] AC 562 (HL) 579 (Atkin LJ).

[840] *Donoghue v Stevens* [1932] AC 562 (HL) 580 (Atkin LJ).

[841] *Donoghue v Stevens* [1932] AC 562 (HL) 580 (Atkin LJ).

[842] *Donoghue v Stevens* [1932] AC 562 (HL) 599 (Atkin LJ).

[843] *Donoghue v Stevens* [1932] AC 562 (HL) 619 (Macmillan LJ).

6. Gray v Thames Trains Ltd

Public policy, pain and suffering, diminished responsibility and the intricacies of criminal sentencing, are all brought to bear in a case broaching tortious claims and unlawful actions. When the victim of a large-scale train crash becomes subject to a manslaughter charge, the latent need for compensatory remedy is awoken with claims for damages stemming from the punishment dispensed by the courts.

In 1999, the now cross-appellant, was one of a number of survivors travelling on the Thames Trains Turbo Train when it collided with a First Great Western High Speed Train near Paddington Station. Known as the 'Ladbroke Grove Train Crash', the aftermath left thirty-one people dead and another five hundred injured. Fortunate enough to sustain only minor injuries, the appellant later attempted to return to normality, despite suffering from panic attacks, mood swings, flashbacks, nightmares and grief symptoms; although within a number of months, he found himself unable to cope with work, travel, social interaction and even close relationships.

After unsuccessfully attempting to hold down a number of jobs, the appellant wound up unemployed and a semi-functioning alcoholic. It was during this period that he was attacked by a drunken stranger while driving his car. After leaving the car to defend himself, the appellant was further subjected to hostile behaviour by a passing group, after which he drove away in state of heightened fear. Shortly afterwards, the appellant stole a knife from his partner's parents, before finding the man and stabbing him repeatedly. After the victim later died of his injuries, the appellant turned himself in, and was summarily convicted of manslaughter on grounds of diminished responsibility.

In passing sentence, the court chose to detain him using a s.37 hospital order and s.41 restriction order under the Mental Health Act 1983. Such decisions were typical in instances where a defendant is found guilty of a criminal act while suffering from a recognised psychological abnormality, which in this case had been established as Post-Traumatic Stress Disorder (PTSD) by a psychiatrist during the trial. Roughly five years after his conviction, the appellant initiated proceedings against the respondents Thames Trains and Network Rail, for lost earnings arising from the PTSD during the period between the accident and his incarceration. However, the claim was then extended to include lost future earnings as well as those during the period before and after the trial.

Relying upon the maxim '*ex dolo malo non oritur actio*', meaning:

> "No court will lend its aid to a man who founds his cause of action upon an immoral or an illegal act. If, from the plaintiff's own stating or otherwise, the cause of action appears to arise *ex turpi causa*, or the transgression of a positive law of this country, there the court says he has no right to be assisted."[844]

The respondents made clear that while they admitted full liability for the period between the accident and the unlawful act, they were protected by public policy not to compensate a party who relied upon their own misdeeds when laying claim.

---

[844] *Holman v Johnson* (1775) 1 Cowp 341 (KB) 343 (Mansfield LJ).

While there had been numerous cases touching upon the indivisible nature of tort and criminal matters, strong argument for the 'novus actus interveniens' principle suggested that tortious claims preceding criminal acts were by virtue of the unlawful event, separable and therefore distinct. This gave rise to the notion that liability could extend only so far as the symptoms directly appropriate to, and displayed by the claimant, in relation to the cause of the tort. However, it was equally held that whatever separating act took place, it must be of such magnitude that it 'obliterates' the wrong doing of the defendant'.[845] On this occasion, it was held by the appellant that without the accident and concluding PTSD, there would have been (i) no loss of earnings, and (ii) no act of manslaughter, and so without sufficient evidence to the contrary, the respondents were still liable for the compensation claimed.

In the first instance, the judge awarded in favour of the appellant, while the Court of Appeal reversed the decision and allowed the respondents' appeal. Taken to the House of Lords, the appellant then cross-appealed, while the respondents pursued the same ends as before. Having examined the position taken by the Court of Appeal, the House gave consideration to the manner of sentencing, and the rights of those convicted to claim for loss of earnings. In *R v Birch*, the principles behind s.37 hospital orders explained that:

> "A hospital order is not a punishment. Questions of retribution and deterrence, whether personal or general, are immaterial. The offender who has become a patient is not kept on any kind of leash by the court, as he is when he consents to a probation order with a condition of inpatient treatment."[846]

However, when coupled with a s.41 restriction order it was noted that:

> "A restriction order has no existence independently of the hospital order to which it relates; it is not a separate means of disposal. Nevertheless, it fundamentally affects the circumstances in which the patient is detained. No longer is the offender regarded simply as a patient whose interests are paramount. No longer is the control of him handed over unconditionally to the hospital authorities. Instead the interests of public safety are regarded by transferring the responsibility for discharge from the responsible medical officer and the hospital to the Secretary of State alone (before 30 September 1983) and now to the Secretary of State and the Mental Health Review Tribunal."[847]

This meant that instead of proving an exception to the rule of unlawful conduct, the appellant was instead denied his right to earnings while detained, as was illustrated in *British Columbia v Zastowny*, where the Supreme Court held that:

---

[845] AM Jones, MA Dudgate (eds), *Clerk & Lindsell on Torts* (19th edn, Sweet & Maxwell 2006)

[846] *R v Birch* (1989) 11 Cr App R (S) 202 (CA) 210 (Mustill LJ).

[847] *R v Birch* (1989) 11 Cr App R (S) 202 (CA) 210 (Mustill LJ).

"When a person receives a criminal sanction, he or she is subject to a criminal penalty as well as the civil consequences that are the natural result of the criminal sanction. The consequences of imprisonment include wage loss."[848]

This line or argument was bolstered by the outcome of *Clunis v Camden and Islington Health Authority*, in which a former patient stabbed an innocent stranger within days of their release, before claiming diminished responsibility and suing the local authority for negligence. There it was held that:

"A plea of diminished responsibility accepts that the accused's mental responsibility is substantially impaired but it does not remove liability for his criminal act . . . The court ought not to allow itself to be made an instrument to enforce obligations alleged to arise out of the plaintiff's own criminal act..."[849]

This decision had been given full support of the Law Commission in its consultation paper 'The Illegality of Defence in Tort'[850] and so it was for these reasons, that the House reversed the decision of the Court of Appeal in lieu of the original judgment, and allowed the respondents' appeal.

---

[848] *British Columbia v Zastowny* [2008] 1 SCR 27 [22] (Rothstein J).

[849] *Clunis v Camden and Islington Health Authority* [1998] QB 978 (QB) 989 (Bedlam J).

[850] Law Commission, *The Illegality of Defence in Tort* (HMSO 2001)

Key Citations

"[W]hile a conviction for an offence punishable with imprisonment is necessary to confer jurisdiction on a judge to impose a hospital order under section 37, the offence leading to that conviction may have no relevance to the decision to make the hospital order."[851]

"Although in general a defendant will not be liable for damage of which the immediate cause was the deliberate act of the claimant or a third party, that principle does not ordinarily apply when the claimant or third party's act was itself a consequence of the defendant's breach of duty."[852]

"The maxim ex turpi causa expresses not so much a principle as a policy. Furthermore, that policy is not based upon a single justification but on a group of reasons, which vary in different situations."[853]

"[T]he sentence imposed by the court for a criminal offence is usually for a variety of purposes: punishment, treatment, reform, deterrence, protection of the public against the possibility of further offences."[854]

"[A] civil court will not award damages to compensate a claimant for an injury or disadvantage which the criminal courts of the same jurisdiction have imposed on him by way of punishment for a criminal act for which he was responsible."[855]

"[I]t would be inconsistent with the policy underlying the making of the orders for a civil court now to award the claimant damages for loss of earnings relating to the period when he was subject to them."[856]

"[A] person is not entitled to be indemnified for the consequences of his criminal acts for which he has been found criminally responsible. He cannot attribute them to others or seek rebate of those consequences."[857]

---

[851] *Gray v Thames Trains Ltd* [2009] UKHL 33 [14] (Phillips LJ).

[852] *Gray v Thames Trains Ltd* [2009] UKHL 33 [28] (Hoffman LJ).

[853] *Gray v Thames Trains Ltd* [2009] UKHL 33 [30] (Phillips LJ).

[854] *Gray v Thames Trains Ltd* [2009] UKHL 33 [41] (Phillips LJ).

[855] *Gray v Thames Trains Ltd* [2009] UKHL 33 [69] (Rodger LJ).

[856] *Gray v Thames Trains Ltd* [2009] UKHL 33 [79] (Rodger LJ).

[857] *Gray v Thames Trains Ltd* [2009] UKHL 33 [85] (Rodger LJ).

7. Grobbelaar v News Group Newspapers Ltd

The perversion of justice through miscalculation of the jury, is a difficult case to prove when the reliability of both witnesses and the courts complicate matters further. On this occasion, a respected footballer is left with his professional integrity in tatters, after entrapment by a tabloid newspaper exposes his questionable conduct both on and off the pitch.

In late 1994, 'The Sun newspaper' ran a series of damning articles around the supposed match fixing activities of a reputable premier division goalkeeper. As part of their campaign, the now respondents went to great lengths so as to not only expose the clandestine dealings of the appellant, but to further ridicule his character and dismantle his popular public persona.

In order to achieve this, the respondents colluded with the appellant's former business partner, on the understanding that secret video taping of their conversations would provide sufficient evidence to seal a conviction for corruption. Over a number of meetings, the agent successfully recorded several oral agreements made by the appellant to participate in providing match forecasts, which later transformed into regular meetings with foreign bookmakers, and the receipt of several cash payments for undisclosed reasons.

When the article was published, the appellant issued an immediate writ for defamation, which followed only after he had faced criminal charges under action taken by the respondents. Having been acquitted before the courts, the civil action commenced with use of evidence used in the trial. In the first hearing, the court opted for jury opinion so as to avoid overlooking the subjective nature of the case, and while it was admitted by the appellant that he had received money from unscrupulous individuals, he argued that his only intention was to establish the source of the racketeering, before revealing their identities to the authorities.

Admitted by both parties within the litigation, the appellant was accused of (i) dishonestly taking bribes before fixing or attempting to fix, the result of matches in which he played, and (ii) dishonestly taking bribes with a view to fixing the result of matches in which he would be playing. Here it was left to the jury to determine if, based upon his testimony and the recordings presented, the appellant was by virtue of his claim, innocent of any corrupt behaviour, and that in light of the respondent's article, owed compensation for the pain and distress cased to both himself and his family.

After listening to the direction of the judge, and allowing for the small number of the appellant's innocuous yet significant lies, the jury returned a verdict in favour of the appellant and awarded a reduced amount of £85,000 in damages. Taken straight to the Court of Appeal, the Court reversed the decision on grounds of perversion by the jury, when in the summing up of the case, Brown LJ remarked:

> "[O]ne is left with an inescapable core of fact and circumstance which to my mind leads inexorably to the view that Mr Grobbelaar's story is, quite simply,

incredible. All logic, common sense and reason compel one to that conclusion."[858]

It was then presented to the House of Lords for final evaluation, where the respondents challenged the rights of the House to question a forgone Appeal Court decision. Here it was explained that under s.4 of the Appellate Jurisdictions Act 1876, the House of Lords (being the highest court in the land) was bestowed the power to "determine what of right, and according to the law and custom of this realm, ought to be done in the subject matter of such appeal". With that sentiment in mind, the House concluded by a majority, that under circumstances where the defamed party had been shown to lie, it would be a perversion of justice to award, or allow to be awarded, damages arsing from alleged defamatory remarks; an act which if unproven in the case of newspapers, is granted qualified privilege, as provided in *Reynolds v Times Newspapers Ltd*;[859] and one where the claimant is shown to be less than deserving of financial remedy when their own behaviour is itself, questionable and unreliable. This is known as the 'Pamplin' principle, as laid down in *Pamplin v Express Newspapers Ltd*,[860] in which:

> "[A] plaintiff is entitled to a verdict in his favour on the justification issue but *the evidence properly before the jury on the issue of justification has disclosed that the reputation to which he is entitled is so depreciated that the damages which he should be awarded for the damage to his reputation by the (ex hypothesi) defamatory publication should be reduced below the level that would be appropriate for a plaintiff with an impeccable reputation*, maybe even to a nominal figure..."[861]

It was for the reasons given, that the House held that the appeal should be allowed, but on the condition that the award was reduced to a nominal sum of £1. And that despite the argument that jury decisions were beyond review, the lower courts had allowed judge and jury roles to overlap, and so in order for justice to be done, the intervention of the House was merely academic.

---

[858] *Grobbelaar v News Group Newspapers Ltd* [2001] 2 All ER 437 [92] (Brown LJ).

[859] [2001] 2 AC 127.

[860] [1988] 1 WLR 116.

[861] *Grobbelaar v News Group Newspapers Ltd* [2002] UKHL 40 [54] (Hobhouse LJ).

Key Citations

"[I]t is a very serious thing to stigmatise as perverse the unanimous finding of jurors who have solemnly sworn to return a true verdict according to the evidence. A jury may, of course, from time to time act in a wholly irrational way, but that is not a conclusion to be reached lightly or if any alternative explanation not involving perversity presents itself."[862]

"The tort of defamation protects those whose reputations have been unlawfully injured. It affords little or no protection to those who have, or deserve to have, no reputation deserving of legal protection."[863]

"It would be an affront to justice if a court of law were to award substantial damages to a man shown to have acted in such flagrant breach of his legal and moral obligations."[864]

"The House is not, like the Court of Appeal, a creature of statute, and in the absence of statutory or judicial restriction has inherent power to exercise any power vested in the Court of Appeal."[865]

"[T]he task of an appellate court, whether the Court of Appeal or the House, is to seek to interpret the jury's decision and not, because of justifiable dissatisfaction at the outcome, to take upon itself the determination of factual issues which lay within the exclusive province of the jury."[866]

"To curtail the right of a satirist to deploy ridicule to the extent and in the manner in which he chooses would be a far reaching incursion on freedom of speech. There is no warrant in our legal history, modern principles of public law, convention principles, or policy for such an approach."[867]

"If a person, believing himself to have been defamed, brings a defamation action and there is no dispute but that the defendant was responsible for uttering the words complained of and no dispute but that the words were defamatory of the claimant, the defendant, in order to rely on the defence of justification, must prove that the words were true."[868]

---

[862] *Grobbelaar v News Group Newspapers Ltd* [2002] UKHL 40 [21] (Bingham LJ).

[863] *Grobbelaar v News Group Newspapers Ltd* [2002] UKHL 40 [24] (Bingham LJ).

[864] *Grobbelaar v News Group Newspapers Ltd* [2002] UKHL 40 [24] (Bingham LJ).

[865] *Grobbelaar v News Group Newspapers Ltd* [2002] UKHL 40 [25] (Bingham LJ).

[866] *Grobbelaar v News Group Newspapers Ltd* [2002] UKHL 40 [26] (Bingham LJ).

[867] *Grobbelaar v News Group Newspapers Ltd* [2002] UKHL 40 [38] (Steyn LJ).

[868] *Grobbelaar v News Group Newspapers Ltd* [2002] UKHL 40 [73] (Scott LJ).

8. Hedley Byrne & Co Ltd v Heller and Partners

Duty of care under accusations of negligence, particularly within the carelessness of speech, forms the basis of a claim between a corporate entity and a merchant bank. On this occasion, the appellant advertising agency had taken steps to ascertain the financial credibility of a new client; which while careless in its execution, left them at a considerable loss when the information proved worthless.

In 1957, the appellants received instruction from a new client requiring a number of advertisements, which was later followed by a request for a structured advertising programme with estimated costs of around £100,000 p.a. Given the short-term trading history between them, the appellants asked their bank to consult their client's bank so as to establish their financial standing.

The reference, which was by no means official, read that their client was 'a respectably constituted company whose trading connection is expanding speedily' and that 'We consider the company to be quite good for its engagements'. Upon this positive note, the appellants proceeded to organise scheduled television and newspaper slots at cost to themselves, on the strength of the bank's statement.

Several months later, the appellants concerns for the financial integrity of their client grew to the point where a second reference was requested. This time, an oral bankers report was provided for by the respondents, that while detailed enough to warrant a sound response, was issued under the express notice that it was given with no responsibility for the outcome of the enquiry. Within this report was knowledge that the client was a subsidiary of a parent corporation in the throes of liquidation, but the bank similarly emphasised that they had confidence in the director and his integrity as a businessman.

With written confirmation of the report sent by the bank to the appellants, the terms expressed were relied upon when in light of their client's liquidation, the appellants suffered losses of around £17,000. It was this somewhat unsurprising event that triggered a claim for damages, based upon negligence by the respondents when offering statements that were contributory to the appellant's extension of credit.

In the first instance, the court awarded in favour of the respondents, and when taken to the Court of Appeal, the outcome remained unchanged on grounds that such principles were unreasonably applied to the unrehearsed statements of a banker, and not an official credit report. Presented to the House of Lords, the principles of negligence peripheral to any contract, were examined for exactness, whereupon the dicta of Sir Roundell Palmer in *Peek v Gurney* initially proposed that:

> "[I]n order that a person may avail himself of relief founded on it he must show that there was such a proximate relation between himself and the person making the representation as to bring them virtually into the position of parties contracting with each other..."[869]

---

[869] *Peek v Gurney* (1871) LR 13 Eq 79 (HL) 97 (Sir Roundell Palmer).

There was also mention of *Candler v Crane, Christmas & Co*,[870] in which a proposed corporate takeover involved the presentation of company accounts to the prospective buyers, accounts that by all intentions had been carelessly prepared, and on which the investors had relied when purchasing the firm. While in *Robinson v National Bank of Scotland Ltd*, a guarantor was left facing huge debts when it was argued he had been falsely induced into signing by the lenders, prior to the borrowers lapsing into bankruptcy. In this matter, Haldane LJ commented:

> "[W]hen a mere inquiry is made by one banker of another, who stands in no special relation to him, then, in the absence of special circumstances from which a contract to be careful can be inferred, I think there is no duty excepting the duty of common honesty…"[871]

While in *Shiells v Blackburne*, Loughborough LJ stressed that:

> "[I]f a man gratuitously undertakes to do a thing to the best of his skill, where his situation or profession is such as to imply skill, an omission of that skill is imputable to him as gross negligence."[872]

In *Cann v Willson*,[873] the claimants sought the professional opinion of valuers when borrowing against the worth of their home; and having provided what was suggested as a moderate valuation, the claimant defaulted on the required payments, whereupon the sale of the property failed to cover the debt owed. On this occasion, the court awarded in favour of the claimant on grounds of negligence, want of skill, breach of duty and misrepresentation.

In *Nocton v Lord Ashburton*, Shaw LJ propagated the principle that:

> "[O]nce the relations of parties have been ascertained to be those in which a duty is laid upon one person of giving information or advice to another upon which that other is entitled to rely as the basis of a transaction, responsibility for error amounting to misrepresentation in any statement made will attach to the adviser or informer, although the information and advice have been given not fraudulently but in good faith."[874]

This translated to a recognition by the House that while there was no question that a duty of honesty was inherent to the words of the bankers, there was no evidence to suggest fraudulent or misrepresentative intention, particularly when at the time the advice or report was issued, the respondents had expressed their abject unwillingness to be held to account for the actions of the company discussed. This left the appellants with no substance upon which to claim damages and so the appeal was uniformly dismissed.

---

[870] [1951] 2 KB 164.

[871] *Robinson v National Bank of Scotland Ltd* [1916] SC (HL) 154 (HL) 157 (Haldane LJ).

[872] *Shiells v Blackburne* (1789) 1 HBl 158, 162 (Loughborough LJ).

[873] (1888) 39 Ch D 39.

[874] *Nocton v Lord Ashburton* [1914] AC 932 (HL) 972 (Shaw LJ).

Key Citations

"[I]f someone possessed of a special skill undertakes, quite irrespective of contract, to apply that skill for the assistance of another person who relies upon such skill, a duty of care will arise. The fact that the service is to be given by means of or by the instrumentality of words can make no difference."[875]

"[I]f in a sphere in which a person is so placed that others could reasonably rely upon his judgment or his skill or upon his ability to make careful inquiry, a person takes it upon himself to give information or advice to, or allows his information or advice to be passed on to, another person who, as he knows or should know, will place reliance upon it, then a duty of care will arise."[876]

"[I]f a banker gives a reference in the form of brief expression of opinion in regard to credit-worthiness he does not accept, and there is not expected from him, any higher duty than that of giving an honest answer."[877]

"A man cannot be said voluntarily to be undertaking a responsibility if at the very moment when he is said to be accepting it he declares that in fact he is not."[878]

---

[875] *Hedley Byrne & Co Ltd v Heller and Partners* [1964] AC 465 (HL) 502 (Morris LJ).

[876] *Hedley Byrne & Co Ltd v Heller and Partners* [1964] AC 465 (HL) 503 (Morris LJ).

[877] *Hedley Byrne & Co Ltd v Heller and Partners* [1964] AC 465 (HL) 504 (Morris LJ).

[878] *Hedley Byrne & Co Ltd v Heller and Partners* [1964] AC 465 (HL) 533 (Devlin LJ).

9. Hunter v Canary Wharf Ltd

The tortious claim for nuisance, and the rights of those in occupation of land have for many years, been exclusively limited in the preservation of common law sensibility. On this occasion, a collective suit for both nuisance and negligence by local residents against that of corporate rights, produced an unexpected outcome.

After the demise of dockland trading in London, the areas once frequented by countless importers and exporters, fell foul of disuse and neglect. After lengthy consideration, both immediate and future plans for the site were subject to the Secretary of State who, recognising the need for both housing and commercial exploitation, took advantage of ss.134(1) and 135(1) of the Local Government, Planning and Land Act 1980, in order to commission urban regeneration of the London docklands area under the formation of the London Docklands Development Corporation (LDDC).

In line with the need for such redevelopment, the 1980 Act allowed the Minister to override typical planning permission requirements, as laid down in the Town and Country Planning Act 1971. This resulted in the construction of the 800ft tall Canary Wharf Tower by nominated contractors Olympia and York Canary Wharf Ltd, along with interlinking roads to the surrounding city over a four-year period.

This ambitious project resulted in two tortious claims by 500-700 local residents, the first of which centred around the interruption and in some cases, total disruption of television broadcast signals after the completion of the tower, and excessive amounts of materials dust invading the homes of the claimants throughout the construction period. The case itself drew mixed, and yet keen attention of the the courts, primarily because the history of nuisance and negligence were to some extents, intertwined, and thus dependant on the principles found within property law.

In the first matter, the rights of those wishing to build upon their land stem from the long-standing principle that in the exception of easements or restrictive covenants, every man has the freedom to build as he pleases, as was stressed by Hardwicke LC in *Attorney-General v Doughty*, when he said:

> "I know no general rule of common law, which warrants that, or says, that building so as to stop another's prospect is a nuisance. Was that the case, there could be no great towns; and I must grant injunctions to all the new buildings in this town . . ."[879]

Furthermore, in a recent German case *G v City of Hamburg*,[880] the Supreme Court had ruled unequivocally that where a resident had suffered diminished television broadcast signals following the construction of a nine-storey hospital, such effects were not subject to the powers of their Civil Code, and so no claim for nuisance could stand. This reflected the stance of the English courts, therefore support for such a claim would not be found, despite the large numbers of complaints.

---

[879] (1752) 2 Ves Sen 453 (Ch) 453 (Hardwicke LC).

[880] 21 October 1983; Decisions of the Federal Supreme Court in Civil Matters, vol 88, 344

Turning to the issue of dust, the principles of property law were again invoked, inasmuch as established academic precedent argued that:

> "In true cases of nuisance the interest of the plaintiff which is invaded is not the interest of bodily security but the interest of liberty to exercise rights over land in the amplest manner. A sulphurous chimney in a residential area is not a nuisance because it makes householders cough and splutter but because it prevents them taking their ease in their gardens. *It is for this reason that the plaintiff in an action for nuisance must show some title to realty.*"[881]

However, this definite founding for claim had seen its critics, when in *Foster v Warblington Urban District Council*,[882] the Court of Appeal had ruled that a person in exclusive possession of land could sue, despite no evidence of title. This principle was further promoted in *Khorasandjian v Bush*, in which a young girl had been subjected to continuous phone calls from a spurned former partner while living with her parents, and where Dillon LJ had also remarked that it was:

> "[R]idiculous if in this present age the law is that the making of deliberately harassing and pestering telephone calls to a person is only actionable in the civil courts if the recipient of the calls happens to have the freehold or a leasehold proprietary interest in the premises in which he or she has received the calls."[883]

Here, the court followed Canadian case *Motherwell v Motherwell*,[884] where it was held by the Appellate Court, that not only was the legal owner entitled to remedy for nuisance, but the wife too, despite her having nothing more than occupational rights.

Unfortunately, the problems facing the claimants was that a large majority of them were spouses, children and in some instances, extended family. This placed the courts in a difficult position, inasmuch as recognising the need to consider expanding upon private claimant rights in nuisance cases beyond that of land owners, especially with similar changes to spousal rights in both the Matrimonial Homes Act 1983 and the Family Law Act 1996.

When first heard, the court held that television signal interference was a claimable right under nuisance, and that exclusive possession of land was the qualifying criteria for claim in both instances. The Court of Appeal reversed the decision, and so it was that the original defendants were appealing to the House of Lords, while the claimants sought to cross-appeal.

With forbearance of the seemingly inextricable limitations of both tort and property laws, it was after lengthy discussion, unanimously held that the despite the changes in modern society and the family units, the strict rule of exclusive possession remained steadfast, not on grounds of unreasonableness, but in the prevention of arbitrary awards

---

[881] FH Newark, 'The Boundaries of Nuisance' (1949) 65 LQR 480, 488

[882] [1906] 1 KB 648.

[883] [1993] QB 727 (CA) 753 (Dillon LJ).

[884] (1976) 73 DLR (3d) 62.

for complainants having little to no proprietary rights. It was for that simple reason, that the House reversed the Court of Appeal's findings in lieu of the original judgment.

Key Citations

"[T]he quantum of damages in private nuisance does not depend on the number of those enjoying the land in question. It also follows that the only persons entitled to sue for loss in amenity value of the land are the owner or the occupier with the right to exclusive possession."[885]

"Nuisance is a tort against land, including interests in land such as easements and profits. A plaintiff must therefore have an interest in the land affected by the nuisance."[886]

"[A] spouse may, by virtue of an order of the court upon a break-up of the marriage, become entitled to exclusive possession of the home. If so, she will become entitled to sue for nuisance. Until then, her interest is analogous to a contingent reversion. It cannot be affected by a nuisance which merely damages the amenity of the property while she has no right to possession."[887]

"[A]t common law anyone may build whatever he likes upon his land. If the effect is to interfere with the light, air or view of his neighbour, that is his misfortune. The owner's right to build can be restrained only by covenant or the acquisition (by grant or prescription) of an easement of light or air for the benefit of windows or apertures on adjoining land."[888]

"English common law allows the rights of a landowner to build as he pleases to be restricted only in carefully limited cases and then only after the period of prescription has elapsed."[889]

---

[885] *Hunter v Canary Wharf Ltd* [1997] AC 655 (HL) 696 (Lloyd LJ).

[886] *Hunter v Canary Wharf Ltd* [1997] AC 655 (HL) 702 (Hoffman LJ).

[887] *Hunter v Canary Wharf Ltd* [1997] AC 655 (HL) 708 (Hoffman LJ).

[888] *Hunter v Canary Wharf Ltd* [1997] AC 655 (HL) 709 (Hoffman LJ).

[889] *Hunter v Canary Wharf Ltd* [1997] AC 655 (HL) 709 (Hoffman LJ).

10. Lister v Hesley Hall Ltd

Vicarious liability and the systematic sexual abuse of children under the care of trained staff, becomes the nucleus of a collective suit against the abuser's employer, in the wake of criminal allegations leading to a conviction.

Between 1979 and 1982, the respondents employed the services of a warden for the purposes of managing a boarding house designated the care of emotionally troubled and vulnerable children. Of the eighteen boys resident to the property, a number of them were subjected to numerous forms of sexual abuse, achieved through careful grooming and insidious manipulations by the offender.

While the acts themselves went unreported, a criminal investigation revealed the identity of the accused, and following summary conviction, he was sentenced to seven years imprisonment. Almost fifteen years later, the appellants issued claims against the owners of the boarding house on grounds of vicarious liability and negligence.

In the first instance, the claim for negligence was dismissed, while the accusation of liability for the abuse fell victim to the existing position as determined by the verdict in *Trotman v North Yorkshire County Council*, in which a disabled pupil had been sexually abused by the deputy headmaster while on a school trip abroad. When assessing the culpability of the local authority, Butler-Sloss LJ concluded that:

> "[I]n the field of serious sexual misconduct, I find it difficult to visualise circumstances in which an act of the teacher can be an unauthorised mode of carrying out an authorised act, although I would not wish to close the door on the possibility."[890]

Subsequently holding that the employers in question, could not be held liable for the individual actions of a sick mind, despite having harmed the child while under the employment of the authority at the time of the abuse.

When heard by the Court of Appeal, who themselves adhered to the principles ascribed in *Trotman*, the decision was taken to award damages based on the wardens failure to report his actions to his employer. This was expressed by Waller LJ, who explained:

> "The simple point in this case is that if wrongful conduct is outside the course of employment, a failure to prevent or report that wrong conduct cannot be within the scope of employment so as to make the employer vicariously liable for that failure when the employer was not vicariously liable for the wrongful conduct itself."[891]

Granted leave to appeal, the case was presented again to the House of Lords, who took issue with the decision in *Trotman*, while clarifying the very principles of vicarious liability.

---

[890] *Trotman v North Yorkshire County Council* [1999] LGR 584 (CA) 591 (Butler-Sloss LJ).

[891] *Lister v Hesley Hall Ltd* Times, October 13, 1999

The essence of vicarious liability rests upon the timeless principles espoused in academic text, and which state that a wrongful act undertaken by an employee in the course of his employment is recognised where 'it is either (a) a wrongful act authorised by the master, or (b) a wrongful and unauthorised mode of doing some act authorised by the master'.[892] This is further supported by the principle that 'a master…is liable even for acts which he has authorised, provided they are so connected with acts which he has authorised, that they may rightly be regarded as modes-although improper modes-of doing them'.[893]

In *Lloyd v Grace, Smith & Co,*[894] a firm of solicitors were held liable for the manipulation of their client by a manager who used the acquired property for his own benefit, while in *Williams v A & W Hemphill Ltd,* it was expressed by Lord President Clyde that:

> "[W]here the workman does some work which he is appointed to do, but does it in a way which his master has not authorised and would not have authorised had he known of it, the master is nevertheless still responsible, for the servant's act is still within the scope of his employment. On the other hand…if the servant is employed only to do a particular work or a particular class of work, and he does something outside the scope of that work, the master is not responsible for any mischief the servant may do to a third party."[895]

However in *Central Motors (Glasgow) Ltd v Cessnock Garage and Motor Co,* Cullen LJ argued that:

> "The question is not to be answered merely by applying the test whether the act in itself is one which the servant was employed or ordered or forbidden to do. The employer has to shoulder responsibility on a wider basis; and he may, and often does, become responsible to third parties for acts which he has expressly or *impliedly* forbidden the servant to do."[896]

While further remarking that:

> "An honest master does not employ or authorise his servant to commit crimes of dishonesty towards third parties; but nevertheless *he may incur liability for a crime of dishonesty committed by the servant if it was committed by him within the field of activities which the employment assigned to him, and that although*

---

[892] RFV Heuston, RA Buckley, *Salmonde and Heuston on the Law of Torts* (21st edn, Sweet & Maxwell 1996) 443

[893] RFV Heuston, RA Buckley, *Salmonde and Heuston on the Law of Torts* (21st edn, Sweet & Maxwell 1996) 443

[894] [1912] AC 716.

[895] *Williams v A & W Hemphill Ltd* 1966 SC(HL) 31 (HL) 44 (Clyde LP).

[896] *Central Motors (Glasgow) Ltd v Cessnock Garage and Motor Co* 1925 SC 796, 802 (Cullen LJ) (emphasis added).

the crime was committed by the servant solely in pursuance of his own private advantage.[897]

In a more recent Canadian case *Bazley v Curry*,[898] involving the sexual abuse of children by an employee of a children's foundation who had been assigned a parental/ carer role, the court found the employers vicariously liable and awarded damages accordingly. In 'Vicarious Liability in the Law of Torts' it was also suggested that 'The master ought to be liable for all those torts which can fairly be regarded as reasonably incidental risks to the type of business he carries on'[899] while in *Dyer v Munday*[900] the court agreed that there was no reason why the doctrine of vicarious liability ought not operate where a tort becomes a crime.

It was for these reasons, as well as the ignorance shown in *Trotman*, that the House agreed the judgment was to be overruled, and that in this matter, the appeal was to be upheld on grounds that the proximity between the wardens actions, his duty to his employers and conversely theirs to the appellants, left no doubt as to where liability lay.

Key Citations

"Vicarious liability is a species of strict liability. It is not premised on any culpable act or omission on the part of the employer; an employer who is not personally at fault is made legally answerable for the fault of his employee."[901]

"[I]t is no answer to say that the employee was guilty of intentional wrongdoing, or that his act was not merely tortious but criminal, or that he was acting exclusively for his own benefit, or that he was acting contrary to express instructions, or that his conduct was the very negation of his employer's duty. The cases show that where an employer undertakes the care of a client's property and entrusts the task to an employee who steals the property, the employer is vicariously liable."[902]

"[T]here is no a priori reason why an employer should not be vicariously liable for a sexual assault committed by his employee, though naturally such conduct will not normally be within the scope of his employment."[903]

---

[897] *Central Motors (Glasgow) Ltd v Cessnock Garage and Motor Co* 1925 SC 796, 802 (Cullen LJ) (emphasis added).

[898] (1999) 174 DLR (4th) 45.

[899] PS Atiyah, *Vicarious Liability in the Law of Torts* (Butterworth 1967) 171

[900] [1895] 1 QB 742.

[901] *Lister v Hesley Hall Ltd* [2001] UKHL 22 [65] (Hobhouse LJ).

[902] *Lister v Hesley Hall Ltd* [2001] UKHL 22 [79] (Millet LJ).

[903] *Lister v Hesley Hall Ltd* [2001] UKHL 22 [81] (Millet LJ).

10. Lonrho Ltd v Shell Petroleum Co Ltd (No.2)

The tort of conspiracy, while certainly relevant to the world of commerce, is one that overlaps with criminal activity, due to the clandestine nature of the offence. On this occasion, the unlawful collusion between corporate entities brought about a claim for damages by a party to a previous agreement, that had since been abandoned due to legislative sanctions by the United Kingdom.

In 1962, a number of petroleum companies came together to draft what was known as 'the shippers agreement', a contract that allowed for the supply of unrefined oil to Mozambique (or Rhodesia as it was also known). The appellants were a Portuguese organisation, while the respondents were both British petroleum companies, all of which had constructed a refinery, that while under Rhodesian ownership, was subject to shareholdings by the appellants, respondents and a number of other investors.

The appellants owned the pipeline itself, while the respondents used their shipping vessels to import the crude oil, before passing it through the pipeline to the refinery in Mozambique. Less than a year after the operation became live, the Government of Southern Rhodesia declared unilateral independence, which prompted Parliament to draft and enact, the Southern Rhodesia Act 1965, from which the Southern Rhodesia (Petroleum) Order 1965 imposed prohibitive sanctions against the supply of oil or petroleum to Southern Rhodesia by British suppliers.

S.2(2) of the 1965 Act expressed the powers to prevent supply, while s.1(1) of the 1965 Order restricted the supply of petroleum to Southern Rhodesia. S.1(2) also provided that any UK registered corporate body breaching the the restriction set down would be guilty of a criminal offence, and subject to fines or imprisonment or both, as explained in s. 4(2) of the 1965 Order.

On this occasion, the respondents had acted together to circumvent the powers expressed by the Southern Rhodesia Act 1965, in order to continue supplying the Mozambique Government their own petroleum by other means. This rendered the appellants pipeline useless, and after two years of neglect, the appellants sued for damages in excesses of £100m under the tort of conspiracy.

The definition of conspiracy was outlined in *Crofter Hand Woven Harris Tweed Co Ltd v Veitch*, when Viscount Simon LC expressed how the tort consists of:

> "[T]he agreement of two or more persons to effect any unlawful purpose, whether as their ultimate aim, or only as a means to it, and the crime is complete if there is such agreement, even though nothing is done in pursuance of it."[904]

While under the established facts of *Cutler v Wandsworth Stadium Ltd*,[905] it was agreed that the failure to act, or to act in contravention of prohibitive statute, renders a party liable both to criminal charges and accountability under tort, where a third party has

---

[904] *Crofter Hand Woven Harris Tweed Co Ltd v Veitch* [1942] AC 435 (HL) 439 (Viscount Simon LC).

[905] [1949] AC 398.

been proven to suffer. The condition to this principle is that it must be shown that the defendant(s) acted in deliberate pursuance of that suffering, as opposed to one borne from self-interest.

In the first instance, the claim for damages were dismissed, and the Court of Appeal followed suit, before being given final consideration in the House of Lords. It was then with deliberate evaluation of the statutory powers conferred, and the exacting nature of tort conspiracies, that the House wasted little time in holding that despite the obvious and unavoidable consequences felt by the appellants, there was no evidence to suggest that the breach of the Southern Rhodesia Act 1965 was anything more than a selfish pursuit by the respondents. And so without unnecessary expansion on the scope of tortious conspiracy, there was nothing with which to endorse the appeal.

Key Citations

"[I]njury to the plaintiff and not the self-interest of the defendants must be the predominant purpose of the agreement in execution of which the damage-causing acts were done."[906]

---

[906] *Lonrho Ltd v Shell Petroleum Co Ltd (No.2)* [1982] AC 173 (HL) 189 (Diplock LJ).

11. McLoughlin v O' Brian

Proximity, foreseeability and nervous shock, are central to a claim for damages when a mother is witness to the fallout of a multiple vehicle collision, which left one of her children dead. At a time when common law and judicial confidence preferred to abstain from extending the scope of award, the need for extension became overwhelming in the face of such distress and protracted suffering.

In 1973, the appellant's husband and three children were involved in a traffic accident involving two articulated vehicles central to the cause of the collision. The outcome left the husband with bruising and shock, the oldest child with severe head injuries, fractures and bruising, the middle child with fractures, bruising and concussion, while the youngest child aged almost three, had died just moments after the crash. The appellant was informed of the accident roughly an hour after the tragic event, and was immediately taken to see her family at the nearby hospital.

On her arrival, the appellant saw her husband in a state of shock and visible distress, after which the hospital staff informed her that their youngest child was dead. She then witnessed her oldest child screaming and shouting while, her middle child was unable to speak and simply clung to the appellant throughout.

Having initiated a claim for damages under severe shock, organic depression and a change of personality, the court dismissed the claim on policy grounds in that despite admitting liability for the death and injuries of the immediate victims, there was no duty of care when allowing for the foreseeability that the appellant would suffer resulting psychological injuries. When heard in the Court of Appeal, the Court ruled that although their was a valid argument that the respondents could have foreseen the impact their negligence would have upon a wife and mother, existing policy denied award to those not present at the scene.

Pursued in the House of Lords, the question in need of address was whether if, by refraining from close analysis and challenge of the existing policy on nervous shock, the judiciary had failed to acknowledge the manifestation of psychological trauma within parties beyond the tragedy, and thereby polluted the course of natural justice.

In *Benson v Lee*,[907] the court had allowed a claim for nervous shock, when a mother who having been told by a third party, ran outside her home to find her son had been run over; while in *Chadwick v British Railways Board*,[908] a nearby resident to a train crash was diagnosed with nervous shock, after arriving at the scene and helping rescue the survivors. On this occasion the court treated the matter as one of special duty, given his willingness to attend and assist.

Contrastingly, it was stated by Reid LJ in *McKew v Holland & Hannen & Cubitts (Scotland) Ltd* that:

---

[907] [1972] VR 879.

[908] [1967] 1 WLR 912.

"A defender is not liable for a consequence of a kind which is not foreseeable. But it does not follow that he is liable for every consequence which a reasonable man could foresee."[909]

Whereas in the American case *Wagner v International Railway Co*, Cardozo J explained that:

"Danger invites rescue. The cry of distress is the summons to relief. The law does not ignore these reactions of the mind in tracing conduct to its consequences. It recognises them as normal. It places their effects within the range of the natural and probable. The wrong that imperils life is a wrong to the imperilled victim; it is a wrong also to his rescuer."[910]

It was this statement that led the House to consider the appellant's attendance at the hospital, as that of a rescuer at a traumatic event, despite the reluctance of the Court of Appeal to widen the scope of award to those elsewhere, as outlined by Griffiths LJ, who stipulated that:

"[T]he closer the relationship the more readily it is foreseeable that they may be so affected, but if we just confine our consideration to parents and children and husbands and wives, it is clear that the potential liability of the tortfeasor is vastly increased if he has to compensate the relatives as well as the immediate victims of his carelessness."[911]

While the House agreed that overextension of scope ran risk of abuse of the principle, the time had come to move the parameters of the law in line with increased medical insight, and with a recognition that many years earlier, Australia had taken the liberty of embracing the right to such claims under s.4(1) of the New South Wales Law Reform (Miscellaneous Provisions) Act 1994. An Act which allowed a parent, husband or wife of a killed, injured or severely distressed party, to claim for nervous shock damages, regardless of the spatial or temporal relationship to the accident or event involved. It was for this reason, along with the obvious need to lead the change required, that the House uniformly upheld the appeal, while clearly noting that legislative reform was now long overdue in this particular field.

---

[909] *McKew v Holland & Hannen & Cubitts (Scotland) Ltd* [1969] 3 All ER 1621 (HL) 1623 (Reid LJ).

[910] *Wagner v International Railway Co* (1921) 232 NY 176, 180 (Cardozo J).

[911] *McLoughlin v O'Brian* [1981] QB 599 (CA) 617 (Griffiths LJ).

Key Citations

"[I]f the effect on this wife and mother of the results of the negligence is considered to have been reasonably foreseeable, I do not see the justification for not finding the defendants liable in damages therefor."[912]

"Space, time, distance, the nature of the injuries sustained, and the relationship of the plaintiff to the immediate victim of the accident, are factors to be weighed, but not legal limitations, when the test of reasonable foreseeability is to be applied."[913]

"I would suppose that the legal profession well understands that an acute emotional trauma, like a physical trauma, can well cause a psychiatric illness in a wide range of circumstances and in a wide range of individuals whom it would be wrong to regard as having any abnormal psychological make-up."[914]

---

[912] *McLoughlin v O'Brian* [1982] 1 AC 410 (HL) 429 (Russell LJ).

[913] *McLoughlin v O'Brian* [1982] 1 AC 410 (HL) 431 (Scarman LJ).

[914] *McLoughlin v O'Brian* [1982] 1 AC 410 (HL) 433 (Bridge LJ).

12. Murphy v Brentwood District Council

Proximation and the scope of special relationships, lie close to the heart of tortious principle, and although the direction taken in *Anns v Merton London Borough Council*[915] was with hindsight, both unnecessary and damaging, it became important to relinquish those shackles through the examination of this case.

During the construction of a number of new homes, it was the decision of the consulting local authority to employ the services of professional and suitably qualified civil engineers, in order to ensure full compliance with the building regulations of the time. Unfortunately, there were two properties that due to inconsistencies with the land, required very detailed and purpose-specific foundations, in order to avoid subsidence or resulting damage of any kind.

The council themselves had no immediate employees instructed enough to challenge the opinions of the engineers, and so when those same professional contractors failed to properly calculate the foundation integrity, the plans submitted were signed off without contest. It was not until after a sale of one the two homes, that the purchaser, who after a period of growing concern, discovered there had been significant movement of the property due to a shift in the footings. This unforeseen issue became the catalyst to a number of structural fractures, as well as utilities supply ruptures of a nature that could have proven dangerous, if not fatal, to the occupiers.

However, instead of using the home insurance proceeds to restore the property back to its correct state, the owner chose to sell the house at a grossly under market value, while issuing legal proceedings against the local authority on grounds of negligence arising from a statutory failure to prevent the faulty construction of the foundations, and thereby the overall property. At the original trial, the judge awarded in favour of the claimant, awarding costs exceeding the value lost through the defects, with allowance for considerable outlay on furnishings and repairs while under the ownership of the original purchaser.

When the local authority appealed, it was ultimately dismissed, while the Court upheld that they had, through the course of their statutory duties, allowed the home in question to become victim to 'physical damage,' that by virtue of its construction, ran serious risk of causing injury and distress to those parties in occupancy at the time such an event happened. This judgment was dependent upon the outcome of *Dutton v Bognor Regis Urban District Council*[916] and in equal share to that of *Anns,* which supported extension of public body liability to where private law remedy could hold them responsible beyond the reach inferred from existing statute.

Having then granted leave to appeal, the case was again presented to the House of Lords, where in many respects the opportunity to reexamine the precedent established in *Anns,* could now encourage departure from the overextension of duty of care principles;

---

[915] [1978] AC 728.

[916] [1971] 2 All ER 1003.

particularly when relying upon *Donoghue v Stevenson*[917] for relationship proximity and vicarious negligence where none existed. After meticulously evaluating the chain of events that led to the purchaser's claim, it became difficult to sustain that a third party to a transaction could be held against a duty of care to those suffering the results of poor construction design (as that incorporated into the overall product), which on this occasion was the finished property. This conflict then provoked a decision which allowed the local authority appeal and overturn the decision in *Anns*; a reversal that emphasised the differentiation of tortfeasor relationships, and the starkness between physical and pecuniary loss within tort law.

---

[917] [1932] AC 562.

Key Citations

"I would hold that Anns was wrongly decided as regards the scope of any private law duty of care resting upon local authorities in relation to their function of taking steps to secure compliance with building regulations and should be departed from."[918]

"If a builder erects a structure containing a latent defect which renders it dangerous to persons or property, he will be liable in tort for injury to persons or damage to property resulting from that dangerous defect. But if the defect becomes apparent before any injury or damage has been caused, the loss sustained by the building owner is purely economic."[919]

"[D]amage to a house itself which is attributable to a defect in the structure of the house is not recoverable in tort on *Donoghue v Stevenson* principles, but represents pure economic loss which is only recoverable in contract or in tort by reason some special relationship of proximity which imposes on the tortfeasor a duty of care to protect against economic loss."[920]

"I cannot see how, in principle, the scope of the liability of the authority for a negligent failure to ensure compliance can exceed that of the liability of the builder for his negligent failure to comply."[921]

"[I]n an uninterrupted line of cases since 1875, it has consistently been held that a third party cannot successfully sue in tort for the interference with his economic expectations or advantage resulting from injury to the person or property of another person with whom he has or is likely to have a contractual relationship."[922]

"[T]here is nothing in the terms or purpose of the statutory provisions which support the creation of a private law right of action for breach of statutory duty."[923]

"It seems to me no less absurd to hold that nevertheless there exists between the authority which failed properly to inspect and the donee of the property a relationship entitling the latter to recover from the authority the expenditure which he cannot recover from the donor."[924]

---

[918] *Murphy v Brentwood District Council* [1991] AC 398 (HL) 472 (Keith LJ).

[919] *Murphy v Brentwood District Council* [1991] AC 398 (HL) 475 (Bridge LJ).

[920] *Murphy v Brentwood District Council* [1991] AC 398 (HL) 479 (Bridge LJ).

[921] *Murphy v Brentwood District Council* [1991] AC 398 (HL) 481 (Bridge LJ).

[922] *Murphy v Brentwood District Council* [1991] AC 398 (HL) 485 (Oliver LJ).

[923] *Murphy v Brentwood District Council* [1991] AC 398 (HL) 490 (Oliver LJ).

[924] *Murphy v Brentwood District Council* [1991] AC 398 (HL) 490 (Oliver LJ).

13. Smith v Littlewoods Organisation Ltd

Foreseeability, and the duty of care for the criminal acts of third parties, seems somewhat overburdening, and so in this matter, the appellants found themselves central to an argument that required brevity, so as to restore the flow of justice.

In 1976, the respondents acquired a derelict cinema as part of their national retail expansion programme. While awaiting the refurbishment process to begin, the site was occasionally occupied by subcontractors and their employees, in order to fully strip the building bare ahead of the main construction stage. Over a period of weeks, the site was accessed by local youths who, on two occasions, started small fires, before having them extinguished by members of the nearby parish church.

Unfortunately, instead of notifying the police or the appellants, those acts went unreported until a third fire was allowed to get out of control, before causing significant damage to a neighbouring property and the church.

Having commenced litigation against the respondents, the now appellants contended that failure to provide adequate security to the site was a breach of duty owed to prevent both access by the youths, and the damage caused to their properties as a result of the fire. In the first instance, the court agreed that insufficient safety measures on the part of the respondents had granted reasonable foreseeability that the vandalism might occur, and awarded accordingly. Having been heard in the First Division of the Inner House of the Court of Session, it was agreed by the appellants that the respondents had no knowledge of the first two fires, and so the decision was reversed.

Presented to the House of Lords, the appellants continued to claim for damages, while the House took time to examine the nature of negligence and duty of care for strangers to property and ensuing criminal acts. In *Dorset Yacht Co Ltd v Home Office*, it was remarked by Reid LJ that:

> "[W]here human action forms one of the links between the original wrongdoing of the defendant and the loss suffered by the plaintiff, that action must at least have been something very likely to happen if it is not to be regarded as novus actus interveniens breaking the chain of causation. I do not think that a mere foreseeable possibility is or should be sufficient, for then the intervening human action can more properly be regarded as a new cause than as a consequence of the original wrongdoing."[925]

While in *Bourhill v Young*, it was argued by MacMillan LJ that:

> "The duty to take care is the duty to avoid doing or omitting to do anything the doing or omitting to do which may have as its reasonable and probable consequence injury to others, and the duty is owed to those to whom injury may reasonably and probably be anticipated if the duty is not observed."[926]

---

[925] *Dorset Yacht Co Ltd v Home Office* [1970] AC 1004 (HL) 1030 (Reid LJ).

[926] *Bourhill v Young* [1943] AC 92 (HL)(Sc) 104 (Macmillan LJ).

However it was well illustrated in academic text that 'the law might acknowledge a general principle that, whenever the harmful conduct of another is reasonably foreseeable, it is our duty to take precautions against it…but, up to now, no legal system has gone so far as this….'[927]. This position was also supported by Sumner LJ in *Weld-Blundell v Stephens*, who explained that 'In general…even though A is in fault, he is not responsible for injury to C which B, a stranger to him, deliberately chooses to do.'[928]

By this it was construed by the House that unless there are exceptional circumstances where the property owner, by virtue of his inaction, created a circumstance in which damage to another property fell under his remit, perhaps by some unique relationship, and that the foreseeability of such damage was little short of certain, there could be no justification for holding that owner to account; and so it was, that for this reason, the appeal was uniformly dismissed.

Key Citations

"Unless the needle that measures the probability of a particular result flowing from the conduct of a human agent is near the top of the scale it may be hard to conclude that it has risen sufficiently from the bottom to create the duty reasonably to foresee it."[929]

"[W]hat the reasonable man is bound to foresee in a case involving injury or damage by independent human agency, just as in cases where such agency plays no part, is the probable consequences of his own act or omission, but that, in such a case, a clear basis will be required on which to assert that the injury or damage is more than a mere possibility."[930]

"[L]iability in negligence for harm caused by the deliberate wrongdoing of others cannot be founded simply upon foreseeability that the pursuer will suffer loss or damage by reason of such wrongdoing. There is no such general principle.[931]

"[T]o impose a general duty on occupiers to take reasonable care to prevent others from entering their property would impose an unreasonable burden on ordinary householders and an unreasonable curb upon the ordinary enjoyment of their property."[932]

---

[927] HLA Hart, Tony Honoré, *Causation in the Law* (2nd edn, OUP 1985) 196

[928] *Weld-Blundell v Stephens* [1920] AC 956 (HL) 986 (Sumner LJ).

[929] *Smith v Littlewoods Organisation Ltd* [1987] 1 AC 241 (HL) 261 (Mackay LJ).

[930] *Smith v Littlewoods Organisation Ltd* [1987] 1 AC 241 (HL) 261 (Mackay LJ).

[931] *Smith v Littlewoods Organisation Ltd* [1987] 1 AC 241 (HL) 272 (Goff LJ).

[932] *Smith v Littlewoods Organisation Ltd* [1987] 1 AC 241 (HL) 280 (Goff LJ).

14. Stovin v Wise

This appeal case discusses the actions, or inactions, of public bodies when operating under the guidance of statute, and an albeit narrow, prerequisite duty of care towards the general public.

After a number of road traffic accidents had occurred in a well-known intersection, the focus of complaint by drivers at the time, centred around a small patch of land on one of the number of corners, which obscured vision and thereby contributed to the now growing number of vehicle collisions.

When consideration was taken by the highways authority, operating under the local authority, to try and remove the affected area, the decision was taken to write to the land owners British Rail, and request that either the State body take steps to remove the blockage, or that permission might be granted for the local authority themselves to carry out the work at cost to the State under s.79 of the Highways Act 1980.

Under the power of this statute, the local authority were at their own discretion, able remove the land at cost to themselves, in order to circumvent any undue objections, and while acting in the interest of public safety. Unfortunately, while the local authority had written to the corresponding public body, and a meeting was held to examine how best to proceed, the letter was ignored by the recipients, while the sender was later reassigned to another council department without explaining to anyone that the matter was under review, and how further action was needed.

When the claim for negligence and breach of statutory duty was initiated by the victim of the accident, damages were awarded, and shared liability placed upon the driver and local authority (in varying degrees), after which an appeal was made by the defendant public body in the Court of Appeal, who dismissed the claim before presentation before the House of Lords.

During the hearing, Hoffman LJ's view of operational policy translated that:

> "The distinction between policy and operations is an inadequate tool with which to discover whether it is appropriate to impose a duty of care or not."[933]

In other words, just because the highways authority and local authority were obligated to provide safe roads and road surfaces to the general public, private land that prevented an unobscured field of view, did not render those same bodies liable for a duty of care, even if they had decided to take steps outside of prescribed statute to remove the obstruction at cost to themselves, hence it was this controversial reluctance that resulted in a narrow judgment in favour of the appellant local authority.

As a closing note, this case ties strongly with the constitutional concept of justiciability, which is to say that because public bodies are created by statute through the democratic process, the court recognises the limitations of their capabilities and subsequently hesitates to challenge them, whether questionable or not.

---

[933] *Stovin v Wise* [1996] AC 923 (HL) 951 (Hoffman LJ).

Key Citations

"I think that the minimum preconditions for basing a duty of care upon the existence of a statutory power, it if can be done at all, are, first, that it would in the circumstances have been irrational not to have exercised the power, so that there was in effect a public law duty to act, and secondly, that there are exceptional grounds for holding that the policy of the statute requires compensation to be paid to persons who suffer loss because the power was not exercised."[934]

"In my view the creation of duty of care upon a highway authority, even on grounds of irrationality in failing to exercise a power, would inevitably expose the authority's budgetary decisions to judicial inquiry."[935]

---

[934] *Stovin v Wise* [1996] AC 923 (HL) 953 (Hoffman LJ).

[935] *Stovin v Wise* [1996] AC 923 (HL) 958 (Nicholls LJ).

15. Taylor and another v A Novo (UK) Ltd

In a similar vein to *McLoughlin v O'Brian*,[936] the boundaries of proximity, and the effects of secondary nervous shock are explored with deliberate force, so as to establish where two related events fall within the passing of time and space.

In the first event, the respondent's mother was subject to a workplace accident involving a stack of racking boards that unexpectedly fell upon her. While recovering at home, the victim unexpectedly collapsed as the result of a deep vein thrombosis and associated pulmonary embolism, which were caused by the accident itself.

In the second event, the respondent daughter was visiting with her mother at the time of her death, and was subsequently witness to her sudden passing. This left the respondent in a state of shock, resulting in Post-Traumatic Stress Disorder (PTSD), a psychiatric injury familiar to both the courts and the medical profession.

In the first hearing, the judge placed focus upon whether, as a secondary victim to an earlier event, the respondent was qualified to receive damages. In order to conclude as to her entitlement, there were seven requirements set forth, namely that:

(1) The respondent's injury was reasonably foreseeable
(2) The relationship between the respondent and the primary victim was a close one
(3) There was a recognised psychiatric injury
(4) The injury was the result of the appellant's negligence
(5) The injury was the result of shock from witnessing the primary victim's death
(6) The respondent was either present at the time of death or the immediate aftermath
(7) The respondent perceived the death with her own senses

While the appellants accepted that all but one of the criteria (4) were satisfied, the judge awarded in favour of the respondent, before the matter came before the Court of Appeal. Here the mechanics of secondary nervous shock claims fell under discussion, in order to both understand the previous findings, and reach an informed conclusion as to the limitations of such developing claims.

The categorisation of primary and secondary nervous shock victims was properly outlined by Oliver LJ in *Alcock v Chief Constable of South Yorkshire Police*, where he remarked:

> "Broadly [the cases] divide into two categories, that is to say, those cases in which the injured plaintiff was involved, either mediately or immediately, as a participant, and those in which the plaintiff was no more than the passive and unwilling witness of injury caused to others."[937]

Before going further to explain that:

---

[936] [1983] 1 AC 410.

[937] *Alcock v Chief Constable of South Yorkshire Police* [1992] 1 AC 310 (AC) 407 (Oliver LJ).

"What is more difficult to account for is why, when the law in general declines to extend the area of compensation to those whose injury arises only from the circumstances of their relationship to the primary victim, an exception has arisen in those cases in which the event of injury to the primary victim has been actually witnessed by the plaintiff and the injury claimed is established as stemming from that fact."[938]

While later posing that:

"[T]he concept of 'proximity' is an artificial one which depends more upon the court's perception of what is the reasonable area for the imposition of liability than upon any logical process of analogical deduction."[939]

In *Taylor v Somerset Health Authority*,[940] a widow was awarded damages when her husband died at hospital following a sudden heart attack at work. Having arrived at the hospital an hour after his death, she waited twenty minutes before being informed by staff of his passing, whereupon she was taken to the mortuary to confirm his identity while still understandably distressed and shocked. At the trial, it was revealed that the hospital had failed to diagnose the severity of his condition, while the widow was now diagnosed as having nervous shock from her experiences in the hospital. On this occasion, the court held the local Health Authority liable for damages, through the months of misdiagnosis leading up to his passing.

In the previous hearing, Halbert J had explained that:

"[T]his was not a gradual decline leading to death, it was a sudden collapse. It was on any practicable view a new 'event' and a very traumatic one...The operative 'event' which traumatised the claimant was sudden and horrifying. She was present at the scene and witnessed it with her own senses. The fact that there was an earlier incident caused by the same negligent act is irrelevant."

However, as had been stipulated by Wilberforce LJ in *McLoughlin v O'Brian*, it was important to remember that:

"As regards proximity to the accident, it is obvious that this must be close in both time and space. It is, after all, the fact and consequence of the defendant!s negligence that must be proved to have caused the 'nervous shock'."[941]

On this occasion, there had been a number of weeks between the first event and the second, therefore while the scope of secondary nervous shock was largely applicable to the core of the claim, there had since been a significant passage of time between both the accident and the death of the respondent's mother. This indisputable and distinguishing element, therefore left the Court with no other option than to allow the

---

[938] *Alcock v Chief Constable of South Yorkshire Police* [1992] 1 AC 310 (AC) 410 (Oliver LJ).

[939] *Alcock v Chief Constable of South Yorkshire Police* [1992] 1 AC 310 (AC) 411 (Oliver LJ).

[940] [1993] PIQR P262.

[941] *McLoughlin v O'Brian* [1983] 1 AC 410 (HL) 422 (Wilberforce LJ).

appeal on grounds of unreasonable proximity and proportionality of the doctrine, thus dismissing the claim outright.

Key Citations

"In a secondary victim case, physical proximity to the event is a necessary, but not sufficient, condition of legal proximity."[942]

"[T]he concept of proximity depends more on the court's perception of what is the reasonable area for the imposition of liability than any process of logic. In the context of claims by secondary victims, the control mechanisms are the judicial response to how this area should be defined."[943]

"The courts have been astute for the policy reasons articulated by Lord Steyn to confine the right of action of secondary victims by means of strict control mechanisms. In my view, these same policy reasons militate against any further substantial extension. That should only be done by Parliament."[944]

"Ms Taylor would have been able to recover damages as a secondary victim if she had suffered shock and psychiatric illness as a result of seeing her mother's accident. She cannot recover damages for the shock and illness that she suffered as a result of seeking her mother's death three weeks after the accident."[945]

---

[942] *Taylor and another v A Novo (UK) Ltd* [2013] EWCA Civ 194 [27] (Lord Dyson MR).

[943] *Taylor and another v A Novo (UK) Ltd* [2013] EWCA Civ 194 [28] (Lord Dyson MR).

[944] *Taylor and another v A Novo (UK) Ltd* [2013] EWCA Civ 194 [31] (Lord Dyson MR).

[945] *Taylor and another v A Novo (UK) Ltd* [2013] EWCA Civ 194 [32] (Lord Dyson MR).

16. Tomlinson v Congleton Borough Council

Reckless endangerment and the scope of relevant statute, are central to a case where the civil liberties of the general public and local authority duty of care, run risk of pollution after a life-altering injury leads to a claim for damages.

Purpose-built from derelict land, the 14-acre Brereton Heath Country Park was home to a lake known as the 'mere'. The lake itself had been created through the flooding of a disused quarry, and while the appeal of the lake drew over 160,000 visitors a year, the controlling borough and local authorities had been pragmatic in their prohibition of swimming through the installation of visible warning signs, distribution of leaflets, lifebelts, throwing lines and constant supervision by park rangers, despite flagrant ignorance by many of those visiting.

On a sunny Saturday afternoon, the 18 year-old respondent had taken it upon himself to enter the lake with the expectation of swimming. Standing in little over two feet of water, he proceeded to dive in, whereupon his head struck the sandy bottom, thus breaking his neck in the fifth vertebrae. Now facing life as a tetraplegic, the respondent sought to claim damages from the local authority under the Occupiers' Liability Act 1957 and Occupiers' Liability Act 1984, on grounds that a duty of care was owed, both as a trespasser and a visitor to the park.

Under recommendation by the Law Reform Commission,[946] s.2(2) of the 1957 Act stated that:

> "The common duty of care is a duty to take such care as in all the circumstances of the case is reasonable to see that the visitor will be reasonably safe in using the premises for the purposes for which he is invited or permitted by the occupier to be there."[947]

While s.2(4) explains:

> "In determining whether the occupier of premises has discharged the common duty of care to a visitor, regard is to be had to all the circumstances, so that (for example) (a) *where damage is caused to a visitor by a danger of which he had been warned by the occupier, the warning is not to be treated without more as absolving the occupier from liability, unless in all the circumstances it was enough to enable the visitor to be reasonably safe...*"[948]

---

[946] Law Reform Committee, *Occupiers' Liability to Invitees, Licensees and Trespassers* (Cmd 9305, 1954)

[947] Occupiers' Liability Act 1957, s.2(2)

[948] Occupiers' Liability Act 1957, s.2(4) (emphasis added).

Later in 1976, the Law Commission[949] gave recommendation to statutory duty of care for trespassers, which was given effect in s.1(1) of the 1984 Act s.1(1), while ss.1(5) and (6) read:

> "(5) Any duty owed by virtue of this section in respect of a risk may, in an appropriate case, be discharged by taking such steps as are reasonable in all the circumstances of the case to give warning of the danger concerned or to discourage persons from incurring the risk.

> (6) No duty is owed by virtue of this section to any person in respect of risks willingly accepted as his by that person (the question whether a risk was so accepted to be decided on the same principles as in other cases in which one person owes a duty of care to another)."[950]

This translated that where no award was found under the first Act, then the same would apply by extension to the second. Leading authority for the conversion from visitor to trespasser was found in *Hillen v ICI (Alkali) Ltd*, in which Atkin LJ remarked:

> "So far as he sets foot on so much of the premises as lie outside the invitation or uses them for purposes which are alien to the invitation he is not an invitee but a trespasser, and his rights must be determined accordingly."[951]

Given the fact that swimming was overtly and historically prohibited, the respondent had no choice but to seek remedy as a trespasser, and with claims that the water had muddied his view of the bottom, mention was made to *Whyte v Redland Aggregates Ltd*, where Henry LJ illustrated:

> "[T]he occupier of land containing or bordered by the river, the seashore, the pond or the gravel pit, does not have to warn of uneven surfaces below the water. Such surfaces are by their nature quite likely to be uneven. *Diving where you cannot see the bottom clearly enough to know that it is safe to dive is dangerous unless you have made sure, by reconnaissance or otherwise, that the diving is safe, ie, that there is adequate depth at the place where you choose to dive.* In those circumstances, the dangers of there being an uneven surface in an area where you cannot plainly see the bottom are too plain to require a specific warning and, accordingly, there is no such duty to warn…"[952]

In the first instance, the judge held that there was nothing remotely dangerous about the lake so as to warrant liability by the local authority, and so dismissed the claim; whereupon the Court of Appeal extended the occupiers liability beyond one of reasonable limits before awarding damages. When appealed by the local authority to the

---

[949] Law Commission, *Liability for Damage or Injury to Trespassers and Related Questions of Occupiers' Liability* (Cmd 6428, 1976)

[950] Occupiers' Liability Act 1984, ss.1(5)(6)

[951] *Hillen v ICI (Alkali) Ltd* [1936] AC 65 (HL) 69 (Atkin LJ).

[952] *Whyte v Redland Aggregates Ltd* (unreported) 27 November 1997; Court of Appeal (Civil Division) Transcript No 2034 of 1997 (CA) (Henry LJ) (emphasis added).

House of Lords, full consideration of the accountability of the respondent, as well as his many years of experience while swimming in the lake, was given before taking issue with the stance adopted by the Court of Appeal.

The House held that while a duty of care for those visiting occupied land fell between autonomy and observance of rules, the principle that individual risk-taking in the knowledge of visible danger was incumbent upon the owner when considering damages, was counter-productive, inasmuch as failure to acknowledge warnings was not a precursor for liability when the claimant suffers harm. It was for this reason, that the House reversed the Court of Appeal's decision and restored that of the first judge.

Key Citations

"I can see no difference between a person who comes upon land without permission and one who, having come with permission, does something which he has not been given permission to do. In both cases, the entrant would be imposing upon the landowner a duty of care which he has not expressly or impliedly accepted."[953]

"[I]n the case of a lawful visitor, one starts from the assumption that there is a duty whereas in the case of a trespasser one starts from the assumption that there is none."[954]

"If people want to climb mountains, go hang-gliding or swim or dive in ponds or lakes, that is their affair. Of course the landowner may for his own reasons wish to prohibit such activities. He may be think that they are a danger or inconvenience to himself or others. Or he may take a paternalist view and prefer people not to undertake risky activities on his land. He is entitled to impose such conditions, as the Council did by prohibiting swimming. But the law does not require him to do so."[955]

"[T]he balance between risk on the one hand and individual autonomy on the other is not a matter of expert opinion. It is a judgment which the courts must make and which in England reflects the individualist values of the common law."[956]

"[L]ocal authorities and other occupiers of land are ordinarily under no duty to incur such social and financial costs to protect a minority (or even a majority) against obvious dangers."[957]

"The pursuit of an unrestrained culture of blame and compensation has many evil consequences and one is certainly the interference with the liberty of the citizen."[958]

---

[953] *Tomlinson v Congleton Borough Council* [2003] UKHL 47 [13] (Hoffman LJ).

[954] *Tomlinson v Congleton Borough Council* [2003] UKHL 47 [38] (Hoffman LJ).

[955] *Tomlinson v Congleton Borough Council* [2003] UKHL 47 [44] (Hoffman LJ).

[956] *Tomlinson v Congleton Borough Council* [2003] UKHL 47 [47] (Hoffman LJ).

[957] *Tomlinson v Congleton Borough Council* [2003] UKHL 47 [48] (Hoffman LJ).

[958] *Tomlinson v Congleton Borough Council* [2003] UKHL 47 [81] (Hobhouse LJ).

17. Topp v London Country Bus (South West) Ltd

Proximity and lack of foreseeability, prevent this tragic claim for damages when a grieving husband argues that the owners of a minibus are liable for the death of his wife.

In 1988, a minibus owned and driven by bus company staff, was left parked and unlocked with the keys in the ignition, in the lay by of a nearby public house. It was considered normal practice for the drivers of these vehicles to leave them there in that state, as literally minutes later, it would typically be collected and driven by a replacement driver.

On this occasion, the replacement driver failed to turn up for work due to illness, which left the bus unlocked and clearly vulnerable to theft. During the time between the driver leaving the minibus and the accident taking place, the original driver had noticed it had not been taken as expected, and promptly notified his employers. At 11.15pm that evening, an unknown person took the minibus, and shortly afterwards ran down and killed the appellant's wife as she was out cycling. This led to action being taken against the bus company, on grounds of breach of duty of care, negligence and foreseeability.

In the first instance, the court dismissed the claim, whereupon the appellant claimed the judge erred in law on three grounds, namely (i) judging the claim unreasonable, (ii) holding that the facts fell outside the scope of award for duty of care, and (iii) not finding the respondents liable for the victim's death.

In *Smith v Littlewoods*, it was cited by Goff LJ that:

> "[E]ven though A is in fault, he is not responsible for injury to C which B, a stranger to him, deliberately chooses to do . . . [that] may be read as expressing the general idea that the voluntary act of another, independent of the defender's fault, is regarded as a novus actus interveniens which, to use the old metaphor, 'breaks the chain of causation.'"[959]

While in *Denton v United Counties Omnibus Co*,[960] the court agreed that although an omnibus belonging to the defendants was stolen from an unsecured storage yard before bring driven into the claimant's car, there was insufficient proximity between the owners, and the party liable for the accident to warrant any duty of care.

This translated that the thief and alleged joy-rider, was clearly in no position to consider the danger his actions posed, and irrespective of whether his identity could be established, and unfortunate as it was to have had his wife killed for no reason, a claim of negligence could not reasonably stand, on grounds of proximity and lack of foreseeability, thus the Court dismissed the appeal.

---

[959] *Smith v Littlewoods Organisation Ltd* [1987] AC 241 (HL Sc) 272 (Goff LJ).

[960] The Times, 6 May 1986; Court of Appeal (Civil Division) Transcript No 421 of 1986

Key Citations

"[T]he determination of the question whether there was a duty of care to protect against the wrongful acts of third parties was a matter for the judges of fact to determine."[961]

"[T]here was in the circumstances of this case a relationship of proximity between the defendants and Mrs. Topp. But I entirely agree with the judge that no duty of care is shown either in principle or having regard to the authority of this court…"[962]

---

[961] *Topp v London Country Bus (South West) Ltd* [1993] 1 WLR 976 (CA) 979 (Dillon LJ).

[962] *Topp v London Country Bus (South West) Ltd* [1993] 1 WLR 976 (CA) 979 (Rose LJ).

Bibliography

AG Guest (ed), *Chitty on Contracts* (26th edn, Sweet & Maxwell 1989)

AM Jones, MA Dudgate (eds), *Clerk & Lindsell on Torts* (19th edn, Sweet & Maxwell 2006)

Civil Service Commission, *Civil Service Order in Council* 1982 (Civil Service Commission, 1982)

FB Fuller, *The Law Relating To Friendly Societies* (William Clowes and Sons 1896)

FH Newark, 'The Boundaries of Nuisance' (1949) 65 LQR 480

HLA Hart, Tony Honoré, *Causation in the Law* (2nd edn, OUP 1985)

Home Office, *Compensating Victims of Violent Crime: Changes to the Criminal Injuries Compensation Scheme* (Cmd 2434, 1993)

Law Commission, *Illegality of Defence in Tort* (HMSO 2001)

Law Commission, *Liability for Damage or Injury to Trespassers and Related Questions of Occupiers' Liability* (Cmd 6428, 1976)

Law Reform Committee, *Occupiers' Liability to Invitees, Licensees and Trespassers* (Cmd 9305, 1954)

Lord Chancellor's Department, *Royal Commission on Civil Liability and Compensation for Personal Injury: Report* (Cmd 7054, 1978)

Mary Warnock, *Report of the Committee of Enquiry into Human Fertilisation and Embryology* (White Paper, Cm 9314, 1984)

Parliament, *Explanatory Note from First Parliamentary Counsel to the Select Committee on the Modernisation of the House of Commons* HC 389 (2nd Report, 3 December 1997)

Parliamentary Counsel to HM Treasury, *The Defence (General) Regulations 1939* (14th edn, HMSO 1943)

Press Complaints Commission, *Editors' Code of Practice* (2012)

PS Atiyah, *Vicarious Liability in the Law of Torts* (Butterworth 1967)

RFV Heuston, RA Buckley, *Salmonde and Heuston on the Law of Torts* (21st edn, Sweet & Maxwell 1996)

Sir Jack IH Jacob (ed), *The Supreme Court Practice 1993* (Sweet & Maxwell 1992)

Supreme Court of Judicature, *The Rules of the Supreme Court 1965* (HMSO 1966)

Index

Printed in Poland
by Amazon Fulfillment
Poland Sp. z o.o., Wrocław